Rituals *in* Families
and Family Therapy

Evan Imber-Black, Ph.D.
Janine Roberts, Ed.D.
Richard A. Whiting, Ed.D.

W · W · Norton & Company · New York · London

A NORTON PROFESSIONAL BOOK

Published simultaneously in Canada by Penguin Books Canada Ltd.,
2801 John Street, Markham, Ontario L3R 1B4.

Printed in the United States of America.

First Edition

Library of Congress Cataloging-in-Publication Data

Rituals in families and family therapy.
 "A Norton professional book" — P. preceding t.p.
 1. Family psychotherapy. 2. Family. I. Imber-Black,
Evan. II. Roberts, Janine, 1947–   . III. Whiting,
Richard Alva, 1944–   . [DNLM: 1. Family. 2. Family
Therapy. 3. Models, Psychological. WM 430.5.F2 R6155]
RC488.5.R58   1988   616.89′156   88-17954

ISBN 0-393-70064-X

W. W. Norton & Company, Inc., 500 Fifth Avenue, New York, N. Y. 10110
W. W. Norton & Company Ltd., 37 Great Russell Street, London WC1B 3NU

1 2 3 4 5 6 7 8 9 0

THIS BOOK IS LOVINGLY DEDICATED TO OUR CHILDREN

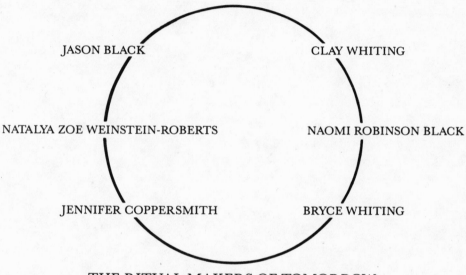

JASON BLACK

CLAY WHITING

NATALYA ZOE WEINSTEIN-ROBERTS

NAOMI ROBINSON BLACK

JENNIFER COPPERSMITH

BRYCE WHITING

THE RITUAL MAKERS OF TOMORROW

Foreword

PEGGY PAPP, M.S.W

THIS BOOK IS NOT only about the use of rituals in family therapy but about a particular way of thinking about families. The therapeutic assumption that informs this thinking is based on what Evan Imber-Black refers to as the "resource model," in which the therapist views families as essentially resourceful and only secondarily and temporarily in need of therapy. In the resource model the therapist searches for and uses the family's own strengths and resources rather than viewing the family as deficient and needing repair from outside sources. This is the underlying concept upon which the metaphorical rituals are developed in this book and it is this concept that lends them their most consistent and distinguishing feature. The key word is "coevolve." The designing and implementation of the rituals involve a collaborative effort between the family and therapist. Rather than being imposed or coercive, the rituals emerge as an integral and natural extension of the therapy.

In this process, the family members' own judgment is validated, their unique talents are mobilized, and their imagination and creativity are used as essential elements in the self-healing ceremonies. They become "co-therapists" in their treatment.

The reader is sure to be moved by some of the poignant and poetic gestures the families show themselves capable of making. Unexpressed thoughts and feelings are tapped and hidden wellsprings of affection and nurturance unexpectedly emerge as they participate in these symbolic acts. Family members exchange gifts that transform the anger and pain of separation into reassurance and comfort; a couple designs its own gameboard and diverts frustrating arguments into an amusing sport; a balloon is released carrying away past hurts into infinity and a mother becomes the ultimate authority on her child by writing her own psychological report. These are testimonies to the often unexplored and unappreciated capacities of clients and will hopefully encourage other therapists to discover and develop them.

As we read this book we become more and more aware of the ubiquity of rituals in our daily lives and the profound meaning they hold for us. Our gender, our identity, our relationships, our traditions, our idiosyncratic preferences are all reflected in our common rituals. They are a natural and powerful source of healing that up until now has been used by therapists only sporadically and in unusual situations. I believe one of the reasons for this is the fact that they have never before been made so clear and available to us. When rituals are presented as "creative leaps," "intuitive hunches," or "flashes of genius," we can only despair and admire them from afar. A debt of gratitude is owed to the authors for giving specific instructions for the designing and implementing of the rituals. The careful outlining of how, when, and where to use them plus the thinking process behind each step in creating them shows great respect for the reader and puts this book in the five-star category of "usefulness." Through a wide variety of subjects, including families, adolescents, children, individuals, adoption, remarriage, sexual problems, gender issues and training, we are shown specifically how to draw on the power of ritualized behavior to produce change.

The book is broad in scope, examining rituals not only within the context of interpersonal relationships but as reflections of our history, culture, ethnicity and social norms. Our consciousness is raised as we become aware of the multiple meanings of weddings, funerals, graduation, birthdays, bar mitzvahs, and their link to the wider social system. It is this wide vision plus the respect for human inventiveness that makes this an inspiring as well as practical book.

Contents

Contributors

"Alexandra" and "Julius"
Massachusetts

Linda A. Bennett, Ph.D.
Center for Family Research
George Washington University
    Medical Center
Washington, D.C.

Judith Davis, Ed.D.
University of Massachusetts
Amherst, Massachusetts

Aaron Noah Hoorwitz, Ph.D.
Unified Services for Children
    and Adolescents
Troy, New York

Evan Imber-Black, Ph.D.
Albert Einstein College of Medicine
Bronx, New York

Jane S. Jacobs, Ed.D.
Center for Family Research
George Washington University
    Medical Center
Washington, D.C.

Cecilia Kohen
Buenos Aires, Argentina

Joan Laird, M.S.W.
Smith College for Social Work
Northampton, Massachusetts

William D. Lax, Ph.D.
Brattleboro Family Institute
Brattleboro, Vermont

Dario J. Lussardi, M.A.
Brattleboro Family Institute
Brattleboro, Vermont

John J. O'Connor, Ph.D.
Unified Services for Children
    and Adolescents
Troy, New York

Janine Roberts, Ed.D.
University of Massachusetts
Amherst, Massachusetts

Gary L. Sanders, M.D., F.R.C.P. (C)
University of Calgary
Calgary, Alberta, Canada

Mary F. Whiteside, Ph.D.
Ann Arbor Center for the Family
Ann Arbor, Michigan

Richard A. Whiting, Ed.D.
Springfield College
Springfield, Massachusetts

Steven J. Wolin, M.D.
Center for Family Research
George Washington University
    Medical Center
Washington, D.C.

Acknowledgments

WE WOULD LIKE, first, to offer our deep appreciation to all of the families who have participated with us in our exploration of rituals. Families have informed us about their normative rituals, participated in therapeutic rituals, co-created rituals with us, and given us privileged access to the meanings of rituals in their lives.

We want to thank all of the authors of this volume. Their ideas and broad applications of a ritual perspective have enhanced our work with rituals. Their colleagueship in this endeavor has made the creation of this volume a pleasure.

We wish to acknowledge the work with therapeutic rituals of Mara Selvini Palazzoli, Luigi Boscolo, Gianfranco Cecchin, and Guiliana Prata and the conceptualizations of Onno van der Hart, as these served as important catalysts for our subsequent work.

We want to thank Pam Colorado, both for her support of our work and for her work in revitalizing Native Indian rituals, which has informed our thinking about the importance of normative rituals in families.

We thank Helm Stierlin for his thoughtful comments regarding therapeutic rituals.

Several people assisted us with the manuscript. We thank Gerry Weinstein and Michelle Patten for their help constructing charts and genograms. We express our appreciation to Marie Mele, Betti Swazey, Nancy Baer, and Louise Whiting for typing the manuscript.

Finally, we have all received the personal support so necessary to the completion of this project. For that we offer our deep appreciation to Lascelles Black, Gerry Weinstein, and Louise Whiting.

Evan Imber-Black
Janine Roberts
Richard A. Whiting

Preface

ORIGINS AND INFLUENCES OF THE BOOK

OUR DECADE-LONG collaboration as therapists, writers and teachers of family therapy has been shaped and guided by our mutual excitement regarding rituals. Beginning in the late 1970s, when Janine Roberts, Richard Whiting and I worked together seeing families in Western Massachusetts, and continuing across great geographic distances through joint teaching and workshops, late night conference calls to discuss rituals in our work, and meetings to develop our ideas, rituals have been our unifying interest. Functioning, as rituals do, to express dualities and resolve contradictions, our immersion in rituals has been both the glue of our collaboration and the expander, both the boundary and the frontier. Our interest in therapeutic rituals began as we read the clinical cases reported by the Milan team; like many others, we began to experiment with such interventions. Little did we know the surprises and gifts we would encounter from colleagues, trainees, and families.

Three major influences informed our decision to create the present volume. First, as we worked with therapeutic rituals and presented our work at conferences and in writing, we began to meet other clinicians and researchers whose interests were similar to our own. Most striking in this developing colleagueship was the discovery of the broad applicability of therapeutic rituals to problems across the family life cycle, as well as to larger social issues confronting families. As we met people who based their own clinical work on models quite different from our own, but who found therapeutic rituals efficacious, we began wondering if therapeutic rituals might be a process capable of transcending specific models of practice. The current volume, which brings together theorists, practitioners, and researchers from many different therapeutic schools of thought, illustrates our belief that rituals are not bound by any one model and that they are explainable from a variety of vantage points.

The second influence came from the participants in our courses and workshops who engaged and challenged us to demystify the design and implementation of therapeutic rituals. We were never at ease with the notion that rituals arose from some "flash of therapeutic genius," and we have struggled to understand the elements involved in creating effective rituals and to make such elements teachable and learnable for both therapists and families.

The third influence came from the families who gave us entry into their naturally occurring rituals, who engaged in the many therapeutic rituals described in our work, and who, in turn, taught us through their feedback that families are creative partners in developing therapeutic rituals. The present book attempts to capture families' responsiveness to a ritual perspective and to communicate the richness that emerges when families are our collaborators.

ORGANIZATION OF THE BOOK

The book is divided into five sections. In the first section, *Defining and Designing Rituals*, the three editors provide a context for the reader which not only introduces the entire topic of rituals but also orients the reader to the editors' model of therapeutic rituals. In Chapter 1, *Setting the Frame: Definition of Rituals, Functions, and Typology*, Roberts defines ritual, provides an extensive review of both anthropological and therapeutic literature regarding rituals, focuses on the multiple functions of rituals, and describes a typology of rituals, including daily rituals, family traditions, family celebrations, life cycle rituals, and therapeutic rituals. The chapter usefully differentiates therapeutic rituals from therapeutic tasks, offers interview questions regarding a family's ritual life that can be used by a therapist, and illustrates the material with clinical case examples.

In Chapter 2, *Ritual Themes*, Imber-Black defines and describes five ritual themes, including membership, healing, identity definition and redefinition, belief expression and negotiation, and celebration. Each theme is elaborated for both normative, naturally occurring rituals and therapeutic rituals in order to guide the therapist's choices when working with rituals. Case material illustrates each theme.

Chapter 3, *Guidelines to Designing Therapeutic Rituals*, by Whiting, completes the first section. In this chapter, Whiting demystifies the design of therapeutic rituals. Readers will learn the design elements of rituals, including symbols, open and closed aspects of ritual instructions, and the uses of time and space. Specific ritual techniques, including letting go, utilizing differences, giving and receiving, ritualizing the game, and documenting are described and illustrated with examples. Finally, other useful design considerations, including the use of alternations, both within a given ritual or in two or more rituals, the use of repetition, combining themes and actions, and the use of teams, including teams involving family members, are described.

The second section, *Rituals for Couples, Children and Adolescents*, provides the reader with many ideas for a ritual perspective and therapeutic rituals for issues at various stages of the family life cycle. In Chapter 4, *Normative and Therapeutic Rituals in Couples Therapy*, Imber-Black attends first to the normative rituals in any couple's life, including weddings, anniversaries, vacations and holidays, demonstrating how the therapist may attend to these for therapeutic purposes, and then describes the use of therapeutic rituals for various issues that couples present in therapy. Specific ritual issues for homosexual couples are discussed.

Chapter 5, *Imitative and Contagious Magic in the Therapeutic Use of Rituals with Children* by O'Connor and Hoorwitz, expands the theoretical underpinnings for therapeutic rituals to include hypnosis and the cognitive theory of Piaget within a strategic family therapy practice. Through four different cases, an efficacious ritual design for children's emotional or physical problems is illustrated.

In Chapter 6, *The Use of Rituals in Families with an Adolescent*, Lax and Lussardi, utilizing a Milan systemic model of practice, demonstrate the applicability of therapeutic rituals for families struggling with adolescent development. This chapter is complemented by Chapter 7, *Mazel Tov: The Bar Mitzvah as a Multigenerational Ritual of Change and Continuity*, in which the researcher, Davis, describes the bar mitzvah ritual in four very different families, considering its effects on individual, family, and community functioning. Implications for therapeutic involvement in other naturally occurring life cycle rituals are described.

The third section, *Facilitating Complex Family Processes Through Ritual*, demonstrates the multiple applications of rituals with often difficult family issues. In Chapter 8, *Therapeutic Rituals with Families with Adopted Members*, Whiting first discusses the importance of attending to rituals in families with adopted members, differentiating their ritual path from non-adoptive families. A full-length case example, utilizing the ritual technique of a document, illustrates the chapter.

Chapter 9, *Assessing Family Rituals in Alcoholic Families*, by Wolin, Bennett and Jacobs, presents the decade-long research outcomes of this group's study of families dealing with alcoholism. This research has generated concepts for examining rituals more generally. Their crucial finding that preservation of family rituals may serve a preventive function in families highlights the importance of a ritual perspective in clinical work.

In Chapter 10, *Systemic Rituals in Sexual Therapy*, Sanders places therapeutic rituals within a recursive model of sexual therapy that includes biological, directive behavioral, and systemic concepts and interventions. His work is illustrated with a full-length case.

Chapter 11, *Creation of Family Identity Through Ritual Performance in Early Remarriage*, by Whiteside, combines research and clinical practice to demonstrate the importance of both normative and therapeutic rituals for the issues faced by remarried couples and families. Several case examples from Whiteside's research with remarried families in their first year of formation and from her clinical practice illustrate the chapter.

The fourth section, *Rituals, Families and the Wider Social Context*, focuses on relationships among family struggles, normative and therapeutic rituals, and influences and forces from larger systems and the broader political and social context. In Chapter 12, *Use of Ritual in "Redocumenting" Psychiatric History*, Roberts and her co-authors, "Alexandra" and "Julius," describe a powerful ritual co-created by therapist and family that interdicted the effects of decades of psychiatric labeling. This chapter is unique as it is written by the therapist with commentary by the clients, consonant with the method involved in the ritual.

Chapter 13, *Women and Ritual in Family Therapy*, by Laird, raises crucial questions about gender in rituals, critiques many normative rituals as these function to preserve traditional sex roles, and offers clinical examples of therapeutic rituals capable of empowering women.

In Chapter 14, *Political Traumas, Oppression and Rituals*, Kohen describes the disastrous effects on family and individual functioning of the Argentinian military dictatorship and, in a deeply moving full-length case, demonstrates the healing power of therapeutic ritual.

The fifth section, *Rituals and Family Therapy Training* contains Chapter 15, *Rituals and Trainees*, by Roberts. This chapter focuses both on rituals in the trainees' families of origin and on the design and use of rituals within a training group. Several exercises developed by the editors are included.

The present volume concludes with a brief Afterword by Imber-Black, pointing to future directions for work with rituals.

—Evan Imber-Black

I

DEFINING AND
DESIGNING RITUALS

Setting the Frame: Definition, Functions, and Typology of Rituals

JANINE ROBERTS

THE PROBLEM OF DEFINITION

RITUAL HAS BEEN USED as such a general term both popularly and across academic disciplines that the problem of definition has to be addressed. For use clinically in family therapy, ritual needs to be defined narrowly enough to distinguish it from other types of interventions, yet broadly enough to encompass the range of ritual interventions that families and clinicians can create. I will look first at how the term has already been used in the field of family therapy, then return to ritual's roots in anthropology, and emerge with the definition of ritual that is used in this book.

Ritual as Used in Systems Family Therapy

Ritual was formally introduced to the systems models of family therapy in 1974 by Mara Selvini Palazzoli in her book *Self-Starvation: From the Intrapsychic to the Transpersonal Approach to Anorexia Nervosa*. This book (much of which was originally published in Italian in 1963) has several chapters at the end, written in the early seventies, in which Palazzoli begins to describe the first work of the Milan group (this included at that time G. Cecchin, G. Prata, L. Boscolo, and herself). All were psychiatrists who had been trying since 1969 to shift from a psychoanalytic mode of therapy to a systems approach. In *Self-Starvation*, ritual in therapy was defined as "an action, or a series of actions, accompanied by verbal formulae and involving the entire family. Like every ritual it must consist of a regular sequence of steps taken at the right time and in the right place" (p. 238).

Two very brief case vignettes were included in *Self-Starvation*. The first was a ritual with a family with an aggressive six-and-a-half-year-old boy who had been treated with massive doses of sedatives. The treatment team was struck by how the boy was allowed to act viciously at home, in ways that would not have been tolerated from other children, because of his "sickness." As a way to frame his behavior differently, the therapists prescribed the following ritual. Together the family members were to go in a procession to the bathroom, and ceremoniously pour the medicines down the toilet one by one. The father was asked to solemnly say to his son. "Today we were told by the doctors that we must throw all these medicines away because you are perfectly well. All you are is a naughty child, and we simply won't take any more of your nonsense." The father also repeated as each medicine was emptied, "You are perfectly well" (Selvini Palazzoli, 1974, p. 237). The ritual created a frame that the son was expected to follow family norms for behavior. The second ritual was prescribed for a family with an anorexic daughter (later identified as "Nora" in a more extensive writeup of the case [Selvini Palazzoli et al., 1977]). In this family, no one could speak ill of the powerful extended clan, so the nuclear family members were asked to lock the door and sit down for an hour with everyone taking an equal amount of time to give his or her opinions about the families of origin. This ritual was designed to implicitly shift the family rule regarding expression of negative opinions about extended family.

In the same year, the Milan group (Selvini Palazzoli et al., 1974) reported on two other rituals. The first was a burial ritual for a family with a young daughter. She had stopped eating after her baby brother died four days after birth. No one had talked directly about his death. The family was asked to acknowledge the infant's death in a way that the little girl could understand. They took some of her baby brother's clothing and buried them, talking about what had happened to him. The other was a ritualized contract with a young boy to stop soiling his pants if the parents stopped all their efforts to have his teeth straightened and special eyeglasses prescribed (efforts that medical specialists did not think would help him that much anyway). The team did not deal with the issue of definition in this article, emphasizing instead the efficacy of rituals, saying, "family rituals of this kind are among the most important and effective therapeutic techniques that we devised in the course of our research into rapid and decisive intervention with dysfunctional families" (p. 438).

In 1977, Palazzoli and her colleagues returned to the problem of definition as they described in more detail the ritual used with the anorexic woman, Nora, focusing on how ritual was used to influence the family myth of "one for all and all for one" of the tightly joined extended family. They defined ritual at this point as actions that are prescribed in detail (time, place, order, etc.) for the family and that are *sometimes* done in conjunction with verbal messages (italics added). They emphasized that the power of the ritual lies in the fact that it is closer to the analogic nonverbal code than to the digital. They also highlighted the difficulties in designing each ritual anew for families.

Descriptions of another shift in the Milan group's definition of ritual were published in 1978. Palazzoli et al. presented the odd days/even days ritualized prescription, where only the formal aspects of the ritual (e.g., on "even days" the father is to do the parenting, on "odd days" the mother) were prescribed and the actual interactions were not. This intervention could therefore be used with a number of diverse families where they felt the parents were involved in symmetrical disqualifications around the behavior of a child. The Milan associates went on in *Paradox and Counterparadox* (1978b) to give several examples of rituals with "schizophrenic families," always emphasizing the importance of presenting the ritual in the larger frame of positive connotation of the family dilemma.

Over time, one can discern a loosening of the Milan group's definition of ritual. There is a movement away from always needing verbal elements, less emphasis on the importance of prescribing a particular place or time to perform the ritual, and some awareness of the importance of open rather than highly prescribed parts to the ritual (e.g., with the odd days/even days ritual, where the family chooses the content).

In the same year that *Paradox and Counterparadox* was published in English (1978), van der Hart's book on psychotherapy and rituals was published in Dutch. Van der Hart, who had become interested in the relationship between rituals and therapy from the work of the Milan group, extended this work with a broader conceptual base through the study of rituals done in anthropology. However, there was not much access to this book in North America until it was translated into English and issued in 1983 as *Rituals in Psychotherapy: Transition and Continuity*. Here, van der Hart defines ritual as:

> . . . prescribed symbolic acts that must be performed in a certain way and in a certain order, and may or may not be accompanied by verbal formulas.
>
> Besides the formal aspects, an experiential aspect of rituals can be distinguished. The ritual is performed with much involvement. If that is not the case, then we are talking about empty rituals.
>
> Certain rituals are repeatedly performed throughout the lives of those concerned; others, on the contrary, are performed only once (but can be performed again by other people). (pp. 5–6)

Van der Hart also discusses the importance of open and closed parts in ritual. Open parts provide enough fluidity so that participants can invest the experience with their own evolving and idiosyncratic meaning. Closed parts provide enough structure to give safety to strong emotional components, pass on important new cultural information, and give form to the actions.

Van der Hart enlarges upon the definition of the Milan group by introducing the notion of "empty" or hollow rituals. This means that a ritual prescribed in therapy cannot be viewed solely from the perspective of what the therapist says about the ritual, but must be understood from the participants' experience of it as well. The importance of involvement in the ritual is also highlighted by the necessity of including both open and closed parts. Finally, van der Hart acknowledges that ritual can occur only once, that it need not be repeated in order to be defined as a ritual.[1]

Ritual as Used in Anthropology

As we turn to anthropology, we find that, although anthropologists do not agree on the operational limits of the concept of ritual, there has been common acceptance of Victor Turner's definition of ritual as "prescribed formal behavior for occasions not given over to technological routine, having reference to beliefs in mystical beings or powers. The symbol is the smallest unit of ritual" (1967, p. 19). Yet Turner himself went beyond this definition in his later work, to look at so-called secular ritual where symbols once crucial to ritual action have migrated into other areas, such as politics, advertising, and the law. In 1974 he even went so far as to organize (along with Max Gluckman and Sally F. Moore) a conference in Burg Wartenstein, Austria, entitled "Secular Rituals Considered." In the book which emerged from the proceedings of this meeting Moore and Myerhoff (1977) make the point that anthropological study of ritual has often been limited to religious and magical aspects of a culture, partly because anthropologists have so often worked in societies "in which everything has a religious significance . . . " (p. 3). However, they note that as societies have become more secular they have continued to carry within them unquestionable tenets that have the same role in society as religion; further, they stress the importance of recognizing the "sacredness" of these tenets and the rituals carried out around them. Their definition of "sacred" goes beyond the traditional religious definition to focus on specialness—something imbued with meaning beyond the ordinary. This fits with Durkheim's (1915) notion that ritual functions as a frame highlighting the sacred as set apart. Goody (1977), while not enamored of the term ritual, notes that Turner's definition can be used for secular rituals by omitting the phrase "having reference to beliefs in mystical beings."

Turner's (1967) definition also highlights *symbols* as the building blocks of rituals. He explains the significance of symbols in three areas: (1) ability to carry multiple meanings and thus contribute to the open parts of rituals;

(2) the ways symbols can link several disparate phenomena that could not be joined as complexly through words; and (3) the ability of symbols to work with both the sensory and cognitive poles of meaning simultaneously.

Rappaport, who has written on cybernetics and rituals, also noted that the term ritual is not limited to religious practices. He elucidates (1971) six key aspects to ritual, especially collective ceremonies, of which family rituals are a part:

1. Repetition—not necessarily just in action but also of content and form.
2. Acting—not just saying or thinking something but also doing something.
3. Special behavior or stylization—where behaviors and symbols are set apart from their usual common uses.
4. Order—some beginning and end and containment for spontaneity.
5. Evocative presentational style—where through staging and focus an "attentive state of mind" is created.
6. Collective dimension—where there is social meaning.

In her later work, Myerhoff (1977) accepts and draws upon these key aspects of ritual, but also highlights the physiological aspects of ritual with its "costumes, masks, colors, textures, odors, foods, beverages, songs, dances, props, settings and so forth" (p. 199). In addition, she discusses the inherent contradiction of ritual, in that a ritual defines reality yet happens in a "sacred" time and space that is outside of the usual "reality." Therapy works with this same contradiction, in that it is seen as a process to rework day-to-day interactions yet happens in a special time and space that is outside of the usual boundaries of daily interaction.

> Critical, analytic thought, the attitude which would pierce the illusion of reality is anathema to ritual. The fiction underlying ritual is twofold: first, that rituals are not made-up productions, and second, that the contradictions embraced by their symbols have been erased. . . . Rituals can be distinguished from custom and mere habit by their utilization of symbols. They have significance far beyond the information transmitted. They may accomplish tasks, accompany routine and instrumental procedures, but they always go beyond them, endowing some larger meaning to activities they are associated with. (Myerhoff, 1977, pp. 199–200)

From anthropology, then, in defining ritual, we gain an emphasis on the power of symbols, the necessity of action, physiological aspects, and the coordination of order and spontaneity. Together, these combine to create a frame of "specialness" beyond the everyday. Also, there has been a common acceptance of the three-part stages of ritual that Van Gennep first wrote about in 1909. In the first stage, *separation*, special preparations are made and new knowledge is passed on as the frame is set for marking a particular event. This time of preparing for the ritual is as important a part of the ritual process as the actual event itself. The second stage is the *liminal or transitional*, where people actually partake of the ritual and experience themselves in new ways and take on new roles, new identities. The third stage is *reaggregation or reintegration* where people are reconnected to their community with their new status.

Before moving into the definition of ritual used in this book, which has its roots in both anthropology and family therapy, an important distinction needs to be made between the use of ritual in cultural contexts (anthropological view) and the use of ritual in the therapy context. Ritual is not just the ceremony or actual performance, but the whole process of preparing for it, experiencing it, and reintegration back into everyday life. This seems particularly important to emphasize when working with rituals in therapy because in a sense all three phases need to be developed. With cultural rituals, the three stages have already been clearly defined and built into the process (for instance, with Christmas, there is the cutting of the tree, the baking of Christmas treats, the buying of gifts in secrecy; then there is the actual celebration of Christmas Eve and Christmas; and then the taking down of the tree, writing thank you cards, etc.). These processes need to evolve in therapeutic rituals. Years of tradition are not necessarily there to draw upon. Also, in therapeutic rituals one is consciously creating new tradition rather than doing it the "same old way."

Working Definition of Ritual

Rituals are coevolved symbolic acts that include not only the ceremonial aspects of the actual presentation of the ritual, but the process of preparing for it as well. It may or may not include words, but does have both open and closed parts which are "held" together by a guiding metaphor. Repetition can be a part of rituals through either the content, the form, or the occasion. There should be enough space in therapeutic rituals for the incorporation of multiple meanings by various family members and clinicians, as well as a variety of levels of participation.

A way to operationalize this definition is to compare ritual to the more common tasks that are given in family therapy (see Table 1).

Case Example: Mixing, Matching and Masquerading with Hats

To elucidate these differences, a case will be described from a team at the University of Massachusetts using Ericksonian hypnotherapy and Milan

TABLE 1

Ritual Differentiated From Task

RITUAL	TASK
1. Works with multiple meanings on behavioral, cognitive and affective levels.	1. More focus on the behavioral level of the task, the actions.
2. Intervention includes both open and closed parts with space for the family to improvise within the more open parts. Therapist is not necessarily so sure what the family will create with the ritual. Nor is the therapist particularly interested in predicting what the family will "look" like after the ritual.	2. More emphasis on doing the intervention as prescribed with a predicted outcome. (Often the therapist has a vision, "if the family does the task in this way, then this will happen").
3. Reliance on symbols and symbolic action.	3. More reliance on the concrete with little emphasis on multivocality of symbols.
4. Preparation, the coevolving of the ceremony, is an essential part of the ritual.	4. Focus on the actual doing, not necessarily the preparation.

approaches, with both a task and a ritual designed for the same presenting problem.

A mother came in for treatment with her teenage daughter and son, age 10. The son was identified by the family as the person having problems. He had frequent outbursts of anger at home and both mother and daughter complained that he did not follow family rules. The ex-husband had just moved back into the area after having been gone for about six years. There was a peripheral boyfriend who lived with them but did not want to come to the therapy sessions or parent the children. He just wanted to be a friend to them.

As we talked with the family, the mother said she and her ex-husband had had some marital therapy before they divorced. At the time, in the therapy, her husband had been identified as "the man with the black hat" and she was the "woman with the white hat."[2] These were roles that each of them brought from their families of origin (the bad child and the good child). The mother stated that making these roles explicit had been helpful in the previous therapy.

As we worked with the family, we saw that the same distinction strikingly occurred in the next generation. The daughter was the "good hat," where the son was the "bad hat." The daughter was mother's confidante and very much a parental child who did a lot of disciplining of the "bad" child. The son was more challenging of family rules, more outspoken, and much more likely to talk about things that were upsetting to him.

In the fourth session, we did a lot of questioning regarding who wore "white" and "black hats" around the house and outside of the house and at what times. We found out that the son wore some "good" hats — he played the trumpet, had a lot of musical talent, and actually did quite well in school. The daughter turned out to wear the "black hat" sometimes when she had babysitting jobs and other responsibilities outside of the house and did not follow through. We also asked what hats the boyfriend wore to bring his presence into the room. Intriguingly, we found out during the discussion that they had a white cat and a black cat and perceived the white cat as the 'good" one and the black one as the "naughty" one.

If we had given a task to this family at the end of this session, it might have been something like this: "Mom, over the next week, watch for when your son is exhibiting positive behaviors and twice thank him directly for it. Write those times down and bring them into session. Also, discuss with your boyfriend at least twice each week how your daughter comments on the white hat behavior of her brother."

Instead, what we gave them was an *identity* ritual aimed at reworking and establishing new roles by promoting role reversals (see Chapter 2 on Ritual Themes). We asked the family, including the boyfriend, to go out and buy two white hats and two black hats, perhaps of different sizes and shapes (this intervention was given the week of Halloween). If they wanted to, they could try on different hats, see which ones they liked on each other — have some fun trying them on. Also, they might even find some hats for the cats. Then, we asked them to put the hats out in a place in the house where they felt the most sense of connection. They said this was a wood stove that they often gathered around. We asked them to then use the hats when they wanted to call attention to roles that they were playing which were different from the usual; say, if the son wanted to call attention to the fact he was being a good hat, he could put on a white hat. Or someone else in the family might take on the bad hat role — or two hats at once, or place a hat on another member. We asked them to mix up who could wear them when and where.

This is very different from the task described earlier in several ways. First, there are the symbols of the hats and the symbolic actions involved in making conscious choices to put them on and take them off (e.g., one can control one's behavior consciously) or to put them on someone else ("I see and interpret your behavior in particular ways"). This opened the possibility of redefining roles, as well as challenging the implicit intergenerational, gender-based rules. There are also many open parts in terms of choosing the hats, whether to get hats for the cats or not, placement of the hats in the house, and deciding when to wear them, further supporting family flexibility as well as introducing humor and play. The ritual was action oriented in

TABLE 2

RITUAL	TASK
1. Multiple meanings of "good" and "bad" hats, who can wear them, put them on and off.	1. Focus on specific behaviors. Mom is to comment twice on positive behaviors of son and to talk twice with boyfriend on how the daughter comments on "good" behaviors of the son.
2. A number of open parts including whether to buy hats for the cats, placement of the hats, times they would shift hats.	2. Family members are directed to carry out actions with few open parts.
3. Key symbols and symbolic actions were the hats and the possibilities of wearing hats different and/or the same in color.	3. No symbols or symbolic actions included.
4. Preparation of going as a family (including boyfriend who was ambivalent about coming to sessions) to buy the hats and selecting a place for them are seen as essential parts of the ritual.	4. Looking for people to carry out the tasks. No emphasis on preparation.

both the going out together to get the hats and the mobility of the hats from person to person. Also, the process of preparing for the ritual — going to get the hats as a family and deciding where to put them — marks family cohesion. Preparation for the ritual is as important as the ritual itself. Finally, it worked with multiple levels of meaning, involving past relationships, current ones, as well as possible future roles.

Crucial distinctions between ritual and task include the multiple meanings embodied in the ritual and its symbols, the emphasis on the coevolution of the ritual process with the family, the inclusion of open parts, and focus on preparation as being as important as the actual performance of the ritual (see Table 2).

FUNCTIONS OF RITUALS

> Ritual is a statement in metaphoric terms about the paradoxes of human existence.
> —C. Crocker (Shaughnessy, 1973, p. 47)

Rituals provide "frameworks for expectancy" (Douglas, 1966) where, through the use of repetition, familiarity, and transformation of what is already known, new behaviors, actions, and meanings can occur. Time is collapsed in rituals. Changes in the present are grounded in past traditions, while future relationships are defined. Particularly important is the action component of rituals, in that they speak not *about* roles, rules, relationships, and world views, but *in* roles, relationships, rules, and world views as these elements are shifted in the ritual (Davis, 1984). Beyond action, rituals have available to them the density and multivocality of symbols. Symbols, as the smallest unit of ritual (Turner, 1967), can hold multiple, disparate meanings as well as describe what cannot be expressed economically in words. For instance, a net can be seen both as a symbol of entrapment, and one of safety. The ability of rituals to link time, hold contradictions, and work with relationship shifts in action offers us particular tools to work with and hold incongruities between the actual and the ideal.

In a retirement ceremony I observed, new roles and relationships were enacted, while the ritual provided a safe space to examine both the complexities of the retiring person's career and the actual process of her retirement. This was a particularly poignant ceremony because the administrator who was retiring, Susan Marks, the head of a school of nursing, had been sick over the last several months and no one knew exactly what the illness was, although rumors had been circulating that it was life-threatening. Further, it was not clear how much the retirement was her choice, and there were many mixed feelings about how successful her administration had been. A number of people who had worked with Susan Marks chose not to attend and the people who were there had lived for some time with the ambiguities of whether this was retirement by choice, of the life-threatening aspects of the illness, and of lack of definition of who was leading their unit. People gathered for dinner, speeches, and the presentation of gifts.

Of the 10 people who spoke during the dinner, most began by telling personal vignettes of their relationship with Dr. Marks. This grounded their roles as nurses together, teachers, grantwriters, and administrators in hospitals. This began to highlight the very important ways some people had connected with Dr. Marks and her work in the context of the absence of many people who had not found this kind of relationship with her. After telling these vignettes, the speakers all went on to talk about the significance of her work. As they described her work on the national level through her writing, at the state level as almost a legislative lobbyist, and at the university through multiple responsibilities, the scope of her work began to emerge. Ultimately, a much larger world view of the retiring person's work was woven than any one person could have presented. Finally, people commented on what they would like their new relationship to be with her and how they might work with her in the future. This included such details as projects they might ask her to consult on, classes she might come back to teach, as well as places they might want to go with her. The transition out of old relationships and roles had already begun as people began to define new possibilities.

In addition, one person who spoke had recently had a bout with a severe illness. His comments on how this affected his life and on his happiness that he had the strength to be there that night provided a very poignant space for people to indirectly experience some of their own fears about Susan Marks' illness that could not be discussed openly.

At the end of the speeches and open comments from the floor, two symbols were presented as gifts from the group. The first was a sculpture of a dancer in an abstract design that held both power and energy moving out into space and a sense of immobilization with one leg gone. It captured the duality of what many saw as an administration overseen by Dr. Marks, which had been very active behind the scenes, but somewhat immobilized in important day-to-day decisions. The other gift was a formal portrait of the retiree which would now hang in the administration's conference room. Upon the unveiling of the picture, various comments were made, such as, "We can look up at you when we are meeting in that room and ask you for advice," and "We know you'll be watching over us." Only her symbolic presence would be in the building now. In marking new statuses and acknowledging the range of the old, the ceremony provided a safe space that could hold for a brief period of time the incongruities between the actual and the ideal of Susan Marks' administration. While the coming together in one space highlighted who chose not to come to honor Susan Marks, it also provided a public forum for other people to acknowledge their close and enduring relationships with her. While her illness could not be openly discussed, Dr. Marks' public appearance in good spirits and the description of her colleague's illness allowed it to be indirectly acknowledged. Clarification of what Susan Marks had done in her work was combined with a clear definition of her movement out of her old status.

Rituals have multiple functions, which have been highlighted by various scholars of ritual.[3] In this section, drawing primarily from anthropology, I will examine the functions of rituals as these help to elucidate what happens as families participate in daily, familial, and cultural and religious rituals.

Structure, Action and Meaning: Ritual as Intercom

> Looked at from the symbolic "inside out" (rather than the functionalist "outside in"), ritual can be seen as a symbolic intercom between the level of cultural thought and complex cultural meanings on the one hand, and that of social action and immediate event, on the other. (Munn as quoted in Doty, 1986, p. 72)

Early social anthropologists highlighted how ritual reflects and sustains a social order and marks specific community links (Hallowell, 1941; Radcliffe-Brown, 1952). Ritual was seen as promoting intergroup stability, as providing a controlled and safe place to solve personal and social problems and validating the ongoing social structure (Comstock, 1972). Turner (1974) proposed going beyond this analysis to look at the tensive relationship of ritual to stability and change: The same time that ritual is marking social order, it can transform and destroy social structure and establish new norms and new traditions. Ritual can therefore not just *mark* a transition, but also *make* a transition at the same time.

For instance, in weddings some parts of the ceremony seem to specifically focus on marking the social order of this new couple coming together in the same ways as millions of couples have done before them (exchanging rings, taking the vows "'till death do us part," announcing the new titles of "husband" and "wife"). In Western culture these are all common ways to indicate the transition to a new nuclear family. This transition is not just marked, but also made at the same time. The parents "give away" the bride and groom, symbolizing their letting go of them from the family of origin unit.[4] During the wedding, the parents' position in relation to their marrying children changes. By the end of the wedding, the couple is walking out together, and later, leaving together to go to a special place for the honeymoon. Besides new roles taken on by the immediate family, new roles may be asked of the community of witnesses who have gathered to celebrate the wedding as well. A newly developed ritual that I have seen recently at weddings involves asking the guests to stand, to put out one hand toward the couple, and to promise that they will provide community support for the couple through both good and difficult times.

At the same time that the transition is made and marked, there is space in the celebration for new traditions to be established. For instance, the couple may choose to honeymoon in a place to which they will then return for their anniversaries. Playing the "Anniversary Waltz" at the reception may not only mark the anniversaries of people attending the wedding but also start the tradition of celebrating the anniversary of the wedding couple. As Turner (1975) critiqued the traditional sociofunctionalist paradigm:

> . . . it is not enough merely to consider the symbolic molecules of ritual as informational storage-units. They are these and more, and in the "more" we move into the field of social dynamics where ritual both maintains the traditional forms of culture and becomes at times of major crisis an instrument for adjusting new norms and values to perennially potent symbolic forms and discarding old ones from the ideological pole of crucial symbols. (p. 80)

For instance, in the case described in Chapter 2 by Evan Imber-Black of a couple with two children who chose to "remarry," four special glasses were bought by the parents with each person's name inscribed upon one. These glasses were used for their toast to each other in their "remarriage" ceremony. The family members then commented on how they planned to use the glasses at other special family times. They also held their "remarriage" ceremony in a hotel, saying "We'll come back to the same hotel next year."

In contrast to the social anthropologists' emphasis on structure and ritual, cultural anthropologists have focused on *meaning* in ritual and how people construct maps of their reality, how they explain those parts of the cosmos to which none of us can be indifferent: birth and death, night and day, changing of the seasons, war and peace, separateness and togetherness (Culler, 1987). Rituals carry cultural meaning passed on through the different experiences of generations, as well as allowing opportunity to create new paradigms and new metaphors.

In the celebration of Easter, there are multiple meanings that have been passed down with the symbols of the rabbit and eggs in terms of fertility, life at a time of year when the earth begins to blossom again, and fecundity. Even the derivation of the word Easter (which comes from the goddess Eostre) signifies awakening. Within the larger culture this holiday can signify a rebirth from the more dormant time of year. In this context, families create new individualized metaphors that operationalize some of these meanings, as well as others that are significant to their own family development. Eggs may be decorated in Grandmother's style, or special painted eggs may be handed down from one generation to the next.

In Massachusetts, a group of 10–12 families have been gathering for several years at Easter near a river south of Amherst College, in a place that looks out over the rolling hills and Holyoke range to the south. Everyone brings food to share in a glorious picnic. One year when I participated, the children played games while the adults hid the eggs and surprises that each of them had made with their children for the hunt. Then the Easter bunny appeared from over the hill and talked with the children about what it meant to be fellow searchers looking for that which could nourish both their body and their vision, and how the older children should share with the younger what they found at the end. Away the children went along the river and into the woods, helping each other to find the eggs, exchanging treats, and letting the smallest children go first. These families created their own meaning about searching, collaboration, and help for their spring festivities.

In her chapter on four families' bar mitzvahs, Judy Davis highlights how each of the very different families (blended, nuclear, Russian immigrant, and Hasidic missionary) found ways to transform the same ritual to create meaning for each of their developmental needs.

Combining both the cultural perspective and social perspective of anthropology: *Ritual works as both a maintainer and creator of social structure for individuals, families and social communities, as well as a maintainer and creator of world view.* It can mediate between the two arenas of structure and meaning so that each defines, reflects, and elucidates the other. As Doty explained in his excellent review of the study of myth and ritual (1986):

> It is not my intention to develop only a sociofunctionalist position in which myth and ritual are appreciated almost exclusively for their constructive roles in providing the societal glue that binds societies and enables them to adjust to the polarities of personal existence. . . . I would like to move beyond such a position by emphasizing that myths and rituals do that *and more*. Specifically they not only provide functional resolutions of such problems but they also are creative insofar as they are a communicative means through which persons find meaningful systems of symbols for identifying their experiences. Myths and rituals carry the traditional societal assessments of values assigned to this or that experience; and they provide an important means of living through one's life experiences when they become resources for identifying, labeling, and relating to the forces experienced as active within one's environment. (p. 127)

The ability of ritual to work as an intercom between structure and meaning provides it with potent possibilities to transform.

Other Functions of Rituals

Ritual can hold both sides of a contradiction at the same time. We all live with the ultimate paradoxes of life/death, connection/distance, ideal/real, good/evil. Ritual can *incorporate both sides of contradictions* so that they can be managed simultaneously. For instance, a wedding ceremony has within it both loss and mourning and joy and celebration. People say, "You're not losing a daughter, you're gaining a son-in-law." Parents give their child away at the same time as they welcome a new member to their extended family.

In Kumasi, Ghana, I once danced in an Ashanti dance funeral where we were all facing the same direction in a large circle and moving clockwise to the rhythms of a drum orchestra. Each person individually bent down and curled over, as if to feel the pain and loss of the person who had died. But this motion was done within the context of the whole group, everyone feeling the hurt and then coming up into the circle to see the others, to move with their energy, and celebrate our own bodies and life. The movement itself held both sides of life and death.

Ritual may provide a way for people to find *support and containment for strong emotions* (Scheff, 1979). For instance, with a wake, or sitting shiva, there are certain prescribed times for mourning. Groups of people come together to support each other with their sorrow, shared foods are brought, certain clothes may be worn, and particular words are said. There is safety in knowing that you can experience the depth of the feelings but with some circumscribed limits and group support. Likewise, the ritualized aspects of funerals can provide some containment for deep feelings.

In my family of origin, I have a younger brother, Mark, who has been missing for five years. He is an alcoholic and disappeared one day from a residential treatment center for alcoholism which he had voluntarily joined. We live with the difficult ambiguity of not knowing whether he is dead or alive. Further, because we do not know whether he is alive, no ritual (such as a funeral) is readily available to allow people to come together and mark his loss. After Mark first disappeared, family members could talk to one another about him in the context of ways they were searching to find him. However, over time, as no clues to his whereabouts emerged, people found it difficult to talk to each other about him. We felt helpless about knowing what to do. Further, there were questions of blame (each of us might have done more to help him), and residual superstitions that if we talked about him as if he were dead, then that would in a sense make him dead. These issues were all compounded by the fact that my parents were divorced, the family was scattered widely geographically, and we seldom all came together.

Then my mother went to an individual therapist to talk about her sense of loss, something that we were having difficulty expressing to each other. The therapist suggested that my mother create some memorial for her lost son that would both honor him and acknowledge her pain. In a rowboat out in the San Juan islands, she told me of her therapist's idea and we began to talk of doing something together as a family. Over a year's time, my mother selected a corner of her garden where she could look out and see whatever memorial was created. We began to weed and clear out this part of the garden. During this time we began to talk about Mark more, as we knelt on our knees, digging into the earth. In August, as family members gathered from different parts of the country, we decided to go to the mountains and pick out a stone from a particular hiking trail he liked in the North Cascades. This rock was then carried out by backpack to the car and brought to Seattle. On the day of the ceremony, my older brother played the south Indian flute as we walked in a processional out of the house and gathered around the stone. Together we lifted it into a place that had been prepared for it among some small evergreens. Then we each shared memories of Mark and what we wished for him in the future. There were many tears and some laughter as people talked and moved closer together. My mother presented a scrapbook with pictures of Mark and written recollections, asking us all to contribute to it. This scrapbook, which my mother keeps at her house, provides an ongoing way in which we can talk safely about our deep feelings about Mark and contribute our continuing memories. It also contains the photos from the ceremony that my brother-in-law took. My four-year-old daughter, who participated in the ritual, chose to name a doll from China that was given to her the day before "Ceremony," and asks often about "the missing Mark."

Social coordination among individuals, families, and communities and among past, present and future can be facilitated by ritual. Davis (1987), in studying bar mitzvahs, looked at how the process of that ceremony defines a place for the individual child who is now becoming more adult and is moving into a different status within his family, peer group, and community. He has to demonstrate competency in the sacred language, Hebrew. He shows that he can lead the congregation for some small period of time. The bar mitzvah "boy" becomes a person of age in the Jewish community who can be counted to form a minyon. At the same time, the new status of the family is acknowledged. Extended family and friends gather at the behest of the family to celebrate these changes. They give gifts to the young man to acknowledge his new status.

The whole community is also connected to the larger religious and cultural tradition of Judaism. Special readings are given from the Torah, and certain structural elements of the ritual are done which have been passed down over centuries. The ceremony works on a number of levels simultaneously: making and marking individual, family, and group transitions. Also, past, present, and future are linked through the historical context of Jewish tradition, the acknowledgment of present accomplishments of the child and family, and the new status of the child/man.

In the national ritual of Thanksgiving, these same themes of social coordination nested in time can also be examined. Individual roles can be marked by particular preparations. For instance, a minister described how his grandfather raised, killed, and cleaned the turkey on the farm in Kentucky, while his grandmother did the cooking. These tasks represented the delineation of gender roles in his family, where his grandfather primarily did work outside of the house and his grandmother the work inside. His grandfather always carved the turkey, and the minister remembered well when this task was passed on to his own father (this included grandfather's giving him the carving knife), marking the movement of his father into the older generation.[5] In addition, there were certain foods that were always made from recipes that were passed down; these linked the family to their families of origin. As Goodman (1987) described her family's Thanksgiving, "Untouchable recipes handed down from one generation to another arrive on the table bearing the names of these ancestors. Each year the Number One Aunt replicates in exquisite detail her own mother's stuffing. She produces it in a tearful ceremony brought on by equal portions of onions and memories."

For other families at Thanksgiving, rituals such as the telling of familiar stories, cooking together, watching football, and gathering in a particular place all help to define roles (including gender roles) and rules and create group cohesion. Further, this happens within the larger community context of a nation which is giving thanks as it honors the first wave of European immigrants, at the same time that it ignores what was done to the original inhabitants of this country.

Rich Cowles (1985) compares his two extended families' traditions at Thanksgiving (his family of origin's and his wife's) to two hand carved music boxes which are passed down through the generations. Looking at the boxes on a shelf, they seem similar, but when opened each plays its unique song.

> The music boxes are what I'm thankful for this Thanksgiving. In spite of deaths, divorce and distance, in spite of hectic lives and mind-spinning life style changes, we still gather together to open our family heirlooms and sing along. I'm thankful for new faces—unsuspecting souls marrying into the tribe, who add freshness to our songs. And I'm thankful for the kids, the future caretakers of our traditions. May they add tunes not yet imagined and may they keep the music boxes playing long after we are gone. (p. E 5)

The past, present, and future, as represented by the various generations and evolving traditions, are connected.

Besides helping to resolve contradictions, face anxiety and strong emotions, and facilitate social coordination, ritual *supports transitions* (van der Hart, 1983; Van Gennep, 1960). There are three stages, identified by anthropologists in rites of passage and healing rituals, that are useful to consider when looking at rituals in the therapy process. In the first stage, the separation stage, the individual or group is severed from his or her own status and frequently isolated from regular ongoing routines or contact. For instance, many puberty rituals involve separating the youngsters from the living quarters of the larger group and taking them to a special place.[6] In our culture, the tradition in the wedding celebration of not seeing the bride and groom before the ceremony begins still prevails; they are off in a special place separated from the group.

In the marginal or liminal stage, the person or group going through the ritual is in neither old status nor the new one. For instance, in a puberty rite the noviate is neither girl nor woman. She can be classified as having no classification. Often in this second stage there is a passing on of new learning, sacred information. The noviates try on new roles, new identities. In the reintegration or third stage, the person or group is returned to the daily life. His or her new status is often acknowledged with a new name, new clothing, community feasting and celebration.

Ritual has the capability of holding multiple points of view, providing support and containment for intense emotions, while facilitating social coordination among individuals, family members and community going through transitions. This is dramatically illustrated in the film "Some Babies Die" (1986) where Tess, whose baby Cosmo lived only a few hours after birth, is encouraged with her family to create memories of Cosmo by holding and looking at her and preparing her for the funeral. In contrast, Donna's grief over the stillborn birth of her first child is hidden away. The baby is taken away, unseen by Donna, and buried in an unmarked, common grave. There is no public forum in which people might come together to share their grief, but also mark that life goes on.

How Rituals Work for Individuals

Focusing even more on how rituals are experienced by individuals, d'Aquili, Laughlin, and McManus (1979) have examined the neurobiological impact of participation in rituals. Drawing on studies of ritualized animal behavior as well as the neurobiology of the brain, they hypothesize that the active parts of certain rituals (repetitions, multiple symbols, music, dance, etc.) produce positive limbic discharges, which lead to increased contact between people and social cohesion. Different parts of the brain are stimulated as well. In fact, d'Aquili et al. speculate that *the two main hemispheres of the brain spill over into each other*. This may be experienced as a "shiver down the back." For myself, while playing music for numerous weddings over the last 10 years, I have often experienced tears in my eyes and that shiver down my back,[7] even when I have known almost nothing about the people getting married.

How ritual may work for individuals can be described in another way. Both *digital and analogic information are combined* in ritual, so that the more verbal and analytical arena of the left brain is connected with the more nonverbal, intuitive right brain. Ornstein and Thompson (1984) reported on a study that compared the brain activity of people while they were reading written material that was either (1) technical or (2) folktales:

> There was no change in the level of activity in the left hemisphere, but the right hemisphere was more activated while the subject was reading the stories than while he or she was reading the technical material. Technical material is almost exclusively logical. Stories, on the other hand, are simultaneous: many things happen at once; the sense of a story emerges through a combination of style, plot, and evoked images and feelings. Thus, it appears that language *in the form of stories* can stimulate activity of the right hemisphere. (p. 162)

Rituals are also simultaneous and may evoke more activity in the right hemisphere.

Another way in which the brain may be stimulated in individuals is through the use of symbols. *Symbols hold a density of meaning* that words alone cannot capture, but that can be held in the right brain. For example, residents of Dixie Valley, Nevada, when forced to leave their homes and land because it was taken over by the military for a target practice site, had a symbolic burial of "things that have been important to their lives in Dixie Valley and are being lost because of what happened" (*Valley Advocate*, September 14, 1987, p. 12). Among the items that they buried were "two articles of the Constitution, water from the artesian wells that kept the valley green, and a hip flask symbolic of the last drink one man (sic) will ever take in Dixie Valley." These items succinctly hold layers of possibility for interpretation that would take many words to explain.

Functions of Ritual and Family Therapy

The functions of rituals have important implications for the use of ritual in family therapy precisely because they offer many possibilities for holding duality. First, with ritual as a connector for structure and meaning, both aspects of family life can be brought into play. If a seven-year-old child is having stomach and headaches in school and at home, it is important to work not only with the interactional sequences surrounding that behavior, but also with the meaning ascribed to it by the child, parents, school, doctor and other significant members of the child's system. Some family therapy models (e.g., Haley strategic or Minuchin structural as described by Sluzki, 1983) focus on the structure of interactional patterns and how people work with the problem. In dealing with the above problem, questions would be asked about who does what when she has the aches, how often she has them, and how people have changed their behaviors to try to solve the problem. Other models (e.g., Milan model as described by Sluzki, 1983) emphasize the meaning of the problem by asking questions, such as who is most upset and least upset, how people explain that he has the problem, who agrees, disagrees, etc.

In working with Minuchin's or Haley's model, the therapist would move in to change the structure by unbalancing, pulling in less involved people, and interrupting problematic sequences of behavior. This might happen right in the therapy room or through out-of-session directives. In contrast, the Milan model would work more at the level of what meaning is given to the child's behavior (is she seen as immature, bad, sick, crazy?) and how this meaning affects family premises about who the family is as a unit and how both the family and school view each other. There would be an in-session focus on generating new meaning through the process of circular questioning. However, both these levels of structure and meaning need to be coordinated in treatment, and ritual provides an elegant way to do it. It has a capacity to cut across models of family therapy to link structure and meaning.

Second, holding contradictions, as rituals do, is the essence of work in therapy. A person who presents with symptomatic behaviors has great influence on the interactional dynamics around him and is out of control at the same time.

Another central duality in therapy is the change/no change dilemma. People come into treatment asking for change, yet change is risky and unknown. It is also useful to consider in treatment the contradiction that symptomatic behavior both helps and hinders people: Symptoms are solutions and problems at the same time.

Ritual allows strong emotions to be safely experienced, at the same time that interpersonal connections are made. Families in treatment have often put a rigid boundary around difficult events in their lives, lacking a way to mark and share events in their larger community. There may be losses in a family for which no cultural rituals exist, such as abortion, birth of a handicapped child, stillborn birth, separation of the family by war, loss of a foster child, or divorce (Imber-Black, 1988a). These events might not be marked by the family because of the sense of stigma absorbed from the larger culture. The use of ritual in treatment can provide a safe place to explore intense emotions, while providing support through connecting people to each other. A link has consistently been found between social isolation and mental health problems.

The linking of past, present and future through ritual also has broad implications for family therapy. Many families enter treatment with seemingly little fluidity between different time frames. For instance, they are so embroiled in past difficulties that they believe there is little hope for the family in the future. Or they are so engrossed in the requirements of day-to-day living that they cannot value their family history and heritage.

Finally, ritual, with its capacities to link both the analogic and digital aspects of communication, offers possibilities for expression and experiencing of that which cannot be put into words. Words cannot carry the weight of all that needs to be worked through in treatment.

Case Example: Parakeets, Shovels, and Rituals of Walking

In the Jensen family, where the 14-year-old daughter, Sara, refused to walk or talk for two years, her parents and other family members were very organized around helping her. Much of their family life centered on moving, dressing, and getting food for her. However, at the most basic level, Sara was also unable to control where her body would take her.

The youngest child in a very close family with five children, Sara stopped walking and talking as she entered puberty, an important marker in this society for children beginning to mature and starting the process of leaving the family more. The solution of her symptomatic behavior kept the family focused inwardly and close together. The family members did not have to face the possibility that this last child would leave home, as she was literally not going anywhere. At the same time, Sara's difficulties created other problems, such as her not being able to go to school and get an education.

In the Jensen family, there was a hidden loss that had important implications for Sara's own leaving home: Some ten years earlier, Sara's oldest sister Diane was diagnosed as schizophrenic shortly after she left home, married, and had a child (and so was defined as separated from her family).

After Sara had been in a residential program for a year, where family therapy was the organizing treatment of choice, she was walking, talking, dancing, horseback riding, and 50 pounds lighter. She was ready to move home and go back to a regular high school. (See Roberts, 1984, for a complete description of this case.) However, the way she left was seen as an essential part of treatment, because Sara had a prior hospitalization in which she was walking and talking within several weeks, was returned home, and within several months had stopped walking and talking again. During that hospitalization, the family had not been very involved in treatment and had in fact not been allowed to see Sara at times. Sara also spoke to the hospital staff first, after refusing to talk to her own family for over a year. Further, an acceptance of the both/and possibilities that Sara might indeed choose not to walk and talk again did not appear to be an essential part of the work done in the hospital.

A transition ritual to mark Sara's leaving the center and moving home highlights many of the functions of rituals that have been discussed. Sara's parents were each asked to bring to the session a written description of the ways each of them had walked Sara when she first entered treatment. (There had been a symmetrical escalation going on between the parents as to who had the best ways to caretake her.) The therapist brought a small tin box with birds on it (Sara had taught a parakeet to talk before she began talking to people again as a way to avoid the dilemma of who she would talk to first), a video segment of the way Sara was as she first entered residential treatment, and a shovel. In the session, time was first spent on making sure that her parents' description of the best ways to walk Sara were detailed enough so that, if Sara ever went back to not walking, they would have these directions available. Mom's style had been to walk her by holding her left shoulder and hitting the back knee with her right hand. Her father's style had been to hold her at the waist with both hands and kick each foot out with his feet at her instep. After the directions were clarified, the children were asked to practice walking the parents in the two ways the parents walked Sara and describe the relative merits of each. All of the children did this, except for Sara who chose only to watch. The parents were also encouraged to walk each other in the two different styles.

Everyone then viewed a 10-minute video of Sara and her parents teaching us how to care for her as she first entered the program. People talked about all the changes she had made and how different she was now. This video segment was then cut off and put into the box decorated with birds as a way to remember the past as well as to acknowledge how far Sara had come. Then we all went outside, and Sara was asked to pick a place on the grounds of the treatment center with some familiar markers. There we would bury the box. She sited a place on the side of the hill across from the gazebo. All took turns digging a hole for the box. Little was said during this time. I placed the box in the hole, saying, "Sara, if you ever choose not to walk or talk, you will know where to find this to get the necessary information on how people can take care of you." People spontaneously took turns shoveling the dirt back over the box while saying things like. "We'll never have to dig it up," and "We're through with this box now."

This ritual functioned in a number of ways. First, it marked the shift to open discussion of differences regarding how to caretake Sara. There were no longer two caretakers in hidden competition about who was the better caretaker. Also, it mixed up who could caretake whom, in what ways. Children were walking parents, parents were walking each other, no one was walking Sara. Third, it held in multiple ways the contradiction of Sara as one who both walked and did not walk. Sara's past as a non-walker and non-talker was combined with her present status as one who chose to do both, with the future as a place where both of these options would be open to her. Further, the symbolic representation of the past was available to her in the future should she need it. It was not in an easy place to reach, but one that was accessible.[8] Finally, the symbols of the birds on the box, children walking parents, and the burial all offered a number of ways in which analogic meaning could be incorporated into this highly charged transition.

Ritual can hold the duality of stability and change simultaneously, while it links time frames, informs social coordination, and captures meaning beyond words. Ritual combines doing with believing. Events are entered into not just as they are talked about, but as they are experienced — a world where doing and believing are intertwined.

Differences Between How Therapeutic Rituals
and Cultural Rituals Work

Therapeutic rituals differ significantly from rituals found in the day-to-day lives of people because they are less embedded in the ongoing history of the family. In therapeutic rituals there may, therefore, be less ease of access to the larger family network (for instance, extended family gatherings, or neighbors coming together to celebrate) or to the built-in traditions of various preparations (for instance, handmade decorations that have been passed down). This creates both advantages and disadvantages for the design of therapeutic rituals. Perhaps there are more flexible possibilities for creating meaning in a therapeutic ritual because one is not necessarily contending with the weight of years of empty rituals. Also, energy can be carefully focused on one or more particular problematic areas, which is not always the case with rituals that already involve a set series of actions. Yet, historical echoes intrinsic to cultural rituals that link people with the past and undergird the future may be lacking in therapeutic rituals. Special consideration must be given in designing therapeutic rituals to find ways to join families with the power of symbols that have a larger meaning beyond just their unit, to help them create traditions in preparing for the ritual enactment, and to involve the larger community. Attention needs to be paid to the power of witnessing through the use of therapists as onlookers, through videotaping and watching it, through inviting special people to the sessions, or through documenting the ritual in some other way that gives witness. In addition, therapists need to devise ways to protect the sacredness of the ritual space — protection that may already be present for cultural rituals through the declaration of a holiday or in the boundary of the church or synagogue, etc. These issues are addressed further in Chapter 3.

RITUAL, FAMILIES, AND THE THERAPY PROCESS

Looking at rituals with families in therapy can be useful in four areas: (1) assessment of ritualized behavior of the family outside of therapy; (2) symptomatic behavior as ritual; (3) ritualization of the therapy process; and finally, (4) therapeutic rituals.

Assessment of Family Ritual Behavior

Before creating rituals with families in therapy, it is important to learn about their current relationship to ritual in their day-to-day life. Expanding upon the work of Wolin and Bennett (1984), a typology of ritual use in families is presented: (1) underritualized: (2) rigidly ritualized: (3) skewed ritualization: (4) hollow ritual as event, not process: (5) ritual process interrupted or unable to be openly experienced: and (6) flexibility to adapt rituals. This typology can be used to organize the complex data that families present as they are questioned about their daily lives. Sample questions are presented to assess each of the six categories.

We are not suggesting in this book that families will be healed by having them experience ritual in only a particular way or that all families must have a certain level of ritual. Each family will have its own unique, "healthful" relationship to ritual. We are proposing this six-part typology as another perspective from which to assess families. If a family is assessed as under-ritualized, it does not mean that one should automatically move to create more rituals with these family members. Rather, their particular connections to ritualizing behavior need to be respected and a range of other issues (developmental life cycle, organization around symptomatic behavior, solutions already tried, etc.) carefully examined, as in any family treatment.

In the treatment of a family, some type of ritual intervention may be used only one or two times. We do not mean to imply that more rituals automatically mean more health.

Typology of Family Rituals

(1) UNDERRITUALIZED. Often underritualized families neither celebrate or mark family changes nor join much in larger societal rituals. This leaves the family with little access to some of the benefits of ritual mentioned earlier, such as group cohesion, support for role shifts, and the ability to hold two dualities in place at the same time. For instance, a couple with two adult sons came into treatment presenting marital difficulties, with the wife questioning whether she wanted to be married. The week before the first session had been their 24th wedding anniversary. They had not celebrated it because their son was leaving for school and they wanted to get him packed and off. They typically did not celebrate birthdays or mark other significant events in the family. For instance, the husband in this family stopped drinking during therapy, but this was not acknowledged or celebrated by the family in any way. In the course of asking about the process of ending the drinking, we found out that four years earlier (and the husband remembered the day well), he had stopped smoking, never to smoke again. This success too was not acknowledged.

Questions for assessment. All questions are interventive (Tomm, 1987). By asking circular questions, such as the sample ones presented below, clinicians can assess the family level of ritualization as well as introduce to the family information about their own use of rituals. Sample *orienting* questions are given first (called orienting by Tomm [1987] because they introduce the therapist to the clients' life experiences as well as orient the client to patterns). *Reflexive* questions, presented second, are designed to have more influence on possible changes. By asking these kinds of questions, the therapist encourages the family members to be observers of their own ritual behavior. Also, the therapist can begin to understand where the family might want to make some changes.

Sample orienting questions:

1. What was the last family event that you celebrated?

2. How do you celebrate Fourth of July, Thanksgiving (some of the more cultural traditions)?
3. How often during the year does the family gather together to mark something?
4. Do you think you get together more or less than other families you know?
5. Who is most/least comfortable with how you currently celebrate and mark events? Rank them.

Sample reflexive questions:

6. If you were to get together more often to share and celebrate events, who would be the most likely to enjoy it?
7. Who would be the most likely to initiate marking occasions more frequently?

In hearing the responses to orienting and influencing questions, the therapist and family can get an idea of whether the family or some members of it see themselves as underritualized, understand what access the family has to the larger societal ritual context for support, hear the ways in which ritual is or is not familiar to the family, and get a notion of where some small windows for change might be opened.

(2) RIGIDLY RITUALIZED. In families that are rigidly ritualized, there are very prescribed behaviors, a sense of "we must always do these things together in this way at this time." There are few open parts in the rituals, and rituals tend to stay the same over time rather than evolving. In the Jensen family described earlier, Sara had not walked or talked for two years. She had been hospitalized for several months, but there were no physiological findings to explain her condition. The family members were very organized around doing many things together, and there were very precise things that they did—certain TV shows that were watched, places where they ate out, specific movie theatres that they went to, etc. If a person stepped outside of these group norms, there were strong pulls to get her back.

We asked the parents, after the third family session, to go out alone as a reward for all the caretaking they had done of their daughter for two years, as well as of a paternal grandmother who was bedridden in the home. The family therapy team said to the parents, "To acknowledge for both of you all that you have done for everyone in the family and to support each other in it, why don't the two of you take a small and well-deserved break and go out alone and just appreciate each other?" The next session, the family reported that they had gone out with *everybody* to the usual pizza place and movie theatre. They told us, "You don't understand our family. We like to do things together. So this is the way we did it and we had a great time." Here, one may hypothesize that, with little or no room for improvisation, family rituals are rigidly defined. Such rigid ritualization served as a metaphor for a narrow range of relationship options in the family. As we understood this, part of the work in therapy consisted of broadening the role flexibility of the parents, viewing the daughter as a teenager making some "stubborn" decisions (rather than as a very young child who needed to be cared for), and strengthening sibling bonds.

Orienting questions that can be asked by clinicians to understand the patterns involved in rigid ritualization include:

1. Does this family have any common day-to-day routines?
2. Are there any ways in which you celebrate birthdays the same for different people?
3. What traditions do you carry over from year to year for Thanksgiving?
4. Who is most comfortable with doing things in the old, known way?

Sample reflexive questions that begin to introduce the possibility of more open rituals are:

5. If you were to change one of your routines in one small way, what might you do?
6. If someone tried to change it, who would that person most likely be?
7. Who would be most likely to go along with the change?

These questions offer a means to assess ways in which families may be rigidly ritualized, as well as to help the family and therapist begin to identify small areas of possible change.

(3) SKEWED RITUALIZATION. Where there is skewed ritualization in families, one particular ethnic tradition in the family, or religious tradition, or even one particular side of the family, has been emphasized—at the expense of other aspects of the family. For instance, the family usually gets together with mother's side of the family for vacations in the summer, Hanukkah, birthdays, etc. There is little contact with the father's side of the family around celebratory events.

In my own family, I was raised as a Unitarian and my spouse-equivalent is Jewish. When we were first together, he wanted no part of celebrating Christmas or Easter or any other holidays with Christian overtones. For several years, we celebrated primarily Jewish holidays. Over time, this became problematic, as I felt that important traditions from my side of the family could not be shared. I felt very lonely on holidays that had been celebrated in my family of origin for years. We had to work out ways in which we could begin to create our own celebrations on those days that were sensitive to the religious issues and each other's differing needs.

Couples from mixed ethnic or religious backgrounds are faced with a unique developmental task regarding rituals. Different values may be inherent in celebrations. For instance, in research by McGoldrick and Rohrbaugh (1987), respondents from Irish families reported that their families valued "self-control, suffering, drinking, strength in women, and respect for Church rules," and that children should be seen and not heard. In contrast, "Jewish respondents more often reported that their families valued education, success, encouragement of children, verbal expression, shared suffering, guilt, and eating" (p. 96). If spouses come together from these two traditions, creating, for example, an anniversary party, may give rise to many differences around the roles children should have, drinking, food, and ways things might be verbally expressed. Couples have to find ways to blend and honor both traditions. They may get into conflict in planning rituals, not even realizing that it is because of different values emphasized in the traditions.

Where families have had skewed ritualization, the therapist may want to examine the issue of balance between ethnic and religious traditions and extended family. Orienting questions that might be asked to assess this area included:

1. If you go to relative's houses for the holidays, where do you usually go?
2. What traditions have been passed down from your families of origin and for what events?
3. What ethnic traditions are most honored in this family and where did they come from?
4. What religious holidays are honored in this family? How is this reflective of family background?

Sample reflexive questions might be:

5. In what ways could you include in your rituals aspects from the other family of origin (or ethnic or religious tradition)? Who would support this? Whom would it upset?
6. How might your rituals change as you did this?

Responses to these questions particularly impart a sense of the family's embeddedness in a wider cultural, ethnic and religious context. How each family has uniquely intertwined various heritages can be brought forth.

(4) HOLLOW RITUAL AS EVENT, NOT PROCESS. When people celebrate events out of a sense of obligation, with little meaning found in either the process or the event, these are called "hollow" rituals (van der Hart, 1983). This may happen because rituals have become too closed, have become degrading, or end up creating more stress for family members. For instance, in most families in this society, women have traditionally been the preparers of family celebrations. They buy and cook the food, decorate, prepare special clothing, mail out cards, etc. Over time, their primary role may become burdensome for them, so that the rituals are followed out of obligation. Also, if creating the ritual process falls on one person, little space is available for all family members to bring their particular contributions to it.

For some families, following protocol rather than creating and working with meaning may be the predominant sense of their marking of events. Orienting questions that one might ask to understand if people are experiencing "hollow" rituals are:

1. Who usually plans parties, celebrations, and holidays in your family?
2. Who is most/least involved in them?
3. Which is more enjoyable — the planning or the event?
4. If you didn't have these events, who would miss them the most?
5. Who least wants to be there?
6. What are people's thoughts and feelings when the event is over?

Reflexive questions might include:

7. What would need to change in planning for the event in order for it to be more meaningful?
8. When might these changes be made?

With the answers to these questions, information can be generated about the energy in the family for various rituals, who is involved in the process of creating them, and whether they are significant to different family members or not. Knowledge about gender differences in family ritual-making can also be articulated.

(5) RITUAL PROCESS INTERRUPTED OR UNABLE TO BE OPENLY EXPERIENCED. At times, because of sudden changes (death, moving, illness) or traumatic events in

the family or larger culture (war, oppression, migration), families may be unable to fully experience the whole ritual process. For instance, Davis (1987) describes a Jewish Russian immigrant family who came to the United States eight years ago. Their son's Bris (circumcision) was held in secret in Russia. The family was not able to openly celebrate with the larger Jewish community, thus depriving the ritual of one of its many levels of meaning—the connection of this particular Jewish family to the community of Jewish families all through history. This then had many implications for meaning, importance, and joyousness attached to the celebration of this son's Bar Mitzvah in freedom in this country.

I also worked with a couple who described the wedding of the husband's parents in Vienna in the late 1930s. Since it was not safe to openly celebrate a Jewish wedding, it was a small, hidden celebration. Their son described the wedding picture as symbolic of a pall that had hung over his parents' 45 years of marriage. The picture shows the happy wedding couple in the middle, with very tense and anxious looking relatives gathered around them. The son grew up with the stories of what had happened to each of the relatives in the picture, whether it was escape to Palestine not to be seen again for 25 years, death in a concentration camp, or escape from a camp and years of traveling before safe sanctuary was found. For his parents, wedding anniversaries, the usual marker of a positive transition into the family, were fraught with another powerful aura altogether—the destruction of families, towns, and Jewish culture.

In addition, when there has been migration, there may not be access in the new country to the foods, symbols, language, and special places of the old culture that are important markers for a ritual. For instance, a Puerto Rican student described the difficulties of celebrating Three Kings Day in Massachusetts when his family first migrated 15 years ago.[9] The special candles could not be found, essential foods had to be mailed from Puerto Rico, and people were not given time off from work for that holiday.

Stigma in the larger culture may also prevent some people from having access to traditional cultural rituals that support transitions (Imber-Black, 1988a). Gay, lesbian, and common-law couples may not have wedding ceremonies; families with an adopted or foster child may not have ways to celebrate the addition of a new child to their family. On another level, Vietnam veterans returned in disgrace in many communities, with no victory parades.

Orienting questions can be asked to understand how ritual process might have been cut off by a major shift in the family's life or by oppression in the larger culture:

1. How do you think any ritual processes were interrupted (by war, death, suicide, migration, etc.)?

2. Who did this interruption affect the most?
3. How do you know that?

Some reflexive questions:

4. If members of your family had been able to celebrate the ritual more openly, or with more support from the culture, how might they have done it differently?
5. If you were to complete the ritual now in some way, what might you do?
6. Who would it be important to include?
7. What other resources can be called in to provide a supportive and safe environment for the ritual?

Responses to these questions can uncover ways in which the shifts in ritual process affected people's lives, while introducing the idea that some of the past rituals can be reworked — something can be done about what was cut off before. In addition, the need for the creation of space to acknowledge important transitions is highlighted, even if the larger culture does not provide this.

(6) FLEXIBILITY TO ADAPT RITUALS. The last area in assessing families is to look at their flexibility to adapt rituals. Bedtime rituals, for instance, are central in families with children. (See Albert, Amgott, Krakow, & Marcus [1979] for an intriguing look at bedtime rituals in 12 different families.) Yet, a bedtime ritual for a two-year-old should be quite different from that for a 15-year-old. The night journey is the first important separation of the child from the family and is repeated over and over again. How does the family work with this small leavetaking and reconnection over the years?

For instance, I worked with a family with two sons, aged six and ten. There seemed to be little differentiation between the two of them. They were often lumped together as "the kids" and unique strengths that each had were not highlighted. When I asked about their bedtimes, I found that the ten-year-old had the same routine and time for bed as the six-year-old. The nighttime ritual had not adapted to the increased autonomy of the older son.

A trainee, in talking about why she did not want to go home to celebrate her birthday with her parents, described how the celebration had remained unchanged over the years. Her mother still made the same kind of cake with number candles (a three and a two candle now for 32), just family members came, and little marked her change in status to an independent person outside of the family.

In contrast, Jim Shaw (a professor at the University of Massachusetts) described how a Christmas ritual kept shifting in his family. When the children were young, they always used to go out for a drive to see if they could find Santa Claus coming to their house. Of course, they always just missed Santa, and when they came home, all the presents were out under the tree (put out by the grandparents). As the children grew older and no longer believed in Santa, they still insisted on going out in the car and stories were passed down about the year "Daddy honked rudely at another car on Christmas Eve," and the time Janice mistook the yellow gas pumps for the carolers. The children, now all in their twenties, still go out in the car each year and exchange memories and stories of Christmas rides in the past.

Some sample orienting questions are:

1. How had bedtime changed for the child/ren over the years?
2. Have birthday parties changed?
3. Are the same people involved in the nighttime rituals? How have their roles changed?
4. When someone has either entered (through birth, marriage, remarriage) or left (through moving away from home, death, divorce) the family, how has it been marked?

Some reflexive questions are:

5. Five years from now, when Maria is living out of the home, how do you think her birthday will be celebrated?
6. If you were to experience a loss in this family, how do you think that you might mark it?
7. What new rituals has the family created?

The capacity to change rituals over the life cycle keeps the rituals vibrant for families, gives families access to special times to mark and rework roles, rules, and relationships, and provides group cohesion. Families are constantly undergoing change, as everyone grows older, new members enter and members leave. Flexibility to adapt rituals means that these changes can be worked with in meaningful ways.

Family Celebrations, Family Traditions, Life Cycle Rituals and Day-to-Day Life

Where, in the day-to-day lives of families, can the therapist look to assess where they might fit with this six-part typology? Four areas of family life can be examined: *family celebrations, family traditions, family life cycle rituals*, and *day-to-day life* that has become ritualized (adapted from Wolin & Bennett, 1984). Family celebrations are defined as rituals that are widely practiced around events that are celebrated in the larger culture, such as Fourth of July, Thanksgiving, Passover Seder, Christmas, etc. Through larger cultural expectations, the society to some extent organizes the time, space and symbols of these rituals. Family traditions are less anchored in the culture and are more idiosyncratic to the family, based on what might be called an "inside" instead of an "outside" calendar. Anniversaries, birthday parties, vacations, etc., all fall into this category. The third area to look at is family life cycle rituals, such as weddings, showers, christenings, graduations, retirement parties, etc. These are events that mark the progression of the family through the life cycle. Finally, it can be useful to examine rituals of daily family life, such as dinnertime, bedtime, recreation—events that are infused with meaning as the family creates its roles, rules, and norms.

As information is gathered about these four areas of family life—family celebrations, traditions, life cycle rituals, and day-to-day life—the clinician and family can understand the ways they may be rigidly ritualized, underritualized, have skewed ritualization, or experience rituals as hollow, interrupted, or unchanging over time. This understanding begins to form the base of the fit between how the therapist will work with clients and ritual interventions in the therapy process. If the family members are underritualized, elaborate rituals are going to seem foreign to them. Perhaps marking some changes with small in-session rituals would be an appropriate place to start. If the family is rigidly ritualized, the clinician might look to create small, more open parts in some already established ceremonies, enabling some news of a difference to then emerge. With skewed rituals, the therapist might help family members gradually introduce some symbols, content, and values from other parts of their heritage. With hollow rituals, a small area needs to be found where some meaning can be infused through changing the process of preparing for the ritual. Rituals that have been interrupted or celebrated in secret can be conversed about more openly; perhaps some parts of them can even be reenacted. Working with flexibility around life cycle rituals, family members can be helped to see where they have successfully adapted rituals over time and where others might need to be modified.

For instance, Dick Whiting and I worked with a man and a woman who, in their three years together, had created a number of rituals for the two of them. They set aside one night a week to go out and be together, they tried to preserve one day on the weekend just for the two of them, and they celebrated a number of familial and cultural events with their families on a regular basis (Christmas, Mother's day, birthdays, etc.). However, one event in the woman's (Marisa's) life was markedly devoid of any rituals. Her brother had committed suicide some 20 years earlier. His death was still something that could not be talked about openly in her family, nor was it marked by visiting his grave or gathering together in any way around the anniversary of his death or birth. The anniversary of his death was approaching in the next month. Marisa was afraid she would be depressed around the time of the anniversary. She also had concerns that, because she had chosen a spouse with the same first name as her brother, perhaps she had unresolved issues around his death.

In the sessions preceding the anniversary, we talked about ways in which the couple might want to make this anniversary more open, as a way to allow more personal support for Marisa and also for her family (visiting the grave, telling the family the two of them were going and inviting any family members to join them, looking at family pictures, honoring her brother somehow in their house). We also asked a number of questions around the ways in which Rand (Marisa's partner) was different from her brother, highlighting them as two distinct individuals. We then left it to Marisa and Rand to come up with a ritual that might work for them. Given that they had already shown a proclivity to using rituals, we felt comfortable leaving this very open-ended. Several weeks later, they described how in their home for several nights preceding and then on the date her brother had killed himself, they had lit a candle and talked some of what his life had given to the world when he was alive. In addition, Marisa had gotten out some pictures of her family, including her brother (typically she had not displayed pictures of him). These pictures were later left up in the kitchen. Rand felt better able to support Marisa at a time he knew was hard for her because there was some structure of openly acknowledging the topic of the other Rand's death, and Marisa described being more in control of her ups and downs during that time. After much discussion, she was also able to call her mother during that week to tell her how she was marking her brother's death. Her mother did not fall apart and was able to talk with Marisa a little about the ceremony Marisa and Rand had created. This was a conversation that Marisa had thought she and her mother would never have. In the therapy process, we found some fit between our and the couple's access to ritual.

In contrast, Dr. Whiting and I worked with another couple that I described earlier as underritualized (they did not celebrate anniversaries or birthdays or mark special events in the family). They were questioning whether to stay married. Much of the content in the first few therapy sessions revolved around past hurts and disappointments in their 24-year marriage. As the spouses clarified their different points of view about the hurts, cleared up misunderstandings, and communicated more directly about them, we asked them to differentiate the hurts into those that they could let go of, those they still needed to work through, and those that needed to continue in some way to be part of their shared history. These lists were brought into a session. We then asked them to transform the hurts they felt they could let go of by doing something at home with them. They talked about burning them outside in their grill (this was in the middle of winter in Western Massachusetts). They never did the burning ritual and came back in two weeks saying that it was not necessary. In retrospect, I think we had not made enough of a fit with their style of working with rituals. Since rituals were not something they typically did on their own, it would have worked better to have the transforming ritual in the session with us. Ultimately, their hurts persisted as a very strong metaphor and after several more months of treatment, they terminated. Several months after that, the wife left her husband.

Symptomatic Behavior as Ritual

A second area in which it is useful to examine ritual in the therapy process is in the rigidly ritualized aspects of symptomatic behavior. For instance, in the Jensen family, where the youngest daughter refused to walk or talk for two years, a series of ritualized behaviors had evolved. First, her father had a particular way to walk her, kicking her feet out as he stood behind her and he propelled her forward. He also carried a supply of small Tootsie Roll candies to give her as a reward after he had moved her from one place to another. Mother had a completely different way to walk her where she held her tightly at the shoulders with one hand and then bent over and hit the back of each knee with her hand to propel the leg forward. The daughter could only wear slippers to walk in (shoes were too heavy) and only Mom or Dad could walk her. Parental differences emerged in bickering about which way was better to walk her. Dad thought his way was better because the person walking her did not have to bend over. Mom thought her way was better because the daughter was stretching the muscles of her leg more as she had to bend her knee. Thus, the rigidly ritualized symptom was supported by rigidly ritualized interactions which were metaphorical for family relationships.

Placement of household things in a particular manner before one can leave the house, eating and bingeing, handwashing, alcoholic drinking, drug abuse, and many different kinds of symptomatic behavior can have intricate rituals attached to them. In our experiences, such rigidly ritualized symptoms often appear in families lacking more meaningful rituals. As Schwartzman (1982) has noted, "Rites of passage function to facilitate individuals' changing their social relationships in a culturally appropriate fashion while symptomatic behavior functions to legitimate failure to make culturally appropriate changes in the life cycle" (p. 3). He goes on to talk about how both rituals and symptomatic behaviors help to maintain their respective social systems, but how rituals work with multiple levels of meaning and organization and open parts, which then makes change possible. He sees rituals (in particular rites of passage) as working with paradoxical messages simultaneously, thus inviting change.

The meaning and symbolism invested in symptomatic rituals can be used for opening up other options. For instance, in the case of the girl who did not walk or talk, we created a new way to walk her that incorporated both and Mom's way particularly for going up stairs. This introduced the notion tial treatment, a videotape was made with Mom and Dad as the experts, showing all of the staff of the center their particular ways to walk her. This videotape was shown to everyone, with the residential center then coming up with a way to walk the girl, using Dad's way particularly for doing turns, and mom's way particularly for going up stairs. This introduced the notion that she could adapt to different ways of "walking." Every couple of weeks the way she was walked was varied, so that gradually one arm was removed from her shoulder, the backs of her knees or feet were not touched, etc. Ultimately, in the weeks preceding when she walked finally on her "own," she was "walked" with the palm of a person's had placed lightly in the center of her back.

Therapy as Ritual

Therapy itself can be looked upon as a ritual. Kobak and Waters (1984) took the three stages proposed by Van Gennep as commonly found in rites of passage and looked at how they apply to the therapy process. The first stage is *separation*. In puberty rites in many parts of Africa, adolescents are separated through special housing for young women menstruating for the first time or a separate camp for the young men being initiated. The physical separation denotes their removal from their old status, yet they are not yet integrated into the group in their new status. In addition, the adolescents accept certain people within their group as guides, who will pass on new information to them. A group connection is also made, as they band together as common travelers going through the changes.

Treatment also takes place in a special, separate place, and in family therapy it often has particular paraphernalia with one-way mirrors, phone hookups, and video equipment. There is a joining with, an acceptance of, the therapist as a guide with whom you have particular conversations where specialized knowledge is passed on. As Tomm (1988) noted, "The therapist can legitimately inquire about the clients' personal and private experiences" (p. 2). Ordinarily, such initiative would be considered inappropriate or bizarre outside the context of an intimate relationship. This can demarcate that in therapy you are *talking about* day-to-day life, but are not *in* day-to-day life.

Also, at the beginning of treatment, work is often done with the family members to encourage all of them to undertake the journey together, rather than designating one person as needing to be "fixed." Sometimes all family members are invited in as common travelers "who are equal in their need and hope for change" (Kobak & Waters, 1984, p. 91). At times, families do not become engaged in treatment because this idea of common travelers is not successfully negotiated. For instance, in one case that Dr. Whiting and I worked on, a 42-year-old man (oldest of three sibs), had been living in his parents' basement and refusing to come out for some eight years. The family presented Herman as the only one with problems. We asked the parents, as well as the two sibs, to come in for several sessions to help us understand Herman's difficulties. We tried to move in these sessions toward looking at the son's problems more interactionally, as we found out that (1) the parents had very volatile fights which Herman tried to stop; (2) the parents had angrily decided to have separate bedrooms for the 10 years earlier; and (3) the parents had very disparate views on how to handle Herman's problems. (Father felt Herman should be forced to come out of the basement and he had called the police to drag him out. Mother felt he should be left alone and talked to in the house, that in time he would get over what was bothering him.) We were unable to successfully negotiate the view of family problems as something shared by them all as common travelers and the pressure was increased to see Herman individually. After the third session, the family refused to come in for more sessions. Several months later I received a Christmas card from the family, commenting that things had stabilized with the son's hospitalization. With his entering an institution, his role as the "sick" one was reestablished.

With the partners described earlier, who created their own ritual to acknowledge the brother's suicide, I ended up meeting with them for the first session in my regular university office instead of the office I work in with Dick Whiting (which has all the regular family therapy paraphernalia). They were eager to start treatment and, because of a snow storm that dumped 10 inches, none of us wanted to drive the 30 miles to the usual office. My university office is not that private (you can hear people talking in the corridor), and upon arriving, the couple ran into one of my students, who turned out to be someone they knew. Later, there was some confusion about the ending of the session, with both clients making phone calls to rearrange commitments due to the storm, and I asked Marisa whether, when her family got together over the approaching holidays, there would be any mention of her brother at all. When we started the second session, Marisa and Rand told me how they were upset about my mentioning this issue when it was unclear as to whether we were still in session or not, but they understood it in the context of not having a special place to meet with a separate waiting room, etc. For the second session, we met at the usual office with the one-way mirror and such. They said it felt much more comfortable. For myself, I wondered whether it was a mistake to even start therapy away from that special place.

Models of therapy themselves seem to have developed their own rituals about this first separation phase. For instance, the Haley strategic model talks about the importance of the social phase (which provides the important bridge between the family's daily life and the specialness of therapy), then the problem phase (which demarcates this time as one in which there is a particular focus), and then the interventions stage (therapist as a guide who can help them with some difficulties) (Haley, 1976). The Milan model has the five-part session: (1) the premeeting of the therapy team to discuss the family and the working hypothesis; (2) the session with call-outs of the therapist in the room; (3) the intersession meeting of the therapist and team behind the mirror to discuss the information from the session and what intervention or comment to present to the family; (4) the presentation to the family; and (5) the postsession discussion to analyze the family's reaction to the comment or intervention (Selvini Palazzoli et al., 1978b). This distinct five-part process seems to mark roles between the therapy team and the family, with special emphasis put on the time when new information is introduced from the team.

Therapists themselves may find they have certain rituals, such as sitting in the same chair, or asking a sequence of questions about why therapy now, or typically starting with a genogram in the first session or two. Or there may be common types of rituals the therapist finds herself using with the family to engage them in treatment and separate them from their day-to-day life. For instance, in cases where there are differing opinions about whether the family needs therapy or not, Imber-Black (1985) has used variations of the odd days/even days ritual of the Milan group. On even days the family members act and talk as if they do not need treatment; on odd days, they act and talk as if they do need treatment. Members are asked to carefully observe how particular problematic behaviors that some people are concerned about differ and change on the odd and even days. In the next therapy session, the main focus is on helping family members come to some decision about whether they want to be in treatment or not.

The first phase in therapy is a time of establishing a level of trust, safety, and acceptance while usual roles and status are up in the air. While the rules and roles are being reworked, family members need some anchors in personal connections that provide the underpinnings for possible changes in the second stage, the liminal period.

The *liminal* or *transitional* stage of the ritual process is one of experimentation, trying on new identities, and learning new information. In cultural rituals, initiates are in the "status of having no status"—neither girl nor woman, neither boy nor man.

This phase in therapy is a crucial time for opening up changes in the family. If the therapist has connected well in the separation stage, he or she now has a window open into the family, for a limited amount of time, to co-create new patterns. If this phase goes on too long, families can become too dependent on the process of therapy itself, rather than accessing their own resources. Also, the longer this phase goes on, the more likely that the therapist and family will become too richly cross-joined and settled into certain interactions, making it harder to introduce new information. The treatment process itself can become rigidly ritualized, especially around time, place, and content. Varying time between sessions, the meeting time, place of the session, and topics addressed can all help to avoid the possibility of therapy becoming a rigid ritual.

In the third ritual phase, *reaggregation*, people are connected back to the community in their new status. In therapy, there is a move away from the special place and time of therapy towards connections to family resources and their day-to-day life.

For several reasons family therapy often seems to be weakest in exploring this third phase of therapeutic process. One, more writing has been done about the initial stages of therapy, with little written on termination. Also, it is easier to write about what happens in the therapy room than about new connections outside of the session. Finally, typically the termination process has been very short in family therapy. This may be connected to systems models wanting to differentiate themselves from other therapeutic models, where working with termination and transference and countertransference issues led to long endings (Imber-Black, personal communication, 1987).

A common ending of the therapy ritual that has evolved in my own practice is to ask the families questions that put them in the role of meta observer to the therapy process. For instance, I ask clients what was most helpful in therapy, least helpful, and what they would recommend for other families with similar problems. This moves the therapist out of the role of meta observer and commenter and invites the family members to participate as colleagues. I also use a coming out from behind the mirror to mark the end of treatment. This can be done either in a formal ritual (for instance, with all team members coming out from behind the mirror, use of food, exchanging symbols or gifts), or more informally, where the family begins to watch more of the team discussions and comment upon them, as in a reflecting team model (Anderson, 1987). Moving out from behind the mirror in these ways shifts who is watching whom, who is helping whom, who thanks whom. It moves towards everyday life and can be an important way to mark the family's own strengths.

In conjunction with asking the family to comment on the therapy process and coming out from behind the mirror, I often encourage exchanges of symbols or gifts that highlight some part of the therapy. This can be done in several ways: the therapist presents something to the family that acknowledges family strengths; there is a mutual exchange of symbols or gifts in session; or some out-of-session ritual gift-giving links the clients more strongly with their community. (See Chapter 3 for more examples.)

For instance, in the final session with the Lawson family, the therapist[10] reconvened the mother, father, and their two twin girls. (She had been doing some couples work with just the parents regarding some stuck parts of their relationship.) As she asked the family what had been most helpful in therapy, Dannielle, the twin who had been school phobic and having learning problems (and whom the mother had been helping continuously every day) said:

DANNIELLE: It was most helpful to have my Mom ask my sister (Davina) if she needed help.

THERAPIST: How did that help you?

DANNIELLE: It made me think my Mom does not just love me but she loves both of us. (Davina and Mom exchange a knowing look. The therapist asks them to let everyone in on it.)

DAVINA: I think it is important for Dannielle to know Mom loves me too so that she won't always be hanging onto Mom. I think Dad not being off on pot jobs (extra part time work) has been real helpful too. I think Dad being home has helped a lot. I can share my feelings with him.

THERAPIST: Thanks, Davina. What was most helpful for you, Karen (Mom)?

KAREN: Making sure I made time for both girls, especially Davina.

THERAPIST: In your heart she was always there.

KAREN: That was one of the big ones—when Davina said she felt like I didn't have time for her. And actually, I think the whole thing cut through the ice.

THERAPIST: What about you, Mark, what was most helpful to you?

MARK: The simple fact that you and your team members were outsiders and wouldn't side with one or the other. That was the biggest help of all because you could look at things neutrally. Good points and bad points from each one of us. That was the big push that Karen and I needed—someone that wouldn't side with either one of us.

THERAPIST: I'm glad you feel that. (to Karen) Do you feel that equally? Of course, it doesn't work if you don't feel that way as well.

KAREN (nodding):   Yes.

The therapist then went on to ask them what was least useful and what they would recommend to other families. She then brought out a giftwrapped box. She said, "I gained a great deal in working with you and I want to give you some small thing in return. I thought about what your family represents for me and the idea of balance kept coming to me. I remember you saying, Mark, that marriage is 50-50. And I was aware of how concerned you were with the twins—maintaining the balance so that each gets what she needs. And so I thought of a mobile. It hinges on balance, yet within it there is a lot of freedom of movement. Yet everything in the mobile provides the balance. If you take one piece away, it does not work. And as I thought of mobiles, a story came to me of a pair of swans that I used to tell my children." The therapist went to tell a parable of a swan family that paralleled the work the family had done in therapy. The children then opened the present—a swan mobile that the therapist had made for them—and, as the thank-you's were passing around, the team also phoned in to the mother and father to thank them for their sharings.

Treatment ended with the marking of a more collaborative relationship. Family strengths were summarized and highlighted, the family was asked to give feedback on the process of therapy, and the therapist gave them a gift as a way of saying thank you for the "gifts" they gave to her. The swan mobile not only embodied powerful family themes, but also served as a reminder of the swan parable, which had been designed to highlight the considerable skills the family had demonstrated in making some changes both in parenting and in the couple relationship.

In a year's follow-up to this case, the father proudly told the therapist that both girls had been on the honor roll that year, and that they were still enjoying the swan mobile, which hung in their living room.

Ritual Typology and the Therapy Process

These three stages of ritual in the therapy process can be analyzed from the point of view of the six-part typology discussed earlier.

(1) Is your therapy process *underritualized*? How is ritual used in the separation, transitional, and reintegration stages? Is there some distinction of these three phases in treatment? In what ways do you mark entering treatment? Look especially at the last phase—reintegration. How do you reconnect the family with its network and resources?

(2) Is your therapy process *rigidly ritualized*? Do you always use the same format for sessions (e.g., one person in the room, one behind the mirror, with the person behind the mirror usually calling in near the end of the session) or same modality (e.g., primarily talking, sculpting, working with genograms)? Are there things that you feel must be done the first session or two? Are there certain types of interventions that you find yourself usually giving (e.g., disengaging the "overinvolved" mother and pulling in the "peripheral" father)?

(3) *Skewed ritualization.* Do you find yourself working primarily with one model, or ideas from one person on the team? Is there a history of past rituals that have been used in therapy with some of your families that keep reemerging to the preclusion of new ideas?

(4) *Hollow ritual as event — not process.* Are there certain kinds of events that you find occurring over and over in treatment, so that there is a predictive quality to them? For instance, in a school setting, does an interdisciplinary team meeting automatically become scheduled when a child is having difficulty (focus on the "ceremony"), rather than various people working with a child having a chance to plan and talk about when and where a team meeting might be appropriate (focus on the process)? The process of organizing the meeting can be just as important as the meeting itself.

Interventions may be experienced by families as events, not process, when they are duplicated over time. For instance, if over a series of five sessions the end-of-session message is always presented to the family as a split team intervention, are frameworks of expectancy or predictable responses being created?

(5) Is your *ritual process interrupted*? For instance, do you plan something with the family but another family crisis erupts and you find it difficult to get back to what you were planning?

(6) What *flexibility* do you have to adapt rituals over time? Does the way you use the phone shift? Does the team exist only behind the mirror or in other realms? When does the family come behind the mirror? How do your therapy rituals evolve?

Typology of rituals can be used not just to examine ritual behavior of the family but also to examine the stages of the therapeutic process.

Creating Therapeutic Rituals

Working with these three areas — assessment of family's current use of ritual, ritualized aspects of symptomatic behavior, and the rituals of the process of therapy — the clinician is then ready to move into considering the appropriate ritual themes for a family in treatment, as well as important design elements. In Chapter 2, to orient clinicians to family issues that can be addressed well with therapeutic rituals, five ritual themes are detailed. Guidelines for co-creating rituals that examine the use of time, space, symbols and symbolic actions are discussed in Chapter 3.

NOTES

[1]As Moore and Myerhoff (1977) stated, "Even if it (a ritual) is performed once, for the first and only time, its stylistic rigidities, and its internal repetitions of form or content make it traditionlike" (p. 8).

[2]We are aware of the connotation that black is "bad" and white is "good" inherent in this

intervention. In this particular instance we chose to pick up on the family's use of the white and black hats, but would not necessarily recommend using this idea with other families, as it indirectly perpetuates racial stereotypes.

[3]For comprehensive reviews of the field of ritual, see Ronald Grimes (1982) *Beginnings in Ritual Studies*, Lanham, Maryland: University Press of America (especially parts I and III) and William G. Doty (1986) *Mythography: The Study of Myths and Rituals*, University, Alabama: University of Alabama Press (especially Chapters two and three).

[4]Unfortunately, it is usually only the woman who is "given away" officially in the ceremony, which reflects the patriarchal remnants of the wedding where the father passes on his "property" to another man. See Tad Tuleja in *Curious Customs* (1987) for fascinating tidbits about other ways this shows up in wedding celebrations, such as the tying on of old shoes to the couples' car. He contends that this is left over from the contractual symbol of shoes in the ancient Near East, where the passing on of a sandal or a shoe signified that the transaction was completed. Among the Anglo-Saxons, the father of the bride gave her new husband one of her shoes to show that his authority was passed on to the new mate. "Significantly, this ceremony was concluded by the husband using the shoe as a mock scepter, tapping his bride on the head with it" (p. 67).

[5]Tad Tuleja notes that it is the senior male who still does the carving in families, no matter how much time the women have spent preparing the meat. He feels that the carving ritual "celebrates the male's role as 'hunter' while obscuring the equally essential contribution of female 'gatherers'" (1987, p. 98).

[6]This is particularly true for boys, since their entry into puberty can be more easily marked as a group event. For girls, the actual onset of menstruation, which can vary widely, is often used as a definite marker for entrance into puberty. This means that there are fewer group celebrations for girls.

[7]In a large survey, half of the Americans questioned said that in listening to music at some point in their life, they had the physical experience of that shiver (Ornstein & Thompson, 1984).

[8]Sara invited me to her high school graduation some three years later. I proudly watched her march in, stand in the first row and grace an audience of several thousand with her singing in the choir. When I gave her a present at a party at her house, she looked over at me and asked, "Is this the box?" "No," I said, "that's only for you to dig up if you ever need it." Meanwhile the parakeet was chirping away in the room, saying, "Hello, hello".

[9]My thanks to Edison Santana for helping me to understand how migration affects ritual development.

[10]My thanks to the therapist in this case, Doris Cohen from the University of Massachusetts, for her very fine work.

REFERENCES

Albert, S., Amgott, T., Krakow, M., & Marcus, H. (1979). Children's bedtime rituals as a prototype rite of safe passage. *The Journal of Psychological Anthropology, 2*(1), 85–105.

Anderson, T. (1987). The reflecting team: Dialogue and meta-dialogue in clinical work. *Family Process, 26*(4), 415–428.

Comstock, W. R. (1972). *The study of religion and primitive religions*. New York: Harper and Row.

Cowles, R. (1985, November 28). Giving thanks for the music boxes. Washington, D.C.: The Washington Post, E5.

Culler, B. (1987). *Change in the context of stability: The design of therapeutic rituals for families*. Doctoral dissertation, University of Massachusetts, Amherst.

d'Aquili, E. G., Laughlin, C. D., & McManus, J. (1979). (Eds.) *The spectrum of ritual: A biogenetic structural analysis*. New York: Columbia University Press.

Davis, J. (1984). Mazel tov: Ritual and discontinuous change in the normal family life cycle. Unpublished paper, University of Massachusetts, Amherst.

Davis, J. (1987). *Mazel tov: A systems exploration of Bar Mitzvah as a multigenerational ritual of change and continuity.* Doctoral dissertation, University of Massachusetts, Amherst.

Doty, W. G. (1986). *Mythography: The study of myths and rituals.* University, AL: The University of Alabama Press.

Douglas, M. (1966). *Purity and danger: An analysis of concepts of pollution and taboo.* New York: Praeger.

Durkheim, E. (1915). *The elementary forms of religious life.* (J. W. Swain, Trans.). New York: Free Press.

Goodman, E. (1987, November 24). Family defines itself by its Thanksgiving ritual. Springfield: Morning Union.

Goody, J. R. (1977). Against ritual. In S. F. Moore & B. G. Myerhoff (Eds.) *Secular ritual.* Assen and Amsterdam: Van Gorcum.

Grimes, R. (1982). *Beginnings in ritual studies.* Lanham, MD: University Press of America.

Haley, J. (1976). *Problem-solving therapy.* San Francisco: Jossey-Bass.

Hallowell, A. I. (1941). The social function of anxiety in a primitive society. *American Sociological Review, 6,* 869–81. Bobbs-Merrill reprint series, A-104.

Imber-Black, E. (1985). Toward a resource model in systemic family therapy. In M. Karpel (Ed.). *Family resources.* New York: Guilford Press.

Imber-Black (1988a). Idiosyncratic life cycle transitions and therapeutic rituals. In B. Carter & M. McGoldrick (Eds.). *The family life cycle: A framework for family therapy.* New York: Gardner Press.

Imber-Black, E. (1988b). *Families and Larger Systems.* New York: Guilford Press.

Kobak, R. R., & Waters, D. B. (1984). Family therapy as a rite of passage: Play's the thing. *Family Process, 23*(1), 89–100.

McGoldrick, M., & Rohrbaugh, M. (1987). Researching ethnic family stereotypes. *Family Process, 26*(1), 89–98.

Moore, S. F., & Myerhoff, B. G. (1977). (Eds.). *Secular ritual.* Assen and Amsterdam: Van Gorcum.

Myerhoff, B. G. (1977). We don't wrap herring in a printed page: Fusion, fictions and continuity in secular ritual. In S. F. Moore & B. G. Myerhoff (Eds.). *Secular ritual.* Assen and Amsterdam: Van Gorcum.

Ornstein, R., & Thompson, R. F. (1984). *The amazing brain.* Boston: Houghton Mifflin.

Radcliffe-Brown, A. R. (1952). *Structure and function in primitive society: Essays and addresses.* Glencoe, IL: Free Press.

Rappaport, R. A. (1971). Ritual sanctity and cybernetics. *American Anthropologist, 73*(1), 59–76.

Roberts, J. (1984). Switching models: Family and team choice points and reactions as we moved from the Haley strategic model to the Milan model. *Journal of Strategic and Systemic Therapies, 3*(4), 40–54.

Scheff, T. J. (1979). *Catharsis in healing, ritual, and drama.* Berkeley and Los Angeles: University of California Press.

Schwartzman, J. (1982). Symptoms and rituals: Paradoxical modes and social organization. *Ethos, 10*(1), 3–25.

Selvini Palazzoli, M. (1974). *Self starvation: From the intrapsychic to the transpersonal approach to anorexia nervosa.* London: Chaucer.

Selvini Palazzoli, M., Boscolo, L., Cecchin, G., & Prata, G. (1974). The treatment of children through brief therapy of their parents. *Family Process, 13*(4), 429–442.

Selvini Palazzoli, M., Boscolo, L., Cecchin, G., & Prata, G. (1977). Family rituals: A powerful tool in family therapy. *Family Process, 16*(4), 445–454.

Selvini Palazzoli, M., Boscolo, L., Cecchin, G., & Prata, G. (1978a). A ritualized prescription in family therapy: Odd days and even days. *Journal of Family Counseling, 4*(3), 3–9.

Selvini Palazzoli, M., Boscolo, L., Cecchin, L., & Prata, G. (1978b). *Paradox and counterparadox.* New York: Jason Aronson.

Shaughnessy, J. D. (1973). (Ed.). *The roots of ritual.* Grand Rapids, MI: William B. Eerdmans. Eerdmans.

Sluzki, C. (1983). Process, structure and world view: Toward an integrated view of systemic models in family therapy. *Family Process, 22*(4), 469–476.

Some babies die. (1986). University of California media extension service. A film by Martyn Langdon Down.

Tomm, K. (1987). Interventive interviewing: Part I. Strategizing as a fourth guideline for the therapist. *Family Process, 26*(1), 3–15.

Tomm, K. (1988). Interventive interviewing: Part III. Intending to ask lineal, circular, strategic and reflexive questions. *Family Process, 27*(1), 1–15.

Tuleja, T. (1987). *Curious customs.* New York: Harmony Press.

Turner, V. (1967). *The forest of symbols: Aspects of Ndembu ritual.* Ithaca, NY: Cornell University Press.

Turner, V. (1974). *Dramas, fields, and metaphors: Symbolic action in human society.* Ithaca, NY: Cornell University Press.

Turner, V. (1975). Ritual as communication and potency: An Ndembu case study. In C. Hill (Ed.). *Symbols and society: Essays on belief systems in action.* Athens: Southern Anthropological Society Proceedings, no. 9, 58–81.

van der Hart, O. (1983). *Rituals in psychotherapy: Transition and continuity.* New York: Irvington Publishers Inc.

Van Gennep, A. (1960). *The rites of passage.* Chicago: University of Chicago Press.

Wolin, S. J., & Bennett, L. A. (1984). Family rituals. *Family Process, 23*(3), 401–420.

$\mathscr{2}$

Ritual Themes in Families and Family Therapy

EVAN IMBER-BLACK

A MAN, MR. KORNER, called requesting therapy for himself. He stated that he was separated from his wife and children and had just lost his job. He said he felt very depressed and wasn't sure that life was worth living. I asked whether he thought his separation was permanent, and since he was unsure, I asked him to invite his wife to the first session. During this first session, Mrs. Korner said she had tried for many years to get her husband to work on their problems, which included conflicts between them and between Mr. Korner and his 12-year-old son, Billy, but that Mr. Korner had always refused. They were now separated and had been for a year and a half, during which time Mrs. Korner had moved into a new house with Billy and their daughter, Sally, 10. Mrs. Korner had gone back to school and had just been hired for a good job. During this time, Mr. Korner had lost his job and was continuing to have very problematic relations with his son. She said she had tried to get him to go to therapy earlier, when their marriage was collapsing, but that he had refused, and she had gone by herself. Mrs. Korner said she did not want to come to therapy with her husband at this time, but that she might be willing to come in "from time to time."

Work commenced with Mr. Korner, focusing on his generally troubled relationships with his wife, his son, and his fellow workers. He allowed that he had been a very critical person and that he saw himself as very hard to live with, as he always put his wife down, often in front of other people. He said that during recent years his wife just refused to have company, and even family dinners had dwindled. He described himself as an unimaginative and uncreative person. Exploration of his own family of origin revealed that

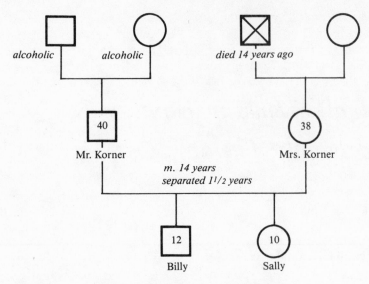

FIGURE 1   The Korner Family: A Family Rebirth

both of his parents drank alcohol to excess and that they were extremely critical of him and had often humiliated him in front of others. During therapy which focused on intergenerational patterns and Mr. Korner's place in those patterns, both as a child and now as an adult, Mr. Korner began to change his behavior, especially towards his wife. He was able to get a new job. He and his wife began to date, and she returned to the therapy, as they decided to reconcile. Here the therapy began to work on "new wedding vows," a ritualized process that allowed the couple to air past differences and set a tone for their future relationship. The couple's first wedding had been marred by the death of the wife's adored father two days after the wedding. Mr. Korner said he had felt he could never measure up to the memory of his wife's father. Their current effort was framed as a "new beginning, a fresh start."

While Mr. and Mrs. Korner were working on their new vows, they appeared for a therapy session looking very upset. They began to describe the children's, especially Billy's, unhappiness with the prospect of father's rejoining the family. Mr. Korner said that when he went to the house, Billy would say, "Who wants you here—go away!" Most recently, both children refused to go on a family outing that the parents had planned. Mr. and Mrs. Korner, who had set a date for Mr. Korner to move back home in three weeks, now felt uncertain. I asked them to bring the children to a session the following night.

Billy and Sally were very articulate and in our conversation they were able to state that, while they loved their father and really liked this "new" man who was coming over all the time, they were also very frightened that the changes would not last. Billy said, "We've become used to living just with our mother. It took a long time. What if we have to go through this again?" At this point, both children appeared more frightened than angry. Billy also described old fights between him and his father, which used to lead to fights between husband and wife, and expressed worry that these would occur again. He also described that in these fights Sally would side with their father, and that only recently were he and Sally able to get along. During the session, Mr. Korner apologized to Billy for all the old hurts, and both parents promised the children that the old way would not return. They described their new wedding vows to the children. They spoke about the sort of parents they planned to be for both children, and as they did so, the children visibly relaxed.

At the end of the session, I requested that Billy and Sally get together without their parents and plan a surprise for their parents on the occasion of their father rejoining the family. I then asked Mr. and Mrs. Korner to get together to play a surprise for Billy and Sally on the occasion of Mr. Korner rejoining the family. All agreed to my request.

When I next saw the family a month later, Mr. Korner had, indeed, moved home. I asked about the surprises and heard the following:

BILLY: We made a wedding cake! We baked four angel food cakes and
stacked them up. It took us all day!
THERAPIST: Were your parents surprised?
SALLY: Yeah!!! And we got frosting all over ourselves!
MR. KORNER (laughing):   And all over the kitchen!

Mrs. Korner said she couldn't fathom how they had done it, since they told her they hadn't greased the pans between each baking! She also said they had put a piece in the freezer for next year's anniversary, as the date of the father's rejoining the family was now their "new anniversary." Billy, previously labeled "unimaginative, like his father," proudly told me that the cake had been his idea.

I then asked about the parents' surprise for the children. Mr. and Mrs. Korner had rented two adjoining hotel rooms and had taken the children out for a special night. When they arrived at the rooms the children found small gold-colored glasses with each one's name on a glass and the date. The parents split a large bottle of champagne and the children split a tiny bottle of champagne. While both parents had worked on most of the ideas for the surprise, the glasses were Mr. Korner's idea and he had made all of the arrangements, something which he would not have done previously. Before dinner, the parents had planned to exchange new wedding rings. At the last moment, they decided to include the children in this ring ceremony. Mr.

Korner gave Sally the ring to hand to her mother, and Mrs. Korner gave Billy the ring to hand to his father, in a ceremony that metaphorically expressed the new relationship options available in the family.

I saw the family again in six months. They were doing well, and were able to articulate many differences from their prior interactional patterns. Mr. and Mrs. Korner were able to discuss issues between them. Mr. Korner no longer criticized his wife or his son. Father and son were going out and doing things together, which they had never done before. They told me that they used the little gold glasses on special family occasions. At this session, I asked about whether they had always been a family that planned such nice celebrations as they had described to me and where they had learned to do such things. Mrs. Korner said she came from a family that always had lovely family events. Mr. Korner said that on holidays in his family, his parents would drink and fight and be verbally abusive to him. He had decided that, when he had his own family, they would not have family celebrations and would thereby avoid a lot of problems. For 14 years, the family followed Mr. Korner's plan, and remained underritualized, with no markers for family events or developmental change. Only when the family reunited with many new assumptions were they able to celebrate themselves with rituals.

The rituals designed by the family in response to my instructions to "make a surprise" functioned to reincorporate the husband and father as a *member* of the family, effectively mark the *healing* process between husband and wife and between father and son, highlight the father's new *identity* as caring, rather than critical, establish a new *identity* for the family as a family able to have special family events together in which all participated, punctuate the *belief negotiation* process involved in the new wedding vows, and serve as a *celebration* of their many personal and interpersonal changes. They chose symbols that defined them as being both like other families, e.g., a wedding cake and wedding rings, and as unique, e.g., special glasses with their names and new anniversary date on them. The symbols and symbolic actions highlighted each individual member (e.g., four cakes, four glasses), dyadic relationships (e.g., the large champagne bottle for the parents and the small one for the children), the shift in available alliances (e.g., the ring ceremony), and the family as a whole. Finally, the entire ritual connected past, present, and future for the family via a process that did not deny the hurts of the past, that marked the new relationships in the present, and that involved symbols to be used by the family in the future.

FIVE RITUAL THEMES

In designing and implementing therapeutic rituals with individuals, couples, families, or families and larger systems, five themes serve to orient the therapist's decision-making: (1) membership; (2) healing; (3) identity; (4)

belief expression and negotiation; and (5) celebration. These themes may also be seen in any family's normative rituals, whether these are daily rituals, family traditions, family and cultural celebrations, or life cycle transition rituals. Any given ritual may include one or more than one theme.

Membership

All human systems must deal with the issue of membership, including the questions of who is in and who is out, who belongs to the system, who defines membership, and how one gains or loses membership. Such membership issues are often difficult for families, as they require complex reworking of family patterns, rules, available relationship options, and previously agreed upon roles.

Membership rituals occur daily in families during family meals, during which seating arrangements, allowable topics and allowable affect metaphorically define and redefine the family's views of itself. Discussion in therapy of the family's dinner time can inform the therapist about membership issues. Thus, in one divorced family, the three sons complained that the family had not had a meal together "since father left." Instead, the mother cooked and ate in her room alone, while the oldest and youngest son ate in front of the television at separate times and the middle son stayed out on the streets during dinner. This daily ritual replaced the one of the family eating together and served as a painful metaphor for the family's current fragmentation. Daily rituals of parting and reentry are also membership rituals, defining issues of closeness and distance.

The membership theme attends to many family life cycle transitions that are marked by normative rituals, such as weddings, in which the membership in two families of origin and in a new couple unit is potentially redefined, baby-naming ceremonies in which a new child is welcomed into the family and extended family and often into a particular ethnic community, Bar Mitzvah, which redefines membership in both the family and the Jewish community, or graduation ceremonies, in which a young adult's relationship to the family, parents' relationship to the young adult and to each other, and the family's relationship to the school system may be redefined. Such normative rituals may mark changes that have been in process, or facilitate needed changes in relationship definitions, or point the way to changes yet to come.

Families with more idiosyncratic life cycle transitions often have no rituals to mark or facilitate membership changes (Imber-Black, 1988). For instance, there are no agreed upon rituals to mark families formed by adoption or for families whose membership is changed by divorce. There are no wedding rituals for homosexual couples to mark the creation of their unit or to connect them with extended family. There are no leaving home rituals for families with handicapped members who are leaving to live in a group home. There are no special rituals to facilitate the complex membership changes required in stepfamily formation; rather, such families most often begin with a wedding ritual which erroneously suggests they are identical to a new nuclear couple. An extreme example of this may be seen in a stepfamily who came for therapy due to stepparent-stepchild conflict that was rapidly leading to the extrusion of a child. This couple's wedding was celebrated with extended family and friends, but their five children from their prior marriage, ages six to twelve, were barred from attending. The wedding ritual had publicly affirmed the new couple, but not the new stepfamily.

MEMBERSHIP RITUALS AND THE THERAPEUTIC PROCESS. Therapeutic membership rituals may be designed to facilitate the expansion or contraction of membership, to redefine the meanings of membership, to facilitate entrances and exits, and to delineate boundaries both within the family and between the family and the outside world. The rituals described in the Korner family allowed for the reentry of the husband and father in a new way, while also redefining alliances. Membership rituals may be designed to mark definitive membership changes, such as the entry of a stepfather into a preexisting family unit of mother and children, to alter the meanings of membership, such as when a young adult leaves home, or to mark more temporary changes, such as the entry of the therapist into the family system.

The membership theme is particularly poignant in the issues brought to therapy by stepfamilies, divorced families, families formed by adoption, families where membership is ambiguous, and families intensely involved without outside helping systems. Conversations between therapist and family can productively focus on normative membership rituals, both as information for the therapist and as a catalyst to revitalizing old or inventing new membership rituals.

BRIEF EXAMPLE—THE THERAPIST COMES TO DINNER. A family was referred for therapy due to an "eating disorder" in the older daughter. The family consisted of a father, Bob Wharton, 33, a mother, Sue Wharton, 30, and two daughters, Sandra, 12, and Ellen, 8. During the first session, which focused on understanding the presenting problem in the context of family, extended family, and helping system relationships, the family members were extremely tense. They answered questions briefly and with much nervous laughter. As therapist, I felt like an extreme outsider to the family.

During a discussion of Sandra's problem, which involved unusual food preferences, to wit, french fries, bread and milk, which she ate to the exclusion of all other foods, I discovered that the only time this provoked conflict was at the family's daily dinner. At breakfast and lunch, which Sandra had

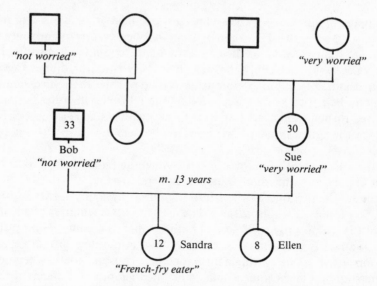

FIGURE 2   The Wharton Family: The Therapist Comes to Dinner

with her sister while their mother stood nearby, Sandra ate bread and milk, but did not get into any struggles. However, at dinner, when both parents were present, Sandra and her mother would fight over Sandra's eating. Father would listen silently for a while, eat his meal, and then leave the table, where Sandra and her mother would remain for upwards of an hour, locked in a conflict in which Sandra's way prevailed.

Thus, the family's dinner had became a daily ritual whose central relational metaphor was triadic. As the family discussed it with me, it was clear that food had come to symbolize covert power and control to the members, rather than many of the other things which food may symbolize in a family, such as nurturance, giving and receiving, expression of ethnicity, etc. In addition, few individual differences seemed available for expression in the family, with the dramatic exception of Sandra's food preferences.

I concluded the first session by asking the family to bring dinner to the next clinic appointment. I relabeled Sandra's "eating disorder" as "having favorites" and, among other instructions, asked that she and her father shop for the dinner and select some of her "favorites" for the family and for me to eat.

The family arrived for the next session with their dinner. Mother asked Ellen to "set the table" just as they sit at home. Sandra's place was between her parents. As Ellen set the table, her mother reminded her that "We have a guest for dinner," and asked, "Where does our company usually sit?" Thus, in the opening moments of the second session, held at the clinic and not at the family's home, the daily dinner ritual had begun to transform my relationship to the family. I was their "guest." I was "company." In short, I was allowed access to the family through their daily ritual of dinner together. The environment was much more relaxed than during the first session, and the family began to show acceptance of the reframe "favorites," which, I suggested through questions, applied to all members and not just Sandra, replacing their prior view of "three normal eaters and one with an eating disorder" (Imber-Black, 1986a).

In this case and other similar ones in which the family is invited to bring dinner to the clinic, the family's daily membership ritual of a meal is utilized to facilitate the therapist's access into the family system in order to form a temporary family-therapist system. The usual complementarity of client and therapist is temporarily confounded both through the unusual complementarity of a family preparing and bringing food to the therapist and through the symmetrical act of sharing a meal together. Thus, a variety of temporary membership options become available for the therapist and the family.

Other membership theme rituals will be illustrated below in the chapters on adoption (Chapter 8), couples' issues (Chapter 4), and remarried families (Chapter 11).

Healing

In every human life, there are times when personal and relationship healing is needed. Rituals to effect healing can be found in every culture's funeral rites, which simultaneously mark the loss of a member, facilitate the expression of grief, and point to a direction for ongoing life. Such rituals frequently require shared meals or visiting the bereaved for a prescribed period of time in order to prevent dysfunctional isolation during the period of immediate grief and loss. Specific steps for reincorporation of survivors into the larger community may be included (Van Gennep, 1960).

Many religious and cultural groups have specific rituals for remembering and honoring a member who has died. For instance, in Catholicism, survivors may request that a mass be said to commemorate the anniversary of a loved one's death. In Judaism, a special ceremony is held to place the headstone on a grave a year following a death, and family members recite the Kaddish prayer both on anniversaries of the death and on certain holidays. Such rituals are time-bounded and space-bounded, allowing for the expression of grief and loss in a manner that simultaneously facilitates ongoing life.

Nations or communities may create healing rituals to deal with the losses sustained by war. A contemporary example is the Viet Nam war memorial in

Washington, D.C., which provides an ongoing healing ritual as family members and friends who lost men and women in the war come, find their person's name on the wall, and make rubbings to carry back home, thus affirming their own personal loss while connecting with a larger community. Such trips to the wall are often referred to as "pilgrimages."

More recently, in the American gay community, a healing ritual has begun with the creation of a quilt consisting of individually-made patches to commemorate persons who have died of AIDS. Each patch is made by a person who has lost someone and contains personal expressions designed to capture some essential aspect of the person who died. Here, the choice of a quilt, rather than, for instance, a painting, may be seen to symbolize the possibilities of warmth available through survivors' connection with each other, thus affirming life even in the face of terrible death. This painfully unfinished ritual functions on multiple levels to memorialize each person who has died, to connect a community that is grieving together, and to serve as a stark and visual reminder to the broader community of the magnitude of loss.

HEALING RITUALS AND THE THERAPEUTIC PROCESS. While prescribed healing rituals to deal with the loss of a person through death do exist, the connection of these rituals to the needs of a particular person or family may be missing. For example, in contemporary society, a eulogy may be given by a clergy person who barely knew the deceased, and the funeral ritual, per se, may be a hollow ritual. Since most people now die in hospitals rather than at home, the earlier proximity with death and loss as part of the human life cycle has all but disappeared, making healing more difficult to accomplish. Thus, a therapist may find that the healing process regarding the loss of member through death has been blocked and replaced by symptoms that function to orient attention away from the need for healing. Here symptoms may also connect to unacknowledged and unhealed losses in previous generations (Walsh, 1983). Therapeutic healing rituals may be designed to begin to deal with such losses, particularly if normative healing rituals have either not occurred or have been insufficient to deal with the complex personal and interpersonal processes connected to death. Losses in a family, including pregnancy loss, suicide, sudden, violent or unexpected death, may especially call for therapeutic healing rituals. Such rituals must respect the magnitude of the loss, and should sensitively involve the client in their co-creation.

BRIEF EXAMPLE – RETURNING HOME. A young woman, Carolyn Bell, 28, came for therapy, complaining of "never being able to finish anything." She had dropped out of college after two years, and had since had a series of jobs at which she felt unsuccessful. She lived alone, having left two relationships since college. In the first session, she said, "everywhere I look in my life, things are incomplete." When we did her genogram together, I found out that her mother had died unexpectedly when Carolyn was 14 and about to graduate from junior high school.

She told me that she had been so distraught that the family doctor recommended that she not be allowed to attend her mother's funeral, as it would be "too upsetting," and that her father followed this advice. Shortly after her mother's death, her father sold the home they lived in to neighbors and moved the family to be near his own mother so that she could help him with childrearing. Carolyn did not attend her junior high graduation, and the entire event was lost, as the family was caught up in grief and in the details of moving. Carolyn was simply enrolled in the new high school and expected to function. Very quickly, teachers began to complain that she was not finishing her homework, but she was given a lot of understanding due to her mother's death. She began to think of herself as "a person who doesn't finish things." During high school, Carolyn asked her father twice if she could go visit their old house. Both times he declined, saying it would be "too upsetting for her." After that she stopped asking. Seemingly, the past was to be sealed off. During our conversation, Carolyn said she believed that her inability to finish things was connected to her mother's death and all that happened after, but that since this was all in the past she did not know what to do about it. I asked her to consider what she felt most "unfinished" about from that period of her life and said that we would discuss this the next session. I said that she could do this consideration in any way that seemed appropriate for her, but that I would suggest that she carefully review each aspect of that time, including her mother's death, the funeral she missed, the graduation she missed, leaving her house, moving to a new area, and not being able to return to the old house. She smiled and said she wasn't sure she could complete the task, but that she would try.

Carolyn returned and told me that she had decided to carefully study each aspect of that time on a different day, feeling that she would at least complete a portion each day. She said the task had been very painful and that she had been tempted to stop but didn't. She told me that she had decided that she felt most unfinished about the house she had lived in and not been allowed to return to as a teenager. This disconnection from her home seemed to be a very vivid metaphor for disconnection in other areas of her life. In a very moving discussion, she said that she knew a lot of people visited cemeteries, but that she felt more of her mother's presence and of her relationship to her mother was in that house. We began to talk of what it would mean for her to return there for a visit.

Between the second and third sessions, Carolyn did a lot of work. She spoke to a friend about the old house and discovered that it had been sold again to people she did not know. She managed to get their name and phone number, but had not called them yet. She wondered if her father would be angry with her if she went back to see the house. As we talked, it seemed as if Carolyn still related to her father as if she were a teen, and that, indeed, their relationship had not matured after her mother's death, but rather had become frozen in time. She decided that she wanted to tell her father that she planned to visit the old house and to invite him to come if he wished.

Between the third and fourth sessions, Carolyn contacted the people who owned the house, explained why she wanted to visit the house, and secured their consent to do so. She still felt scared about her father's response. I coached her to thank her father for his protection of her when she was younger, rather than to express anger at him, which a former therapist had encouraged. Carolyn then said that perhaps she had been protecting him, too, since not finishing her schoolwork and other chores had distracted him from the pain of his loss. I suggested that, since she was an adult now and since 14 years had passed, perhaps neither needed so much protection now.

By the fifth session, Carolyn had spoken to her father and had invited him to see the old house with her. He declined, but said he understood that she would want to do so. He also gave her several photographs that had been taken in the house and which they had not looked at since her mother's death. She brought the photographs to the session and we looked at them together. Several were of her mother obviously enjoying this home. Carolyn cried and said she had seen no photographs of her mother for so many years. Towards the end of the session, she said she was ready to go see the house by herself. I suggested that she might want to take some new photographs of the house.

Carolyn returned in a month. She had been to the house and walked through each room. She drew a picture for me of the floor plan of the house, and we talked about what she remembered. The memories were both happy ones and painful ones, replacing her earlier sense that the past only contained painful memories. She had also taken a photograph of the outside of the house. It looked quite different from when she had lived there, as the owners had done some remodeling. She said this upset her at first, but that she realized that, of course, things must change. She felt proud of herself for going and for talking to her father about it afterwards. She said she wanted to take some time to consider all that had happened and that she would call me. I was left wondering if therapy was not "unfinished," but decided to wait and see.

Carolyn called me in four months. During that time, she had made one more trip to see the house with her father accompanying her. They cried together for the first time. She had decided to reenter college and had made application and been accepted. She had never before been able to focus on what she wanted to do with her life, but had decided since I had seen her last to follow a strong interest in anthropology. She said her sense of herself as a person who "could not finish things" had "faded away."

In this case, Carolyn and I co-created the healing ritual of her returning home. Rather than assume that what was required was, for instance, a cemetery visit, I carefully followed her direction and served primarily as a coach and as a person to whom she could report her own developments. Just as pain and loss are intensely personal and individual, so is the healing of pain and loss. Thus, while there are certain symbolic actions that appear common to many healing rituals, such as visiting a grave, burying, burning, etc., the particulars must be highly individualized to suit the requirements of the person or the family. In this therapy, I distinctly chose to underplay Carolyn's view of herself as a "person who doesn't finish things" and refocus on an opportunity for her to choose to finish a very crucial time of her life and to move on with a sense that she no longer needed to seal off the past, but could carry aspects of the past with her in a new way. Since unresolved loss frequently functions in ways that keep people anchored in the past, even when they are working very hard to deny the past, and prevent a sense of present and future development, healing rituals are often designed to provide a temporal connection of past, present, and future.

THERAPEUTIC HEALING RITUALS FOR OTHER LOSSES. Healing may also be needed for losses resulting from the irreparable break in a relationship, such as separation and divorce or the end of nonmarried relationships. In Western culture, there are no agreed upon rituals to mark the end of a marriage and to facilitate the healing that is needed to reestablish oneself or to promote a new kind of relationship between spouses after the end of a marriage, especially necessary when they will remain as parents to children. One client cynically commented that going to court was her divorce ritual, and that the court experience left her feeling bitter and empty. There are also no rituals to ease the way for extended family relationships in cases of divorce.

Certain religions do have religious divorce rituals, as, for instance, the Jewish *get*. Granted by rabbinic authority, and marking the end of a marriage as that which occurs within the context of a larger community, the *get* involves the actual tearing of the marriage contract or *ketuba*, which is usually a very beautiful document decorated with handdrawn artwork.

Therapeutic healing rituals are especially efficacious for the end of relationships that are not confirmed by the wider community. The end of a nonmarried relationship not only has no healing ritual, but also often is not acknowledged as a loss by family and friends, or is considered "less serious" than a divorce. This very lack of confirmation of loss makes healing more difficult, as there is no context for the expression of pain and sadness.

For both divorce and the end of nonmarried relationships, therapeutic healing rituals frequently begin with an affirmation of loss and then lead to a gradual process of letting go that carefully respects the client's pace. Very often, periods of holding on are symbolically alternated with periods of letting go, enabling the client to examine both aspects and to determine the pace. Symbolic action, such as burying or burning metaphors for the old relationship may be utilized to symbolize finality when the client indicates a readiness for such finality.

Therapeutic healing rituals may be efficacious for losses of bodily parts and functions due to illness and the often attendant loss of roles, life expectations, and dreams. The lack of any such rituals that can acknowledge the losses and begin to facilitate alternatives has been hypothesized as a contributory factor in the rapid deterioration of older people who suffer multiple unmourned losses. Here healing rituals should involve aspects that mourn the loss while simultaneously pointing to what is possible in the future.

Therapeutic healing rituals may be designed for deep cultural losses, such as the losses due to migration. Here the healing rituals may be designed both to incorporate unrecoverable aspects of life, such as when a person or family cannot return to the country of birth, and to make ongoing cross-cultural connections possible through affirming memories, traditions, stories.

BRIEF EXAMPLE—EL SALVADOR AND THE BRONX. A family, consisting of a single mother, Ms. Torres, and two adolescent children, a boy, Manuel, 15, and a girl, Maria, 13, were referred for therapy due to the son's problems in school. In recent weeks he had begun cutting school and hanging out on the streets. The family was from El Salvador, which they had fled four years earlier following the imprisonment and subsequent death of the father for political activities. The children spoke English, while the mother spoke primarily Spanish. They were living in the Bronx.

In the first session, the mother said that they had been very close, both in El Salvador and during the first two years in the Bronx, but that now they were distant. She said she could not understand her children anymore, and that she was very afraid of losing them, especially her son. The children both stated that they could no longer understand their mother. They said they wanted to be American and that she wanted them to be Salvadoran. They were angry that she had not learned more English, and the son said, "My mother lives in the past!" While the children spoke, the mother cried. When they finished, she said that they refused to listen to her when she wanted to talk about home. The son immediately said, "Home is in the Bronx now!"

They described a daily pattern in which the mother would try to speak about El Salvador, and both children would leave. When the children tried

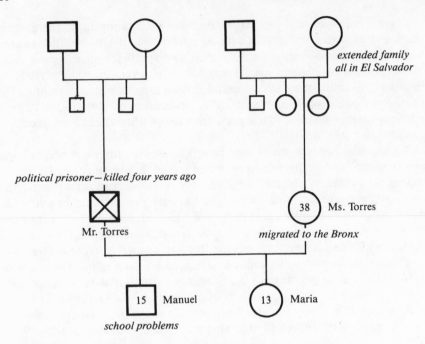

political prisoner—killed four years ago

Mr. Torres

38 Ms. Torres

migrated to the Bronx

extended family all in El Salvador

15 Manuel

13 Maria

school problems

FIGURE 3   The Torres Family: El Salvador and the Bronx

to talk about what was happening to them everyday, the mother would get upset. Mother and children were becoming more and more separate. At the same time, the children's care and concern for their mother became evident when the conversation shifted to their dead father, as both children moved swiftly to protect their mother, changing the subject to issues that would upset her in more manageable ways! Thus, the children's seeming refusal to affirm their connection to El Salvador not only expressed fairly typical adolescent rebellion in situations of migration, but also served a protective function, albeit misguided, to keep their mother angry rather than sad.

At the end of the session, I asked them all to bring items to the next session that would represent El Salvador and the Bronx, in order to begin a process that would affirm the connection of all three members to both places. In the second session, time was spent with each member sharing their items. The mother was surprised that both children brought items from El Salvador that represented very tender memories, including photographs and toys. She said that she had no idea that they had kept anything. Their items from the Bronx were a rock and roll tape and a poster from a concert. The son expressed surprise that this did not upset his mother, since at home they frequently fought about the music the children wanted to hear. The mother brought Salvadoran food she had made. She also brought a small pizza that she had bought to represent the Bronx, and said that lately the children were always eating pizza instead of the food she prepared. We sat and ate both the Salvadoran food and the pizza together.

At the end of this session in which both cultures were affirmed by all family members, I asked them to pick a time once a week for "storytelling," when the children would listen to their mother's stories about El Salvador, followed by the mother's listening to the children's stories about the Bronx. This storytelling ritual was designed to interdict the previous pattern of distance and struggle, to affirm both cultures, to connect mother and adolescent children, and to allow for continuity of past and present. The family continued this storytelling ritual beyond the three weeks I had asked them to try it, and it became a part of their family life. Over time, the stories allowed for the expression of all of the members' loss and sadness and fear involved in their forced migration, while at the same time anchoring them in a new life that could include many elements of their heritage. Also, stories which the children told about the Bronx enabled the son to begin to discuss his school problems, which he had been afraid to raise with his mother earlier.

This two-part ritual began with the family members' bringing the items that represented El Salvador and the Bronx to the session. During this in-session portion, the mother was able to discern that her children were still connected to El Salvador and the children were able to realize that their mother was not closed to their new experiences in the Bronx. A small dose of symmetry was able to interdict the previously escalating complementary pattern. The at-home storytelling ritual continued this pattern shift, while allowing for the healing process needed in a family that had been forced to flee their own home.

Therapeutic healing rituals to assist families who have experienced political terror will be discussed and illustrated in Chapter 14.

THERAPEUTIC HEALING RITUALS FOR RELATIONSHIP RECONCILIATION. Over the course of adult couple relationships, parent-child relationships, and close friendships, issues of forgiveness and reconciliation may be salient. Extramarital affairs, marriages or parent-child relationships in which years of resentments have built up, and the emergence of long-held secrets all may be times when therapeutic healing rituals are useful. Here such rituals may begin a process of forgiveness and reconciliation or may mark the accomplishment of reconciliation, as in the case of the Korner family, in which the rituals marked the reconciliation of husband and wife, and father and son.

BRIEF EXAMPLE – PARENT-CHILD RECONCILIATION. The Simpson family, consisting of two elderly parents, George, 74, and Carrie, 73, and two grown daughters, Catherine, 48, and Ellen, 47, who lived separately from the parents,

came to therapy due to the mother's compulsive handwashing. The relationship between parents and daughters seemed stiff and frozen. The mother's
handwashing was the only topic family members would discuss with each
other. Members were distant from one another. During the course of the
therapy with the older couple, a 40-year secret emerged. Before the couple
had married, the woman had become pregnant, and they were sent away by
their families of origin. After the first daughter was born, the couple married. No family came to their wedding, and they felt they had married in
shame. They had no wedding celebration and no celebration for the birth of
their daughter. They decided it would be best to keep the origins of their
marriage a secret from their children. They avoided anything that would
touch on this secret. Thus, they never celebrated their anniversary. More and
more topics became off-limits, until only the mother's handwashing was safe
for discussion. The couple was increasingly cut off from extended family
and the outside world. Until discussing this secret in therapy, they had told
no one, although they believed that, in fact, their daughters knew and were
pretending not to know in order to protect them.

   An in-session healing ritual of reconciliation was co-created by the couple
and me. They invited their daughters to a session and brought symbols of
their wedding, including the marriage license which they had kept hidden in
the bottom of an old trunk for nearly half a century. The session was
comprised of each parent's telling the daughters their story. As the parents
spoke, the daughters cried and said they had known this secret for years and

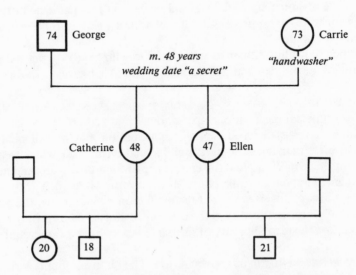

FIGURE 4   The Simpson Family: Parent-Child Reconciliation

had always felt so terrible that they could not discuss it with the parents, but felt that it would be wrong to bring it up. After the parents told their story and listened to their daughters' responses, many issues that had never been discussed began to pour out. The whole family's reconciliation of relationships was further marked by the parents' subsequent celebration of their anniversary for the first time in almost 50 years. (See Imber-Black, 1986b, for a complete description of this case.)

In this case, the beginnings of reconciliation between parents and children occurred in an in-session storytelling ritual, in which symbols of a formerly forbidden past were brought out into the open. After this occurred, other hidden issues were able to emerge as well, replacing the pattern of distance with one of involvement. The parents' reclamation of their own anniversary ritual may be seen as a punctuation of the reconciliation process.

Identity Definition and Redefinition

Individuals, families, and larger systems are known to themselves and others through particular identities. Such identities may be positive, broad, and flexible, or they may be negative, narrow, and constraining. Normative rituals in families facilitate shifts in identities for both individuals and families. Thus, a wedding operates not only to redefine membership, but also to redefine identities, as two individuals become husband and wife and several family members become in-laws. A rite of passage ritual, such as a Bar or Bas Mitzvah, is intended to change the identity of a person from child to young adult with new responsibilities within the Jewish community. A colleague told me a story of marking this change in identity by having her children pick new bedroom furniture on the occasion of their bar mitzvah in order to metaphorically express the shift from child to young adult. The children were told to pick the furniture that they thought they would like to take with them when they left home, thus connecting the current life cycle and identity change to a future one in which their identity would again shift, this time to independent adult. When the children left home and took the furniture with them, the parents were then visibly confronted with the change in their own identities from parents of children at home to a couple with grown children who no longer lived at home.

Many family traditions and celebrations touch on issues of identity. Birthday parties involve the identity theme, as they include aspects that symbolically allude to the change in age and development of a person. In my own family, we celebrate my daughter's adoption every year with an adoption day whose specific content varies year to year, enabling the affirmation of her growth and development to be an element in the ritual. For instance, when she was very young, her adoption day was marked by a family party at home. As she has grown into a young woman, she has selected special ways to mark this celebration, such as going to dinner and a show with family members. Unlike a birthday party, this ritual is attended only by family members. This ritual, which also contains the membership theme, celebrates her identity as an adopted person and as a daughter and a sister in our family.

Family religious and ethnic celebrations may contribute to a sense of identity. Here specific foods, dress and ceremonies may serve to symbolize the identity theme. Such celebrations define an individual's identity as part of a larger cultural group. In the multi-ethnic society of the United States, participation in such rituals as the Chinese New Year or Greek Orthodox Easter allow even highly assimilated persons to stay connected to their ethnic and religious identity.

Cultural rituals, such as Veteran's Day, Mother's Day, and Father's Day, all involve the identity theme, as these mark and celebrate particular aspects of people's identities. Alcoholics Anonymous meetings involve a ritualized process that may contribute to a person's identity as a "recovering alcoholic." Such activities as adopted persons' searching for their biological parents, or historical genealogy searches to discover one's origins, or making distant trips to countries where one's ancestors came from frequently take on identity definition and redefinition ritual qualities, as prescribed steps are followed, including reclaiming one's "roots" and reunions.

IDENTITY RITUALS AND THE THERAPEUTIC PROCESS. Families may reify the identity of their members. Thus, a particular member may be known in a family as "the stubborn one" or "the sick child" or "the one with a temper" or "just like father." Children may be labeled with complementary roles, such as "bad" child and "good" child. Members may strive for particular identities and become unhappy when these prove impossible to reach.

BRIEF EXAMPLE – BECOMING "IMPERFECT" PARENTS. A family consisting of two parents, Mr. and Ms. Ellis, and two adopted children, Andy, 11 and Cathy, 8, came to family therapy due to problems with Andy. The parents said they found him hard to manage, that he misbehaved at home and at school. Often Andy would not follow rules. He frequently got into fights with other children, including Cathy. The parents felt that Andy was the "instigator" of these fights, and they described how Cathy would come and tell them when Andy was "picking on her." They did not attribute the problems to Andy's adoption, since Cathy was also adopted and she was a "very good girl." During this discussion, the team observed that Cathy was smiling, while quietly kicking Andy under table!

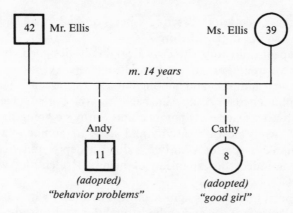

FIGURE 5   The Ellis Family: Becoming "Imperfect" Parents

The parents were religious and felt that they had a special responsibility to be "perfect parents" to these children whom they had adopted. This pressure of being "perfect parents" seemed to be contributing to their current upset, since they felt that Andy's behavior was a strong indication that they were far from "perfect parents." Thus, they felt bad about themselves and about Andy. Their confidence seemed to be eroding every time Andy misbehaved, and they felt less and less able to handle him.

During the second session, the team suggested that perhaps Andy, through his misbehavior, was trying to teach the parents that they did not need to be "perfect parents." During this discussion, Andy smiled. The parents were asked to stage a mock fight between the children, in which they were to instruct Andy to start and Cathy to come and tell them that he was picking on her. At this point, the parents were to say to both children, "Thank you for teaching us that we don't need to be perfect parents!"

The family returned in a month. They began by reporting that Andy was doing much better in school, that he had made several friends, and that the children were fighting less. The mother said they had decided against the mock fight, but that every time Andy did something that upset her, she simply said to herself, "Thank you for teaching me that I don't have to be a perfect parent," and then went about her business. The father then described an amazing ritual, planned and executed by the children, under Andy's leadership. The parents had come home from their church two weeks earlier to find their house filled with neighbors. The children had made snacks for everyone. On the wall as they walked into the house was a huge sign that read, "Happy Parents Day To Our Imperfect Parents!" The father got tears in his eyes and said, "I just had no idea, I had no idea he was so creative," and both parents went on to describe aspects of Andy they had been noticing that they had not noticed before.

This therapeutic identity ritual was originally designed to offer a new identity to the parents, and in so doing to interdict the escalating patterns between parents and son and among brother, sister and parents, which frequently culminated in Andy's misbehaving, the parents' feeling increasingly bad about themselves as parents, and Cathy's owning the position of "good child." Andy's own creativity and sense of humor and play, which became available as patterns shifted, added a depth and richness to the ritual that continued the expansion of members' identities with self and others.

Children born following a significant loss in a family may be expected to follow a particular identity and embody qualities of the dead relative. Often behavior that does not fit the role goes unobserved or unnoticed. Therapeutic identity rituals may be designed in order to help differentiate the individual from the dead relative. Such rituals, which often involve specific affirmation of qualities that are *not* associated with the dead relative, affect both individual and family functioning.

A similar issue frequently arises in divorced families when a parent insists that a particular child is "just like the other parent," usually in negative ways. Unfinished aspects of the old marital conflict begin to emerge between parent and child, freezing the individuals and the system in its development. Aspects of the child that differ from this definition go unseen. Here a therapeutic identity ritual may be designed that highlights both the child's uniqueness and ways that the child shares traits of both parents.

Larger systems may contribute to narrow and constraining identities, as when schools describe children as "just like his brother" or "children from a broken home." Referrals for therapy may identify a family as a "hopeless case." An individual's or family's identity is subsumed and totalized by a phrase that carries with it implications for subsequent interactions and expectations.

Many individuals and families are limited in their sense of identity by rigid roles or by stigmatizing labels. Physical and mental illnesses and disabilities all carry labels that frequently function to define a person's identity in ways that limit rather than expand possibilities both for the individual and for relationships. While diagnostic categories may be useful for certain treatment planning and implementation, and while they have become a required aspect of the therapeutic establishment in our culture, therapists must always remember that labels become toxic when they are understood to capture the essence of a person or a family.

Therapeutic identity rituals function to remove stigmatizing labels and enable new identities to emerge. The ritual designed by the Milan team in which a family was instructed to throw away their son's medication while telling him that he was a normal boy is an example of an identity redefinition ritual (Selvini Palazzoli et al., 1977). Such rituals operate at an individual, family, and family-larger system level.

BRIEF EXAMPLE – FROM HYPERACTIVE TO NORMAL BUT NAUGHTY. The Wells family came to therapy presenting their 11-year-old daughter as "hyperactive." The girl had been so labeled for eight years. The family, consisting of two parents and the child, was referred by her pediatrician, who had been prescribing Ritalin for the girl but felt it was time to explore other options. In the first session, it became clear that all interactions with the girl involved her label of "hyperactive." She was not disciplined for misbehavior either at home or at school due to her hyperactivity. The mother spent a lot of time going to appointments with her daughter, while father remained distant from both mother and child.

Feeling that various options with the girl were not being tried, the team suggested an experiment – the parents were to drop the label of "hyperactive" for three weeks and to treat her as they would treat a normal child. At this juncture, the father began to become more involved. The pediatrician agreed to a trial without Ritalin. The parents went jointly to the school to explain the experiment and to ask for the teachers' cooperation. This very direct approach, which involved explaining to the parents the possible effects of labels, had brief success, followed by a relapse. The mother called, very upset, saying that the experiment was not working, the girl was misbehaving, and the father was ready to give up.

The therapy team decided that a more symbolic and dramatic approach was needed. The family was asked to come to a session and to bring the remaining medication. The session began as the therapist gave out to each

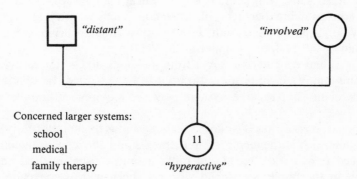

FIGURE 6   The Wells Family: From Hyperactive to Normal, but Naughty

member index cards titled, "Old Roles." These included "hyperactive girl," "busy mother of a hyperactive girl," and "distant father of a hyperactive girl." The family members agreed that these indeed were their roles. The therapist asked if they felt ready to give these up, even though it was not yet clear what might take their place, and the members agreed that they were more than ready to try something new. The therapist then invited the girl to burn the index cards. She did so very carefully and put the fire out. The ashes were then mixed with the remainder of the Ritalin and put into a large envelope, which the family then buried, while the therapist witnessed their ceremony.

Six weeks later the girl had to have minor surgery. The mother reported that she was an excellent patient, both in the hospital and at home. The school was treating her as a normal child and disciplining her like other children when necessary. Mother was looking for work outside the home and father was more involved with both his wife and daughter. The parents agreed that their daughter was simply a normal child who sometimes did naughty things (Imber Coppersmith, 1982). (See Chapter 12 by Janine Roberts for a more extensive identity redefinition ritual involving psychiatric labelling.)

Therapeutic identity definition and redefinition rituals are especially useful for families and individuals with severe or chronic illness or other disabilities. In such instances, the person's whole identity may become fused with the illness or disability, such as "cancer patient," "AIDS victim," etc. Other aspects of the person may become lost. In a television movie about Down Syndrome, "Kids Like These," the boy, 11, with Down Syndrome, who appears frequently while his mother gives lectures to other parents, finally says to her, "I'm sick and tired of all this Down Syndrome stuff!", expressing his own conviction that he is more than his label.

The L'Arche Community, an intentional community with chapters in many countries involving persons with handicaps and persons without obvious handicaps living together, utilizes several rituals whose principal aim is to provide all participants with the identity of human being, rather than constraining labels (Imber Coppersmith, 1984).

After a family member recovers from a serious illness, the member and the entire family's identity may also need to be redefined. In addition, the family's relationship to larger systems may also require redefinition.

BRIEF EXAMPLE – THE THERAPIST COMES TO DINNER (CONTINUED). In the Wharton family described in the membership theme section above, with the little girl who liked french fries, bread and milk, a salient issue involved Sandra's position in the family as a child who was born with a congenital heart condition, requiring that the family interact with many specialists from outside systems over many years. Her heart condition, corrected a year and a half before therapy ensued, contributed to her position as a "special child" in the family. Even after successful surgery, her identity as the "sick" member continued due to her eating problem, and she was labeled by her mother, maternal grandmother, and dietician as "anorexic." In the first session, both parents predicted that she would stop eating altogether and would die in a couple of years. Here it may be hypothesized that the girl's identity as a "sick" child with a congenital heart condition that threatened to shorten her life had never been redefined following her surgery. Further, the family's involvement with outside helpers simply continued, with new helpers tackling the eating problem rather than the heart condition. Thus, the family's own definition of itself as a family requiring outside help remained unchallenged.

Two rituals were used initially to challenge the girl's identity as "anorexic," replacing this with a common family identity of people who have "favorites." These rituals included the dinner at the clinic, during which all family members' "favorites" and disliked foods were discussed at length, and an at-home dinner ritual which focused first on the expression of each member's disliked foods as a permission-giving metaphor for the discussion of other differences, and then on the transformation of this disliked food to something more palatable through the joint efforts of family members. The family's reliance on outside helpers attenuated through a ritualized process in which the parents became the "therapists" for the girl by designing and implementing a plan for her to "broaden her food repertoire." As the parents redefined their own identity as "experts on their daughter," they fired the dietician when she criticized their plan and tried to put Sandra on a different plan. This was the first time that the parents saw themselves as people who could challenge outside authority. In the final session, a second family and therapist dinner was held. During this meal ritual, a discussion of the future resulted in the family's redefinition of Sandra as a girl who would become a woman and a lawyer, rather than a girl who would soon die (Imber-Black, 1986a).

The identity definition and redefinition theme is further exemplified in the chapters on adoption (Chapter 8), families and larger systems (Chapter 12), and families and political oppression (Chapter 14).

Belief Expression and Negotiation

Normative rituals frequently function to express beliefs and to shape and negotiate new beliefs. Religious and cultural rituals, in particular, allow for the expression of a group's beliefs. Those rituals that remain alive and meaningful have space for variations that express changing norms and beliefs while affirming a connection to the past (see Davis, Chapter 7). The Passover Seder is an example of such a ritual. Variations in the Seder, both among the three branches of Judaism and in particular families, allow for the expression of both general and specific beliefs. For example, in a recent reform Judaism Haggadah (the book containing the order of the Passover Seder), a fifth cup of wine has been added to the traditional four cups. This cup, called the "Cup of Redemption," is set aside for the future, connecting those who celebrate the Passover with those who are still not free, thereby expressing the belief that the Seder per se is not simply a commemoration of a past event, but a living celebration of present and future as well (Bronstein, 1974). In many families, including my own, following that portion of the Seder when the 10 plagues are recited, a time has been added for participants to express their beliefs about contemporary "plagues," such as racism, sexism, poverty, and war.

As beliefs are expanded, altered, or challenged, new rituals may emerge or significant aspects of existing rituals may change. A vital example may be seen in the Roman Catholic Mass following Vatican II. While the Mass per se remained unchanged, the change from Latin to the vernacular and the change in the priest's position from one where his back was to the congregation to one where the priest faces the congregation exemplifies a change of belief regarding the participation of the laity from passive to active.

Certain cultures have rituals that are designed to negotiate beliefs between parties who cannot come to agreement. A colleague, John Rolland, related such a ritual to me that clients had imparted to him. In an African tribe, the covers of cooking pots are used to negotiate conflicting beliefs between a wife and husband. On occasions when a wife is angry with her husband over differences between them, she will replace the usual cover on the cooking pot with one upon which pictures have been engraved that express proverbs applicable to their conflict. The wife will have a variety of such covers given to her by her mother when she marries. When the husband sees the new cover, he understands the meaning of the particular proverb and the issue being raised by his wife. At this juncture, the husband has two choices. He can affirm his wife's position and apologize, or he can turn down her position by replacing the cover his wife has placed with one of his own from a collection given to him by his father at his wedding. If the available covers are not sufficient to settle the differences or if they do not quite fit the situation, then the couple may go to a specialist, a sculptor of new covers, and have one made to order to address the differences! In our own culture, many couples and families turn to therapists when they have run out of "available pot covers" to deal with their conflicting beliefs.

BELIEF EXPRESSION AND NEGOTIATION RITUALS AND THE THERAPEUTIC PROCESS. Therapeutic belief expression and negotiation rituals are especially useful when clients present conflicting beliefs about a particular issue. They may be manifesting such conflicting beliefs through behavior, as when one parent disciplines a child and the other parent protects a child, or the conflict may be largely verbal, as when one member of a couple expresses a wish to separate while the other expresses a wish to remain together. Often family members ascribe badness or blame to certain beliefs of members and goodness or correctness to other beliefs, usually their own. Therapeutic belief expression and negotiation rituals provide an opportunity for family members to hear and experience each other's positions without blame, thereby creating a new context for relationships.

One example of the belief expression and negotiation theme may be seen in the Milan team's ritual "odd days and even days" (Selvini Palazzoli et al., 1978). In this ritual, the Milan team used time to draw a distinction between one parent's approach to a child's behavior and the other parent's approach to the same behavior, in families where it appeared that the parents were undermining each other while sending conflicting messages to the child. In such symmetrical conflicts, each parent's way of handling the child was given implicit credence by a ritual that gave each parent an equal number of days to "be in charge," while the other parent was to observe.

BRIEF EXAMPLE – THE THERAPIST COMES TO DINNER (CONTINUED). In the case of the Wharton family, in which Sandra ate french fries, bread and milk, the mother believed that Sandra had a "big" problem, while the father believed she had a "small" problem. These beliefs were expressed in action by the mother's remaining at the dinner table every night, urging Sandra to eat, while the father left to watch television. An early intervention utilized was the "odd days-even days" ritual. When the family returned, they reported that "Sandra ate better on the nights when Dad was in charge." The mother stated that she believed this was because it was so different to have him involved and that she was glad for his involvement. This ritual ultimately led to negotiations between the parents regarding the whole issue of parenting, resulting in the emergence of a new belief that two parents working together were needed to solve the problem.

Variations on this ritual may be created to express and negotiate beliefs in many circumstances.[1] Utilizing time and action as key variables, family members may be asked to behave and believe according to one set of beliefs for a particular time period and another set of beliefs for a different time period. This process interrupts endless symmetrical struggles, allows members to listen to each other, promotes empathy, and communicates the therapist's belief that there is merit in both positions.

BRIEF EXAMPLE – ENABLING A NEW CONVERSATION. A couple, Mr. and Ms. Colling, came to therapy regarding a single issue. For four years they had been split regarding whether or not to have a third child. The couple, in their late thirties, had two children, ages seven and nine. Ms. Colling wanted another child, while Mr. Colling did not. The spouses were very committed to each other and felt that most areas of their marriage and family life were sound.

They described the following pattern: Every few months, Ms. Colling would raise the issue of having another child. She would present all of the reasons why this was a good idea and what it meant to her. Mr. Colling would respond with all of the reasons why having another child was not a good idea and why he did not want another child. Ms. Colling would then present answers to all of his objections. Each would become more adamant and defensive as the conversation continued. Mr. Colling would then withdraw and there would be distance and quiet anger between them that would last for several weeks. Each felt unheard by the other on this crucial issue.

At the end of the first session, I asked them to have two conversations at home. During one conversation they were each to discuss all of the reasons why it would be a good idea to have another child. Mr. Colling was asked to suspend his usual position and to fully enter on his wife's side of the issue. During the other conversation, they were each to discuss all of the reasons why it would be best to not have another child. Ms. Colling was asked to suspend her usual position and to fully join her husband's side of the issue. They were asked to choose a particular time and place for these conversations, in order to highlight them as special and unique. Such utilization of

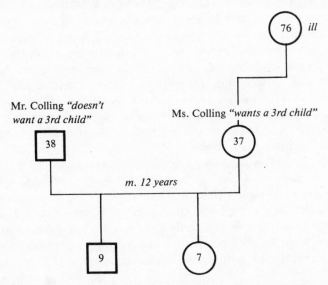

FIGURE 7   The Colling Family: Enabling a New Conversation

time as an element in belief expression and negotiation rituals provides safety for the participants to explore new territory, knowing such exploration will be for a limited time.

When they returned, each expressed that they felt understood by the other in a way that they had not previously felt. Ms. Colling said she was extremely moved by what her husband had expressed regarding having another child and what his children and family meant to him. She said she felt closer to him than she had in a long while. Mr. Colling expressed surprise at how clearly his wife understood his present career issues, which he felt she had dismissed in their previous discussions of the issue. Ms. Colling had also been able to express her own concerns about her aging and ill mother, a subject she had not previously raised for fear it would be used by her husband as another reason not to have a third child. They were able to begin to examine this very important issue for the first time. While they had not reached a mutual decision regarding a third child, both husband and wife saw new qualities in the other, particularly empathy and sensitivity, that were hidden by the previous pattern. The usual end to their discussion of the issue, distance and anger, was replaced by a sense of connection. This conversation ritual allowed each to present his or her own views without defensiveness, to hear the other's views without distancing, and to feel understood.

Variations on such a conversation ritual may be developed for situations where competing beliefs are deadlocked, whether between spouses, other family members, a family and outside helpers, or within an individual. Specific actions may also be part of the ritual. For instance, a single-parent mother expressed her feeling of being caught between a school system that was pushing her to hospitalize her school-refusing adolescent son and a family therapy program which was counseling her to "go slow." The school's belief was that he was a psychiatric patient, while the family therapist's belief was that his behavior was related to family issues. Unable to choose between the competing beliefs, she felt paralyzed and less and less capable. She was asked to divide up the week. On Mondays, Wednesdays, and Fridays, she was to behave and believe as if hospitalization were the best course of action. This was to involve her calling people, getting information about the hospital, and relating to her son as a patient. On Tuesdays, Thursdays and Saturdays, she was to take the position that no more treatment was needed. On these days she was to review all of the treatment failures, which were considerable, to cease conversations with those urging hospitalization, and to relate to her son as a normal boy who needed some time to think. She did the ritual as instructed and decided not to hospitalize her son (see Imber-Black, 1985, for a complete case description). Perhaps even more important than the content of the mother's immediate decision was the reemergence of her ability to be active in a family-larger system configuration in which she previously felt paralyzed and unable to express her own beliefs.

When people become locked into seeing only their own belief as correct and other beliefs as wrong or blameful, humor usually disappears. Belief expression and negotiation rituals often utilize humor in order to intervene in rigidities and facilitate problem-solving.

BRIEF EXAMPLE – "MOUTHY" AND "EVIL." A young couple, Mavis and Ken Sutter, came for couples therapy. Married for four years, they felt unable to discuss differences of opinion without getting into heated, protracted, and unfinished arguments. Regardless of topic, the process between them would deteriorate to name-calling. Mavis's most common word for Ken was "evil," while Ken referred to Mavis as "mouthy." Once these terms were hauled out by either, their fights deteriorated further. They stated that they thought they argued about ten percent of the time, that their marriage was satisfying in many ways, and that they both felt concerned that the fights could destroy a positive relationship.

I asked them to go on a shopping trip together to a nearby mall. There they were to go to the store that made T-shirts with words and pictures on them.[2] Together, they were to pick out a shirt that symbolized "mouthy" and a shirt that symbolized "evil." They both began laughing. I asked them if they would agree that during the next fight, rather than calling names, they would put on their shirts and continue the fight. They agreed.

At the next session, Mavis and Ken entered carrying a bag in which they had brought their shirts to show me. Together they had picked a shirt for Ken that had a huge viper on it, symbolizing "evil," and a shirt for Mavis that had giant red lips on it, symbolizing "mouthy." They had used the shirts in two fights. In the first, they had handed the shirts to each other, just short of their usual name-calling. In the second, each had gone and retrieved his or her own shirt and put it on! They described laughing and then settling the issue in a new way. Name-calling had ceased, and each felt better about the other.

Belief expression and negotiation rituals may be particularly useful for families involved with multiple helpers from several larger systems, each with its own beliefs about the nature of a problem and the appropriate treatment. In such circumstances it is not unusual for an individual or family to deteriorate in its own capacity to solve problems or to express paralyzing confusion regarding a course of action. Simultaneously, the multiple helpers may become locked in a struggle with each other regarding the "correct" belief. Here rituals may be designed to clarify and draw distinctions among the beliefs of various helpers, while reempowering the client to make decisions and to take action. The rituals may function to challenge rigid beliefs about a family, such as when a single-parent family and helpers all believe "single-parent families cannot function well." Such rituals may follow family-multiple helper consultations, or may emerge when a therapist discovers that a family is currently seeing multiple helpers or has seen many helpers in a serial fashion.

BRIEF EXAMPLE – A THIRD OPINION. A single-parent family, Ms. Montero and her two children, Ida, 11 and Joseph, 8, were seeing multiple helpers due to problems identified in Joseph, such as temper tantrums and refusal to listen to adults. The helpers included a family therapist, a pediatrician, a psychologist who tested Joseph, and a Big Brother for Joseph.

The psychological testing of Joseph resulted in a very pessimistic report which stated that Joseph would likely need residential treatment. Markedly different beliefs among the helpers towards Ms. Montero were visible in the dissemination of the report, as the psychologist refused to show her the results directly, stating that, "she would not be able to handle seeing the report," while the pediatrician did show her the writeup. At this juncture, conflicting beliefs regarding Joseph's future emerged both among the helpers and in Ms. Montero's extended family, various members of which insisted that Joseph go for a "second opinion."

In a consultation, Ms. Montero expressed great confusion regarding the advice she was receiving from the various helpers. She said she felt com-

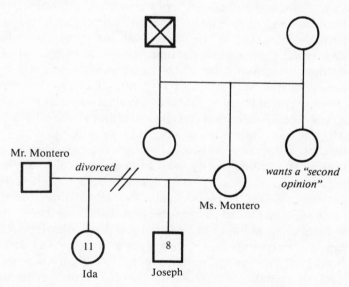

FIGURE 8   The Montero Family: A Third Opinion

pelled to follow her family's suggestion regarding a "second opinion," although she really did not want to put Joseph through more testing. She also informed the consultant that, in fact, Joseph had been improving, both at home and at school, but that there had been little opportunity to discuss this with any of the helpers.

Ms. Montero was asked by the consultant to collect information about her children and herself, the transitions and changes they had undergone and to construct a written "third opinion" to be used to guide her work with helpers and her interactions with her family of origin. This document ritual was designed to reempower Ms. Montero as the expert on her family, to inform all of the helpers about noted changes in Joseph, and to place Joseph's behavior in the context of his family (Imber-Black, 1988).

Other belief expression and negotiation rituals will be illustrated in the chapters on couples' issues (Chapter 4), the Bar Mitzvah (Chapter 7), remarried families (Chapter 11, and women's issues (Chapter 13).

Celebration

The theme of celebration attends to many normative rituals. While the term "celebration" generally conjures up festivities, it also may refer to more solemn and sacred rituals. Thus, all of the rituals attendant to life cycle transitions, such as weddings, birth of children, adolescent rites of passage, and funerals, involve celebration as one theme. The celebration theme is also attendant upon religious and cultural holidays and many family traditions, such as birthdays and anniversaries. The celebration theme involves that aspect of rituals connected to affirming, honoring, commemorating, and demarcating regular time from special time. Rituals of celebration frequently involve ethnic expression, special food and drinks reserved for certain celebrations, unique music, gifts, and particular clothing. The celebration aspect of rituals is often the most visible and dramatic marker of individual, family and community definition and change, although the celebration, per se, is usually only the culmination of a much longer process.

Rituals involving celebration often have familiar and expected aspects, existing both in the culture at large and in one's particular family. These expected and familiar processes function as abbreviated metaphors for family and cultural rules and roles. As such, they may express the warmth, comfort, support, and human connectedness available in celebrations. They may allow for the expression of key cultural and family development. Conversely, they may poignantly announce a sense of loss, such as during holiday celebrations following a family member's death, or signal cutoffs through lack of invitation or refusal to participate in a celebration, or silently express relational stagnation and hypocrisy, as when the form of the celebration remains unchanged despite vital, though often unspoken, relationship changes.

CELEBRATION RITUALS AND THE THERAPEUTIC PROCESS. Similar to the membership theme, the celebration theme is readily available for conversations between therapists and families. As one gathers genogram and life cycle issues from a family, discussion of particular life cycle celebrations can begin to inform both therapist and family about participation, decision-making, relationship connections and cutoffs. For instance, one couple who were planning to marry, but whose plans were put off due to a high level of conflict, responded to a question about their potential guest list by telling me that the man's grown daughters would not be invited and that the woman's mother would be invited "out of sheer politeness." This information led to a broader discussion of family-of-origin issues and the ways in which the couple's current conflicts could be viewed as existing in this wider context, of which the couple had not been aware.

Discussion of specific holiday celebrations, such as Thanksgiving or Christmas, can be relevant grist for the therapeutic mill, both informing about conflicts and leading to new rituals capable of transforming relationships. Such discussion easily brings family-of-origin issues into the open. During my graduate student days, I sold Christmas trees one winter and listened to endless variations of, "We have to have a scotch pine, dear, because that's what my family always had," answered by, "Scotch pines are nice, honey, but we have to have a douglas fir, because that's what my family always had!" Clearly, such arguments over appropriate symbols of the celebration are fraught with issues of loyalty, power, "correct" beliefs, etc., and can be usefully examined and reworked in therapy.

Ethnically and religiously intermarried couples face particular challenges during celebration rituals. In therapy, religiously intermarried couples may describe how they get along well until December, when they are faced with issues of difference, or how they could "ignore" the issue until children were born. Some families attempt to resolve the struggle by opting out of celebrations altogether, but find they must then deal with a sense of emptiness and cutoffs. Celebration rituals in ethnically intermarried couples may highlight differences that are not usually discussed. Here the therapist can effectively assist the partners in a key developmental task of being able to affirm their differences through celebration rituals that respect the heritage of each and facilitate the creation of new rituals, symbolic of their unique family system.

Therapeutic celebration rituals may be designed with couples to mark a new beginning to their marriage, such as with the Korner family. Gay couples, for whom legal marriage is not possible, may wish to design a celebration ritual that publicly proclaims their relationship. The celebration theme may attend to therapeutic rituals to mark particular achievements, normative or idiosyncratic life cycle transitions, or may be used to reframe as a cause for celebration that which a family has previously hidden, such as the couple that had not celebrated their anniversary for nearly 50 years. Since therapy is often about painful issues, the therapist must take care to watch for moments when celebration rituals are appropriate and not leave celebration outside the therapy room. Since a therapeutic celebration ritual often punctuates a key turning point for an individual, couple or family, and may be likely to become a part of family's ongoing tradition, such as the Korner family's gold glasses used for subsequent family celebrations, these rituals tend to rely heavily on family input for their design and implementation.

CELEBRATION AND LOSS. A discussion of holiday celebrations with families in therapy may reveal issues of loss. The loss of members through death or through separation and divorce is often experienced acutely at times of celebration. Families' attempts to deal with such losses at times of celebration may inadvertently prevent both an affirmation of the loss and an opportunity to experience the support and connection available in celebration. Thus, some families establish an unspoken rule to not acknowledge the loss or, as one mother described, "to pretend that we're happy." Here, paradoxically, the sense of loss and bereavement often floods and overcomes any sense of celebration. Other individuals or families place a moratorium on celebration and exist in a permanent state of grief. Family members may be out of sync with one another regarding a sense of resolution of a loss, resulting in celebrations that are fraught with tension. In all of these situations, a well-designed therapeutic ritual incorporating both loss and celebration may open the family to new possibilities.

BRIEF EXAMPLE—"WHAT ABOUT CHRISTMAS?" A family, consisting of Mr. and Mrs. Franco, 58 and 57, and their son, Alan, 33, came to the crisis unit of a community hospital in early December. Alan lived at home and did not work or go out of the house. He had a long history of seeing therapists with no change in his behavior. Over the previous week, Alan's negative behavior towards his mother had been increasing, resulting in the family's coming to the hospital.

As the therapist gathered the genogram, the parents related that they had had another son, Michael, who died suddenly 15 years earlier of virulent cancer. Two years older than Alan, Michael was a star student and athlete. He had married in December, just before Christmas, and died in February, leaving a pregnant wife. The family members related to the therapist that each had grieved the loss of Michael alone. Mother went to church to grieve, father went to the cemetery frequently, and Alan, who became intensely depressed after his brother's death, went to individual therapy! Mrs. Franco remarked that her previous encounters with therapists had made her feel like a bad mother. Sensitive to each other's grief, they did not discuss the subject of Michael's death together. Rather, the family became distracted by Alan's increasingly bizarre behavior, which seemed to function to postpone mourning and to obviate individual and family development.

In early sessions, regardless of topic, Alan would insist, "The story of Michael! The story of Michael! We have to discuss the story of Michael!" Gradually, many painful aspects regarding Michael's death were discussed, including the cutoff from Michael's wife and child, who was now a teenager. Then, in a session focused on current family relationships, Alan insisted, "Christmas! What about Christmas? We have to talk about Christmas!" What emerged was a description of a very bleak Christmas, for while the family decorated the house and Mrs. Franco made a special dinner, the specter of Michael's death permeated the holiday, but was not discussed. Alan always disrupted the dinner and would act up in ways that made the

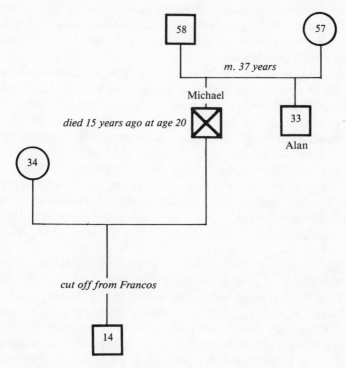

FIGURE 9   The Franco Family: "What About Christmas?"

parents feel that they could not have company over, nor could they leave to visit others. During the discussion of decorations, Mrs. Franco described childhood decorations that Michael had made and that she always put up. Then she said, "They really aren't made well, and if he were alive, I think I would have stopped putting them up years ago. I don't think I'm going to put them out this year." This was the first indication that this Christmas might somehow be different and might be a vehicle for expressing that the family was not stuck 15 years in the past.

The therapist then discussed with the family the possibility of a ritual that would allow for their joint discussion of Michael *and* their celebration of Christmas. She asked if each would be willing to bring a symbol of Michael to the next session, which was scheduled three days before Christmas. They agreed. During the next session, the therapist asked each to bring out his or her symbols. Father brought a ring belonging to Michael, Mother brought a poem, and Alan brought a photograph. She asked them to exchange their symbols with one another, thus connecting them in their previously solitary grief. She then asked each to relate a favorite memory of Michael. Alan, who was often tangential and distracting, sat quietly and attentively while his parents talked. Discussion of favorite memories led to a spontaneous sharing of formerly hidden guilt of each member regarding Michael's death. The family members cried together for the first time. Mrs. Franco hugged the therapist with appreciation.

Following this very moving ritual, the family began to discuss Christmas. Alan agreed that he would not disrupt the holiday and that he would not try to stop his parents from going visiting, as he had for many years. He then began to discuss his own future.[3]

This ritual, combining the human needs for healing and celebration, offered the family a way to share its profound loss of a son and a brother together and openly, enabling the possibility of reconnection and celebration at Christmas for the first time in 15 years. The case illustrates more generally the often hidden, but exquisite, interplay between loss and celebration and demonstrates that celebration rituals may become viable for some families when losses can be affirmed.

CELEBRATION AND GIFTS. Many normative celebration rituals involve the giving of gifts. Birthdays, anniversaries, and holidays such as Christmas, Hanukkah, or Valentine's Day all involve gift-giving. Many families develop their own traditions for such gift exchanges that heighten elements of surprise or creativity. Often, the process of such gift-giving alters as children grow, serving as a metaphor for developmental change. In other families, the gift-giving aspect of celebration serves, rather, as a symbol for disappointment and resentment, as, for example, the wife whose husband gave her an intercom set for Christmas so "she could hear better when the children needed her," or the couple who told me sadly that their gifts to each other were never appreciated, as he always returned what she gave him, and she always left whatever he gave her to hang in the closet, unseen and unworn. Discussion of gifts with families in therapy near appropriate holidays can be a useful therapeutic topic, revealing family rules regarding giving and receiving, and often opening previously taboo areas for discussion.

In our work with families, we have found that gifts may be an important element in therapeutic celebration rituals. In particular, a ritual that we have used repeatedly called "the giving of gifts" has proven to be effective to reframe precipitous or angry leavings, such as when a child leaves to go live with another parent, or to ease difficult transitions, such as when a young adult child with handicaps leaves home to live in a group home. For this ritual, family members are asked to bring gifts to the next session. Each member is asked to bring a gift for the member who is leaving. The member who is leaving is asked to bring a gift for each other member. Family members are told not to buy the gifts, but to either make something or bring something of their own that they wish to give. The ritual is conducted with the suggestion by the therapist that the gifts be exchanged with little conversation, except for any explanation of the gift, per se, that might be necessary. This is done to interdict usual patterns, especially where anger has been high, and to provide a tone of receptivity for the family.

BRIEF EXAMPLE – "THE GIVING OF GIFTS." In a recent case utilizing this ritual with a family whose daughter was leaving home to go to a group home, and in which the parents were very worried about her well-being, the father gave the young woman his favorite frying pan, which she always wanted to use but had not been allowed to, and the mother gave her perfume, which she had also not been allowed to use, and earrings belonging to the mother's mother. In short, the gifts from the parents were signals of permission to grow up and leave home, while still maintaining an important connection to the family. The daughter, in turn, gave her father a photograph taken of her at the group home, surrounded by young men and women, and gave her mother her favorite stuffed animal, which she had slept with since childhood, signaling in her own way that she was, indeed, growing up (Imber-Black, 1988).

CELEBRATION RITUALS TO END THERAPY. Celebration rituals may be useful to mark the end of therapy or the end of a family's protracted relationships with larger systems in general. Such rituals may be co-created by the therapist and family, and/or may involve actions of the therapist in some kind of surprise.

BRIEF EXAMPLE – THE THERAPIST COMES TO DINNER (CONCLUSION). In the work with the Wharton family, a second in-session dinner was held as a marker of the changes that had occurred in Sandra and in the family. In keeping with the theme of "favorites" used throughout the therapy, the family agreed that each would bring a "favorite" item for this celebration dinner, thereby communicating in action the now more symmetrical nature of relationships in the family, replacing the previous escalating complementarity. Following the meal, I brought out two items for the family – a potato (Sandra's all-time favorite) and a kiwi fruit (Sandra's nemesis, pushed on her by a dietician) – representing the themes of likes and dislikes, favorite and disfavored items, the capacity to state preferences directly, etc. The potato and the kiwi fruit brought laughter from the family members, and father joked that these were two things that Sandra loved! Linking the potato and the kiwi fruit to a variety of normal family developmental issues, I then told the family members that I wanted them to freeze these items with the understanding that, in the future, when any member of the family felt a family discussion was needed, the thawing out of the potato and the kiwi fruit would signal the call for such a meeting. The family thanked me and left therapy with both a celebration and the symbols of the work in their possession.

CONCLUSIONS

The five ritual themes discussed in this chapter, including *membership, healing, identity definition, belief expression and negotiation* and *celebration*, are key aspects of normative rituals and as such provide direction for the therapist both for the discussion of rituals with families and for the design of therapeutic rituals. Throughout a given therapy, one or more of these themes may be addressed. The themes may also interact in any particular ritual. Finally, while as therapists we may have a theme we are seeking to address in our work with a family, the family, through its own unique implementation of a ritual, will ultimately determine the theme's meanings.

NOTES

1I want to express my appreciation to Karl Tomm, M.D., with whom I worked in collaboration on variations of the "Odd Days-Even Days" ritual.

2I want to express my appreciation to Richard Whiting for his humorous innovations with "T-shirt" rituals.

3I want to express my appreciation to Donna Wolf, therapist, and Ellen Landau, supervisor, who worked in collaboration with me on this case.

REFERENCES

Bronstein, H. (1974). (Ed.). *A Passover Haggadah: The New Union Haggadah* (new ed.). New York: The Central Conference of American Rabbis.

Imber-Black, E. (1988). Idiosyncratic life cycle transitions and therapeutic rituals. In E. A. Carter & M. McGoldrick (Eds.). *The changing family life cycle*. New York: Gardner Press.

Imber-Black, E. (1986a). Toward a resource model in systemic family therapy. In M. A. Karpel (Ed.). *Family Resources: The Hidden Partner in Family Therapy* (pp. 148–174). New York: Guilford Press.

Imber-Black, E. (1986b). Odysseys of a learner. In D. Efron (Ed.). *Journeys: Expansions of strategic and systemic therapies* (pp. 3–29). New York: Brunner/Mazel.

Imber-Black, E. (1985). Women, families and larger systems. In M. Ault-Riche (Ed.). *Women and Family Therapy*, (pp. 25–33). Rockville, MD: Aspen Systems Publishers.

Imber Coppersmith, E. (1984). A special "family" with handicapped members: One family therapist's learnings from the L'Arche community. In E. Imber-Coppersmith (Ed.). *Families with a handicapped member* (pp. 150–159). Rockville, MD: Aspen Systems Publishers.

Imber Coppersmith, E. (1982). From hyperactive to normal but naughty: A multisystem partnership in delabeling. *International Journal of Family Psychiatry, 3*(2), 131–144.

Selvini Palazzoli, M., Boscolo, L., Cecchin, G., & Prata, G. (1978). A ritualized prescription in family therapy: Odd days and even days. *Journal of Marriage and Family Counseling, 4*(3), 3–9.

Selvini Palazzoli, M., Boscolo, L., Cecchin, G. & Prata, G. (1977). Family rituals: A powerful tool in family therapy. *Family Process, 16*(4), 445–454.

Van Gennep, A. (1960). *The rites of passage*. Chicago: University of Chicago Press.

Walsh, F. (1983). The timing of symptoms and critical events in the family life cycle. In H. A. Liddle (Ed.). *Clinical implications of the family life cycle* (pp. 120–133). Rockville, MD: Aspen Systems Publications.

Guidelines to Designing Therapeutic Rituals

RICHARD A. WHITING

QUESTIONS RANGING FROM "How did you design that ritual?" to "Why did you decide to do an in-session ritual as opposed to an out-of-session ritual?" have been asked of my colleagues and myself over the last several years during our workshop presentations on therapeutic rituals. Such questions have helped us to think more deliberately about what is actually involved in the design process and have highlighted the fact that, with the exception of van der Hart (1983), no one has published suggestions related to the design and creation of therapeutic rituals. This chapter, which reflects discussions and presentations of nearly a decade with Evan Imber-Black and Janine Roberts, will offer guidelines much more specific than Palazzoli's (1974) suggestion that it takes "flashes of genius" (p. 239) and will expand upon van der Hart's pioneering recommendations. These guidelines are intended to offer clarity and direction and to demystify the process of designing therapeutic rituals. Three major categories will be described in detail: (1) design elements common to all rituals; (2) ritual techniques and symbolic actions; and (3) other design considerations. An outline of the organization of this chapter appears in Table 1. It may serve as a checklist of things to be considered as you venture into the creative process of designing therapeutic rituals.

DESIGN ELEMENTS

In 1977 the Milan team, in an article published in *Family Process*, concluded that "the intervention of a ritual always requires a great effort on the part of

TABLE 1

Category I Design Elements	Category II Ritual Techniques and Symbolic Actions	Category III Other Design Considerations

A. Symbols
  1. Client language
  2. Therapist directive
  3. Client choice
B. Open and Closed Aspects
C. Time and Space
  1. In-session rituals
  2. Position of therapist
  3. Out-of-session rituals
  4. Alternating in-session
    and out-of-session
    rituals
	A. Letting Go
	B. Utilizing Differences
	  1. Reversals
	C. Giving and Receiving
	  1. Between family members
	  2. To the therapist
	  3. Between the therapist
	    and family
	D. Ritualizing the Game/
	    Prescribing the Symptom
	E. Documenting
	  1. To enhance commitment
	  2. To alter patterns of
	    interactions
	  3. To solidify change
		A. Alternations
		B. Repetition
		  1. Of actions
		  2. Of content
		    a. Via speech
		    b. Via letter
		    c. Via playful actions
		C. Combining Themes and
		    Actions
		D. Use of teams
		  1. Family as team

the therapists. First an effort of observation and then a creative effort" (p. 453). It is from the position of observation and data collection that the themes and issues for a ritual emerge. Although therapists have different theoretical orientations and models, the ideas for the ritual should fit with the emerging issues and problems that are presented by the family, couple, or individual. To assist in the creative design, the following elements are offered.

Symbols

As van der Hart (1983) asserted, symbols and symbolic actions are the building blocks of rituals. As a design element, symbols form the foundation of the design process. It is important to note that symbols are meant to include either the *objects* or *words* which represent the possibility of altering beliefs, relationships, or the meaning of events. Because symbols play such a significant role in the design process, it is critical that they connect and fit with the individual, couple, or family. The selection of the appropriate symbols is typically achieved in one of three ways: (1) explicit client language, (2) therapist choice based upon themes and issues, or (3) client choice.

CLIENT LANGUAGE. Imber-Black (1986) described a case in which the mother spoke of having to treat her daughter with "kid gloves." The daughter, who was living at home, had been recently discharged from a psychiatric hospital after leaving college during her freshman year. Although the mother believed she needed to provide some structure for her daughter and to push her to move on with her life, the idea of treating her daughter with kid gloves prevented such direction. Using mother's language, Imber-Black advised mother and daughter to buy a pair of kid gloves and to freeze them. The next time the mother was aware of treating her daughter with kid gloves, she was to remove them from the freezer, let them thaw, and treat her daughter based upon her instincts. In this case, the choice of kid gloves obviously came from mother's own use of language.

THERAPIST DIRECTIVE. While clients can directly give therapists the appropriate symbols to use, occasionally the therapist provides the symbols. In Chapter 8 I describe a ritual which involved themes related to membership and adoption even though they were not seen as explicit problems by the family. In that case, I wrote a letter which the parents agreed to copy, sign, and post in a room in their home. The symbols were the words and phrases in the letter, which I believed needed to be seen and heard by members of the family to facilitate a shift in beliefs and relationships. Depending upon the outcome of using symbols prescribed by a therapist, the choice of continuing, modifying, or completely changing the symbols becomes a therapeutic decision between clients and therapist.

CLIENT CHOICE. A third possibility for the selection of appropriate symbols can rest solely with the clients. Very recently I saw a graduate student who sought help for his drinking. Although he defined his behavior as less problematic than during his undergraduate days five years ago, he had been in a car accident and arrested for driving while intoxicated during his Christmas vacation. He did not believe he was an alcoholic, nor was abstinence his goal. He wanted to be able to drink moderately and to stop drinking before he became intoxicated. In my mind, conceptualizing his drinking as a ritualized behavior, I began to think to myself about ways of altering this problematic ritual. Since no concrete symbols emerged in his language in this initial interview and I believed he needed to assume responsibility for his behavior, I asked him to bring to the next session all of the symbols he could think of that were associated with the positive/social and negative/destructive aspects of his drinking. Smiling, he said he liked the idea, and I believe he will come to the next session with a variety of items. Giving him the choice of symbols will enable him to select relevant items, while helping both of us better understand the meaning of his drinking behavior.

Regardless of how the symbols are selected, it is through the ongoing process of assessment and treatment that they will emerge in the themes, metaphors, and issues which are presented. Because of the emerging process, the symbols used in the ritual itself will then appropriately fit into the issues, language, culture, religion, values, and world view of the people with whom you are working.

Open and Closed Aspects

Once the appropriate ritual theme and symbols have been determined, the question of open and closed aspects to the design becomes critical. It is critical because these variables will greatly affect the ritual process. Since a ritual should be designed to include room for improvisation and spontaneity (open) as well as specificity (closed), the question remains as to which aspect is to be emphasized in the design. I believe the answer lies primarily with the style of the individual, couple, or family and how they present themselves and the problem, as well as how they approach the therapeutic process. A couple of brief case examples will highlight these points.

I was working with a couple who had been married 22 years. For more than half their marriage, these spouses had been in therapy together and separately with a variety of different therapists. They felt that, although they had had a lot of therapy, not much had really changed and they continued to have problems together. They both reported that they frequently felt disappointed and hopeless, and they were both wondering if they would be better off divorced. By coming to therapy they hoped the situation could improve, but they were not sure if they could get beyond this feeling of "Oh no, here we go again. This relationship isn't worth it!" Their tone was somewhat desperate as they approached therapy requesting me to do something that would help them. I suggested that the next time they had that desperate "here we go again" sense, they stop what they were doing and write down on file cards what had happened that had led up to that feeling. After a few sessions, with three-week intervals between sessions, they both had accumulated a two-inch stack of file cards.

At the next session we discussed the possibilities of letting go of the cards in some fashion. After hearing that they had an urn, at my suggestion they each agreed to burn the cards one by one in the office. In a smoke-filled room, the couple agreed to take the ashes home and put them in the urn and place it upon their mantel. They were told that the next time either one of them began feeling hopeless, they were to take the other by the hand and go stand together for a minute of silence in front of the urn. After a minute, whoever initiated going to the urn had to say what led up to feeling hopeless and to offer three things that he or she would like the other to do to improve their marriage. The other, who was to be silent during this time, would listen, and after hearing the other's request would say "thank you" and leave to consider which one of the three requests he or she would do in *his or her own* way that would fulfill the request. At the next session the spouses reported that they had gone to the urn on two occasions and that they had been able to problem-solve and meet each other's needs in some new ways.

The closed aspects emphasized here are reflected in the specificity of all the directives: writing issues and feelings at specific times, burning the cards, placing them in the urn, putting it on the mantel, and, when feeling hopeless, the ritual of holding hands in silence in front of the urn for a minute, listening to the three requests, saying thank you and leaving to problem-solve. This closed, prescribed process included, however, the opportunity for spontaneity, as each, in his or her own way, would attempt to honor a request to improve the marriage.

In contrast, spouses who had been married seven years, both of whom were introspective, creative artists, complained about how they cycled through a pattern of feeling close to one another, which led to a deep sense of distance, which led to a "huge blowup," which resulted in making up, leaving them feeling close again. They described it as a "game" they played with each other and said that it could take anywhere from a month to six months for it to go full cycle. In the third session, after I gave them a very rough sketch, I asked them if they could further design a circular board game that highlighted all the moves that were involved in this pattern. They returned to the following session with an elaborately designed board game, dice, and the rules of how to play. Additionally, they had created stacks of "relationship cards," each containing aspects they valued in the relationship and "forgiveness cards," as they believed they needed to forgive each other for a number of issues. They described how, if they landed on a space on the board marked "relationship" or "forgiveness," they would pick up the appropriate card and discuss the identified theme. The spouses indicated that they had already played the board game on several occasions and that they intended to further refine the rules of play. The closed parts of the ritual design included their word "game" and the idea that it was cyclical. Providing them with a rough sketch of a circular board game was a closed prescription. Asking the couple to further design the board game and better identify what was involved in playing it highlighted and emphasized the open aspects.

In both of these examples, elements of closed and open aspects were included in the design of the ritual intervention. In the first example, the emphasis was placed on closed aspects because it fit more with the spouses' style and how they approached the therapeutic process. They wanted to do something more specific than just talk about their difficulties, as had been the case in their previous therapies. Additionally, the specificity also attempted to introduce more clarity and modify a sequence and pattern that had become unwieldy and problematic. If I had designed a ritual with an emphasis on openness and improvisation with this couple, I believe it would have had little therapeutic value, as it would not have afforded a unifying anchoring point, which the closed aspects provided. In contrast, the artist couple presented themselves as creative, innovative people who were not expecting directives in the therapy process. When I emphasized spontaneity, the couple created a ritual far beyond my imagination.

These examples highlight the idea that all rituals should be designed to include aspects of openness and closedness. Which aspect is emphasized becomes a clinical judgment related to such things as how people approach therapy, their personal styles, and feedback from other interventions. Achieving the appropriate balance of openness and closedness is part of the ongoing treatment process. If people report that doing the ritual feels constraining, discussing ways to increase openness is indicated. If doing the ritual feels too unwieldy, it may need to be revised to include more closed aspects. As with any intervention, there is a trial and error component to the design of therapeutic rituals.

Time and Space

Time simply refers to when the ritual is to be done — in the morning, every other day, on the weekend, 30 minutes in the evening. At home, in the woods, in the living room are phrases marking the space where it is to be done. How the elements of time and space are emphasized is often related to the previous elements of open and closed aspects. For example, in a ritual where the closed aspects are emphasized, the time and space ingredients are generally prescribed in specific ways. The specificity may be presented to the participants in such a way that everyone knows exactly when and where the ritual is to occur and who is to do what and in what sequences during the ritual time. In contrast, the participants of a ritual where openness has been emphasized may not know the exact time when or place where the ritual may occur. As an example, it might be suggested to family members that they decide to do the ritual at a time and place of their convenience before the next session. Thus, how time and space are emphasized is related to how the ingredients of open and closed are being balanced. Beyond these specifics, a few general comments related to the concepts of time and space are relevant.

Probably one of the most important concepts related to time has to do with marking the experience as distinct and different from the usual activities of daily living. This time boundary serves to highlight the experience as ritual time and in some instances makes the ritual more manageable. Healing rituals can produce intense emotional reactions in the participants, thus having a time boundary around the experience often offers a degree of safety for emotional expression. Just knowing that the ritual may last only 30 minutes can provide an important boundary of safety and comfort. Beyond comfort and safety, time parameters often facilitate participation. "Ritual time" becomes a specific time when participants experiment with new behaviors and try new solutions. In effect, it provides some participants with a sense of freedom and permission to act or think differently.

Finally, in relationship to time, the ritual experience is seen as a temporary intervention. Participants should not be given the impression that this will be something they will need to do for the rest of their lives. In most instances, the ritual provides the participants and the therapist with new information which influences modification of the original design as changes, interactions, and experiences occur around the presenting problem.

A key element in ritual design and enactment may be the place where the ritual occurs. In normative life cycle rituals, the place is often prescribed in the culture. For instance, religious weddings in Western culture usually occur in a house of worship. Changing the traditional place for a wedding, for instance, holding it in a woods, is an important way to "speak" about shifting norms and beliefs. Families may develop specific traditions involving the "appropriate" places for Thanksgiving or Christmas, such that changes in the place are noticeable and may provoke much discussion, as for instance when young adults begin to hold celebrations at their own home rather than at parents' homes.

In therapeutic rituals, the choice of place should be given careful thought by the therapist, and may be an area for discussion between therapist and family. Two broad choices are *in-session* rituals and *out-of-session* rituals. Further refinements of these choices may be made depending on the particular ritual.

IN-SESSION RITUALS. Several authors have described rituals held *in* the therapy session (Imber-Black, 1986; Imber Coppersmith, 1985; Kobak and Waters, 1984; Papp, 1984; Seltzer & Seltzer, 1983). All describe utilizing the therapy session in an unusual and unexpected way to engage families, to break up rigid frames, and to introduce change. The decision to create an in-session ritual generally emerges from the therapist's assessment that (1) actually performing the ritual is important, and that this is more likely to happen in the session than at home; (2) having a witness to the ritual is important in order to add elements of confirmation and verisimilitude; (3) therapy per se has become "rigidly ritualized" so that an in-session ritual may be capable of introducing new patterns in the therapist-family system; and/or (4) strong affect attendant to the ritual requires a "safe" place.

In-session rituals may be a complete surprise to the family. For instance, one couple often referred to a secret past that was interfering with their present relationship, but refused to discuss this in therapy. In a session, the usual conversation was stopped and they were unexpectedly asked to write the past issue on paper. Following the writing of the secret, the couple was invited to bury the secret on a frozen hill behind the clinic (Imber Copper-smith, 1985). In this case, the element of surprise helped to break up a rigidly ritualized therapy, in which the couple complained about their past, while refusing to discuss it, in session after session. As the couple first laughed and then solemnly buried the secret with the therapist serving as witness to the ceremony, the former struggling relationship between therapist and couple and between husband and wife was recontextualized as one now marked by sharing a most unusual event!

When using the element of surprise in an in-session ritual, the therapist must closely gauge the responses of clients in order to avoid forcing people into actions they would rather not do. The surprise elements of in-session rituals must always be contained in a context of respect. At the same time, the therapist must be comfortable with taking some risks, trying the unfamiliar, and utilizing humor and the unexpected.

Some in-session rituals may include instructions for preparation in between sessions. Such preparation may include directions that will shift alliances and interdict escalating patterns, while uniting the family in a common enterprise and heightening curiosity in ways that provoke the family's own problem-solving capacity and creativity. Here, as in preparing for a normative ritual, preparing for the in-session therapeutic ritual becomes "special time," contributing to a larger context of change. For example, preparation for the in-session ritual, "the giving of gifts," described in Chapter 2 generally operates to introduce symmetry, as each member is involved in the act of gift selection, and to interdict anger that is often connected to precipitous or unanticipated leavings.

The therapist's directions for preparation for an in-session ritual can also highlight changes in the family. For instance, in the Wharton family, described in Chapter 2, in which the daughter, Sandra, preferred french fries, bread and milk, instructions for the first in-session meal ritual were precise and were intended to comment openly on existing alliances and begin to introduce greater symmetry into a system marked by escalating complementarity. These instructions were planned by the therapist and team. By contrast, instructions for the second meal ritual, held at the end of therapy, which simply invited each member to bring favorite food to share, announced both the disappearance of Sandra's "eating disorder" and the more symmetrical relationships now available in the family.

Since in-session rituals tend to be unusual and dramatic, they can easily become part of a family's shared mythology, lending a "staying power" to therapy that may be less available in regular sessions. Symbols and meta-phorical action are brought into the therapy session. As families and thera-pists participate in in-session rituals, such as meals, weddings, burials, gift exchanges *in the therapy room*, the question "Are we pretending or are we not pretending?" implicitly and powerfully frames the activities. In-session rituals generate a kind of "creative confusion," as the therapist's position shifts from session conductor to witness and/or participant, team members may enter the room, and otherwise ordinary daily events, like a family meal, become extraordinary.

POSITION OF THE THERAPIST. In-session rituals call upon flexibility, a keen sense of timing, an attitude of acceptance, and an ability to shift positions by the therapist. Such rituals may reverse the usual therapeutic hierarchy, placing the therapist in the position of following and taking directions from the family, as in in-session rituals in which family members become part of the consultation team advising the therapist. Or these rituals may eliminate hierarchy altogether, as when therapist and family become coparticipants in a ritual, for instance, a gift exchange ritual marking the end of a particular therapy. The therapist may serve as a witness, as when couples exchange new wedding vows in the context of a therapy session, or may sign documents that have emerged from the therapeutic endeavor (see Roberts, Chapter 12, and Kohen, Chapter 14 for full-length cases involving the therapist as wit-ness and document signer in in-session rituals). Finally, just as in-session rituals are often powerful for families, so they are frequently deeply moving for therapists who may be honored by access to a family's otherwise hidden places.

OUT-OF-SESSION RITUALS. Out-of-session rituals are utilized more frequently than in-session rituals. The choice to prescribe or co-create an out-of-session ritual in therapy is made when (1) location of the ritual in a place outside of therapy is deemed important, such as when a ritual is to be held in the backyard, in a place of worship, or in a special space at home; (2) the effects of repeating the ritual over several days or weeks is considered to be an important aspect; and (3) connection to people who do not come to therapy is important, as in out-of-session rituals that involve extended family.

The specific place of an out-of-session ritual may be suggested by the therapist, may be negotiated by therapist and family, or may be left entirely up to the family, such as when the therapist simply says "pick an appropriate place" and finds out in a subsequent session where the family chose to do the ritual.

ALTERNATING IN-SESSION AND OUT-OF-SESSION RITUALS. In a given therapy, one may use both in-session and out-of-session rituals in a meaningful sequence.

For instance, an end-of-session ritual to work on some aspect of healing may be followed by an agreed upon in-session ritual furthering the healing process through a witnessed burial or burning. Conversely, an in-session ritual, such as the final meal session held with the Wharton family (Chapter 2), may be followed by an end-of-session ritual, such as asking the Whartons to freeze the potato and the kiwi fruit, with particular instructions for their subsequent use at home.

RITUAL TECHNIQUES AND SYMBOLIC ACTIONS

It is the symbolic actions in combination with the previous ingredients of symbols, open/closed, and time/space which bring the ritual intervention to life. Every ritual must have some symbolic action included with the design. The choice of the appropriate symbolic action depends upon the ritual theme or themes being utilized and the kinds of actions available to those in treatment. Through their language, metaphors, and issues, people will typically provide the symbolic actions to be incorporated into the design of the ritual. For example, people have made comments like: "We would give anything to be able to put this to rest," "The issues in the past freeze us from going anywhere," "We need to shelve some things." Such comments suggest some of the actions that might be used as part of a ritual technique. The following categories of letting go, utilizing differences, giving and receiving, ritualizing the game, and documenting represent types of ritual techniques/symbolic actions frequently incorporated in the design process.

Letting Go

The symbolic actions described within the letting go category are commonly, yet not exclusively, utilized in healing and identity rituals. The letting go actions facilitate a cleansing and healing process. Over the years we have asked people to burn, freeze, bury, flush, or send up in balloons a variety of symbolic items, such as photographs, rings, letters, written memories, psychiatric records, and clothes. Such ritual actions have assisted people in moving beyond traumatic events and meanings that have interfered with their living in the present.

Often in healing rituals, especially if there has been a lengthy period of suffering and agonizing, these actions may be used as part of several rituals. Years ago, in working with a couple where the husband had had an affair, they were asked to experiment with this painful issue from their past. On different occasions they were to bury, burn, freeze, and flush a variety of symbols that represented this painful past. Symbols included photographs of this couple during the time of the affair, a Christmas card, and angry feelings the wife had written on file cards. After each ritual action, they were to discuss how it felt to do that activity and to rank the effectiveness of each action. This couple decided that flushing was the most appropriate and effective ritualized action. Having some symbols submerged in their septic system provided the couple, especially the wife, with a new sense of pleasure and relief.

In some instances the letting go ritualized activity needs to be combined with some form of holding on action. A college student recorded several traumatic childhood life experiences on separate pieces of paper. She placed them all in a helium-filled balloon and attached the balloon to a string. On prescribed occasions, she experimented with letting the balloon go and pulling it back in again. As she grew more comfortable with the idea of letting go of her past, she found that she was able to let out more and more string. Eventually, she was able to let the balloon fly away. This ritualized action combined the need to let go and the need to hold on in a manner that respected her pace and decision-making.

Both of these examples also highlight how rituals are part of the therapeutic process. Rituals are typically done over a period of time and modified with therapeutic setbacks and gains. They are not seen as quick and simple solutions to therapeutic problems.

Utilizing Differences

Ritual actions which utilize differences are typically belief negotiation rituals as they address conflicting beliefs and symmetrically escalating conflicts. The authors have used the Milan team's odd days/even days prescription (Palazzoli, Cecchin, Prata, & Boscolo, 1978a, 1978b) as a foundation for many ritualized actions dealing with dichotomous beliefs and themes. It has been our experience that, when people present differences regarding solutions, gender and sex roles, cultures, or world views, the ritualized action of odd days/even days is very appropriate. People often report that through this ritual technique that they have gained an appreciation for the "other" point of view and modified their own behavior.

When designing a ritual that uses the odd days/even days technique, you have the flexibility to emphasize either the closed or open aspects or to offer them in combination. The original Milan prescription emphasized closed aspects, as certain behaviors or points of view were to be carried out by one parent on Monday, Wednesday, and Friday while the other parent attempted his or her solution on Tuesday, Thursday, and Saturday. Open aspects were made available with the "be spontaneous" prescription on Sunday and with each parent's choice of behavior. Open aspects would be emphasized if you asked a wife, without announcing to the husband, to think and act like the husband on any three days during the week, and asked the husband to do likewise on three other days. Such a ritual would be open, as the people would decide when they were to behave like the other. The closed aspects would include the number of days being specified.

The odd days/even days ritual technique can be used effectively any time differences are being negotiated in therapy. Couples who are struggling with separating or remaining married can be asked to act "as if" they were married on specific days and act "as if" they were separated on the remaining days of the week. Parents have been asked to relate to their children on different days according to such dichotomous points of view as: being biologically depressed vs. situationally depressed; genetically flawed vs. needing guidance; needing psychological help vs. needing no help; planning for the child's death (substance abuser) vs. planning for the child's future. Without question, this ritual technique has many clinical applications.

REVERSALS. Reversals are also helpful in situations where differences are being negotiated. The reversal is discussed here, because it is generally used within the framework of an odd days/even days ritual. Reversals are used when you are attempting to expand role repertoire and behavioral options. Differences presented in therapy can reflect either a skewed complementarity or symmetrical escalation. The balance of a skewed complementarity may involve an overfunctioning/underfunctioning spousal relationship. Other examples may include relationships where one person primarily leads and the other follows, or one usually teaches and the other learns. In relationships marked by a symmetrical escalation, each participant feels that his or her ideas are "the best," producing a competitive escalating struggle. Regardless of how the differences are being manifested, asking people to think and act like the other during specific times can facilitate similarities in the face of differences.

A few years ago Janine Roberts and I were working with a couple whose relationship was based on stereotypical sex roles. This configuration had served them well in the past but had recently become problematic as they were struggling over the best way to parent their young daughter. In an attempt to modify their escalating struggle, we asked them to experiment with the following reversal embedded in an odd days/even days ritual action: On Mondays, Wednesdays, and Fridays the wife was to announce "Today we think like a woman," and she was to teach her husband what it meant to think as a woman; on Tuesdays, Thursdays, and Saturdays he was to announce "Today we think like a man," and he was to teach his wife what it meant to think as a man; additionally, before the next session in a month, he was to take his wife out for a "man's night out" and she was asked to take him out for a "woman's night out." The spouses returned to the next session highlighting their similarities as people and as parents and reporting fewer struggles over their differences, which they were better able to appreciate.

Giving and Receiving

As actions, giving and receiving are common to a variety of normative rituals. Many family celebrations and family traditions are marked by the exchanging of gifts, food, and cards. In day-to-day life, kissing a child or spouse good night can be a way of giving and receiving love and affection. In therapeutic rituals, the exchanging of gifts can be used in a variety of ways: (1) family members exchanging with one another, (2) the family members giving symbolic items to the therapist, (3) gifts being exchanged between therapist and family members.

BETWEEN FAMILY MEMBERS. Janine Roberts supervised a case, where Linda Lewandowski was the therapist, in which the family members reported they were in a crisis. Alice, 15, had been living with her mother, stepfather, and their two younger children, ages seven and five, since the parents' divorce 10 years ago. Very recently Alice had decided, with her father, to move from Massachusetts to live with him in Oregon. This decision, which her mother and stepfather supported, was based almost entirely upon the fact that they had been in conflict with one another for many years. Their relationship was marked by frequent arguments and tension. Alice's stepfather and mother felt there was a crisis because Alice was leaving so angry that they feared they might never see her again. Although Alice already had a one-way flight ticket to Oregon and was scheduled to leave in 10 days, her mother and stepfather came to the initial session with Alice. At the end of the session, the therapist suggested a "transition ritual" and asked Mrs. Malley, her husband, and Alice to bring special things to the next session to help them say goodbye. During the session Mr. Malley acknowledged that, although

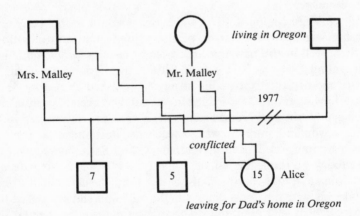

FIGURE 1   A Leaving Home Ritual

there had been much conflict between him and Alice, there had been some harmony as well. The therapist suggested that he bring a symbol of that harmony which Alice could take with her to Oregon. Mrs. Malley was asked to bring a symbol of her love that Alice could also take with her. The younger boys, who were invited to the next session, were to bring something special for Alice's new home. During the session Alice said she hoped that someday she would be able to apologize to her mother and stepfather for some of her behavior. She was asked to bring two things: (1) a creative symbol of what her apology might be someday if she could make it; and (2) something she would like to leave behind that would be left out in the open in the house to remind the family of her.

The following week, Mr. and Mrs. Malley, the boys, and Alice came with wrapped items to share. The therapist/team brought juice and fresh strawberries and the members of the family gave and received their gifts. Mr. Malley presented Alice with one of his favorite shirts, which she had previously borrowed, without his permission, on many occasions. Alice's mother read and then presented Alice with a letter in which she talked about forgiveness, acceptance, freedom and joy. She also gave her *The Prophet* by Khalil Gibran (one of the themes in this book is the letting go and acceptance by parents of their growing children). The boys each presented Alice with a favorite stuffed animal. Alice presented the family with her radio, which was an important symbol for Alice, as the family lived in a commune and had no radio or television. Additionally, she presented the family with a drawing which said, in bright bold colors, "I love you." This drawing represented her apology. At the end the therapist actively participated in the ritual by giving each member of the family a purple tulip, saying that, although they were the same, each was unique and different.

Without question, this in-session ritual, which emphasized giving and receiving, provided the family with the opportunity to mark Alice's leaving home feeling connected and concerned as opposed to cut off and angry. The ritualized action of giving and receiving served to access feelings of tenderness and vulnerability and made available the beginnings of a healing process which had been previously unavailable.

Similar to the "giving of gifts" case reported by Imber-Black (1988a, b), in which family members exchanged gifts to mark Karen's departure into a group home for retarded adults, a new, positive meaning was created for Alice and her family. As Alice's mother said at the end of the session, "This ritual cleared a lot of stuff for me."

GIVING SYMBOLIC ITEMS TO THE THERAPIST. Timing and pacing are important considerations in the therapeutic process, particularly in designing healing rituals. I have found that one way to respect the pace at which people are able to let go of the memories of painful events in their lives is for me to be the keeper or holder of the symbols of these events. A few years ago a woman student sought help as she was struggling with many painful memories from her past that were interfering with her ability to have meaningful relationships with men. An abused foster child, who had lived in several homes, she began to share her pain and anguish for the first time in her life. As time went on she was able to write down negative and angry feelings about herself and other people, as well as many traumatic events. I kept the cards in my office and over a period of months we were able to put them in two envelopes, one marked "let go of" and the other "hold on to." As an accomplished and skilled hiker and backpacker who had led several wilderness trips in the White Mountains, she described to me one day how whenever she led a trip with young people she would have a ceremonial campfire on the last night. On these occasions she would ask each person to describe everything he or she saw, smelled, heard, touched, and tasted during the trip that was negative as well as positive. After each person talked about his experiences, she gave him a piece of charcoal from the fire.

As you might imagine, we spent three hours one summer night in the woods, by a fire, talking and occasionally crying about each one of the cards in the "let go of" envelope before we burned them. The next day she, alone, returned to the site to take some pieces of charcoal and to cover over the remaining ashes with dirt. I have my pieces of charcoal at home and a few cards in the "hold on to" envelope in my office.

BETWEEN THERAPIST AND FAMILY. Mutual exchanging of gifts and symbols can be a way to mark family problem-solving strengths and to terminate therapy (Imber-Black, 1986). Janine Roberts and I focused on marital and parenting issues with a couple and their two young children for approximately 10 months. For the last session we asked them to bring symbols which represented the treatment process. They appeared at the session with a laundry basket full of clean folded clothes (who did household chores had been an issue); copies of *The Velveteen Rabbit* and *Dr. Gardner's Stories about the Real World*; and an imperfect, unfinished, yet special, box that had all handmade joints. One of the central issues in therapy had been the parents' expectation that they and their children should strive and achieve perfection. We presented each of the parents with a T-shirt, one which said, "Celebrate imperfectly special mothers," and the other, "Celebrate imperfectly special fathers."

The session was spent talking about the meaning of these different symbols and the ways they could be used at home to solidify the numerous changes the family had made. Just as we were ready to end, Mrs. Burke said, "We have one more thing for you out in the car." She left and returned with a gallon of double chocolate fudge ice cream, bowls, and spoons. This clearly marked the end of therapy as we finished talking with each other socially.

Ritualizing the Game/Prescribing the Symptom

This ritualized action attempts to alter a symptomatic or rigid pattern of behavior by prescribing the patterned behavior in an explicit fashion. Asking people to do the patterned behavior within a prescribed ritual introduces an element of confusion, absurdity and humor, which alters the pattern and its meaning. With the pattern and meaning altered, new options for problem-solving emerge. This ritualistic action has been well-documented and has been shown to be an effective intervention with individuals, couples, and families (Andolfi, 1979; Madanes, 1981, 1984; Palazzoli et al., 1978a, 1978b; Watzlawick, Weakland, & Fisch, 1974; Weeks & L'Abate, 1982).

A few years ago, Janine Roberts and I worked with a family in which the 12-year-old son was identified as the presenting problem (see Figure 2). He had recently been caught stealing tapes at a record store. The parents also reported he had been doing poorly academically in school and had recently been suspended for a day for being in a fight. This behavior was alarming to the parents, as their daughters were defined as excellent students who were active in sports and school organizations. The parents, loving and compassionate people, had a parenting style which was relaxed yet supportive. After a few sessions, the parents felt comfortable that the son's stealing was no

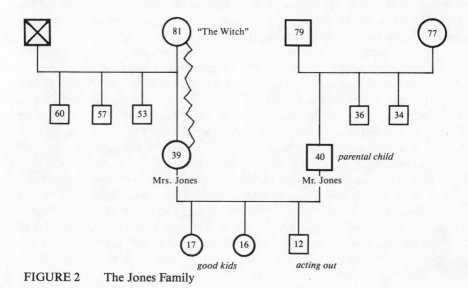

FIGURE 2   The Jones Family

longer a problem, yet his effort regarding his schoolwork was inadequate. In a discussion about consequences regarding their son's behavior in relationship to school, the parents became increasingly anxious. They indicated that they rarely disciplined their daughters, as they typically cooperated with their parents' requests. They recently had attempted to be stricter, set limits, and create consequences for their son's behavior, but they both felt they were unable to follow through. They had attempted to restrict his privileges around time away from the home and the amount of time spent watching television or using the telephone.

When we asked the parents how they understood this difficulty of wanting to set limits yet feeling uncomfortable doing so, two important pieces of information from the parents' background emerged. Mrs. Jones was the youngest of four siblings and had a very conflicted relationship with her own mother. She believed her relationship with her mother had been poor, was currently poor, and would continue the same way into the future. She "hated" her mother, and Mrs. Jones' children described their grandmother as a "witch." Mrs. Jones acknowledged that she worked very hard to have a loving relationship with her own children so they would not feel towards her as she did towards her own mother. This belief clearly influenced her parenting style. Mr. Jones, the oldest of four children, functioned as a parental child within his family of origin. He had worked hard to help his brothers, his mother, and his father, who was an alcoholic and a family physician. Mr. Jones recalled how he regularly drove his father to people's homes in rural Maine for emergency calls since his father had lost his license for driving while intoxicated. Mr. Jones believed that in his youth no one had pushed him to strive for excellence and that now, as an adult, though content with this life, he rarely pushed himself to achieve.

With this important information we designed a ritual incorporating these beliefs, which seemed to prevent the parents from sustaining a limit-setting approach with their son. After the next appointment was set for two weeks, the parents were asked to do the following: The first week, they were not to do anything different in relationship to their parenting styles, only to be aware of how mother's ideas about the importance of having a good relationship with her children and father's idea of not being pushed himself influenced their behavior; the second week mother was to say daily, "I realize I am running the risk of your having a relationship with me like I have with my own mother; however, until you complete your English and social studies homework, you cannot go out, use the telephone, or watch television." Father was told to say, "I realize that I am running the risk of pushing you in ways that I wish I had pushed myself; however, until you complete your math and science homework you can not go out, use the telephone, or watch television."

At the next session the parents indicated that things were going much better in school, as their son had done his homework and scored well on several tests. The parents had given him assistance in their areas of academic competence only after the son had said, "I'm not doing anything until you read your speech." On a daily basis, the parents read their "speeches" and their son did his homework.

This ritualized action incorporated the existing parental beliefs and made them explicit. In voicing their beliefs in this fashion, the parents began to experience their fears more explicitly and hence less powerfully, which enabled them to exercise their parental authority in a more consistent and sustained fashion.

Documenting

There are countless examples in everyday life of how the documenting process marks events as official and often as legal. Making a will, receiving a diploma from preschool or graduate school, and getting a marriage license or a fishing license require the signing of official documents for record keeping, legal, and ceremonial purposes. Recently, my godson, who is preparing to be confirmed in the Catholic Church, called and informed me that I needed a sponsor certificate from our parish priest. After nervously quizzing my wife on the differences between venial and mortal sins, I met with our priest. Although he did not test me, he handed me an envelope which contained a document which bore the stamped seal of the parish as well as his signature. This official document meant that I was a good, practicing Catholic and was worthy of actively participating in my godson's confirmation ceremony. Without this document, I could not be his sponsor.

Because of the powerful and serious nature of the meaning which documents carry, documenting can be a ritual action used in the design of therapeutic rituals. Although there are other creative ways to use documenting, three are offered here as examples.

DOCUMENTING TO ENHANCE COMMITMENT. Because most people regard signed documents as official and serious, there are situations when it is helpful to have people sign agreements regarding their behavior. A few years ago Janine Roberts and I were working with a couple who sought help because of their fighting and uncertainty about remaining married. Their relationship was marked by violent, intense outbursts, which included slapping each other, yelling, cursing, and destroying property within their home by throwing objects and punching doors and walls. Although each person had his/her own explanations for how the fights began, we attempted to set some limits on this behavior by means of a contract. Most of the initial session was spent having the partners agree on what they would be willing to do to prevent an angry outburst as well as something that would communicate a sense of appreciation for the other. Once the list was drawn up, copies were made for each person and signed by the couple, myself, and Janine, who came from behind the one-way mirror. The partners were asked to keep the contract in their possession at all times, and in the event of a breach, they were to call me immediately regardless of the time of day. This documenting of ownership for their own behavior served this couple well, as there were no violent outbursts and significantly fewer hostile interactions, even though they chose to separate during the course of treatment.

DOCUMENTING TO ALTER PATTERNS OF INTERACTIONS. Documenting also functions for the purpose of record keeping. Through the years I have asked people to audiotape at home sequences of interaction that they define as problematic. Frequently this has been asked of parents reporting arguments or fights with or between their children. If the family does not own a tape recorder, I will provide blank tapes and a recorder for their use. Family members are told to leave the tape recorder readily accessible. When they find themselves beginning to enter into the problematic interaction, anyone in the family can announce, "This will be a good one for Dr. Whiting to hear," and turn on the tape. This announcement marks the subsequent interaction as "special." Typically the interaction that follows is quite different from the usual, as the sequence of interaction has become interrupted by the audiotape documentation.

As video cassette recorders have become popular, more people own their own video cameras. Many people are replacing the traditional wedding album with hours of videotape. When available, home video recording equipment can be used to document similarly as audiotape. Having people film unsatisfactory as well as satisfactory interactions has proven to be a useful ritualized action.

DOCUMENTING TO SOLIDIFY CHANGE. Occasionally therapists are requested to submit reports to the courts, social service workers, or school personnel regarding the progress of clients and families. On such occasions I have asked family members to assist me in co-creating the document to be sent to the outside system. Such a process serves to announce, in an official fashion, to the family and others the various ways that behavior and relationships have changed during the treatment. Additionally, it marks the therapy experience as co-evolutionary, since no secret, confidential reports are being exchanged among the "professionals."

Documenting can also help solidify changes at various transitional points in the therapy. Shifting the focus of treatment from child to marital issues may be marked by presenting the child and family with a document acknowledging all the changes that have taken place during the child-focused treatment. Such documentation serves to highlight the ending of one phase of treatment and the beginning of another. Marking the termination of therapy with a document is included in Roberts' case in Chapter 12.

OTHER DESIGN CONSIDERATIONS

The previous sections have focused on the elements which are necessary to the design of therapeutic rituals as well as some of the more common and frequently used symbolic actions or techniques. In this section I will discuss additional concepts and ideas which are not always needed yet are worthy of consideration.

Alternations

Rituals which combine both letting go and holding on actions or suggestions to behave certain ways on specific days and differently on remaining days or identity rituals which include a celebration have the concept of alternation common to their design. As systems have the tendency to remain the same while simultaneously changing, the design of some rituals will incorporate this dichotomy by providing room for alternative thoughts and/or actions. Alternations not only serve the purpose of respecting this dichotomy of sameness and differentness but also help communicate that change is a process that occurs over time.

For example, a graduate student had been experiencing difficulties eating, sleeping, and concentrating on her schoolwork. She reported that her first "significant" relationship with a man had ended, as he had broken up with her a month earlier. After a few sessions, she agreed to bring in a large picture of him. During the session I asked her if she would be willing to let go of it. In response, she tore it into hundreds of tiny pieces. She agreed to carry the pieces with her at all times, representing her desire to hold on to the relationship. She also agreed to ask herself twice a day, "How much am I ready to let go of today?" Depending upon her answer she would reach into her bag and take out a few or several pieces of the photograph and throw them away. After a period of three months she was left with a few remaining pieces, which one day she decided to let go of in a nearby mountain range where she had spent a lot of time as a child. By including the alternations of holding on and letting go in this healing ritual, we respected the timing and pacing of her healing process. Although alternations are not common to all rituals, they can be an important ingredient in the design of some rituals.

Repetition

Repetition is generally associated with religious and cultural rituals rather than therapeutic rituals. Most religious services have prescribed repetitive actions which the clergy and members of the congregation participate in individually and collectively. These actions are repeated behaviorally and verbally. In the Catholic Church, parishioners kneel, sit, or stand during different phases of the mass. There are also various verbal responses that are either spoken or sung. These actions are almost universally adhered to and some Catholics repeat this same mass ceremony daily. There is an expectation of repeated performance of the ritual in prescribed ways throughout one's life. This is an important distinction between religious and therapeutic rituals as there is neither the expectation of repeated performance nor, as Tomm (1984) indicated " . . . any insistence that the ritual actually be carried out, only the claim that to do so may be very useful" (p. 266). Yet with this significant difference regarding expectation and frequency of performance, there is a place for repetition in some therapeutic rituals.

REPETITION OF ACTIONS. An odd days/even days ritualized action has a repetitive component in its design, as certain behaviors are suggested to be carried out by the participants on certain days over a period of time. Regardless of whether the ritual was designed with an emphasis on open or closed aspects, the foundation of an odd days/even days ritual has a repetitive quality whose purpose is to add clarity and facilitate new problem-solving behaviors.

REPETITION OF CONTENT. There are situations where the content or statements regarding beliefs as opposed to behavior become identified as the problem. In these cases, repetition via (1) speech, (2) letter, or (3) playful actions has been used to work creatively with the clients' language or beliefs.

REPETITION VIA SPEECH. In the case described earlier in the section entitled Ritualizing the Game/Prescribing the Symptom, it was suggested that the parents repeat a very specific message on a daily basis to their son. This content came directly from their beliefs, which were affecting their ability to parent effectively. As you may recall, the mother daily said to her son, "I realize I am running the risk of your having a relationship with me like I have with my own mother; however, until you complete your English and social studies homework, you cannot go out, use the telephone, or watch television." Father also repeated a specific message regarding his feelings about "pushing" his son. The feedback of this process was interesting: After one day of the parents' reciting their messages, their son, in a playful manner, began to simultaneously verbalize the message with his parents. By the end of treatment, the parents reported a variety of changes and the mother indicated that sometimes she would look at her son and he would say, "Ya, I know. I realize I'm running the risk," and they would laugh.

REPETITION VIA LETTER. In Chapter 8, Whiting describes in detail a case in which the parents posted a signed letter in the bathroom of their home as part of therapeutic ritual. The message in the letter was powerful, as it contained ideas and beliefs that were different from what the parents usually presented. Because it would have been difficult for the parents to verbally communicate the contents of the letter, it was decided to post it as a way to repeat the message to the children as well as to the parents. It was suggested that several copies of the letter be made so the message could be repeated in the event the letter was removed and destroyed. After the letter was removed and the parents posted new copies on two occasions, one of the sons wrote, "I have already read this" and decided to write his parents a letter.

REPETITION VIA PLAYFUL ACTIONS. A few years ago I saw an unmarried couple who had been dating for approximately a year and a half. The individuals, who were single and in their mid thirties, had met in a local restaurant/disco. During the first nine months of dating, Gary talked a great deal about Sandy, the woman he had dated previously. Jean became increasingly upset at any mention of Sandy and the experiences Gary and Sandy had had together. They sought therapy as they had been arguing and experiencing a great deal of conflict. No matter how much Gary insisted he preferred being with Jean, not Sandy, Jean refused to be convinced. After a few sessions, I asked the couple if they would be willing to purchase customized T-shirts. They were to go to the store together and Gary was to buy a shirt which said, "You are the best thing that ever happened to me." Jean's was to say "I believe you." Anytime they began arguing about the importance of their relationship or about the meaning of Sandy, they were to put on their shirts and continue.

Like Ken and Mavis in the case reported by Imber-Black in Chapter 2, where the couple purchased the "viper" and "lips" T-shirts, Gary and Jean were able to wear their shirts with a new sense of humor and playfulness. Though Gary and Jean eventually stopped dating, wearing the shirts provided them with opportunities to modify their escalating interactions in relationship to each other and with Sandy. In these examples, T-shirts were used to repeat messages and beliefs in a playful manner. Writing statements or beliefs on "customized" underwear, balloons, or "business cards" has been used to interject humor and play into relationships that have been marked by seriousness and anger.

All of the preceding cases highlighted different ways of using repetition in therapeutic rituals as a way of working with people's behaviors, state-ments, or beliefs. Although repetition is not a necessary element in the design of therapeutic rituals, there are situations where it is a helpful ritualized action.

Combining Themes and Actions

Frequently rituals may draw upon symbolic actions and concepts from two or more ritual themes. Such combination rituals generally occur at the later stages of therapy when separate rituals have been used during the treatment process. Imagine a couple who has been struggling for years with a painful event which occurred in the past. An effective combination ritual may in-clude ritual actions of letting go in combination with giving and receiving actions common to celebration rituals. Such a combination ritual would mark the healing of an event and an old interactional process, as well as the beginning of a new interaction and a renewed commitment to the relation-ship.

The extent to which ritual themes and actions are combined into an elaborate ritual depends upon the diversity of the issues and the designing skills of the therapist. The signing of a "health" document by every member of the family after giving and receiving gifts at a party celebrating the burial of all the labels and beliefs about the "unhealthy" member might be an appropriate ritual. Such a ritual would address concepts from all five of the theme categories and utilize several different types of symbolic actions. With an understanding of therapeutic issues, the ritual theme categories, the design ingredients, and the symbolic actions, designing rituals combining different themes and actions becomes possible.

Use of Teams

Although working in teams is certainly not required to design therapeutic rituals, it does provide the opportunity to gain ideas and concepts beyond one's own experience. The sharing of rituals which have been a part of team members' experiences is a rich source of data to be incorporated in the design process. A "team" source which probably has been underutilized has been the family members or individuals in treatment.

FAMILY AS TEAM. I believe that as my colleagues and myself have evolved in designing rituals, there has been greater collaboration with families regard-ing their input into the design of any intervention, including rituals. Previ-ously, we were inclined to leave for an intersession break, design a ritual, and then return to the family and prescribe it without any assistance from family members. Currently, we are more likely to discuss, both directly and through circular questions in the presence of the family, their thoughts and ideas about doing a ritual. Whether the ritual should be done at all becomes a collaborative effort between the family or individual and the therapist/team. Frequently this process not only results in collaboratively designing a ritual that "fits" the family better, but also provides immediate feedback for acceptance or rejection of existing systemic hypotheses.

CONCLUSIONS

This chapter was designed to offer principles and guidelines for the construction of "tailor-made" therapeutic rituals that meet the unique needs of each family, couple, or individual. While the emphasis has been placed upon the elements and ritual techniques and symbolic actions needed to create the ritual, it is important to remember that the process of preparing to perform the ritual is therapeutic as well. The graduate student asked to bring in symbols of the positive and negative aspects of his drinking is having to examine his behavior as he is preparing for new, yet to be designed rituals. Although there is uncertainty as to the exact nature of the rituals, it is certain that they will be designed to include all of the common elements, some ritual techniques or symbolic actions, and an ingredient or two from the other design considerations. I am certain of this because I ask myself questions related to the three categories each time I design a ritual.

For example, with the student concerned about his drinking, questions about Category I, design elements, might include:

1. Does the student feel good about his choices of symbols and do they capture the meaning of the positive and negative aspects of his drinking?
2. What would be the best place to perform an initial ritual and does it include both open and closed aspects and how are these emphasized?

Possible questions which reflect Category II, ritual techniques and symbolic actions, might include:

1. Which of the symbols could be let go of most easily and through which ritualized actions?
2. Would it be helpful to have him document all of the symbols on audiotape so that he could listen to this recording at different intervals when he chose to drink?

Category III, other design considerations, could be considered by questions such as:

1. Does the ritual reflect the dichotomy of the positive and negative aspects of his drinking, and should it include alternations?
2. What would happen if after each time he finished a drink he were asked to stand in front of a mirror for a minute, decide whether he wanted another drink, and then put on a T-shirt which had a positive or negative symbol on it. (This has potential!)

Honestly, it is interesting what just happened. I'm dead serious!! Right now, the idea of using T-shirts just came to me as I was asking myself questions related to Category III. Just listing possible questions which reflected concepts from each of the three categories has helped to provide a lot of direction to a previously unknown ritual. Become familiar with the categories listed in Table 1 and use it as a guide to generate questions to be asked of yourself and of your families, couples, and individuals, and you, too, will be designing creative therapeutic rituals.

REFERENCES

Andolfi, M. (1979). *Family therapy: An interactional approach*. New York: Plenum Press.

Imber-Black, E. (1986). Toward a resource model in systemic family therapy. In M. A. Karpel (Ed.). *Family resources: The hidden partner in family therapy*. New York: Guilford Press.

Imber-Black, E. (1988a). Celebrating the uncelebrated. *The Family Therapy Networker, 12*(1), 60–66.

Imber-Black, E. (1988b). Idiosyncratic life cycle transitions and therapeutic rituals. In B. Carter & M. McGoldrick (Eds.). *The changing family lifecycle: A framework for family therapy*. New York: Gardner Press.

Imber Coppersmith, E. (1985). We've got a secret: A non-marital marital therapy. In A. Gurman (Ed.). *Casebook of marital therapy*. New York: Guilford Press.

Kobak, R., & Waters, D. (1984). Family therapy as a rite of passage: Play's the thing. *Family Process, 23*(1), 89–100.

Madanes, C. (1981). *Strategic Family Therapy*. San Francisco: Jossey-Bass.

Madanes, C. (1984). *Behind the one-way mirror: Advances in the practice of strategic therapy*. San Francisco: Jossey-Bass.

Papp, P. (1984). The creative leap: The links between clinical and artistic creativity. *The Family Therapy Networker, 8*(5), 20–29.

Seltzer, W., & Seltzer, M. (1983). Material, myth, and magic: A cultural approach to family therapy. *Family Process, 22*(1), 3–14.

Selvini Palazzoli, M. (1974). *Self-starvation: From the intrapsychic to the transpersonal approach to anorexia nervosa*. London: Chaucer Publishing Co.

Selvini Palazzoli, M., Boscolo, L., Cecchin, G., & Prata, G. (1977). Family rituals: A powerful tool in family therapy. *Family Process, 16*, 445–453.

Selvini Palazzoli, M., Boscolo, L., Cecchin, G., & Prata, G. (1978a). *Paradox and counterparadox*. New York: Jason Aronson.

Selvini Palazzoli, M., Boscolo, L., Cecchin, G., & Prata, G. (1978b). A ritualized prescription in family therapy: Odd days and even days. *Journal of Marriage and Family Counseling, 4*, 3–9.

Tomm, K. (1984). One perspective on the Milan systemic approach: Part II. Description of session format, interviewing style and interventions. *Journal of Marital and Family Therapy, 10*(3), 253–271.

van der Hart, O. (1983). *Rituals in psychotherapy: Transition and continuity*. New York: Irvington Publishers, Inc.

Watzlawick, P., Weakland, J., & Fisch, R. (1974). *Change: Principles of problem formation and problem resolution*. New York: W. W. Norton.

Weeks, G., & L'Abate, L. (1982). *Paradoxical psychotherapy: Theory and practice with individuals, couples, and families*. New York: Brunner/Mazel.

II

RITUALS FOR COUPLES,
CHILDREN,
AND ADOLESCENTS

Normative and Therapeutic Rituals in Couples Therapy

EVAN IMBER-BLACK

MANY OF THE ISSUES which couples bring to therapy can be approached effectively with a perspective that utilizes both normative, naturally occurring rituals and therapeutic rituals.

The developmental life cycle of married couples is filled with opportunities for normative rituals, beginning with the engagement, which announces an intention to marry. The wedding ritual draws a publicly proclaimed boundary around the couple, delineates membership in the couple system, highlights the nature of connections to extended family and friends, and announces a belief in a shared future. Specific religious, ethnic or personal beliefs about the concept of marriage can be expressed in the wedding ritual. Subsequent anniversaries offer a yearly opportunity for a ritual to reflect upon and celebrate the couple's relationship. Since there are few definitive norms for anniversary rituals, other than celebrations for those anniversaries considered to be milestones, such as the 25th and 50th, wedding anniversaries offer an opportunity for the couple to develop their own ritual traditions.

Cohabitating heterosexual and homosexual couples may develop rituals to mark and celebrate their relationships. The creation of relationship-confirming rituals is especially important for committed gay male or lesbian couples, for whom there is no culturally accepted wedding ritual, and who frequently live in a wider context of disconfirmation (Roth, 1985).

All couples create daily and weekly rituals, such as rites of parting and reentry, meals, evenings out, and sexual rituals. Holidays, special outings, and vacations as a twosome may be part of a couple's ritual life.

While life cycle rituals, such as weddings and anniversaries, and many of the daily or seasonal rituals of couples tend to conjure up images of pleasure and delight, in fact, for troubled couples these rituals are often connected to unhappy memories, cutoffs with extended family, unmet expectations, and current stereotyped, unsatisfying interactions. The therapeutic exploration of a couple's ritual life can allow both therapist and couple access to key developmental, existential, and interactional issues. Revitalizing stagnant rituals that have become metaphors for stuck relationships, changing destructive and demoralizing rituals, and participating in unusual therapeutic rituals can facilitate new relationship patterns in couples therapy.

EXPLORING RITUALS IN COUPLES THERAPY

The starting place for utilizing rituals in couples therapy is the interview per se. Here the therapist can easily inquire about the nature of daily, seasonal and life cycle rituals, and can listen to the couple's descriptions of the current situation in a manner that places appropriate information into a ritual framework.

Brief Example—A Weekend Ritual

In the second session of therapy, a chronically unhappy couple, Mr. and Ms. Polk, told the following story in response to my question about how they spent their free time: Married for 23 years, they had spent the weekends of the last 15 years locked in an unsatisfactory pattern. Every Friday evening, Ms. Polk would tell Mr. Polk about tasks that needed to get done over the weekend. Both would agree that after the tasks were done, they would go out together. On Saturday morning, Mr. Polk would find myriad reasons not to do the tasks. Ms. Polk would get angry and the couple would fight. The tasks remained undone and the couple would not go out, but, rather, would go their separate ways in the house. The unfinished tasks remained as a metaphor for smoldering anger throughout the week until the ritual was repeated the following weekend. The couple agreed that there was "15 years of dust on the shelves!"

It is noteworthy that Mr. and Ms. Polk also told me that they had almost no celebrations between them. They ignored their anniversaries and birthdays. Holidays with extended family were a struggle. During the week, Mr. Polk worked late and the couple did not eat dinner together. The rigid ritual of the weekend struggle provided their main contact with one another. During our discussion, I connoted their weekend pattern as a reliable, albeit unsatisfying, ritual. I gave no homework assignment. I did nothing to restrain change. In the subsequent session, the couple described how during the previous weekend, Mr. Polk, after delaying for one hour on Saturday morning, began his portion of the tasks for the first time in 15 years. Rather than express her anger with the delay as she usually would, Ms. Polk joined him in the tasks. Later that day they went out together and had a good time.

This example is one of many in which the therapist listens to couples with an ear for rituals as a major conceptual underpinning for organizing information. Couples who lack satisfying daily rituals will create unsatisfying ones. They may develop individual rituals that function to avoid contact, such as couples who seldom eat a meal together. Therapeutic discussion regarding a couple's current daily rituals can lead to spontaneous change, as in the foregoing example, or to the design of a therapeutic ritual.

During an interview which is focused on collecting genogram information with a couple, a therapist can easily inquire about life cycle rituals. The question, "What was your wedding like?" can impart a wealth of information to the therapist and the spouses regarding their views of their origins as a couple, their expectations of one another and of marriage, issues of commitment, and the wider context of extended family and friends in which the couple exists. Questions regarding when a couple's anniversary is and the pattern of celebrating or not celebrating can lead to utilizing the anniversary date as a context marker in therapy and to the creation of therapeutic rituals involving "new wedding vows" as a metaphor for relationship exploration and change.

Brief Example — "Our Wedding Was The Pits!"

A couple, William and Ellen Coburn, were seen for a consulting interview. The therapist presented as his reason for seeking the consultation that the couple "could not seem to get committed to therapy." He described that they had seen several therapists during their marriage, that they had had three separations but always reunited, were currently on the verge of a fourth separation, and vacillated in their sessions with him between discussing their own relationship in one session and then wanting to focus on their children's behavior in the next session. The couple had two children, a daughter, 14, who was born with a cleft palette and cleft lip, and a son, 12. The therapist said the sessions were often marked by bitter exchanges between husband and wife and that little progress was occurring.

After hearing the spouses' views of their problems, which closely matched the therapist's, I asked them to describe a typical day. The husband worked the night shift and the couple spent little time together. They did not eat together, except on Thursday, the husband's only day off. When they were together, they argued often. I then suggested that we move back in time a bit, and asked them to tell me about their wedding. Ellen responded, "Our wedding was the pits!" She then elaborated that she was pregnant with their first child when they got married. They chose to marry in a church that was unfamiliar to either family of origin. Ellen said, "We didn't have a rehearsal, and when we arrived, the priest said we should turn around to the congregation to say our vows. I said "No way! I'm not going to say my vows facing my parents and his parents!"

This description was followed by a moving discussion of her sense of shame. William said that this was the first time he had ever heard her talk about these feelings, and he appeared very supportive of her. He then told me that when their daughter was born, there was no celebration because they felt overwhelmed by her disability. Extended family distanced. Ellen said she felt "punished by God." The couple said they told their children that their wedding was on an earlier date in order to hide that the pregnancy occurred before the marriage. Ellen said they usually were so confused about the two dates that they simply didn't bother to celebrate their anniversary.

The material gathered in this consulting interview, which yielded a picture of a couple whose major life cycle events and the rituals to mark those events had been derailed, and who shared few satisfying daily rituals, was utilized to offer a new direction for the therapy. I asked the couple when their actual anniversary was, and they replied that it was six months hence. I asked them if they would be willing to *commit* to a therapy for the next six months whose only focus would be their relationship, interdicting the previous pattern in the therapy and in the marriage that had precluded commitment of any kind. They agreed. I suggested to the therapist that the major task of this therapy would be to explore new wedding vows, since the context of the original wedding vows was obligatory rather than participatory and was fraught with difficulties and disappointments. I concluded by suggesting that this format would enable the couple to decide whether or not they wanted a future as husband and wife.

In this example, a discussion of the major life cycle events and the rituals of wedding, childbirth and anniversaries enabled an exchange of support rather than bitterness between husband and wife in the session, a tender exploration of the aura of shame that had permeated the family, and the design of a new direction for the therapy.

THE DISCUSSION OF FUTURE RITUALS

In addition to discussing past and present rituals with a couple in therapy, as described above, it is often useful to discuss upcoming rituals. Here the focus tends to be on such rituals as holiday celebrations, such as Thanksgiving or Christmas, or on vacations, as these are often ritualized.

Exploring holidays in couples therapy often leads to a focus on the couple's relationships with extended families. Both therapist and couple are able to discover patterns through a discussion of a couple's holiday practices. Such patterns may include cutoffs, celebrations skewed to one side of the families of origin, or participation in obligatory, but tense holiday celebrations. Unresolved issues regarding ethnic and religious differences frequently emerge during such discussion. Often the couple has not had an opportunity to examine these issues with a third party other than extended family members who may have shed more heat than light. Framing the couple's dilemma regarding holiday celebration as a normal developmental task facing all mixed ethnic or religion couples can assist the couple in creating rituals that will work for them. Since relationship patterns are often intensely available at holiday times, these provide opportunities for coaching couples in ways to alter participation in the ritual and in turn alter the patterns for which the ritual practice is a metaphor.

The regularity of holiday rituals for many couples may also allow a member of a couple to notice changes that had gone unnoticed in day-to-day routines. For example, just before Christmas, a wife noticed that her husband was feeling depressed because he was not participating in the holiday preparations the way he always had. During the session, the husband said that he had, in fact, been feeling down for many weeks, but that he had not told his wife, nor had she been able to notice, since their usual daily routines had not changed.

Vacations, like holidays, are a break in "regular time" for a couple. Similar to holidays, each new vacation exists in the context of previous vacations, calling forth memories of satisfaction or dissatisfaction, a sense of success or failure. Many couples have vacation rituals that repeat every year. These may include particular roles regarding planning, such as a husband or a wife making all of the travel arrangements, arguments the night before the trip, favorite places to visit and revisit, stereotyped struggles regarding time together and time apart during the trip, or arguments after returning home from an otherwise satisfying trip. Some couples will state that no matter how they are getting along otherwise "vacations are *always* miserable." Discussion of vacation rituals during couples therapy can allow for the creation of new and more satisfying patterns.

Brief Example — The Therapist as "Travel Agent"

Eugene and Ella Carne came to couples therapy while they were separated. They stated that they wanted to reconcile, but that their relationship was extremely volatile. As our work commenced, a picture emerged of two people who were quite similar in needing a lot of autonomy and interpersonal distance to be comfortable in a relationship. At the same time, each strongly believed that couples *should* spend nearly all of their free time together, and that there was something wrong with their relationship because they were clearly unable to be together so much without fighting. The early sessions of therapy were spent exploring and challenging these beliefs, and normalizing a different style of relating, one that would allow for more distance. Eugene and Ella relaxed and began to work out a more optimal rhythm of being together and being apart that worked for them.

In the fifth session, they came in very concerned about an upcoming vacation to California. The trip was planned both for pleasure and to explore the possibilities of relocating to California. I asked them to tell me about previous vacations. As they related the stories of other trips, it became clear that vacations had been a condensed metaphor for the issue of needing distance while believing that "good" couples spend all of their time together. Previous vacations all included huge fights just prior to leaving and many unhappy interactions during the trips regarding how to spend time. Each felt that his/her separate interests were disrespected by the other, marring even the time to do things that they both enjoyed. I raised with them the possibility of planning a different sort of vacation. Both said that they had never planned how their vacations should unfold and agreed to try to do so now. The remainder of the session was spent exploring what each one liked to do separately, as well as what they liked to do together. I asked them to work out a plan for the trip that would make this vacation different from previous ones before the next session.

They returned and said they had talked through how each of them would like to spend the vacation. Such a discussion was a new experience for them. They agreed on particular blocks of time each day for each to pursue separate interests and particular blocks of time to be together, including dinner. Previous dinners on vacations had often been unhappy events, as they were usually angry. They said that they anticipated that their evenings together would be better on this vacation!

In the session following the vacation, they described that most of it had gone better than any previous trip. They kept to their plan for separate time, and had looked forward to getting together in the evening. They enjoyed each other sexually for the first time on a trip. Eugene remarked that when the relationship got tense, Ella said they needed to follow the "itinerary planned with their 'travel agent' in therapy" and that they were able to laugh and go their separate ways for a while. Their ability to alter their previous vacation ritual bolstered their sense of themselves as a viable couple.

The arena of couples therapy also provides an opportunity to discuss future life cycle rituals, especially with couples who may be planning to marry. As with already married couples, the concept of "wedding vows" can form an effective part of therapy. Discussion of the couple's actual wedding plans may provide information regarding the couple's context, potential relational minefields, and the possible need for healing, while also allowing for the co-creation of a wedding ritual that truly belongs to the couple.

Brief Example—"Since We Set The Wedding Date . . . "

A couple, Karen, 42, and Will, 48, came to therapy prior to a planned wedding that was to occur in six weeks. Each had been married and divorced. Will's divorce was seven years earlier, but Karen's had occurred only a year ago. They said that they argued a lot and were considering calling off the wedding. Karen said, "Since we set the wedding date, things have become worse!"

I asked them whom they planned to invite to their wedding. Their responses indicated many cutoffs and painful, unresolved losses. Will said that he didn't think his grown children would attend, as this might make their mother unhappy. Karen said that while she wished she could invite her stepchildren from her prior marriage, she believed they, also, would not attend. Each expressed surprise when hearing that the other one's children or stepchildren would likely not attend, as they had not discussed this together. Will said his parents would come, but that his father did not approve of the marriage. Karen's father had died a year and a half earlier. She described feeling very confused regarding her grief for her father and her grief from her divorce. As we discussed this guest list, Karen and Will's arguing began to make a different kind of sense, as that which protected them from so many difficult relationship issues. Empathy for each other emerged in the session. Rather than call off their marriage, the couple decided to postpone it to a later date, enabling work in and out of therapy on the many individual and relationship issues raised by our discussion of their potential guest list.

THERAPEUTIC RITUALS IN COUPLES' THERAPY

In the course of couples therapy, therapeutic rituals may be efficacious for issues involving any of the five ritual themes of membership, healing, identity, belief expression and negotiation, and celebration, discussed in Chapter 2. Couples therapy, per se, may be considered as an extended belief expression and negotiation ritual, capable of altering a couple's identity. Thus, a couple may enter therapy with a narrow and constraining identity as "partners who always fight," or "who don't communicate." Through the process of a therapy which provides a time and space boundary for the expression and negotiation of beliefs by couple and therapist, a new and broader identity can emerge.

The particular issues which couples bring to therapy, however, often lend themselves to more dramatic and specific therapeutic rituals, regarding the often overlapping themes of healing, membership and celebration.

ISSUES OF FORGIVENESS AND HEALING IN COUPLES THERAPY

Many couples come to therapy immediately following a specific rupture in the fabric of the relationship. This may include extramarital affairs, revelation or discovery of a secret, or feeling betrayed in a crucial interaction with extended family or friends. Other couples may come to therapy many years after such a happening, and present that they are unable to get past it and that all of their current interactions occur in the context of a sense of betrayal or lack of trust. Such couples' sense of identity regarding what kind of couple they are is most often negative. Here a therapeutic ritual may be designed to facilitate forgiveness and healing.

Case Example—Putting an Affair on Ice

A couple was referred to therapy by social services. Their children were currently in foster care, and a condition of their placement back in the family was that the couple receive marital therapy.

The couple, Joan and Sam, were a remarried couple. Joan had two children from a previous marriage, Sam had one child from a previous marriage, and they had a baby from this marriage. The couple had been married for four years, and had lived together for one year before marriage (see Figure 1).

The referral stipulated that Joan and Sam were a "chaotic" couple, and that the prognosis was "poor." Sam had a history of alcoholism. Joan had recently had a very dramatic and public affair, resulting in the couple's separation, as she "ran off" with her lover. Their children were placed in foster care, and Sam, at the time unemployed, became suicidal. At the time of the referral, the couple had recently reconciled, and Sam had stopped drinking. He was attending Alcoholics Anonymous.

During the first interview, the couple gave me the following information. They had met at a time when each was just emerging from a painful and bitter divorce. Each had sworn that they would never again get involved with "a member of the opposite sex." Having said that to each other, they began living together the night they met! Their new unit included each of their children, and was what Joan called "instant family!" Their families of origin disapproved greatly of their choice to live together and of their choice of a new mate. Predictions of failure were rife. Joan became pregnant and the couple married. They described that most of the members of their families

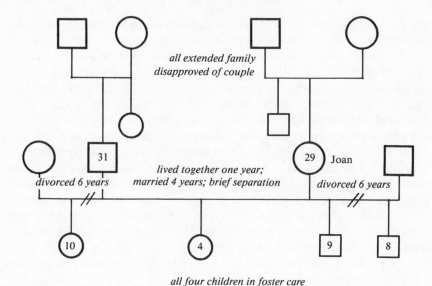

FIGURE 1   Joan and Sam: "Putting an Affair on Ice"

refused to come to their wedding, and that they felt somewhat ashamed that Joan was pregnant. Thus, the initial ritual of couple formation, a wedding, was derailed, and the couple was defined as a "bad couple" by relatives. Shortly after their marriage, Sam lost his job and began to drink heavily, adding further weight to the predictions that the couple and new family were not viable. When their baby was born, most relatives refused to come to the christening. The couple felt isolated and unsupported, and in turn, did not participate in extended family rituals, such as Thanksgiving, Christmas, or family reunions. Their own functioning as a couple deteriorated, culminating in Joan's affair and the subsequent removal of the children.

Although Joan and Sam had reconciled, they felt that they had no outside support for their marriage. Their identity as a couple in their families of origin was as the "crazy" couple. Their identity as a couple among larger helping systems was as the "chaotic" couple unable to follow through on directions for change. Their current view of themselves was that they were struggling to reestablish their marriage, but each feared that the views of family and helpers were probably correct. Part of their basis for this view was a pattern of fighting that had emerged between them since Joan returned home, which involved beginning a fight about a given topic and then fighting in a loud and insulting manner about the affair. Both felt that it was crucial to change this pattern, but did not know how to do so. I suggested the following ritual, intended to address both healing and identity issues:

Once home, each was to separately find an object or symbol that reminded him or her of the "unhappy time that had arisen between them." They were to meet jointly, discuss their chosen symbols, and then place these objects in a large bowl, put water on them, and place them in the freezer. The couple was then asked to agree to try an experiment. The next time they had a fight on any topic, they were asked to stop the fight, go to the freezer and take out the bowl, and wait for the items to thaw before beginning to fight about the affair. During the thawing out period, they were asked to discuss the positive qualities of their relationship, both past and present. They were told that they might want to enhance this discussion by soliciting opinions about them from anyone whom they knew supported them as a couple, as they did have a few relatives and friends who thought well of them. After the items thawed out, they could then fight about the affair if they so wished. The couple laughed for the first time in therapy, and agreed to try the "experiment."

When they returned in three weeks they reported that they had followed most of my suggestions, with a few variations of their own. They decided to talk to people who supported them *before* a fight ensued, and to write down what people said about them and keep this in a special place. For their items, Joan brought a "family of broken dolls" and told Sam that this was how she felt just before and during the affair, and that she felt similarly now when they fought about the affair. Sam brought several dollar bills, stating that the affair had made him feel so ashamed that he had been unemployed. When they got together to freeze their items, Joan apologized to Sam for the affair, which she had not done previously, and Sam, in turn, apologized for hurting her in his verbal responses to the affair. Each talked for the first time about his/her own individual sadness *prior* to the affair. They said they had had two fights. During the first one, while the symbols were thawing, they followed the suggestion to discuss positive aspects of their marriage. When the thawing was done, they had a brief discussion of the affair, but did not fight about it. Rather, they were able to successfully finish the prior argument. During the thawing period of the second fight, they decided that they needed to use the time to discuss strategies for getting their children home from foster care. They came to therapy with a list of issues and questions to begin planning for the children's return.

Discussion of the Ritual

This couple was defined by themselves, significant extended family members and helpers from larger systems as a "bad" couple when they entered therapy. Their behavior before, during and immediately after the affair often served to emphasize and reify this definition. Their own important life cycle rituals had gone awry. They had been unable to heal the hurts from the affair and the context in which it occurred. Continued attempts to discuss the affair simply continued the vicious cycle which culminated in their feeling bad about themselves.

The therapeutic ritual called upon their creativity, sense of humor, and playfulness, all elements that appeared missing when I met them. By asking them each to choose symbols and freeze them together, the ritual introduced symmetry into a system in which the husband had previously been viewed as the victim and the wife as the villain regarding the affair, and vice versa regarding the husband's alcoholism. Their thoughtful selection of personal symbols facilitated a new kind of discussion about the affair, one marked by empathy for each other's pain, rather than anger and defensiveness. As co-participation in the ritual recontextualized the affair, the couple's own problem-solving capacity emerged. This healing ritual facilitated mutual forgiveness and provided Joan and Sam with a new sense of themselves as people who were capable of solving problems, having fun, and working on a future for themselves and their children.

CHRONIC RESENTMENTS AND HEALING RITUALS

Many couples come to therapy presenting years and years of unhappiness, disappointments and bitterness. Attempts to focus on present interactions or future possibilities are met with responses describing decades of resentments. Often such couples have remained together "because of the children," and enter couples therapy for the first time as children are leaving home. One member of the couple, often the wife, may have been requesting that they go to therapy for many years, such that going or not going to therapy has become part of their ongoing struggle. Therapeutic healing rituals may be designed with such couples in order to provide a new forum for the airing and gradual letting go of resentments.

Case Example — The River of Resentments

A couple, Sara and Carl Jackson, came to couples therapy following a six-month separation that had recently ended. They had been married 22 years and were facing the leaving home of their eldest child. Carl was a physician and Sara was a school administrator. The tone in the first session was one of bitterness and acrimony, especially from Sara. She had agreed to come to therapy at Carl's request, though he had refused many similar requests from her over the years. She said she was willing to "give it one last try." As therapist, I was unsure whether she believed that therapy could help anymore. When I asked them to tell me about a time when their marriage had been good, both said that it had never been good. They described a decision to marry that had been filled with ambivalence. Sara said she nearly called off the marriage, but that her mother "talked her into it." During the first two sessions, each complained bitterly about the other. Sara complained that Carl had never been there for her, he would not talk things over with her, he was a workaholic, he had frequently been sarcastic towards her and the children. She allowed that since the separation he was making an effort, but her anger for all the prior years remained high. Carl, in turn, complained that Sara did not support him in his career struggles, interfered in his relationship with their two children, and confided more in her individual therapist, whom she had seen for many years, than she did in him. At one point Sara said, "As you can see, we have a river of resentments."

I asked the two of them to write out their resentments separately at home and bring them to the next session. Carl did so, but Sara refused, stating that she needed time in therapy to discuss all that had happened to her in the marriage.

Over several sessions a painful story emerged that involved Sara's addiction to prescription drugs for many years. Both she and Carl agreed that he had ignored her addiction. He acknowledged that his position had been that the addiction was "her problem" and that this had enabled him to deny both the seriousness of Sara's addiction and his own responsibility as her partner. Ultimately, she had to be hospitalized. During her recovery, she went to Narcotics Anonymous, but Carl refused to go to the partners' group. As therapy continued, more and more bitter memories emerged, primarily from Sara. Issues were discussed that they had never been able to talk about before. Carl's position shifted from one of distance to one of being willing to hear Sara. He expressed a sense of shame for his behavior towards her. While this telling of the past was occurring in therapy, the couple reported getting along much better in the present than they ever had in their entire marriage. Talk of separating ceased. My attempts to focus more on the present and the future, however, were met with refusal from Sara. She said she simply wasn't ready yet.

At this juncture, I requested that each bring symbols of their remaining resentments to the next session. Sara brought an empty pill bottle and said that, while she knew, intellectually, that it was wrong to blame Carl for her addiction, she still resented that he had ignored her during those years. She also brought an old appointment book of his, indicating the years and years that he had worked every night until 10 or 11. Finally, she brought a model car kit, which she said he had given her as her first Christmas gift after they had married. She described how hurt she had been by this gift, which she had never told him before. Carl expressed surprise that she still had it and that she had not seen it as a joke, which he had intended. Carl brought a business card from Sara's individual therapist, stating that he felt resentment that the therapist seemed turned against him without ever meeting him. He also brought an old report card of one of their children and said that he had felt shut out of parenting, while allowing that he had also distanced from the children. Finally, he also brought an empty pill bottle. He said he had felt very tentative about bringing the pill bottle, because he had never wanted to express anger at Sara for her addiction. Sara said she was glad that his feelings were finally out in the open, as she had felt his resentment and anger for many years, but that he had always refused to acknowledge it.

I asked them to take the items home and to think about what items or parts of items they were ready to let go of and what items or parts of items they still needed to hold on to for a while. I also asked them to have a conversation together after they had thought about my question. Finally, I asked them to bring all of the items back to the next session in three weeks.

When they returned, they first told me that during the three weeks Carl had taken time off work to take their oldest child to see colleges. Prior to this, only Sara had taken the daughter on these trips. Sara had made plans to go on a trip with a woman friend. Carl had been upset at first, but they discussed it together, replacing the previous pattern of Carl's pretending something didn't matter and showing his anger tangentially through distance and sarcasm. Finally, they had gone away for a weekend with friends and had had a terrific time for the first time in many years.

They brought their items in two bags. One bag contained the items they felt ready to let go of, and included the appointment book, the model car kit, the therapist's business card and the report card. It also contained the top half of one pill bottle and the bottom half of the other. Sara explained that, in their talk together, both felt that the time of her addiction was not something they could totally let go of, but that neither wanted to hold onto the whole bottle. Carl said he felt that he owned a part of what happened to them during that period, and that he could finally say that to himself and to Sara. Both agreed there was more work to do together regarding that time of their lives. At this point, I reminded them of Sara's phrase in the first session, "a river of resentments," and suggested that when they were ready to do that they might want to float the items they were ready to let go of down the river. Sara said she was afraid of "polluting the river" and they both laughed. At the next session, they told me that they had gone to a small stream near their house, and had, indeed, let the items go. Therapy shifted to a discussion of the future and work commenced on new wedding vows.

Discussion of the Ritual and Comparison to the "Freezing Ritual"

In this therapeutic healing ritual, timing and a respect for client readiness were crucial elements. Early in therapy, I had hoped to separate old resentments from present issues. Sara's and Carl's responses were indications of a pattern in their marriage in which Carl's eagerness to let go of past hurts was met by Sara's insistence to hold on to past hurts. Each one's position led to an escalation of the other's. Therapy proceeded in a manner that shifted this pattern to one where both could examine the pains of the past. Carl's previous denial of problems dissipated and Sara's insistence of focusing on the past gradually lessened. The ritual then punctuated this process and enabled mutual decisions regarding holding on and letting go.

In the case "Putting an Affair on Ice" described above, the freezing ritual occurred early in therapy in response to an acute crisis for the couple. In the present case, the ritual occurred much later in therapy, following and confirming other changes.

In both cases, the couples were asked to choose the symbols for the rituals, and in both cases, wife and husband were asked to do this symbol selection individually and then come together to share their selections. This process facilitates individuation, confirms separate viewpoints regarding a joint dilemma, provokes curiosity regarding the other's choices, implicitly highlights effective symmetry, and communicates in action that the ritual belongs to the couple.

In both cases, I, as therapist, suggested the symbolic action (e.g., freezing the affair and floating the resentments down the river). In the first case, the couple had been viewed by others and viewed themselves as "impulsive" and "out of control." Additionally, an aspect of their relationship, that of arguing nonproductively over the affair, had become stuck or frozen. Participation in the freezing (and thawing) ritual both highlighted the stuckness in an absurd fashion and enabled qualities of patience, planfulness and problem-solving to emerge. In the second case, the initial symbolic action involved holding on and letting go, which is an element both common to many healing rituals and particular to the issues of this couple. The subsequent symbolic action of floating the resentments down the river was selected in keeping with Sara's initial metaphor of a "river of resentments." The ritual symbolically highlighted that this "river" no longer flowed *through* their relationship, but rather was separate from it.

The place of the actual ritual differed in these two cases. In the first case, the search for symbols, the sharing of symbols, and the freezing and thawing occurred *in* the couple's home. This immediacy of place allowed the couple easy access to the ritual process and recontextualized their home as a place where humor and problem-solving, rather than catastrophes, could occur. The partners had also been beseiged by larger systems who thought poorly of them. Placing the ritual at home enabled them to demonstrate mastery of a difficult situation *without* a helper present. In the second case, the ritual was developed and occurred in multiple places. The couple searched for and discussed their symbols at home. They then brought the symbols to therapy for further discussion and to accentuate the holding on/ letting go issue. Finally, a stream located *outside* their home enabled greater remoteness from old resentments.

RITUALS AND HOMOSEXUAL COUPLES

Lesbian and gay male couples present issues regarding rituals that are both similar to and different from those of heterosexual couples. While daily and weekly rituals, such as meals, partings and reentries, and outings, may be quite similar, the therapist and couple will often find poignant differences regarding life cycle rituals, and participation with families of origin in family traditions and celebrations.

The initial couple life cycle ritual, the wedding, which publicly defines and affirms a couple and highlights connectedness to and support from extended family and friends, is not generally available to lesbian and gay male couples. The subsequent traditional anniversary ritual is thus also missing. Many committed homosexual couples create their own ritual to publicly announce their commitment, and many create an anniversary date, based on initial meeting or beginning to live together, or some other important date. Inquiry regarding the creation or lack of such rituals enables the therapist to discover issues regarding difficult relationships with extended family, differences between one partner's family of origin's acceptance and affirmation of the couple and the other's, and available support for the couple. Such discussion may also lead to the creation of rituals to celebrate the couple as a couple, including a union celebration or an anniversary party.

Discussion of family traditions and celebrations frequently opens painful areas regarding cutoffs from extended families. Coaching work to facilitate coming out to family or to reconnect may ensue. One member of a couple may be invited to family celebrations without his/her partner, thus preventing participation in family rituals that lend support to a couple's existence. In situations where one family of origin is open to the couple and the other is not, therapist and couple may find rituals skewed to the one family of origin that accepts the couple. In such circumstances, the partner who is cut off from extended family experiences a double loss of both relationships and familiar rituals, and the couple may remain unable to create rituals that borrow from both extended families and include new elements of their own. Here, the therapist should encourage an examination of rituals from both families and the creation of and participation in rituals that affirm positive aspects of the histories of both partners.

An especially painful and crucial aspect of life cycle rituals for committed homosexual couples emerges regarding the death of one partner. A family of origin that has refused to accept the couple may, at this juncture, refuse to allow the living partner to participate in funeral arrangements or the funeral ritual. Members of couples who have lived together for many years may find themselves shut out at the time of death. This issue has become particularly salient and poignant for gay male couples because of the AIDS epidemic. Here, one partner may provide loving care, nursing, and support for the dying partner, and yet be legally unable to participate in the traditionally sanctioned rituals of grieving. Therapists working with couples where AIDS is involved should raise these issues. Work to reconnect with family of origin whenever possible should be done. The therapist may also want to raise the idea of the couple's creating a living will that spells out the wishes of the dying person regarding the funeral ritual. Such a living will and any last will and testament should be written in language that marks emotional connections to family of origin, while affirming the primacy and legitimacy of the couple (David Barr, personal communication, 1988). General discussion of life cycle rituals in therapy with lesbian and gay male couples may also lead to such processes well ahead of a time when the couple is facing death.

Therapy utilizing a ritual perspective with homosexual couples should encourage the development of rituals that heal cutoffs and splits whenever that is possible. Like therapeutic rituals for any couple whose life cycle path differs from the majority, rituals with gay and lesbian couples should celebrate the couple's uniqueness and difference, while simultaneously affirming the universal.

RITUALS AND ISSUES OF SEPARATION AND DIVORCE

In many couples' cases, issues of separation and divorce pertain. The ritual themes of *membership*, both in the couple system and in the larger system of the couple, their children and extended family, and *healing* are most common in situations of considered separation, actual separation and divorce.

When Couples are Considering Separation

Some couples come to therapy presenting extreme ambivalence regarding separation. At a given session, one partner appears to want to separate, while the other appears to want to maintain the marriage or relationship. Within a given session or at a subsequent session, these positions are reversed. Or both partners talk of separation, but back off immediately when the therapist begins to talk of separation, too. As the therapist shifts ground to work on present issues to enable resolution, the couple becomes more adamant about separation. This quickly reversing pattern prevents either involvement to solve problems or genuine disengagement and separation. Therapy is most often stalemated.

A ritual utilizing the odd days/even days format (Selvini Palazzoli, Boscolo, Cecchin, & Prata, 1978) is useful in these circumstances. The couple's problem is first conceptualized as the difficulty in deciding whether to remain together or to separate. The couple is asked to try an experiment with the following instructions, tailored for the particular couple's issues: On Monday, Wednesday and Friday, you are both to behave and believe as partners who are committed to a future together. On Tuesday, Thursday and Saturday, you are both to behave and believe as partners who have separated. On Sunday, you are asked to discuss the week's experience.

This ritual functions in a number of ways. It interdicts the quickly reversing positions of the couple, and offers instead an experience where both remain on the same side of the issue for an extended period of time. It frees the therapist from the couple's struggle regarding separation or remaining together, placing the issue with the couple where it belongs. Finally, it shifts the issue from discussion to action, as the couple actually behaves in a "committed" way or in a "separated" way.

When couples do this ritual, clarity is promoted regarding direction for the couple and for therapy. For example, partners may say that they have decided, after truly entering the option of separation, to remain together, work on the issues between them, and drop the threat of separation. Other couples may describe that fully entering the option of remaining together enabled them to finally decide to separate, and choose to use therapy to that end. In still other couples, a previously hidden agenda of one spouse, to use therapy to facilitate separation, comes into the open. When couples choose not to do this particular ritual, therapy may shift from the rapid reversal regarding separation or commitment to a discussion of the "decision not to decide."[1]

When Couples Separate and Divorce

Couples may come to therapy already separated or may decide to separate during therapy. When reconciliation is not a possibility, such therapy is usually focused on the emotional aspects of separation and divorce for the couple, their children and other family members and friends, and on the practical, though often highly charged aspects of financial support, custody, and visitation. In the face of the enormity of changes involved in separation and divorce, a ritual perspective can serve to guide both therapist and couple.

Normative Rituals in Separation and Divorce

During separation, all of the familiar daily rituals that spouses may have shared with each other and with children are missing. While there is often initial relief that particular familiar and rigid rituals of fighting and hostility are gone from the daily scene, many couples quickly resurrect these during separation and divorce. For a period of time, those more comfortable daily rituals that were sustained despite discord may not be replaced by new rituals. Discussion of this aspect of separation in therapy can often assist in the design of new rituals, as well as interdicting the process of continuing the rigid rituals of fighting.

Seasonal or religious rituals, such as Thanksgiving and Christmas, and subsequent life cycle rituals, such as other family members' weddings or graduations, may pose particular problems for separated and divorced couples. The power of such rituals is evident in the hostilities that often erupt between the ex-partners regarding attendance and participation in particular rituals. Simultaneously, the loss of the marriage or couple relationship and the frequent loss of relationships with in-laws and friends is often poignantly experienced at times of such rituals. Effective therapy for separating and divorcing couples should spend a period of time discussing and anticipating these normative rituals. By normalizing the experience of loss and anger often attendant to such rituals, couples may be able to abandon blame and arrive at new ritual patterns.

Therapeutic Rituals in Separation and Divorce

In our culture, there are no common rituals for separation and divorce. The relationship of marriage, which has an entry ritual, has no exit ritual.

When separated or divorced couples are coming to therapy together in order to work out issues and reach agreements regarding finances, child custody, visitation and relationships with in-laws, a therapeutic ritual which documents these agreements can be useful. Here the therapist may serve as witness to the document signing. Similarly, some divorce mediation asks couples to sign documents in a manner that ritualizes the agreements completed during the mediation process.

In rare instances, both members of a divorcing couple may come to therapy together to deal with particularly painful aspects of the separation. Such couples have usually moved beyond issues of blame and guilt. In such circumstances, the therapist may assist the couple in designing a divorce ritual capable of capturing the dualities of sadness regarding what has been lost and affirmation of a new life for each. Since the issues for each divorcing couple are unique, and since a renewed sense of empowerment is crucial for divorcing couples, it is important that the therapist not impose a ritual, but rather invent one with the couple.

Following separation and divorce, many people come to therapy individually to deal with the issues of the breakup. While the therapy may involve a individual, the issues are often couples' issues, or the movement from being part of a couple to being single. Therapeutic rituals are useful in this process. Such rituals usually involve healing; however, they may also involve other ritual themes, including membership, identity and celebration.

Case Example — The House-Cooling Party

Brent and Candice Meyers, 30 and 29 respectively, came to couples therapy for one month following Brent's announcement to Candice that he "didn't know if he wanted to be married anymore." The couple had been married for six years and were considering having their first child when this crisis occurred. In the first session, Brent said he no longer felt attracted to Candice and felt very unsure about their relationship. He said he had been feeling that way for over a year, but had kept his feelings to himself until recently. Candice appeared devastated and said she had no idea that he was feeling this way until two weeks earlier. As therapist, I had the uneasy feeling that Brent had, in fact, already made his decision to leave and was coming to therapy to soothe Candice, but attempts to discern this were unsuccessful. I proceeded on the basis of their mutual definition of the therapy, which was "to find out if our marriage can be saved." Between the second and third session, Brent moved out, leaving Candice a note that he was going. In the third session, he announced that the marriage was over and that he was leaving therapy as well, as he no longer saw a need for it. He also told Candice that he was seeing another woman, and that he would like to proceed with a divorce "as quickly as possible." Candice asked if she could see me individually and I agreed.

Our work initially focused on support for Candice through the beginnings of the separation. Her concerns focused heavily on a sense of loss, not only of the marriage and hopes for a future with Brent, but of his family and mutual friends. Her main metaphor for these concerns centered on her house. She and Brent had bought the house three years earlier with much excitement and hope. Shortly before their separation, she and Brent had discussed designing a nursery. She told me that their house had been a center of activity for both extended family and friends. They had developed a monthly dinner ritual with both sets of in-laws, and frequently had friends over. Since both sets of in-laws were elderly, Thanksgiving and Christmas celebrations had shifted to this home. Since Brent had left, Candice had had no company over. She felt uncertain about inviting people over, and she felt frightened that she was going to lose all of her social supports. She said the house was "her loneliness and her memories." She also said it was too soon for her to consider selling it, as she felt she had experienced enough changes for a while.

We spent a session discussing ways that she could re-enliven the house, and alter it in ways that would express her new life as a single person. She decided that the first step was to change some of the furnishings. Brent wanted a lot of their furniture, and they were able to negotiate a deal that enabled her to buy some new items. She did not invite anyone over to see these changes. Her own parents asked repeatedly to come over, but Candice made excuses and visited them at their house. She put away special mementos of their relationship that made her especially sad. She said she wasn't ready to get rid of these, but that she didn't want to look at them every day. Over time, many of their friends, who had at first distanced, called her to get together, but she met them at their houses or at restaurants, rather than at her own home. She said that inviting them over and entertaining them by herself would somehow finalize the divorce, and that she felt frightened to do so. She said she felt like a "strange sort of prisoner" in her own house, stating, "I'm not locked in, but other people are locked out."

At this juncture, I asked Candice if she would be willing to get a new lock for her front door. She looked at me quizzically but agreed. I then asked her to buy the lock, but not to install it just yet. I asked her to bring the lock to the next session. At that session, I requested that she set aside an hour each day. During the hour, I asked her to consider the question "What would it take to put this new lock on my door — a lock that I could open to my family and friends?" Finally, since the entire house had become Candice's "prison," I asked that she conduct this hour in a different room of the house each day.

When she returned, she told me that the first three days had been very sad. Everytime she thought of "putting in a new lock" that she could open to family and friends, she cried, remembering all the earlier good times. On the fourth day, she became aware of feeling very angry. This was the first time she had talked about anger over Brent's actions. On the fifth day, an idea came to her. She decided to have a "house-cooling party" to announce her new life and her new availability to family and friends. She said people usually have "house-warming parties" when they move to a new home, and that she had decided that a "house-cooling" party could mark her divorce with some bit of humor. She spent the hour on the sixth day designing an invitation and sending them out to family and friends. Part of the invitation read "Please do bring gifts appropriate for the lovely home of a single woman — I need to replace the 'his and her stuff'!" On the last day before our session, she had the new lock put on the door.

Following the house-cooling party, Candice recommenced having family and friends to her home.

Discussion of the Ritual

I worked with Candice for three months before she came up with the delightful idea for her own divorce ritual, the house-cooling party. Many of her conversations with me indicated a pattern of holding on and letting go common to the healing process. The central issue regarding having friends and family over to her house was indicative of the change required in normative rituals following a divorce. Candice felt that to continue the old rituals, minus Brent, was simply too painful. Her first solution, frequently utilized by people dealing with great loss, was to abandon familiar rituals altogether. As often happens, this ritual abandonment made her equally sad, reminded her constantly of her loss, and underscored and exacerbated her loneliness.

The at-home ritual, utilizing the new lock as symbol for Candice's possible new identity as a single person with new normative rituals, and involving each room in her house as the chosen place for her deliberations, enabled grieving, expression of anger, and the rediscovery of a sense of humor. Candice then designed her own divorce ritual in the house-cooling party, one that announced her new identity, furthered the healing process, and stated her right to have celebrations.

CONCLUSIONS

Couples' issues lend themselves well to examination of normative rituals and to the creation of therapeutic rituals. Conversations in therapy about the normative rituals in couples' relationships facilitate appreciation for the daily patterns, life cycle path, issues of shame, and connections and struggles with extended family of any given couple. The naturally occurring rituals in the lives of couples, together with a life cycle and ethnic perspective, offer direction for each partner and for the therapist for the design of therapeutic rituals. The rituals described above are indicative of a process in which a couple or individual involved with couple issues and a therapist work *together* to revitalize existing rituals, rework unsatisfying rituals, or enable new rituals.

NOTES

[1] I want to express my appreciation to Karine Rietjens, M.S.W., at the University of Calgary Family Therapy Program, for her idea of posing to couples the option of "deciding not to decide."

REFERENCES

Barr, D. (1988). Personal communication. Lamda Legal Defense, New York, New York.

Roth, S. (1985). Psychotherapy with lesbian couples: Individual issues, female socialization, and the social context. *Journal of Marital and Family Therapy, 11*(3), 273–286.

Selvini Palazzoli, M., Boscolo, L., Cecchin, G., & Prata, G. (1978). A ritualized prescription in family therapy: Odd days and even days. *Journal of Marriage and Family Counseling, 4*(3), 3–9.

Imitative and Contagious Magic in the Therapeutic Use of Rituals with Children

JOHN J. O'CONNOR

AARON NOAH HOORWITZ

THERE WAS ONCE A DOCTOR famous for curing warts by turning on an impressive machine and painting the warts a bright color. The machine and the paint were irrelevant to the cure except insofar as they helped to constitute a therapeutic ritual. Wise old grandmothers craft the same kind of healing ritual when they get rid of the pain from a bumped knee by having the child turn around six times, count to ten, and then pinch the other knee. The examples are endless, whether they are exotic or mundane, whether they are taken from the shamanic and cultural practices observed in other cultures by anthropologists or from the formal and informal rituals existing in everyday life in our own culture.

The purpose of this chapter is to describe how rituals can be used with good effect in therapeutic work with children. Four case examples will be presented to illustrate a particular type of ritual which utilizes principles of imitative and contagious magic. In rituals of this kind, we utilize a "magical reality" and draw from the field of anthropology to obtain clues and examples about ritual. We depend on the field of hypnosis to help guide the crafting of interventions and to conceptualize why rituals seem to work when they do. Also, we utilize theory and research on cognitive development

The authors would like to acknowledge Linda Ford, ACSW, of Unified Services, who was the therapist in one of the cases.

to understand the logic children employ and why the use of ritual is particularly appropriate for them. Before proceeding to discuss these topics, it is
important to articulate our understanding of ritual and the aspects of it that
we believe to be responsible for therapeutic change.

WHAT IS A RITUAL?

Our definition of ritual is a working one, derived from a number of sources
(Hoorwitz, 1987; Jilek, 1982; O'Connor & Hoorwitz, 1984; Palazzoli,
1986). For our purposes, a ritual is a specific sequence of acts which is
believed to punctuate or promote a change in the life of an individual, a
family, or a social group. In the therapeutic rites which we construct, a ritual
also has a clear beginning, a structure, and a sequence of actions organized
around a theme; also, it is often performed repeatedly. It may mark the end
of one phase of life and the beginning of the next, or it may bring about a
change, such as the solving of a problem or the healing of a wound. We are
interested in both of these types in therapy.

The first, which provides some punctuation in history, may sometimes be
used to alter the world view or reality of the family, much as a bat mitzvah or
bar mitzvah may alter the family's view of a daughter or son. This altered
view may then facilitate behaviors and interactions which help the family to
transcend a particular phase of life. The second type consists of a prescribed
set of acts believed to bring about a change in a problem. Since these are the
ones we more commonly employ in our therapeutic work and which we
intend to illustrate in this chapter, our discussion will focus on this latter
type.

A crucial ingredient in ritual is the belief that it will effect a change or
maintain a desired status quo. An example of the latter is a Sunday dinner in
a family, which maintains the beliefs, values, and cohesion of the family.
Belief in ritual is enhanced when the set of acts constituting the ritual makes
sense within the logic or belief system of the child, family, or culture. When
crafting rituals with children and their families, belief in change is enhanced
in several ways. First, it is essential to utilize the child's world view and the
ways of thinking characteristic of the child's stage of development. Second,
belief in change is enhanced by a social consensus that the set of acts is
effective; specifically, this refers to a consensus between family and therapist
about the reality of the belief. Belief is additionally enhanced by the authority of the therapist as a person from whom the parents have requested help.
The therapist is paid a fee, has diplomas on a wall, is licensed by the state,
has a routine of appointments, and so forth, all of which enhance authority
and belief in the therapist's prescriptions. Similarly, in other cultures, shamans or medicine men and women derive their authority from a social

consensus, reinforced across generations. Shamans behave in a prescribed way and utilize certain objects to enhance belief in their efficacy.

Another characteristic of ritual is that it communicates a message about the process of change that is identical to a hypnotic message (Hoorwitz, 1987). The message is that, if a set of prescribed acts is performed, then a desired or curative effect will be achieved. The relationship between the prescribed set of acts and the curative effect involves a causal link which is questionable within propositional or Aristotelian logic.

This dubious causal link is contained in any suggestion which takes on the following form: "If you count to 10 slowly while concentrating on the air going in and out of your lungs, then you can notice your eyelids becoming heavier." Counting to 10 slowly while concentrating on breathing, by itself, simply does not cause the hypnotic effect. It is *presumed* to cause the hypnotic effect; it is this presumption, contained in the language of hypnotic suggestion, that facilitates the effect. The counting to 10 and the participation in a ritual are identical in the sense that they constitute a presumed cause for an intended therapeutic effect. Even more so than adults, children utilize concepts of cause and effect that render them open to the "logic" of a hypnotic suggestion. The causal link contained in any hypnotic suggestion is not as dubious to children as it is to adults. As will be explored later, children think in prescientific ways about the world and usually persist in these ways of thinking about their problems even after their usual cognitive styles and structures more closely resemble adult thinking.

Another characteristic of rituals is that they tend to contain metaphors and symbols which stand for or refer to events, actions, and objects not immediately present. In the simplest form, a ritual is intended to cause some effect and by doing so is assumed to share some identity with that effect. Therefore, rituals are inherently metaphorical or analogical for something else. In ritual's most complex forms, every aspect of every act in a ritualistic sequence is replete with potent and redundant symbols referring to various aspects of a person's or a culture's history, values, and world view (Turner, 1969). When the symbols are numerous and redundant enough, the ritual's symbolic resonance serves to validate and perpetuate that history and world view.

In using rituals with families, it is important to employ sequences of action and objects which symbolically refer to things meaningful to the family members. The purpose of the intervention may be to interdict habitual problem-maintaining interactions, but this can be accomplished only if the intervention can be integrated within the values and world view of the child or family, so that it reinforces the strengths of the family.

Rituals may also be enhanced by some degree of incomprehensibility (Hoorwitz, 1987; O'Connor & Hoorwitz, 1984). This incomprehensibility may simply reflect an unclear link between the ritual and its intended effect. Rituals may appear more incomprehensible if they are exotic, possess unpredictable procedures, or engender mystery and confusion. To the degree that this element of incomprehensibility exists, attention is distracted from the question of whether the presumed cause (i.e., the ritual) will produce the intended effect. In other words, incomprehensibility distracts from the question of whether the ritual does indeed contain an efficacious ingredient. It is ironic that rituals are likely to be most effective when they are incomprehensible and when they simultaneously possess an overriding appearance of validity.

From the hypnosis literature, we can see that the characteristic of incomprehensibility serves the function of depotentiating conscious sets of expectation. That is, it immobilizes a person's usual conscious set of strategies and expectations for negotiating reality demands, such that the person is poised to be influenced by suggestions. It is important to distract attention from, or to depotentiate, these usual strategies, because they might result in conscious and critical scrutiny of the dubious causal link between a presumed cause and an intended effect. Distraction renders the person more open to implied suggestions that change will occur and allows time for the person's cognitive, autonomic, and other internal processes to respond to the suggestions for change. Children in general are more easily distracted from their habitual solutions than adults and are usually posed to accept a therapist's suggestions. The characteristic of incomprehensibility, in addition to serving a distracting function, may also lend an air of mystery which engenders awe and respect; this, in turn, can facilitate belief in the efficacy of the ritual.

These, then, are the characteristics which we believe to be crucial in defining and understanding healing rituals. They are applicable to use with adults as well as children, though we have focused our discussion mainly on children. There is, however, a factor which makes ritual a particularly appropriate modality for children. That factor consists of children's unique stages of cognitive development.

Children's Thinking

Children naturally concoct rituals in play, in games, and in daily routines. Rituals are comforting and healing for children. They allay anxiety and provide a sense of mastery in a harsh and incomprehensible world. Children's predisposition to use of ritual can be explained by the fact that earlier forms of logic are more accessible to them than to adults.

It is not until adolescence that we develop what Piaget and Inhelder (1969) have described as formal operational thinking, the formal propositional logic which we employ as adults. Many of these forms of logic are available during the stage of concrete operational thinking (from about the ages of seven to twelve), but can only be employed on objects which are physically present. The stage most characterized by magical thinking and a predilection to ritual is that described by Piaget as preoperational thinking, typically seen between the ages of two and seven.

Throughout these stages of development, children progress from magical and animistic reasoning to a more scientific approach. To a certain extent, the history of scientific thought is recapitulated in the epistemology and ontology characteristic of each stage of development as children continually redevelop their world views. Children are cosmologists in miniature, inventing and reinventing the universe, until their world view has finally evolved to what we as adults share as a consensually validated reality. However, a residue of the superstitious thinking of earlier stages remains even in adults. During times of stress and emotional upheaval, children of any age and even adults can temporarily revert to or access aspects of preoperational thinking. Yet, because preoperational thinking is so far removed from our adult forms of reasoning, adults can be viewed as cognitive aliens in their attempt to understand children's ways of thinking at this stage of development.

Preoperational thinking is characterized by syncretic reasoning, which means that a causal connection is believed by the child to exist between two events by virtue of their appearing together or in sequence. For example, a child might believe God made her bump her knee because she didn't wear a jacket like her mother told her to. Thinking at this stage is also animistic, for example, believing that the moon is alive because it follows you as you walk. Like gods, children give life to inanimate objects and are themselves the center of the universe. Magical thinking is also characteristic of this stage. In children's minds, a thought is equivalent to a deed. That is, if they wish in anger that a parent were dead, then they feel as if they have performed the act and may feel as guilty as they would if they had actually attempted murder. Because they think something in their heads, they believe it is so in reality. This confusion between inner and outer reality would make a four-year-old's thinking appear psychotic if in an adult body.

It is easy to see, then, how magical ritual is a natural expression of preoperational thinking. When a child wishes her mother dead and fears that as a result of the wish that the event will occur, it is natural for the child to invent a ritual to undo the event, such as pretending to resuscitate a doll that she has "killed." As can be seen, children of this age vacillate between a felt sense of omnipotence and a sense of fragility. It is only over time and through continued testing of beliefs and feedback from the world that children gradually learn that they are neither as powerful as they wished nor as fragile as they feared.

As children enter the stage of concrete operational thinking, they develop greater cognitive capacities for coping with the world and for defending against anxiety. They exercise these new capacities by making things, collecting things, counting things, and doing many other things which have the appearance of compulsive activity. It is natural at this stage to develop obsessions, compulsions, and idiosyncratic anxieties reflecting repeated sequences of thought or action. Compulsion and repetition, combined with a bit of magical thinking, is all that it takes for the creation of a ritual which will undo whatever it is the child fears. Children create rituals to play, to ward off danger, to test beliefs, and to test the limits of their power and powerlessness.

For example: "Having my teddy bear with me at bedtime will protect me from bad dreams or from a monster coming in the night." "If I hold my breath long enough between thunderclaps, my parents will be safe. If I cannot hold my breath long enough, I could breath three times quickly and they will be safe." "I will be safe if I confess my sins ritualistically and recite three prayers in a row." Whether rituals are formal or informal, collective or idiosyncratic, they often reflect and organize childhood themes of loss, injury, power, social concerns, play, revenge, retribution, and the undoing of vengeful acts or feelings.

Rituals also often involve the use of a transitional object, that is, an experience or object which reminds them of an absent parent and thereby brings comfort. A good illustration might be a child singing a song his mother sings to him at night when she is unable to be with him. A child's relationship with a blanket or a teddy bear can metaphorically replace a relationship with a missing parent. The development of rituals incorporating transitional objects helps children to feel more comfortable, to feel in control, to be active rather than passive, and to perform actions that diminish helplessness and powerlessness.

To summarize, rituals are particularly appropriate for children because the repetitive sequence in many rituals accesses the compulsive coping mechanisms which are so frequently used by children. More importantly, children are predisposed to accepting the validity of a ritual. They are less likely than an adult to scrutinize the dubious causal link between a presumed cause (i.e., the ritual) and the intended effect. To the degree that the child thinks with syncretic logic, or reverts to it, there is no doubt about the causal connection at all.

IMITATIVE AND CONTAGIOUS MAGIC

Imitative magical rituals (Frazer, 1959) utilize the law of similarity or "like produces like." The assumption is that one can produce an effect by imitating it in advance in a metaphoric or symbolic form. For example, some cultures possess the collective belief that a person can be injured by injuring an image or effigy of the person. One can facilitate childbirth by dropping rocks or dolls from the genital region of a woman. To melt someone's heart, melt a waxen image. To resolve marital problems, tie two effigies together with the thread of the woman's girdle. To cure jaundice, throw yellow objects away.

The principle of contagion contains the assumption that things which have been in contact continue to act on each other. The properties of one object are transferred to another. For example, an Indian initiate is struck with a "power"-filled cane in a spirit dancing ceremony and a power then possesses him (Jilek, 1982). On a spirit quest, an initiate is visited by a vision of his totem, an animal-like spirit from whom he derives qualities characteristic of that animal. A child holds a rabbit's foot, absorbing from the object its "luck."

In examining these two principles, one can see that they are both characteristics or concepts which connect events, objects, or actions. They are not "causal" connections in any formal way, but because they can be used to categorize, organize, or relate events, it is easy enough to see why they would be perceived as causal from a child's perspective. They are a way of establishing identity between events.

To us the significance of these principles is that they help to dictate the choice of objects or actions in a ritual. By connecting discrete objects, actions, or events, they appeal to a child's type of reasoning and help to provide a sense of validity for a ritual.

Utilizing these principles to guide the process of crafting healing rituals for children and families, one can begin to generate possibilities. A timid and insecure child could eat his father's favorite cereal, to be similar to his father, to share his strength, courage, and confidence. A young girl who yearns for her absent father could be given a ring he wore, as a transitional object which allays separation anxiety by making the father metaphorically present. A child with a headache could transfer the pain to a stuffed animal by touching the forehead with the animal. A child who hears voices can squeeze a little-girl doll and transfer the voices from herself into the doll, and so forth.

The kind of intervention we are describing may on the face of it appear to be deceptively simplistic. That is because we are describing what may be considered to be a type or form of ritual whose use is highly similar for a variety of problems. We do not, by any means, intend to minimize the complexity of children's problems and the complex ways in which family interactions become entangled in these problems.

Children's Problems

When children have problems, there are always two problems: (1) the family's relationship with or entanglement in the problem, whether that problem consists of a fear, an obsession or a compulsion, or pain; and (2) the child's conflict with or relationship to the problem. The first of these refers to the actions taken by family members to address the problems and the child's responses to these actions. Repetitive sequences of interaction usually occur in which parents attempt to help a child with a problem and fail. For example, a child develops a phobia about ceasing to breathe, thinking that, if she stops thinking about breathing, she may in fact stop breathing. The child calls out to the parent, who then reassures the child but unsuccessfully. The parent tries harder and the child is temporarily relieved, which reinforces the parent's solution of providing reassurances. The child's fear returns and the parent tries and fails to reassure the child. In this way, the family can become organized around the problem.

In situations of this kind, the parents' solutions to addressing the problem are often serving to maintain it (Fisch, Weakland, & Segal, 1982; Watzlawick, Weakland, & Fisch, 1974). This is a "strategic" view developed by the research of the Mental Research Institute in Palo Alto. Other compatible views are also possible. For example, the problematic situation can also be viewed in "structural" terms as a hierarchal incongruity (Madanes, 1981), in which the parents, who ordinarily play superior roles of protectors to the children, are in the incongruous position of being helpless to have impact on a powerful problem. Typically, strategic, structural, and other kinds of family therapists help the family to get beyond this impasse by altering the structure of family relationships or by interrupting the sequences of interaction. A common approach would be to provide some task which blocks the parent's problem-maintaining solutions.

What is sometimes neglected in family treatment is a consideration of the child's relationship to the problem. Children may try hard to prepare to face their fears or to avoid their symptoms, and these measures frequently fail; these measures may indeed maintain the problem. The result is that children feel they should try even harder to solve their problems but at the same time feel hopelessly defeated and tyrannized by them. A child's relationship to the problem is a struggle of painful conflict.

Clinicians sometimes develop interventions which simultaneously address both the family's relationship to the problem and the child's relationship to the problem. Elegant condensations of this kind sometimes take the form of family rituals, but it is not necessary for effective therapy to address both targets in one fell swoop. Often, instructions to parents on how to alter their problem-maintaining solutions are useful in conjunction with prescription of a ritual the child can use to alter his or her relationship with the problem.

Enactment of rituals accomplishes a number of objectives. Problem-maintaining solutions utilized by the child are blocked, the child is moved from the passive stance of victim to the active one of participant in solving the problem, and the child is distracted from usual cognitions and feelings connected with the struggle to overcome the problem, cognitions and feelings which may be serving to maintain that struggle. The child establishes a relationship with the ritual which alters the child's relationship with the problem; no longer struggling with the problem, the problem is left behind, no longer central in the child's focus of attention.

The therapist does not ask the child to try harder or to think good thoughts, which would only be a prescription for an obsession. Instead, the therapist asks the child to do something to some object, such as squeeze a button or wear a bracelet belonging to a parent, or transfer a symptom to a transitional object by touching the object. For example, " . . . as you squeeze your mother's amulet tighter and tighter, you can also notice feeling less nervous." The ritual is novel, mysterious, and, to a child, intuitively logical.

CASE EXAMPLES

Four case examples are presented below. Each illustrates the use of ritual we have described here, specifically the use of imitative and contagious magic. Rather than attempt to illustrate the diversity that exists in the use of ritual, we have deliberately chosen a collection of cases characterized by a striking degree of homogeneity: In each case an object is used or worn which alleviates a problem. Our intent is to show that a ritualistic intervention, essentially the same in each case, can be used as a solution to a variety of different kinds of problem.

Case 1: The Monster versus Ralph the Raccoon

Matt was eight at the time of referral for treatment. He was terrified of a monster coming into his room, and his fearful behavior was becoming an increasing problem for his mother. For the previous six months, he would become frightened at bedtime, would fall asleep, and then would wake up terrified. He woke up screaming five or six times a night. Each night either he slept in his mother's room or she slept in his; this was the only way she could get a restful night. If Matt's mother did not sleep with him or blocked his being in her room, Matt ended up on the floor in his older brother's room, whose age was 11.

Matt's father had recently returned home after a six-month hospitalization for complications secondary to multiple sclerosis. He was debilitated physically and mentally, and his care dominated the family routines. The family even ate each meal around his bedside. Mother was a nurse and had set up an in-home hospitalization for father in the family room. Father suffered an organic deficit with fluctuating levels of consciousness. The level of care for father was fairly involved and mother had worked out a schedule to provide this care as well as care for her two sons. She left herself for last and usually dropped into bed exhausted; however, she did not get much rest due to Matt's problem.

The therapist meeting with this family hypothesized that Matt's fears were related to his father's illness and disability. Matt could not call upon his father at night to comfort him, but could only turn to his already exhausted mother to help ward off fears of an incomprehensible and harsh world. Because of father's "dementia," and mother's strong wish that father not be "troubled" by any problem that she might be experiencing with their sons, the therapist concluded that it was not possible to involve the father in making decisions in the therapy. The mother also blocked the therapist from asking that father give his son a message, which might have realigned the hierarchy and provided for Matt an increased sense of protection. Therefore, the focus would have to be on Matt and his mother.

In the first session, Matt looked anxious and sad. He very much wanted to solve the problem of his terror that a monster would come into his room. When asked if he had ever seen a monster, he replied that he had only seen one on TV. He was unclear whether his own monster was "real" or "part of his imagination." Yet this ambiguity did not help to mitigate the terror for Matt each night.

Near the end of the first session, the therapist asked Matt to decide which night in the coming week he wished to spend in his room. The rest of the nights he could sleep with his mother. Mother was asked to double the amount of time she spent putting Matt to bed.

Mother and son did as they were told and Matt spent three hours that night in his room singing himself to sleep. He made up words to songs, saying that "he was a chicken with no muscles, had no friends, and did not feel loved." Mother was frightened, yet fascinated, by this glimpse into Matt's thinking. It made her feel even more helpless and frustrated, since she had made heroic efforts to give Matt a sense of feeling safe, protected, and loved.

That first night he kept the overhead light on and called out to his mother several times, but he stayed in his room. He was cautious but proud of himself for spending a night in his bed; yet he castigated himself for being afraid.

In the second session, the therapist suggested a magical ritual for Matt. She first asked Matt what stuffed animals he had in his room and learned that Ralph the Raccoon had connotations of power for Matt. The therapist then asked mother to continue to spend double time putting Matt to bed and to read a heroic story to him in bed. In addition, Matt was to decide how he wanted his room set up so that he would feel safer, that is, how his stuffed animals should be arranged.

The therapist then told Matt that Ralph the Raccoon could help him. She said that Ralph was a powerful raccoon who could take Matt's fears at night. The therapist asked Matt to remember other times when Matt might have punched or squeezed Ralph, and that Ralph could take anything Matt might give him. The therapist told Matt that he could give Ralph his fears in any way he wished, for instance, by squeezing Ralph's torso or stomach or by holding Ralph close to his own body and squeezing. The therapist repeated several times that Ralph was a strong raccoon and could take anything Matt gave him. The therapist also said that, when Matt squeezed or held Ralph to give him his fears, Matt could also notice himself feeling less afraid and stronger, and he might also notice himself getting sleepier. The therapist said that if Matt gave his fears to Ralph in this way, his fear would be gone. At this point, Matt looked suspicious, but he agreed to do what was asked. Mother was nodding in agreement to these suggestions.

By the third session, two weeks later, Matt had slept each night in his room, with Ralph placed on the floor next to his bed. He said that he woke up a few times but forgot about his fears when he heard his mother talking to a friend on the phone. He also said that the ritual with Ralph did not really work because Ralph was not alive. He still was not sure if the monster was alive.

Despite Matt's claim that Ralph was not helpful, his mother reported that Matt squeezed, punched, and threw Ralph around whenever he was frightened. During this session, Matt also said that he also felt stronger and had begun to lift weights in his room. Mother reported that Matt looked more self-confident and that he had been doing better in his schoolwork.

The therapist congratulated Matt on solving his problems and told him that she thought it was a great idea for him to lift weights in order to get stronger. The therapist also suggested that Matt and his mother continue the rituals as specified, even though Ralph was not alive.

By the fifth session, several months later, Matt's mother reported that his fears were "about all gone." Matt did say that he still liked hearing his mother talk on the phone when he was going to sleep, but he was falling asleep right away each night and was not waking up. He was also lifting weights three nights per week. Mother and Matt were also relating to each other in different ways, for example, by watching National Geographic specials on TV, rather than sleeping together. Mother said that Matt looked stronger emotionally and that she noticed a "big difference in Matt." As he listened to this, Matt was beaming. He then said that he was not afraid anymore. When asked where the monster went, Matt said, "to another kid." He was maintaining his good performance in school and his soccer coach had said he was the most improved player on the soccer team. Matt had dressed Ralph in a soccer outfit with cleats and taken him to school to show his friends. Overall, the adjustment to father's return home was proceeding.

Father had started to see a neuropsychologist and mother had returned to work.

The case represents a common problem with children. It is easy to speculate about why Matt's problems arose when they did: Matt was possibly feeling unprotected by a disabled father and an overwhelmed mother, by the return and uncertain position of father in the family, by mother's feeling isolated and needing to talk to friends, by the hierarchical reversal between father and son, and so forth. If one looks for functions of a symptom, Matt's symptom could be seen to distract his parents from father's disability or to attempt to engage his father and mother in being more competent than Matt felt. Matt and his mother had both become entangled in relationship to one another and to the problem. Attempts by them both to sole the problem were serving instead to maintain it. By introducing a ritual in which mother could participate, which supplanted her usual ineffective methods of helping, and by introducing a ritual for Matt, which blocked his usual attempted solutions, the therapist helped this mother and son move past an impasse. By the follow-up phone call one year later, Matt was doing fine, feeling competent and confident.

The treatment of Matt illustrates a usual by-product of the use of ritual: namely, that children and families often transform or tailor the ritual to better suit their unique world view. At times, a ritual need only fit approximately to be accommodated by that family and be useful.

Case 2: David

David was a bright, well-behaved, precocious and energetic five-year-old before he contracted cancer of the spine and brain. His mother had called because she was feeling depressed and overwhelmed by a sense of grief. She did not feel entitled to "burden" her husband with the immensity of her distress. David, the youngest of two children, had a seven-year-old sister. Mother was also pregnant, which added a certain poignancy to David's life and to this family's tragic situation.

In a brief period of time, it became clear that David would die and relatively quickly. The cancer was particularly virulent. Most of the therapy was with the parents, and it attempted to help them through this great tragedy in their lives. They were helped to be compassionate with themselves, to make enough time to be together and to talk, and to share their anguish, anger, and great sadness; also, they were helped to talk to their young son about his impending death.

The mother asked that the therapist see David. He was in great pain and would moan weakly each time he moved or was moved. He was weak and debilitated but could tell his parents how he wanted his room and world set up and what routines he could tolerate.

The therapist met David on two occasions. The first was in the hospital, where he was watching TV. He was receiving radiation treatment to shrink the tumors but remained in pain when he moved. He also received Tylenol as needed. Upon meeting the therapist, David started fixedly but somewhat vacantly at the TV. He made eye contact briefly and returned to watching TV.

The therapist asked David's mother if he could meet with David alone. She said, "Of course," and left the room. The therapist introduced himself as a doctor who only talks to children. He said that he did not give needles or shots but that he talked to children about how they felt and played games sometimes and that children often felt better after talking with him.

The therapist asked David if he were in great pain and he said "yes" and that "it got worse" when he moved. He asked him about the stuffed animals and toys in his room and learned that he had received several as gifts. His parents had already arranged his room in just the way David wanted. The therapist asked about a two-foot rabbit and David told him it was just a gift that he had not yet named. The therapist asked him to go ahead and name it. David did so, naming it "Fluffers."

The therapist told David that Fluffers looked very special and that he seemed to be very strong. He asked David to remember other "animals" he had at home and how they were very strong as well and could take anything David could give them. The therapist asked him to remember when he squeezed them, hugged them, hit or punched them, and how they did not break, but "fluffed" back to normal, ready for more. They could take anything David could give them.

He said Fluffers was like them except he was very, very strong and could take some of the pain that David had now in his head and neck. David asked him how Fluffers could do that and the therapist said in any way David wished — by touching Fluffers to his head or neck or in some other way that David wished. He repeated that Fluffers was a very strong animal and could take his pain. He said that, if David touched Fluffers to his head and counted 1 to 10, which he could do, he could see that his pain would lessen and lessen. The therapist asked David to do this now and he did it. After he had done so, David said he wanted to watch TV again. The therapist said "fine" and that any time he wanted help from Fluffers to make his pain go away, he could touch Fluffers to the part of his body that had pain, count to 10, and the pain would lessen and lessen as he counted.

The therapist saw David two months later at home. As reported by the mother, Fluffers was constantly with David. The therapist noticed that David was weaker and smaller, and could move only slowly and with pain. The therapist had lunch with him and his parents and afterward met alone with David again to reinforce the ritual he had prescribed. David said he had done the ritual, but he then talked about his parents and his schoolmates, and he talked metaphorically about his dying. We spoke and played with some toys and then he became tired and the visit was ended. He died three weeks later.

Was the magical ritual helpful to David? His mother said that Fluffers was with him constantly. When the therapist was with David, it was inappropriate to evaluate precisely the effects of the ritual on his pain. He was too weak and distracted and it was more helpful to follow where he led.

Three points are important to highlight in this case. First, within the ritual, the therapist did not tell David his pain would be gone, but instead that it would just lessen and lessen. He did not frame the suggestion in this way to preserve his credibility as a therapist in the event that the pain might persist at its previous intensity. He did so, instead, out of a sense of powerlessness and humility that a ritual he was offering for pain was too little for this young boy facing the enormity of his death.

Second, the therapist did not use a previously empowered transitional object. One reason was that a transitional object was not available; also, in previous applications (O'Connor, 1984), children have sometimes not wanted to harm a favorite stuffed friend. Third, when David asked how Fluffers could take his pain, the therapist did not embark on arcane or magical logic or even a pseudo-scientific explanation. David's concepts were derived from a preoperational causality, a universe of psychologically-motivated physical phenomena. The therapist believed that in David's mind Fluffers could accomplish the therapeutic goal in any way David wished, by touching his head to Fluffer's head, squeezing him, and so forth. These last two points clearly illustrate the need, when crafting interventions, to appreciate the cognitive status and world view of the child.

Case 3: "Will I Stop Breathing If I Don't Think About It?"

Dottie was 10 years of age, the eldest of three, with a brother of seven and a sister of one. She did well in school, had normal peer relationships, was a gymnast, and enjoyed cheerleading. However, Dottie had numerous fears and worries. She was afraid to go to bed for fear that she would stop breathing. When eating a potato chip, she thought it would catch in her throat and choke her. When staying over at a friend's house, she usually developed stomachaches and had to return home. On hearing about a kidnapping in the news, she became fearful of walking down the street. She was often worried about dying and contracting diseases. She feared she was developing cancer and was going blind when either a TV show mentioned diseases or she heard that a relative was sick or disabled in some way.

Both parents viewed her as too serious, too worried about diseases, and unhappy. They wanted her to enjoy herself more and they did what they could to encourage this. A pattern evolved in which Dottie would come to her mother in terror and share her worry, mother would reassure Dottie and attempt to diminish the worry by saying it was silly or unrealistic, and Dottie would continue to worry. Of the two parents, mother was more often worried about Dottie and was involved most with her. Dottie rarely sought out her father since he worked long hours.

Yet, Dottie's father was also concerned, although he was involved less frequently in trying to help her. He disclosed that when she was younger, he was obsessively overprotective and constantly told his wife to take her to the doctor, fearing that she may have contracted a disease or would stop breathing. He said he used to call his daughter his "delicate, little flower," or "angel." He related that his family of origin was "ridiculous," being populated by people who were plagued by "hypochrondria." After his other children were born, father became more relaxed and his overconcern diminished. Now he very much wanted Dottie to relax and enjoy her life.

Prior to therapy, Dottie obsessed and worried approximately one to three times per week, but looked tense and unhappy at other times as well. Treatment included eight sessions, which are sketched below. Session one ended with the therapist's asking Dottie to keep track of her worrying episodes and fears and to begin to worry 30 minutes a night in a special "worry chair."

Mother and Dottie were also asked to look for a special object that "contained mother's power to reassure Dottie." Father had mastered his fear but, according to Dottie, her mother had more power to reassure. Mother was asked to continue her reassurances until a magical object was found. The rationale was that Dottie needed to master these fears on her own but did not yet know how to do it.

In the second meeting, the therapist explored the systemic consequences of improvement, thinking that Dottie's worries might reflect the presence of marital problems; however, he concluded that the marriage was fine. Mother emerged in this session as a worrier, like Dottie, whereas father had given up that role and become a problem-solver, viewing problems as challenges. In this session, mother and Dottie also identified a "star" from a necklace father had given mother.

At this point, the therapist prescribed that for 30 minutes per day, Dottie was to worry in her special chair about contracting a disease. If Dottie could not think of any particular disease to worry about, she could consult with her parents, who could name any dread disease they wished. Previously they had studiously avoided mentioning diseases for fear that Dottie would obsess.

The therapist told Dottie that the star was a special star from her mother who had received it as a gift from her father. As such, the star had all of her mother's power and reassurances within it as well as all of her father's mastery over his own fears.

The therapist said, "If you wish, you can use the star to lessen your fear and worry. When you notice yourself starting to worry, you can hold and begin to squeeze the star. The harder you squeeze, the more you can help yourself to master these fears. As you let go of the star each time after you've squeezed it, you can notice feeling more relaxed and worry free. By the time you completely let go of the star, your worry and fear can be gone."

These instructions were repeated and embellished. Mother was also asked to refuse to provide verbal reassurances beyond "remember the star," since Dottie needed to master these fears alone.

In the third session, three weeks later, it was reported that Dottie had used the star a number of times. She said that the star was like her mother's reassurance, like "blood going up your arm . . . the star turns your brain around." The therapist congratulated her on already beginning to master this very difficult problem on her own. During the previous three weeks, Dottie had worried only twice, once about going blind and once that her throat would close. She did not have the star to use on either occasion, having left the star at home. The therapist asked mother to give Dottie a smaller star she had as an earring, which Dottie could always have with her. The therapist repeated the instructions about the star's power, adding that now Dottie had a new, smaller one that was as powerful as the first.

In the fourth session, mother said that Dottie seemed much happier and more relaxed, dancing and singing around the house a great deal of the time. Dottie's worrying in the chair on a daily basis had not been regularly followed. The therapist talked with them about planning a "relapse," which is a strategic maneuver to consolidate change that has occurred. He prescribed the relapse by congratulating Dottie on solving her problem but giving her permission to worry some time in the next two weeks. He said this would be perfectly all right since this often happens when people are solving their problems about worrying.

By session five, Dottie had seen the movie "Mask" and she worried about contracting neurofibromitosis, the disease depicted in the movie. Again, she could not find the star when she needed it. She looked for it for two hours, but didn't find it until the next day. Since the symptom prescription was not regularly followed, the therapist suggested an ordeal (Haley, 1984) of obsessing for one hour contingent upon a "worry episode." Dottie hated the worry time and said she was totally bored with it. The therapist said she only needed to worry in the chair if she worried about her health elsewhere. Then it would be clear that she had to worry in a planful way. Before the end of this session, the therapist also repeated the magical injunction connected with the star.

At the sixth session, it was reported that Dottie had had no further episodes of obsessive worrying or engaging the parents in the ineffective solution of reassuring her. The therapist learned that a serious drop had occurred in Dottie's school performance; the parents openly quarreled about this and resolved their differences during the session. During the argument, the therapist blocked Dottie's efforts to triangulate herself; both therapist and Dottie remained removed from the parents' argument. Afterwards, the therapist told Dottie that her parents had done a wonderful job of talking through their differences and it was clear they did not need help from Dottie or from the therapist.

No further problems emerged in sessions seven and eight. Dottie wore stars patterned on her blouse to one of these sessions and she looked happier and more relaxed. Parents and Dottie had discussed AIDS and other diseases, when these topics had naturally arisen, without this leading to obsessive worry and fear. At the last session, she said her brother needed to come to sessions because he was a pain and that she'd like to stay home and play ball. A follow-up call six months later revealed that Dottie continued to be problem free.

It is important to discuss three issues that emerge in this case. First, a magical ritual is not usually used by itself alone and is more likely to be effective when used in the context of other methods and techniques. As Dottie's treatment evolved, use of a magical ritual was buttressed by the strategic uses of symptom prescription, interdiction of usual solutions of family and child, ordeal therapy, and other techniques and skills in the therapist's repertoire.

Second, children with obsessions think in idiosyncratic and peculiar ways. They appear precociously verbal but communicate poorly. A therapist attempting to understand an obsession in rational or logical ways will be led into a confusing maze of pseudo-logic, which almost seems logical but is not. The child's fluency is in the service of creating a logical fog, not in clearly communicating ideas. Children with obsessions overvalue words, clinging to verbal rituals and mental maneuvers as if they were people or real objects. In dysfunctional ways, children with obsessions engage in magical and dubious causal thinking: "If only Daddy tells me I will not have a bad dream, then I will not." Such a child may fear not just the disease, but also thinking about the disease, which, to the child's magical way of thinking, may be equivalent to contracting the disease. Thus, a child's fear may quickly lead to an obsessional fear of the fear.

The therapist counters or supplants the child's dysfunctional magical ritual with a magical healing ritual. The structure of the child's obsessional logic is preserved while the performance of the ritual interferes with the child's usual style of either obsessing or trying to avoid obsessing. The new ritual shifts the child's relationship with the symptom by establishing a relationship between the child and the magical object or magical action.

Third, the implied hypnotic suggestion conveyed by ritual was made particularly explicit in this case. The prescription of Dottie's ritual contained the "if . . . then" causal connective that was intimately resonant with her own thinking process. "If you squeeze hard, then you can help yourself. As you let go, you can notice yourself feeling more relaxed." If she lets go of the star, there is no formal logical reason why she would be more relaxed. Yet she was. The "letting go" of the star also was meant to suggest metaphorically the "letting go" of her worry, tension, and so forth.

Case 4: The Boy Who Wanted to be Good

Philip and his parents were seen twice. He was six, an only child. The parents' marriage appeared fine. According to his father, Philip "cried about things that don't matter." He cried when his father put a peanut butter sandwich in his lunch because he feared his classmates might laugh at him. He cried at school and later at home because he felt guilty that he had seen the lace of his teacher's slip and the outline of her legs through her skirt. He constantly worried that he might get into trouble at school.

He was plagued by "what if" contingencies: "What if I drop my lunch sandwich?" "What if I trip?" "What if I run in the hall?" Philip was afraid he might do what he thought of doing and then get into trouble; he felt guilty and cried as if he had done the act, as if thinking were doing. He started crying at 6:30 a.m., and by 7:45 his crying was relentless. He generally stopped crying after he walked into school, but mornings for the family were dreadful. Philip returned from school with questions which his parents described as his "all consuming obsession with whether he's good or not." He asked his parents, relentlessly, whether they loved him, whether he was good, and whether he was bad for doing or thinking certain things.

Philip had early difficulties in kindergarten with a particularly rigid, unempathic teacher. He spent most of his time in the hall. Philip's parents had changed his program and his current teacher was empathic, friendly, and understanding. Yet, his experience with the previous disapproving teacher had probably exacerbated an obsessive worry about his adequacy. Philip described a "funny feeling inside" when attempting to identify his undifferentiated feeling states.

Philip appeared to be developing within normal limits in most respects, judging from his activities and accomplishments. He played hockey, got along well with other children, and played well alone. He had been bedwetting for years, but his parents were not concerned about this since he was a deep sleeper.

The parents had attempted a number of solutions to address Philip's fears: to try and cheer Philip up, to explore his guilt rationally, to change the subject, and to scream at him to "lighten up." Philip responded to these measures by continuing to express his fears, to which his parents responded by providing more of the same ineffective solutions.

By the end of the first session, the therapist had asked the father to change the time and context of Philip's usual crying time from 1 hour 30 minutes in the morning to 1 hour 30 minutes in the evening. The therapist asked the father and son to list exhaustively in writing all the things that Philip could worry about. Philip was told that he needed to cry at night because in the morning there was not enough time to do his worrying justice while getting ready for school, whereas in the evening his father could give him his full attention. If he needed to cry and worry, father would be willing to sit with him. If Philip did not need all that time to cry and worry, his father and he could do other things like play catch, watch a movie, or play a game. But the men could only do this if Philip had done enough crying that night.

The therapist also asked father to sit with Philip during this time at night and to share feelings that men have. The therapist asked father to act like a consultant with Philip and suggested to Philip that he could talk with his father about any worry or feeling he had. He told Philip that his father knew about feelings of being excited, and that feeling excited about seeing his teacher's legs was natural for men to feel. Philip was told that feelings and thoughts were different from doing things.

Philip was also told that the more he talked to his father about feelings men had, and whatever worries he had, the more relaxed he would be and that he would worry and cry much less. The therapist asked father to give Philip a coin from his pocket. The therapist told Philip this was a special coin of his father's and that he could use the coin to help him not worry. Philip was told that, in school or when his father was not around, he could take this coin and squeeze it. The more he squeezed it, the more he could notice that he was worrying less and less, and when he let go of the coin, his worry would be gone. The therapist embellished this injunction, repeated it several times and ended the session.

The session scheduled for two weeks later was rescheduled by the parents for three weeks later. At that session, the parents reported the problem to be solved. Philip cried when he did something wrong and was caught but this was seen as appropriate. According to the parents, the quantity of crying diminished a "great deal," like "magic, the problem stopped." All the injunctions had been followed and Philip was spending fun time with his father at night. He said he did not want to "waste time" by crying. Follow-up in six months found Philip doing fine.

The interventions used in this case brought about a rapid change in the presenting problem. This may be due to the choice of interventions, since these have been effective much of the time with similar problems. Several of these interventions can be clearly identified in Philip's treatment. First, the context in which the problem occurred was changed from morning to evening. Philip was also, paradoxically, given permission to cry in this context, rather than being asked not to cry. These changes altered the transactional meaning of the problem. Second, the injunction to cry during prime time constituted something of an ordeal.

Third, the therapist suggested increased involvement between father and son to foster a structural balance in the family. Fourth the usual solutions employed by the parents were interdicted by providing guidance for different behaviors, such as father listening to Philip's worries, making a list of things to worry about, providing consultation to Philip about things important to men, and having fun together.

Lastly, Philip was given several hypnotic injunctions during the prescription of a ritualistic use of his father's coin. These were intended to enable him to begin to experience mastery and competence. The coin was meant to become a representation of Philip's father and as such to take on the power of a transitional object. This power was probably augmented by having also fostered more of a relationship between Philip and his father. Now, Philip's relationship with the coin, and his magical actions towards it, could replace his relationship with his problem.

The therapist erred in assuming that Philip as a five-year-old knew how long 1 hour 30 minutes was. He may not have, and if his concepts of time were unclear or undifferentiated, the time could have been communicated as the length of three TV shows or one movie or a whole bunch of cartoons.

Discussion

The rituals illustrated by these case examples all share a high degree of similarity in form. Each ritual involves a child's mastering a problem. Each involves interdicting the parents' and the child's previous solutions. Each uses preoperational logic and an "if-then" causal construction that is isomorphic to the child's dysfunctional magical construction, which has framed and perpetuated the problem. The child establishes a new type of relationship with an object that is either old or new. In most cases, the use of ritual occurs in the context of other directives and interventions, and the ritual is modified to suit the child's unique style or tempo.

We should again point out that this use of ritual is not confined to children. One of our colleagues has also utilized this type of ritual with an adult who experienced migraine, where the transitional object was not presented as a source of power and magic but rather as an opportunity to "vent" or express feelings. The hypnotic message and the form of the ritual were identical to those described here and the migrainous pain in the adult was eliminated. It may be that in times of stress adults can more easily revert to the preoperational logic which renders ritual so effective.

A few words about transitional objects should be made. Transitional objects are implicitly powerful within children's experience and represent a resource that is usually underutilized. The power of the object is derived from the child's developmental stage, thinking style, and psychosocial needs. A transitional object was available for Matt in the form of Ralph the Raccoon. One was not available for David. His use of Fluffers could be construed as use of a transitional object only insofar as Fluffers constituted a source of comfort and a medicinal object to which he could transfer pain. However, both Dottie's use of a star from her mother and Philip's use of a coin from his father can be understood as the construction of transitional objects. These objects came to represent the power and security provided by the parent in the parent's absence.

The use in these last two cases of objects which represent parental power and security are applications of the principle of imitative magic. These applications are imitative in form in the sense that the objects symbolize someone else with powers greater than the child's, powers which the child would like to possess. These are examples of symbolic imitation, since the star and coin used by Dottie and Philip are symbolic of, rather than physical representations of, parents and parental power and security. The imitative principle is also applied when Dottie lets go of the star and Philip lets go of the coin; these actions imitate or are metaphoric for the letting go of fear and worry. The imitative principle is more obvious in cases where there is actual representation rather than symbolization of an object or person, for example, in the use of effigies. In the exorcism of hallucinatory voices by transmitting them to a doll, the doll physically represents the person suffering from hallucinations (Hoorwitz, 1987).

The first two cases of Matt and David more clearly reflect an application of contagious magic. In these cases a child transfers a symptom or problem out of self and into an object. The child is not imitating an action which is a metaphor for a desire effect, but is instead projecting the problem to something outside of the child. On the other hand, the principle of contagion was not applied in the last two cases. Dottie's star and Philip's coin were not used to absorb the fears and worries. Instead, they were acted upon, squeezed and let go. These actions on the object were intended to facilitate the lessening of the problem in the child.

The similarity of form in the use of ritual in this collection of cases suggests that the same basic intervention can be used for a variety of problems. This suggestion is somewhat at odds with a basic assumption in strategic therapy that the strategy should be tailored to fit the unique aspects of the problem and of the family rather than the reverse. As a result of this assumption, the literature has flourished with creative and unique solutions. A creative and unique solution to a problem is commendable, and we take delight when we have formulated an effective one. However, a unique solution may not be generalizable for use in future cases or by other therapists.

As we all know, most family therapy does not involve the sparkle and flash of the kinds of approaches that are typically published, but rather involves repeated attempts to apply over a number of cases that which has been described in the literature. Most family therapists quietly test the generalizability of models or approaches described by others. There is special value to discovering methods which can be used repeatedly across a variety of cases. deShazer (1985) and his colleagues in Milwaukee are experimenting with a number of solutions that are applicable across a range of problems. Palazzoli (1986) recently reported on her use of an invariant ritual, that is, a ritual that is prescribed in the same form to family after family despite the first order differences in pattern, configuration, or structure. This research effort is a bold but needed effort to map more precisely the generalizability or external validity of therapy approaches.

This chapter summarizes and illustrates some of our work with rituals that are similar in form across a number of families with a range of problems. The children treated in these ways had difficulties with anxiety, obsessions, compulsions, fears, and pain of various types, both organic and functional. With children, we find rituals using a transitional object and other "magical" objects a natural extension of play, pretend, fantasy, magic, symbol and metaphor, that is to say, a natural extension of children's thoughts, beliefs, and actions. This form of intervention simply capitalizes on the "magical reality" with which children experience the world.

REFERENCES

deShazer, S. (1985). *Keys to solution in brief therapy*. New York: Norton.
Fisch, R., Weakland, J. H., & Segal, L. (1982). *The tactics of change: Doing therapy briefly*. San Francisco: Jossey-Bass.
Frazer, J. (1959). *The new golden bough*. New York: Criterion.
Haley, J. (1963). *Strategies of psychotherapy*. New York: Grune & Stratton.
Haley, J. (1984). *Ordeal therapy: Unusual ways to change behavior*. San Francisco: Jossey-Bass.
Hoorwitz, A. N. (1987). *Hypnotic methods in nonhypnotic therapies*. New York: Irvington Publishers.
Jilek, W. G. (1982). *Indian healing: Shamanic ceremonialism in the Pacific Northwest today*. Washington: Hancock House Publishers.
Madanes, C. (1981). *Strategic family therapy*. San Francisco: Jossey-Bass.

O'Connor, J. (1984). The resurrection of a magical reality: Treatment of functional migraine in a child. *Family Process, 23,* 501–509.

O'Connor, J. (1983). Why can't I get hives: Brief strategic therapy with an obsessional child. *Family Process, 22,* 201–209.

O'Connor, J., & Hoorwitz, A. N. (1984). The bogeyman cometh: A strategic approach with difficult adolescents. *Family Process, 23,* 237–249.

Piaget, J., & Inhelder, B. (1969). *The psychology of the child.* New York: Basic Books.

Selvini Palazzoli, M. (1986). Towards a general model of psychotic family games. *Journal of Marital and Family Therapy, 12,* 339–349.

Turner, V. (1969). *The ritual process: Structure and anti-structure.* Ithaca, NY: Cornell University Press.

Watzlawick, P., Weakland, C. E., & Fisch, R. (1974). *Change: Principles of problem formation and problem resolution.* New York: Norton.

6

The Use of Rituals in
Families with an Adolescent

WILLIAM D. LAX

DARIO J. LUSSARDI

ADOLESCENCE IS A TIME of great change for both the adolescent and his or her family. It can be a stage filled with confusion and ambiguity regarding what behaviors are appropriate and/or acceptable. Former "rules" and expectations are questioned as both new behaviors and new ideas are introduced into the family system and as parents and the adolescent begin to adjust to these changes. Familiar forms of encouragement and discipline may no longer be useful or appropriate: A formerly exciting planned family activity may be viewed as a burden to be endured by an adolescent, while a "time-out" in his/her room may be experienced as relief not only for the adolescent, but also for the parents.

During this stage new behaviors and experimentation can possibly lead to more serious consequences. Younger children are usually more carefully supervised in their activities. They do not have the freedom or accessibility to the adult world that is available to most adolescents. Adolescents are exposed to new activities which can include driving, drinking, sex and drugs, with potentially devastating results.

While these changes are occurring, families may be faced with other developmental transitions. For example, grandparents are often approaching the age of retirement and old age, and many families experience the death of older family members. This challenges the family in other ways, such as having to deal with health problems and/or increased dependency of the family's elder members.

Meanwhile, parents may be facing individual mid-life transitions. Career and lifestyle changes may also be in question as the implications of the children's departure are considered. Sometimes dealing with the erratic moods and behaviors of the adolescent may provide a welcome distraction from the larger, sometimes overwhelming, changes that family members face. These accompanying changes can lead to additional stress within the family while it is preparing to launch its adolescent.

In our Western culture, one of the main tasks of adolescence is to develop a sense of one's identity apart from the family of origin, attaining independence, yet still remaining connected to one's family (Zilbach, Bergel, & Gass, 1968).[1] Adolescence itself is generally considered as the stage occurring between childhood and adulthood: The adolescent is no longer considered a child, yet is not an adult. This description of adolescence highlights one of the central dilemmas of the stage: There is confusion and ambiguity regarding whether the individual is a child or an adult. Are they "neither/nor" or "both/and" children and adults? In this "in between" state, the adolescent is not accorded the rights and privileges of adulthood, yet is expected to be more responsible and to behave differently from a child. It might be more accurate to consider the adolescent as sometimes a child, sometimes an adult, or some combination of the two, yet always occupying the same body.

Traditionally adolescence was defined by the individual's age, with the beginning marked by the onset of puberty, including dramatic physical maturation and the development of secondary sexual characteristics. The end of adolescence was more formally marked by the adolescent's reaching the "legal" age, graduating high school or entering the workforce as a self-sufficient adult.

However, chronology does not seem to be the determining factor anymore. Young children are trying to grow up faster and are assuming roles of older adolescents, including becoming more concerned with fashion fads like wearing designer jeans and makeup and being "sexy." Conversely, the time that an adolescent remains dependent on the family has also increased. At many levels of our culture demands for specialization and needs for further education have greatly increased the length of time required to complete an education. Thus, the definition of adolescence becomes less dependent on chronological age and more dependent on "meanings" that the individual, family, subculture, and larger social system ascribe to it. It is becoming more apparent that world views of many families "have given way to a more vague and meaningless set of adolescent expectations and affirmations" (Quinn, Newfield, & Protinsky, 1985). This only serves to increase the ambiguity and confusion regarding the definitions and expectations during this stage of development.

RITES OF PASSAGE AND RITUALS

While different views of adolescence exist across cultures, religions and geographical areas, there are also differences within cultures and between families. Different families have different meanings, rules, and behaviors regarding this stage of development. Individual and intergenerational histories and relationships are very important factors in determining a family's view regarding what may be appropriate for the adolescent (Carter & McGoldrick, 1980). Some parents may wish to maintain or discontinue the values and ways with which they were raised. Those wanting maintenance may find that these older values are not suitable in today's world; "what worked for my parents should be good enough for you" often does not work now. Families seeking to change old values may find they have no familiar map for development.

While some recognizable rituals and rites of passage exist for adolescents and their families, very few of them are clear and/or "appropriate." These may include school graduation, driving an automobile, reaching the "drinking age," and having one's first sexual encounter. These are more often equated with later adolescence and early adulthood.

Haley (1973), while discussing the transition of adolescent to adult, commented on the paucity of appropriate rituals at that stage:

> In many cultures, the weaning of children and parents from each other is assisted by a ceremony that defines the child as a newly created adult. These initiation rites give the child a new status and require parents to deal with him differently from that point onward. In middle-class America, there is no such clear demarcation; the culture has no way of announcing that the adolescent is now an individuated adult. (p. 60)

Due to the seeming lack of appropriate rituals at this stage of development, families may create their own rites to facilitate and mark transitions from one stage of development to another (Quinn et al., 1985). A friend once described how his family addressed the adolescence transition: When a child was considered "responsible enough" he or she moved downstairs to the "kids' section" of the house. This transition was marked by a special dinner attended by all family members and by the older children's instructing the new member in the "rules" of their living quarters. This was a desired change for each family member and all children made it.

RITUALS IN THERAPY WITH ADOLESCENTS

When transition and change become difficult and symptoms develop, parents often try "more of the same" (a formerly successful approach) to solve the dilemma. In families seeking treatment, rituals may be lacking or may have become too rigid.

Families who come into therapy with their adolescents are often confused and sometimes angry about their children's behavior, as are the adolescents about their parents' behaviors toward them! Parents may differ with each other about what they should expect of and how they should deal with their adolescent. In addition, often there is an absence of clarity regarding what the roles and expectations are for the adolescent. This may come from discrepant experiences with parents, peer groups, and teachers, as well as messages from the larger cultural influences such as television and advertising.

Families present themselves with some form of symptom, whether it is described as residing within the individual or within a relationship. Whatever the problem, the symptom or pattern can be viewed as a behavioral and contextual ritual that is attempting to lead the family through a transition or prevent it from continuing on its current way (Schwartzman, 1983). It may be an attempted solution to other dilemmas surrounding a life cycle transition. Keeney (1983) described how "this perspective views a symptom as part of the organizational logic of its ecology. . . . The important point, sometimes obscured, is that symptomatic behavior always provides the direction for therapeutic change" (p. 8). The "symptomatic ritual" thus can be viewed as a pattern that "fits" the clients' world by linguistically and contextually restricting participants in their interactions, distinctions and choices. This ritual itself takes on meaning, may need attention, and/or can be viewed as a metaphor for other processes within the social system (Haley, 1980).

When viewing symptomatic patterns as rituals, our work as psychotherapists is to try to understand these rituals within the context of the family system, begin to reflect these understandings to the family, and offer potential new rituals that contain possibilities for altering the symptomatic behavior. The underlying metaphorical qualities of the symptomatic ritual must be respected without our casting blame or pejorative connotations upon them. The therapeutic rituals must also address these other underlying processes within the family system to which the ritual may be connected, either as a solution or as a metaphor.

We have found that therapeutic rituals can be used very effectively in families with adolescents. Most adolescents want to make the transition from child to adult, more clearly marking themselves as independent individuals. They often feel blamed, are angry, and are experiencing excessive confusion about their dilemma. Like many other therapeutic interventions, rituals offer the families clear distinctions, different from what had existed. In addition, most of the adolescents that we have encountered have a good (although sometimes dormant) sense of humor, and the idea of rituals often brings this into play.

In designing rituals, several factors must be considered. Our primary guidelines include (Imber Coppersmith, 1985):

- respecting the values of the family;
- having the ritual "fit" with the family's world view;
- including all members of the "meaningful system."

We attend carefully to that system that has developed around the problem (Anderson, Goolishian, & Winderman, 1986).

CASE EXAMPLES

Case 1: The Walkers—Different Styles of Parenting

Mrs. Walker called us, stating that her daughter was "defiant" and would not listen to her. The family included her husband, 37, and herself, 35, two daughters, Kim, 14, and Debbie, 8, and a son, Mike, 6 (see Figure 1). We requested that all members of the family come, so that we might obtain their views of the situation. At the initial appointment Mr. Walker made it clear that he did not have any difficulties with his daughter. He said that he and Kim were close, and she was just as "sweet" and thoughtful as she had always been. He could not understand his wife's difficulties with her. Kim would always do what he asked of her, and he thought that she was doing fine. The younger daughter agreed with her mother and said that Kim "spites" her mother any time she can and that, while Kim does not refuse to baby-sit for her and her brother, she always puts up a lengthy vocal argument about having to do it.

Kim stated that her mother treats her like a "slave," always asking her to take care of the younger two kids. She resents her mother and feels that she

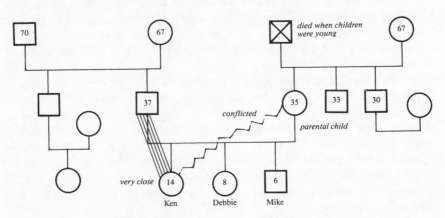

FIGURE 1   The Walker Family

treats her like an infant, but then asks her to be "grown-up" and assume responsibilities appropriate to the oldest child. Kim stated that she can't wait until she is 18, when she will leave home. Mr. Walker did agree that he treats Kim differently from the way his wife does and does not make as many demands of her.

During the first interview Mrs. Walker reported that she was the oldest child from a family of three children. Her father, a factory worker, had died when she was very young, and she and her mother shared the responsibilities for the other two children. Mr. Walker stated he was the youngest of two children. His parents were professionals and he had very few responsibilities at home.

Both parents agreed that Mrs. Walker first started to notice difficulties at about the same time that she had considered going back to work. All of the children were in school then, and she had much more free time than she had ever had before. Mr. Walker did not like the idea of her working, as he felt that she should be available to the children at all times, particularly when they came home from school at the end of the day. When the difficulties with Kim began, Mrs. Walker gave up the idea of returning to work.

During the first meeting the therapists took a short break and discussed in front of the parents the thought that it would be important to find out if the parents could agree that there were some difficulties for family members, even though they might not agree on their extent.[2] The parents did agree that Mrs. Walker was having troubles with Kim, that Kim's grades were starting to drop at school, and that she was not as social as she had been in the past. They also agreed that they both had Kim's best interests at heart.

The parents stated that they had conflicting expectations of her, due to their own different backgrounds. Mr. Walker said he often related to her as a child younger than she was, and thought that it was fine for her to stay young and not grow up so fast. Mrs. Walker thought she should have more responsibilities at home. Kim was confused and just wanted to be more independent.

At this point the therapists wondered if Kim may be "voicing" her father's thoughts and wishes about Mrs. Walker's returning to work. It was not possible for him to more openly disagree with or "forbid" his wife from doing what she wanted. We discussed this with them, and they agreed that father may have had reservations about her going to work. However, he said that he would never stand in her way and had "resigned" himself to her returning.

We thought that it would be best to focus on the issue with which they were all concerned and which they had presented to us: Kim's problems. We considered the dilemma from Kim's perspective as well as the parents': Given the parents' confusion about how to treat her, each having a different model in mind, Kim might feel confused as well. She would hear "act older" from her mother and "be younger" from her father. The problem that the parents faced seemed to mirror their ambivalence and desires regarding their own issues of growing up: Father wanted to be able to act younger with her and mother wanted her to grow up and go to work!

We developed with them a variation of an "odd days/even days" ritual (Selvini Palazzoli, Boscolo, Cecchin, & Prata, 1978). We divided the week into three-day slots. On day one they would treat her as an older daughter, as mother would want her to be; on day two they would treat her as a younger child as her father wanted; and on day three there were no set arrangements as to how to relate to Kim or how she should act.

All liked the idea and Kim agreed to follow her parents' requests on each day and act accordingly.

When the family members came for the next meeting, they reported that they had done the ritual for the first few days and then stopped. Kim stated that she liked doing it a lot. Being with her parents was easier when their expectations for her were clear. However, on "younger days" she missed having the kind of conversations that she had had with her mother when she was treated as an "equal." On "older days" she missed the kind of contact that she had with her brother and sister and the attention that she received from her father. Mr. and Mrs. Walker started to talk more with one another and less through Kim. They "spontaneously" began to discuss the possibility of Mrs. Walker's going back to work and decided on a date. Mr. Walker realized that he had been trying to keep his "baby" a little girl, while Mrs. Walker felt that she was placing Kim in a too adult role, as had happened to her when she was a child. Kim became closer to her sister and during the following summer spent a great deal of time with her. We talked about what aspects of each other's behaviors that they liked and wanted to keep and what they wanted to change.

We met for two more meetings to continue the discussion that they had been having at home, and we met once with just the parents to discuss the issues between them about Mrs. Walker's work. We saw them for a total of six times. A year later, we met once with the parents when they became concerned about possible drug use by their daughter. Mrs. Walker had been working fulltime, 3:00 to 11:00 p.m., and Mr. Walker had been taking care of the three kids while she was at work. They had found a note written by a friend of Kim's about drugs that were being sold at school and the possibility of buying some. They discussed their differences regarding drugs, teenagers, and their daughter, and decided that they would just keep an eye on her and not make a big deal out of the note. We spoke with Mrs. Walker a year later and she said that all was still going well.

Discussion

This case highlights the confusion of roles that many adolescents experience, which in this family was heightened by the parents' disagreement. Until Kim had reached adolescence Mr. and Mrs. Walker's ways of parenting had not been problematic: Their different ways had not been challenged, all the children could be treated like younger children, and there had not been any indication that they should be treated differently. However, as Kim reached adolescence and began to strive for more independence, and Mrs. Walker was considering other changes (going to work), the family's view was challenged. Prior to the introduction of the ritual they had been stuck in an either/or position of mother's or father's view. The ritual allowed them to move to a both/and position. Their solution was not a matter of either mother's or father's way being the correct one, but of the family's finding a new way in which aspects of both mother's and father's ways could be considered useful. They had moved from positions of competition to collaboration.

Prior to therapy the family was at a point of transition, but having difficulties making a shift. Kim was caught in the middle both of the differences between the old ways and the new and of the differences between her mother and her father. The ritual was able to highlight these differences, helping the family make an important developmental transition. Family members were able to determine what old behaviors they wished to carry into the future with them and what they wished to leave behind. This was done without feeling the need to drop all of their prior behaviors while adding new ones to their existing repertoire.

Case 2: The Marks—The Quarter In The Jar

The following case study is an example of how we designed and modified a simple ritual with a family with a 14-year-old boy who was stealing money from other family members. The family was seen for six sessions with a follow-up phone conversation a year later.

The Marks family consisted of the parents, Helen, 38, and Steven, 39, and three children: the identified patient, Jack, 14, his sister, Susan, 12, and an older half-sister, Sarah, 20 (see Figure 2). In the initial phone call the mother reported that she was "scared and nervous" and that there seemed to be a "family mystery": There had been "chunks of money" missing at home and at her workplace. Suspicious of Jack, they had initially confronted him about the missing money and objects, but he denied taking anything. She said that several days ago she and her partner caught Jack stealing money, and he said that he was "glad he was caught."

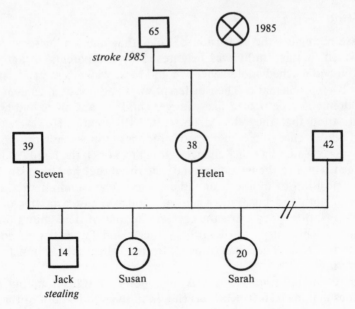

FIGURE 2   The Marks Family—Missing Money

Mother and father both commented that they do not move easily into new situations, such as coming into therapy, and that all family members are "private people" and find it "difficult to talk about things." While they all agreed that money had been missing for approximately two years and that this was a serious problem for them, Mr. Marks reported the step of coming into therapy was very difficult for him. They were "used to taking care of these kinds of problems at home in our own way"; talking with a stranger was very uncomfortable.

The family reported that the stealing began about the same time that Mrs. Marks became involved in a retail business and Mr. Marks started working fulltime. One reason for these changes was that their children were "getting older." They described that summer as a period of many adjustments, including Mr. and Mrs. Marks' not seeing one another very much.

Prior to this change, the family had "OK" ways of communicating with one another, although these were not always in words. They said that they knew one another well and did not always have to be "saying stuff to one another." They agreed that prior to two years ago they "communicated" well with one another in many nonverbal ways.

Sarah reported that she understood what Jack was doing—when she was Jack's age she had sold beer to friends from the back of a store to obtain money and was picked up by the police. Her stepfather attended to the situation and resolved the matter without her having a criminal record.

Both therapists noted that there had been significant changes in the family over the past two years. These included the following: older sister leaving for college; mother beginning a fulltime summer business; father starting to work on a fulltime basis; Jack beginning junior high school; Mrs. Marks' father recently having a stroke; and the death of her mother two months prior to the opening of the retail business. One thought the therapists had was that something might have been metaphorically "taken" from this family, as there were so many losses and transitions. The therapists chose not to comment on this at the time.

After the third session, the family members reported that they had been having "family meetings" at home and that no money had been missing since the beginning of therapy. Once during the week someone discovered that money was missing from a dresser, and the parents immediately thought of Jack. After a brief search of the house, they found the money somewhere else without ever asking him.

We began to think that stealing may possibly be part of a ritualistic communication, either assisting the family in its transition to a new stage of development or attempting to slow it down, indicating that the family may not be ready to make this transition so rapidly. All family members had agreed that it was difficult for them to be "heard" and to make their thoughts and feelings known to each other, and that they were having difficulties "adjusting to all the changes." They were not pleased with the current arrangement because they spent very little time with one another.

We wondered to ourselves whether Jack had become the voice of this discomfort and whether he learned this "signaling mechanism" from his sister Sarah when she had been in trouble before and her stepfather had helped her out. We thought that the family's communication system had been altered when mother and father went to work fulltime and Mrs. Marks' mother died.

Since the family had previously introduced the idea of stealing as some form of communication, we decided that we would introduce stealing in the form of a ritual designed to parallel the problem and fit with the world view of the family system. We said the following to the family:

> We were wondering if it might be useful to all of you if you were to place a quarter in a jar someplace that is obvious to all family members. We would ask all of you to pay close attention to each other and see if anyone, including yourself, is wanting to communicate something to someone else, but having difficulty doing so. If you notice this, take the quarter from the jar! Whoever first notices that the quarter is missing calls a family meeting. You may even want to take turns watching the family and the jar. It would be at this family meeting that you could

discuss anything that you may want to talk about, as you did at other family meetings and as you do here.

The family liked the idea and decided to place the quarter in the jar over the sink in the kitchen, making it obvious, but "hard to steal."

Part of this ritual was based on the idea that the family meeting had been beneficial to all family members and that they felt they had been able to communicate with one another in a different way. It also made everyone equal (each had the same power to "steal" the quarter), provided a different connotation of the stealing, and normalized the stealing. A session was scheduled for a month later.

The next session began with mother stating "the quarter didn't leave the jar!" Father made some jokes about removing it to purchase a stamp, but no one took the quarter. Mother reported that she was tempted to take the quarter, as there was some "increased unpleasantness," as there was before the summer vacation, but decided not to. Both parents reported that there still had been no stealing of any money throughout this time. They stated that when there were miscounts of money at the business mother still thought of Jack.

Mrs. Marks reported that it was hard to know how to use the quarter, and then entered into a lengthy discussion of the losses that they had suffered over the past two years, including her mother's death and her father's stroke. We discussed how the family had addressed these distresses over the past two years, and how the children and parents communicated and signaled one another about their feelings and responses to these losses. Given the depth of this conversation, we began to believe that the losses were central to the stealing and that the family members may have started to find another way of communicating with one another without the overt symptomatic pattern.

The team commented to the family that "signaling" had been somehow important for members of this family. We decided to alter the ritual slightly, hoping to expand its use. We suggested that they use the ritual in "whatever broad way they may like" and that any family members could use it to signal *whatever* they might like to signal. The family members all agreed that this was less confining to them and easier.

Seen three weeks later, the family reported that there had been no stealing incidents during that time, and no need to signal in any way. It was agreed that the meetings had been useful to them and that they would like to continue having meetings on their own. They stated that they are now able to discuss the past more openly with one another and to move on to the future. It was agreed that we would meet again in four months for a "check-up." Mother suggested that they keep the quarter in the jar in the kitchen, so that they would always have a reminder if anyone in the family felt that some signaling needed to be done.

When they returned four months later, father began the session by saying that "the quarter is missing." He said that he had taken the quarter and three days passed before anyone noticed that it was missing. The family discussed how in the past it had been very difficult for each of them to discuss their thoughts and feelings with one another. Mr. Marks said that recently they had begun to find a "close enough distance" and a new balance with one another, similar yet different from the one they had years before. They all felt that they had a much better idea of how they would like to communicate with one another. They were ready to stop coming to therapy. It was agreed by all family members that they wanted to continue to have the quarter in the jar in the kitchen, and that they would actually assign a week to each family member over the next four weeks to watch and signal other family members.

We decided to modify the ritual slightly at this termination point. We agreed with them that this would be a good time to stop and suggested that, while they might keep the quarter in the jar as a reminder, possibly someone could merely say "someone has taken the quarter" and the family would know that someone thinks that something important is not being recognized by the family.

The family was contacted by telephone one year later. Mrs. Marks said that "no one is stealing." Her father had moved in with them and he was doing much better. She had stopped the retail business and had been working for a year at another job with regular hours, allowing her to be home at a "reasonable" hour with the family. Jack worked after school during the past winter and summer to earn money for a trip to France. He was more social and both Mr. and Mrs. Marks had stopped wondering if he would fall back on his old behaviors. She said that Mr. Marks mentioned that since they had been in therapy with us they were more "aware of clues" and "how to watch" in the family. She said that "something's happened for the good," they are all "more aware than before" and we got them through a "tough time." They kept the quarter in the jar until they renovated their kitchen.

Discussion

The ritual was a modification of a pattern of interaction and communication that had developed through a specific behavior (stealing). Prior to the onset of this pattern this family had a smoothly functioning, unstated way of communicating with one another. When they experienced a life cycle transition consisting of a series of losses, including a death, a family member's having a stroke, and one child going off to college, this pattern was altered. Our view was that the stealing was part of a pattern that had developed during this transition in the family life cycle. The symptom was construed as a metaphor for these past and possible future losses—"something being taken" from the family. Since their normal transition had been truncated by their losses, the symptom could be framed as an attempt to help move the family through this difficult transition.

The therapeutic ritual itself introduced a different meaning to the stealing within the system and helped to alter the pattern of communication and interaction within the family. The ritual was similar to the presenting problem, yet different enough from the family's view of the situation to begin to generate a change in the family system. This simple modification allowed the family members to develop a new method of communication that fit their new stage of development, as well as their world view, and to continue their transition. The ritual was introduced with a positive connotation of the stealing behavior which the family had suggested—stealing as a form of communication—altering the blaming nature of the family interaction and freeing the family to make other choices. It also introduced symmetry into a complementary system by giving all members equal opportunities to take the quarter. All voices were equal, giving validity to each one's desires, loss and grief.

Case 3: The Longs—"The Pizza Party" (A Leaving Home Ritual)

The father of the Long family called requesting counseling for his youngest daughter, Dotti, who was 14 and had begun acting in a rebellious manner. He explained that recently she had been cutting classes, socializing with older boys, staying out late, and "hanging around with the wrong crowd." She had also come home intoxicated on at least two occasions. He stated that he and his wife were particularly upset by the drinking. The parents were invited to come in for an initial session with their daughter so the therapist could better understand all of their concerns.

As the family described their concerns about Dotti, there were many references and comparisons made to their oldest daughter, Tina, who was 19 and had been in and out of the home over the past year and a half (see Figure 3). The parents were upset with Tina because she was currently in an "immoral" relationship, living with her boyfriend for the past five months. They had only occasional contact with her by telephone. Her leavings were always preceded by intense conflicts regarding her refusal to obey her parents' wishes. They described Tina as having been a good girl who was particularly close to her father and whose sudden departures after repeatedly refusing to comply with her parents' curfews left them in turmoil. The parents remarked how Dotti's behavior was particularly disturbing in light of the difficulties they had undergone with her sister.

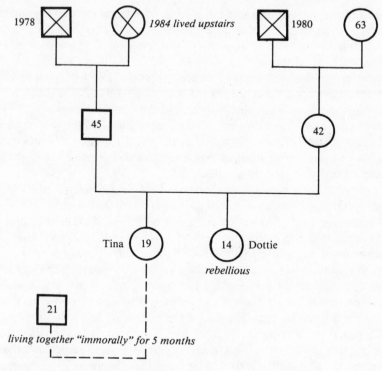

FIGURE 3   The Long Family

The family also reported that they had experienced another loss two years ago, when the paternal grandmother had died. They described their family as "very close" and talked at length about how difficult this loss had been for all family members. The grandmother had lived upstairs from the family and was a part of their day-to-day life. Dotti stated that since her grandmother's death her father had become more "quiet and cranky." She went on to explain that he also started "picking" on Tina and giving her a hard time every time she wanted to go out. Dotti complained that her parents never liked any of her or her sister's friends. The parents retorted that the girls had made bad choices for friends and that "there were many bad influences out there."

They also discussed how they used to do things as a family, like going on picnics, but had not done so lately. They rarely engaged in activities with other families because they "liked to keep to themselves."

Since much of the discussion was focused on Tina, the parents were asked if they would invite her to the next session. They readily agreed. The therapist at this time was wondering if this family might be having difficulties related to the developmental stage of having adolescents and to the prospect of losing a daughter. The therapist was also wondering how Dotti's (and Tina's) behaviors and difficulties might be a way of asking a question: How does one leave this close family?

Tina attended the next session and several others. Discussions focused on the parents' hopes and expectations for their daughters and on plans for the future. This included ideas the parents had for their future when the children were grown up. They expressed the desire to have Tina return home and also discussed the different expectations they had for each of their daughters. Tina was not sure that going home again was a good idea but said she had been considering that possibility.

After several meetings, Tina announced that she had obtained a fulltime job and, after much discussion with her boyfriend, had decided she would not be returning home. Although the parents expressed skepticism and still had concerns that she might not be ready to live independently, they were somewhat more accepting of the idea. After some discussion about what signs would indicate readiness, the idea seemed more palatable. The mother then commented about how hard it had been for her husband to lose his mother and that this may make it more difficult to now also lose his daughter. Dotti at this point suggested that if the parents didn't let go they would lose Tina anyway. The parents agreed and Tina remarked that they would always be their daughters. The father became teary and responded that he just wanted the best for his girls and he knew that they were growing up.

Respecting the difference in tone and understanding, the therapist suggested that a ritual might be considered if the parents were in fact prepared to accept Tina's decision. It seemed to the therapist that it would be important for this family to establish a marker at this point in time if the decision was being made that Tina would be leaving home. When they indicated that they were, partly because they had no choice, it was suggested that the family plan a goodbye party for Tina.

This ritual was suggested with the idea that it might be important to create a different punctuation about leaving home for Tina and this family both in light of the previous failed attempts and because it was particularly hard for this close family to say goodbye. The discussion of the ritual in the room served to punctuate the decision and the actual "event" would formalize, in a positive way, a transition which had been nebulous and painful in the past. The idea was that this leaving could now be different, but not so different as to go against the family's values regarding closeness. In suggesting this ritual the therapist talked about how they had been a close family and how they might remain so. For this reason, the therapist also thought that a home-based ritual made more sense than an in-session one.

Tina said that she wanted her boyfriend to be accepted by the family and feel comfortable visiting them. The parents replied that they always thought that both girls seemed not to like to bring their friends home, and that they would make an effort to have her boyfriend feel more comfortable. The discussion then turned to how to introduce "outsiders" while at the same time not threatening the closeness.

As the discussion continued they liked the idea of a goodbye party more and decided to make it a pizza party, since that was something they had all loved. They also decided to invite only a few close friends and some relatives. The therapist suggested that each family member present Tina with a "small but lasting tribute."

A follow-up meeting was held several weeks later without Tina, who was at friend's bridal shower. Dotti reported that the party was a success. She had given Tina a favorite tape and Tina had given her a blouse that she had asked to borrow in the past. Dotti's mother mentioned that she and her husband gave Tina a necklace and a ring which "had been laying around." The father then modestly remarked that the ring had belonged to his mother.

Dotti also reported that her parents were not on her "case" as much anymore and they had met her boyfriend. Her parents reported that she had invited some of her friends to their home and that her behavior had improved, but that she "had a ways to go."

Discussion

In retrospect it seems significant that in the case (as well as in case 2), as the family was preparing for the departure of the children, other losses contributed to the amount of emotional pain connected to the imminent change. The more child-centered a family is, the more difficult this loss is likely to be. In Dotti's family the emotional charge was compounded by the loss of the paternal grandmother, which occurred at a time when the family was preparing for Tina's departure and Dotti's entry into adolescence. In a family which defined itself as close, losing a grandmother and daughter just as Dotti was beginning to separate may have been too threatening.

The ritual was intended to punctuate Tina's departure as a normal developmental step, separate from other events. It could also be considered a model for Dotti's eventual leaving. The ritual marked this event as different from other leavings: The family gathers, shares food, friendship, gifts and implies continued connectedness. The family can remain close, although in different ways. The gift of the grandmother's ring to Tina seemed to be a significant statement about accepting the loss of the grandmother and passing things on to the next generation. The parents' statement about Dotti having "a ways to go" also signified that she was now recognized as being at a different developmental point than Tina and that the family had time to prepare for her eventual departure. This delineation might also reduce the "stakes" or emotional charge ascribed to Dotti by the family, defining her role as different from Tina's and grandmother's and giving her some time to grow. Having seen Tina's eventual success and knowing that there *is* a way to achieve independence, she may be less "in a hurry" to grow up. She also saw that her parents could change their views.

CONCLUSION

During the stage of adolescence there are numerous issues and transitions taking place which include changes for the entire family. As demonstrated in the above cases, these may include changes in rules and expectations for all family members, as well as different ideas regarding such life stage transitions as careers and losses of both children and grandparents.

Rituals are useful ways of assisting individuals and families make life cycle transitions, providing a different punctuation within their existing situation. Given the paucity of naturally occurring rituals in our culture, therapeutic rituals are a useful technique to help adolescents and their families negotiate these transitions.

As in the cases above, we often view the presenting problem as a ritual in itself, attempting to lead the family members through their transition or to a new solution. Families who come to therapy have often tried their best to solve their dilemma, but often their focus has been only on the symptomatic ritual, which is in itself an attempted, but failed, solution.

Our use of rituals is directed at these two "layers" of the family system: the presenting problem and underlying processes to which the ritual may be connected, as either a solution or a metaphor. This other problem may be a life cycle transition or some other process, with the presenting problem connected to it reflecting an unstated premise or even a direction for a solution.

The first case (the Walker family) demonstrated the use of a therapeutic ritual directed toward both the "disobedient" adolescent and the parental disagreement, which were both connected to the difficulties surrounding a life cycle transition. In the second case (the Marks family) the ritual addressed both the stealing and the underlying issues of loss and transition for all members of the family. Again, in the third case (the Longs), loss and transition were the covert subjects of the ritual.

Rituals are particularly useful with families with adolescents because the rituals can make punctuations and delineations at a time when many changes are occurring, helping to create more clarity in times of confusion and distress. This is evident in the first case, where confusing and conflicting parental messages were separated, allowing the family to develop new possibilities for parenting and relating to one another in different ways. The Marks had experienced several losses over a short period of time and a "stealing" ritual allowed them to address these in their own way. Like the Marks family, the Longs were overwhelmed by their losses, yet separating out the events, behaviors, and people made the changes seem more manageable. In the Long family, confusing messages were also addressed regarding the parents' desires for their daughters to stay or leave home.

It is particularly important to help adolescents be considered in a relationship to their parents different from what they had been in before. Clearly adolescents are not adults, but require some demarcation from their status as children. Rituals involving "growing up" or reversals of too symmetrical or too complementary relationships are useful. In a system that has been in emotional pain and filled with recriminations, a ritual that is acceptable to a family can be enjoyable and can introduce humor and play.

NOTES

[1]When we discuss adolescents and their families and describe the work we do, we are generally referring to white, lower-to-middle-income families who live in a suburban/rural environment. This is not out of any exclusionary prejudice; it just happens that these are the families that live within the area in which we work and who are referred to our institute.

[2]The therapeutic model used in this paper is an expansion of the Milan approach (see Tomm, 1984a, 1984b) developed by Norwegian psychiatrist Tom Andersen (1987) and his colleagues.

REFERENCES

Anderson, T. (1987). The reflecting team: Dialogue and meta-dialogue in clinical work. *Family Process, 26*(4), 415–428.

Anderson, H., Goolishian, H., & Winderman, L. (1986). Problem determined systems: Toward transformation in family therapy. *Journal of Strategic and Systemic Therapies, 5*(4), 1–11.

Breunlin, D. (1983). Therapy in stages: A life cycle view. *Family Therapy Collections, 7*, 1–11.

Carter, B. & McGoldrick, M. (1980). *The family life cycle: A framework for family therapy*. New York: Gardner Press.

Haley, J. (1973). *Uncommon therapy: The psychiatric techniques of Milton Erickson, M.D.* New York: Norton.

Haley, J. (1980). *Leaving home*. New York: McGraw-Hill.

Imber Coppersmith, E. (1985). Families and multiple helpers: A systemic perspective. In D. Campbell & R. Draper (Eds.). *Applications of systemic family therapy: The Milan approach*. London: Academic Press.

Keeney, B. (1983). *The aesthetics of change*. New York: Basic Books.

Quinn, W. H., Newfield, N. A., & Protinsky, H. O. (1985). Rites of passage in families with adolescents. *Family Process, 24*(1), 101–111.

Schwartzman, J. (1983). Family ethnography: A tool for clinicians. In C. J. Falicov (Ed.). *Cultural perspectives in family therapy*. Rockville, MD: Aspen.

Selvini Palazzoli, M., Boscolo, L., Cecchin, G., & Prata, G. (1978). A ritualized prescription in family therapy: Odd days and even days. *Journal of Marriage and Family Counseling, 7*, 3–9.

Tomm, K. (1984a). One perspective on the Milan systemic approach: Part I. Overview of development, theory and practice. *Journal of Marital and Family Therapy, 10*, 113–125.

Tomm, K. (1984b). One perspective on the Milan systemic approach: Part II. Description of session format, interviewing style and interventions. *Journal of Marital and Family Therapy, 10*, 253–271.

Zilbach, J. J., Bergel, E. W., & Gass, C. (1968). The family life cycle: Some developmental considerations. Proceedings of the IVth International Congress of Group Psychotherapy. *Verlag der Weiner Medizinischen Akademie*, Vienna, 157–162.

7

Mazel Tov[1]: The Bar Mitzvah as a Multigenerational Ritual of Change and Continuity

JUDITH DAVIS

THE FAMILY WHOSE first child is entering adolescence is, by definition, beginning to struggle with the issue of "letting go." Most families eventually get through this struggle, some more easily than others.

Jewish families have a natural tool to assist with this letting go; it is the ritual known as "bar mitzvah,"[2] a ceremonial rite of passage evolved over centuries which marks the male child's 13th birthday.

For the most part, the value of this ritual in contemporary Western society has been ignored and unexamined, if not explicitly denied.[3] Despite widespread acknowledgment of the need for ritual (e.g., d'Aquili & Laughlin, 1979; Forssen, 1980; Gelcher, 1983; Haley, 1973; Kimbali, 1960; Quinn, Newfield, & Protinsky, 1985; Schwartzman, 1982; Stevens, 1981) and growing interest in the clinical possibilities of therapeutic rituals (e.g., Culler, 1987; Imber Coppersmith, 1982, 1986; Palazzoli, 1986; Quinn et al., 1985; Tomm, 1984a, 1984b; Wolin & Bennett, 1984), this uniquely tenacious[4] cultural ritual continues to receive little serious attention. With the important exception of Friedman's systemic approach to ceremonies (1980, 1981, 1985), the psychological literature on the bar mitzvah per se is not only scant, but written generally from a psychoanalytic perspective which focuses primarily on the bar mitzvah child (e.g., Arlow, 1951; Zegans & Zegans, 1979) and essentially ignores the ritual's impact on the child's family.

In contrast, the research described here focuses directly on the family system and the relationship between that system and the ritual process. As one whose own son's bar mitzvah had had surprising interpersonal and intergenerational consequences, I began to study the literature on systems change and on classic ritual process. Perhaps my family's experience was not simply idiosyncratic; perhaps there was more to this event than the cynically comic stereotypes and the seemingly universal disregard would suggest. Eventually I became convinced — in theory — of the facilitative relationship between ritual and normative developmental transitions. What I wanted to do was research that would put flesh and blood on the theory. I wanted to see how the process actually worked. It was my hope that by close study of a few nonclinical[5], functioning bar mitzvah families, I would begin to understand more about what was going on below the surface and behind the scenes of the public performance.

In order to explore the premise that the bar mitzvah facilitates developmental change, I observed four families (a "blended" Conservative family, a third-generation Reform family, a Russian immigrant family, and a Hasidic[6] family), over six months during which they planned, participated in, and reflected on their first child's bar mitzvah[7]. I observed family interaction through the use of semi-structured interviews beginning approximately three months prior to the ceremony and ending approximately three months after the ceremony, and through participant observation of the bar mitzvah ceremony/weekend ("researcher-as-guest").

The six-month period was divided into three phases: planning; ceremony/ weekend; and aftermath. These phases theoretically parallel the traditional tripartite ritual process of separation, transition, and incorporation (Van Gennep, 1909/1960), and their associated preliminal, liminal, and postliminal emotional conditions (Turner, 1969, 1982). Phase I focused on decisions and decision-making in preparation for the ceremony and on themes that emerged as central to the family system. Phase II focused on the emotional climate and observed impact of the ceremony. Phase III explored the family's own interpretation of the experience. Throughout the process I was, to paraphrase Tomm (1985), exploring the circular connections between who the families were, what they were doing, and what it all meant to them.

The result of the study was a series of detailed ethnographic portraits that chronologically revealed how each family used the ritual process to negotiate normative developmental change. As a secondary outcome, the portraits and embedded analyses revealed the way in which the researcher, as one coevolving element in the dialogical process of research (Keeney & Morris, 1985, p. 101), "constructed" the findings.

What follows here are brief sketches of these family portraits. Though they highlight the major events and themes, they omit the details, nuances, subplots, and voices of the original work as well as any discussion of the interactive nature of the research. Presented here are the conclusions of the study rather than its life. Such a partial presentation has its dangers. In presenting these excerpts one risks doing a real disservice, both to the richness of the families' experience and to the research.[8]

FAMILY SKETCHES

"The Hospitality Suite"

The Steinbergs,[9] a divorced, second-generation family in which father (Ken) and mother (Stacy) shared custody of their only child, was the first family in the study. After a long separation and a difficult divorce, Ken had remarried. His new wife (Janet) was not Jewish and was feeling very much an outsider in relation to the bar mitzvah. Early in the observed period, she became pregnant. Micah, 12-3/4 years old, alternated monthly between his parents' homes, which were equally involved in planning the event but with dramatic differences. For the single Jewish mother, the bar mitzvah was marking the end of her childrearing years. For the newly married couple, it was marking the beginning of their preparation for a new family. For Micah, the major task was to remain equally loyal to his two families while learning his *haftorah* [prophetic reading the bar mitzvah boy chants] and preparing for the ceremony.

Despite the obvious difficulties, the parents were, from the beginning,

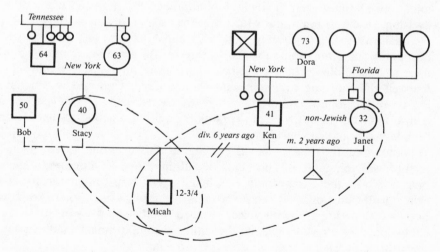

FIGURE 1   The Steinberg Family

determined to make this bar mitzvah a positive experience—no matter how tense the situation might become. One early planning detail illustrates both the inherent tension in the system and the way in which it was repeatedly resolved. As the date of the bar mitzvah was approaching, pressure to send out invitations was mounting. The wording, however, was a problem. From whom was the invitation to come? Stacy's name could not appear without Ken's name and his could not appear without Janet's. ("After all," said Janet, "I'm paying for part of this shindig!") But Stacy was adamant that Ken's new wife's name not appear. ("Micah's my child, not hers. She didn't change his diapers or take care of him when he was sick!")

For weeks the stalemate seemed intractable and quite threatening. It was Stacy, in charge of designing the invitations, who finally came up with the compromise. It was a perfect solution that both Ken and Janet agreed to readily. As it happened, the child's middle name, Lerner, was Stacy's maiden name (which she had never relinquished) and his last name (Steinberg) was Ken's surname. By using the child's full name and beginning the invitation with "The family of Micah Lerner Steinberg fondly invites you to . . . ," the biological parents were named without being named, and the stepmother was neither named nor excluded. It was this kind of delicate balancing among the adults that the family worked so hard to maintain. The wording of the invitation was a creative resolution that not only set the tone for all of the decisions yet to come, but also implicitly informed the guests-to-be of the family's commitment to cooperation and instructed them about supporting that commitment.

The "hospitality suite" was another detail that showed the family's determination. Despite severe financial limitations that determined many other decisions, the decision about which hotel to reserve for out-of-town family was made very differently. The hotel they chose was the one with the best hospitality suite, the room in which all three of the extended families would meet and have dinner on the Friday night before the service, would relax between the morning ceremony and the evening party, and would have brunch on the following morning. Stacy was determined that this space be a comfortable one in which all of the families could be together so that Micah "would not be pulled apart."

Although at the time it seemed as if an inordinate amount of energy and anguish was going into this particular detail, in retrospect it became a metaphor for how the bar mitzvah was being used. Both pragmatically and symbolically, the hospitality suite spoke of this family's intention to keep the bar mitzvah period a "sacred space," a space in which all parts of the system could come together to celebrate the child's accomplishment (and in doing so celebrate the shared accomplishment of the family).

In keeping with this intention, the planning period became one in which the discussion of "hard things" (such as changing visitation schedules, finances, and "adolescent rearing" philosophies) was postponed. It was as if everyone had implicitly agreed to use the time for consolidating and nurturing the system's strengths before tackling the next set of difficult issues that the child's increasing maturity and the subsystems' evolutions were precipitating. In this context, planning for the bar mitzvah became an opportunity for the adults, with their histories of ambivalence regarding both the Jewish religion and their families of origin, to intensify their connections to both. Stacy became increasingly involved with and supported by her Tennessee family (and their "incredible Jewish spirit"). "I've always known," she said, "that this family was meaningful to me but this reinforces it. . . . They love Micah, but it is for *me* (that they are coming)." And Ken's increasing emotional connection to his parents (and their history) was equally apparent. Speaking months later about what he had learned from the experience: "I felt a lot of link between generations. . . . I think a lot of the bar mitzvah for Micah and for me was that, as he grows up, then I need to grow up . . . and part of that is to maintain more history and tradition and ritual."

Not surprisingly, the process became, as well, an opportunity for the child to begin realigning himself both with his parents and with the larger culture of which they and he were a part. As the bar mitzvah date approached, Ken and Micah became visibly closer, sharing "a bar mitzvah secret," shopping together for the bar mitzvah suit, talking about Judaism and about growing up.

By the time the planning period was over and the weekend was upon them, a sense of compromise and accomplishment permeated the system. All three adults had moved closer and were appreciative of each other's efforts. Ken was talking about mutual respect between his ex-wife and new wife, Janet was feeling much more included, and Stacy was acknowledging Ken's generosity and the importance of the process they had been through. "Even if we swallow a lot and get some ulcers out of it, we want it to work. We want it to be nice for Micah. We want the families to have *nachas* [pleasure]."

And *nachas* is what they had. Micah's performance surpassed everyone's expectations and his dramatic sigh of relief at the end of his *haftorah* was echoed throughout the congregation. He had passed the test. "Mazel tov! Mazel tov!" everyone shouted as Micah grinned with pleasure and the president of the congregation came up to "welcome him into the adult community."

The emotional highlight of the event, however, was Ken's speech following his son's ordeal. Barely choking back the tears, Ken presented his son with his deceased father's *tallis* [prayer shawl] and *teffilin* [phylactories] and with his prayer book in which four or five generations of bar mitzvahs had been recorded. As he handed over each item, Ken talked about what his father would have wished for his grandson had he been alive on this day. "What I think he would say is that you should . . . live your life to the fullest . . . and always do what *you* think is right. . . . And what my father gave me above all else was a feeling that I was always loved. That I was always good and the world was a safe place. And if I could give you anything, it would be that." Few eyes were dry when Ken kissed his son and walked off the *bimah* [stage].

The party that night was especially festive, with everyone remarking about how well the family had done, and all going out of their way to be gracious and hospitable. "Bar mitzvahs," said one aunt with whom Stacy hadn't always been close, "bring families together. That's what they're all about." But it was Ken's mother, with her thick Yiddish accent and sparkling eyes, who summed it all up: "The three of them worked it out wonderful. I really mean it. For a divorced couple and a new wife. It really worked out remarkable."

As a way of bringing closure to the successful event (and symbolically celebrating the way in which they had all moved in relation to each other for the good of the system), the three adults (with Micah) planned to meet for dinner together on the Monday following the weekend, after all of the guests had left. This dinner was cancelled and the sacred and celebratory space it was marking abruptly cut short by tragedy. The son of Stacy's man friend, Bob, had been critically injured in a traffic accident in Florida that day and she flew with him to the hospital. By the time Stacy returned five days later, the bar mitzvah had become a thing of the past and there was deep sadness surrounding its loss.

Three months later, Stacy was still mourning the tragedy and the loss of the bar mitzvah's "afterglow," but feeling comforted by the way in which her parents and extended family had rallied around both her and Bob during the trauma. She attributed this support to their having experienced the bar mitzvah together.

In the other household, Ken and Janet were busy moving to a new home and preparing for the birth that was imminent. A suggestion by the researcher that the three-month interview be a joint session (replacing the cancelled dinner) was accepted by Stacy, who still wanted to recapture some of what she had lost, but rejected by Ken and Janet, who were more clearly ready to move on. All had begun tentatively dealing with the difficult child-rearing issues that had been postponed, and it was obvious that a return to the liminal euphoria of the weekend was impossible.

"The Family Project"

The Goldsteins, consisting of mother, Sandy, father, Mark, bar mitzvah boy Seth, and his 10-year-old sister Cindy, were the second family in the study. This was an assimilated, financially comfortable, Reform family with exceptionally clear boundaries around the nuclear system. On Mark's side, this was the first bar mitzvah in many generations. On Sandy's side, only her father had strong feelings about the religious event.

For this family, largely disconnected from the culture's emotional pull, the bar mitzvah was "a family project" and, like all such projects, planned by them "together as a family." Although Sandy was in charge of the details, both parents were equally involved in making the major decisions and the children were appropriately involved in those decisions that affected them directly. Although they worried somewhat about the deficiencies in Seth's Hebrew education and his subsequent ability to learn the *haftorah*, they

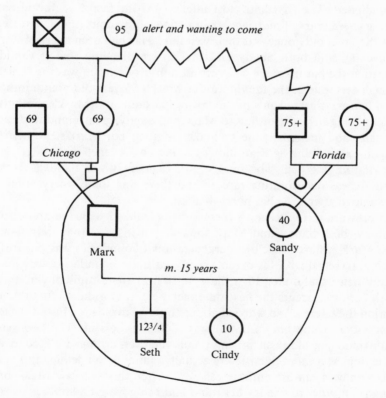

FIGURE 2   The Goldstein Family

were, ultimately, confident that he would do well and that all of the plans they had made with the caterers, the photographers, the florists, and the musicians would go smoothly.

The major focus of planning and excitement was the formal dinner party to be held Saturday night. This was to be attended by the large number of friends they had made and stayed close to over many years. At some level, it was this party rather than the religious ceremony that took on the aura of sacredness. This was the only party to which I was not invited. Even when pressed, they would not allow a researcher into this space. "I'm really sorry," said Sandy, "Mark and I really didn't think you were interested in the party. The service you are welcome to, but we really don't want our guests to be . . . it's just that some parts are private. . . . You can see the video tape."

For this family, the axis of tension during the planning period was not within the nuclear unit but at the level of the grandparents' generation. In addition to the sadness of realizing that their extended families were small and getting smaller as aunts and uncles were aging and dying, three issues predominated: The first and most intense was the fact that during Sandy and Mark's 15 years of marriage, their two sets of parents (living in different states) had met only once—at their wedding! This had been a terribly stressful meeting, and both Sandy and Mark were dreading that it would be repeated at the bar mitzvah. The second source of tension was the fact that, although everyone in the family wanted Mark's 95-year-old grandmother to attend her great-grandson's bar mitzvah, her daughter (Mark's mother) refused to bring her. (According to Mark and Sandy, great-grandmother was physically and mentally able to make the trip, but Mark's mother, they thought, either didn't agree or didn't want to be burdened with the responsibility of bringing her.) The final source of anxiety was Sandy's mother's health. It was deteriorating rapidly and there was some worry about her being able to attend the bar mitzvah at all.

As pressure in reference to these issues escalated with the approaching ceremony, both Sandy and Mark took action in ways that were new for them. Mark, whose sense of intergenerational boundaries was particularly strong, intervened with his parents such that those boundaries were pushed beyond their usual limits. First, he went to his parents and convinced them to visit Sandy's parents the next time they were in Florida, so that the tense situation they were all so worried about could be avoided. This intervention (months before the bar mitzvah) was highly successful. The two sets of grandparents got along surprisingly well and even arranged a second visit. By the time Mark and Sandy were actually planning the details, this source of tension was almost entirely relieved. After this success, Mark began urging his mother to change her mind and bring his grandmother. When it was clear that his appeals were failing, Mark allowed and appreciated his younger brother's uncharacteristic efforts to intervene on his behalf. Although this action did not result in his grandmother's attendance, it did strengthen the bond between the two brothers.

Not only did they become closer to each other but the importance of their children being close to their cousins and to the extended family became increasingly clear. "I think," said Mark after the bar mitzvah, "(that) it did some more to bring the extended family closer together . . . a little bit of a chance for continued family relations. That probably was the biggest thing. The kids got to know a sense of the family outside just the immediate first cousins."

For her part, Sandy visited her parents by herself (three months before the ceremony) for the first time since she had married. Ostensibly, she went to see if her mother's deteriorating health required the hiring of additional help (to insure that she'd be well enough to attend the bar mitzvah). But at another level this visit was an opportunity for Sandy (and her parents) to begin preparing psychologically for the impending shift in caretaking roles that the parents' age and failing health would soon be necessitating. " . . . It was quality time," Sandy reflected, "I spent it with *them*. I didn't go to the pool or visit friends. It was very interesting."

The most significant feature of this family's bar mitzvah ceremony was the fact that the entire nuclear family sat on the *bimah* [stage] throughout the event. Although at first the researcher had interpreted this as a missed opportunity for enacting and facilitating the child's increasing autonomy, it was significant that the parents felt most positive about their decision to take part in the ceremony in this way. "Some people like to watch their son being bar mitzvahed [sic] and not sit behind him. . . . (But) we wanted the whole family . . . (to be together). . . . It made the service warm and people really liked it that way." Upon reflection, it became clear that this arrangement, in effect, had allowed Sandy and Mark to have (vicariously) the bar and bat mitzvah they had missed as adolescents. Having matured in relation to their own parents, they were now symbolically celebrating their own rites of passage. And in doing so, they were simultaneously able to acknowledge and celebrate their son's passage. In addition, this seating arrangement allowed them to symbolically celebrate their boundary as a unit at the same time that they were preparing for the increased permeability of that boundary which their son's growing maturity was requiring.

Not surprisingly, Seth's passage was demonstrated more clearly during the party than during the religious ceremony (in which his *haftorah* had been shortened and thus had presented relatively little challenge). Here Seth surprised everyone with his social skills and capacity as an entertainer. Singing and dancing with the sexy lead singer, the son looked and acted more like a young man than a boy. This was a performance in which he was the sole star (i.e., he wasn't sharing the stage with his parents) and in which he was demonstrating a competence more highly valued in this system than that of *haftorah* reading.

Related to this change, it was significant that at the three-month post bar mitzvah interview, Seth was not present. He had already left for camp and the parents had forgotten to mention it to me when I called to schedule the appointment. It was as if the system had incorporated the son's new distance and was taking it for granted — but not without some regret. "I guess I kind of learned," said Mark, reflecting on the bar mitzvah, "a little bit about my emotions about my kids growing older. How I felt about it. The pluses and minuses. I felt good about seeing them (Cindy had had a part in the service also) become more mature and to a certain extent more self-sufficient. On the other hand, I guess it bothered me a little that they're getting close to leaving the nest." With that, both Mark and Sandy grabbed for their daughter, who was sitting between them on the couch, and Mark laughingly exclaimed, "But we're never letting you go!"

"Baruch Hasham [Thanks be to God]"

The Sheinmans, with their six children and huge interlocking families of origin, were the third family in the study. They were ultra orthodox Hasidim. Both mother, Leah, and father, Yaakov, had come from many generations of Hasidic rabbis, and the couple had been sent to Massachusetts as missionaries by *der Rebbe*, the world leader of the Lubavitcher[10] movement.

For this family, faith in God and belief in Jewish law were absolute and all encompassing. For them, Jewish life and family life were synonymous and completely prescribed by divine decree. Within this law and the world it creates, all roles and rules are prescribed in detail and with great clarity. There is little room for ambiguity about such things as interpersonal boundaries, generational hierarchies, or developmental transitions. Expectations for behavior are explicit, shared both across and through the generations, and reinforced by the enactment of ritual.[11]

All blessings both great and small come directly from God and Hasidim acknowledge this fact constantly. The phrase "baruch hashem," which seems to appear in almost every other sentence of even the youngest speaker, refers not only to their gratitude, but implicitly to their relationship with all that is holy.

Unlike the other families in this study, where the bar mitzvah stands out as one of the few religious rites the family enacts, this was a family for whom the bar mitzvah was only one among thousands of rituals it performs ("a mere blip on a graph," said father, early in the planning process). For Hasidic Jews, there are rites and rituals that structure every aspect of exist-

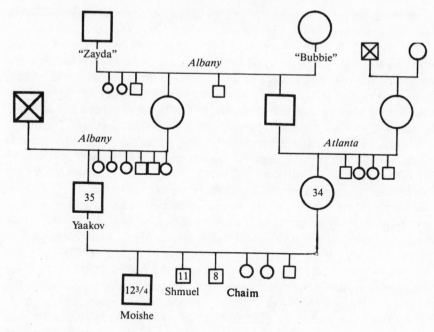

FIGURE 3   The Sheinman Family

ence. Not only do these rituals function to maintain prescribed behaviors, but the behaviors, in turn, maintain the rituals' effectiveness. For Hasidic Jews, ritual is a way of life rather than one aspect of it.

Within this context, the emergence of a first child's adolescence is generally much less stressful than it is within secularized families. Expectations for the child's behavior and the behavior of family and community members in relation to him are clear and uncontested. The rules for his transition into Jewish adulthood are concrete, and the markings of his new status are dramatic and unmistakable. After his bar mitzvah, young Moishe would wear *teffilin* each morning, would be counted as a member of the *minyan* [quorum], would sit at the head table with the men, and would be spiritually responsible for his actions.

Both in terms of emotional focus and effect, the bar mitzvah in the Hasidic family seemed to be different from those in the other families. In secular families, the bar mitzvah essentially announces the fact that the child is "getting ready" to become an adult, i.e., he is becoming a teenager. In secular families, the locus of energy during the preparation period is generally less on the boy's change in status and more on other dynamics in the family's emotional system. But in this family, as in all Hasidic families, the bar mitzvah actually did mark the child's change in terms of his relationship to God, to Jewish law, and to the community. Here the emotional energy wasn't diverted by other issues. The ritual (and preparation for it) worked primarily (though not exclusively) for the celebrant's passage rather than for developmental issues elsewhere in the system. In the Hasidic world, where ritual is so powerful and where there are other rituals for the needs of the other family members at that time, the bar mitzvah ritual seemed to work directly rather than indirectly on the child's change of status. Neither a family crisis in mother's extended family, nor father's difficulty in completing for his son the *pilpul* [Talmudic discourse in Yiddish] that his deceased father had written originally, nor the needs of any of the other children were able to deflect energy from the central purpose of the event.

Once this Hasidic child, whose fundamental beliefs and values were identical to those of his parents and their parents before them, had had his first *aliyah* (i.e., blessed the Torah for the first time in the Rebbe's congregation the day after his 13th birthday), his passage was indisputable. This fact was impressed upon me dramatically as I stood in the family's kitchen a couple of days before the bar mitzvah, chopping vegetables for the luncheon. In the process of stirring some noodles that I was helping him cook for his lunch, Moishe handed me what he quickly realized was the wrong fork. (It was a fork for meat and the pot was dairy—a violation of the dietary prohibition against mixing milk and meat.) Grabbing the fork away from me before I could use it, he apologized profusely and seemed very upset. Trying to comfort him, I joked that it was OK, he wasn't "responsible" yet—since his bar mitzvah was still a couple of days away. I had forgotten that he'd already had his first *aliyah*. "What do you mean?" he asked incredulously, "that I'm not responsible? I'm a bar mitzvah!"

It was during the larger, more public ceremony almost a week after the first Torah blessing that the emotional focus of the transition was able to be shared. Here, as in the first family's bar mitzvah, it was father's speech that brought the congregation to tears. After his son's brilliant performance, which surpassed even his parents' exacting standards ("The whole city was talking about it. All of the connoisseurs [of Torah reading] said they'd never heard a Bar Mitzvah like it!"), Father evoked the memory of his father "standing in heaven" and, with tears streaming into his beard, blessed the entire congregation with the joy of children following in the footsteps of their parents and grandparents. Even in this ceremony, where the primary focus was on the boy's passage, this father, like the father in the first family, was making use of the ritual not only to reinforce the connections between the past and the future, but also to mourn the loss of his father and implicitly the loss of his son's childhood as well.

During the luncheon, it was the dancing that had the most impact. Once the food was eaten and Moishe's recitation completed, the singing began. Before long the men were on their feet circling around Moishe and his great-grandfather, who were dancing together in the middle of the room. The old man, with long beard and stooped shoulders, held hands and danced with his rosy-cheeked great-grandson to celebrate the child's coming of age. The image of the two males so remarkably alike despite the vast difference in age (not only were they dressed identically in black suit, black hat, and white shirt, but they were almost the same height) was visual verification of the connectedness of the generations. And all of the black-suited men dancing around them, with little boys on their shoulders and babies in their arms, were celebrating and reinforcing those connections. (It was a scene out of a Sholom Aleichem story. I could hardly believe my good fortune at having stumbled on to this family. I felt as though I'd accidentally discovered a civilization thought to be extinct.)

Immediately after the bar mitzvah, the family had moved on to ritual preparations for the next Jewish holiday, and by the time of the follow-up interview three months later they were already talking about plans for their second son's bar mitzvah. When I asked them about the significance of Moishe's bar mitzvah, talk returned to intergenerational connections. After acknowledging that, of course, the bar mitzvah had been most significant for the child, father talked about his great-grandparents. He told a story about how they had come to this country afraid that they would not be able to raise their children as real Jews. "For my grandmother to see her great grandchild raised precisely as her brothers had been raised . . . for her to see this, she'd say there is nothing more she can ask out of life than to be able to see what she's seen."

"Grow up (and Accomplish), But Stay Close"

The Gordovskys were the last of the research families. This was a single-parent Russian immigrant family in which the child's *bris* [circumcision] in Russia had been held in secret. The mother, Lena, had divorced the boy's father, Felix, shortly after emigrating to America, almost seven years earlier, and with the help of her parents, who had emigrated with her and who lived around the corner, raised the child, David, without much assistance from the father. Shortly before the planning period, Felix married a woman who was not Jewish, further weakening his already attenuated relationship with his son.

Although the grandparents lived in a separate household, the three generations composed one emotional unit with complex and confusing roles. Often the grandparents functioned as parents to both Lena and David, who interacted as siblings. Although these multiple roles may be more the norm

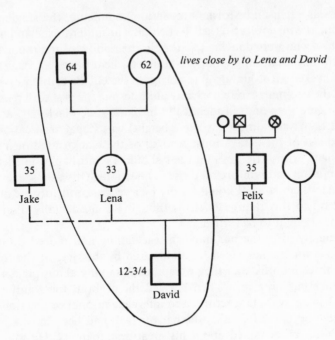

lives close by to Lena and David

FIGURE 4   The Gordovsky Family

in Russian culture, and more functional than dysfunctional in single-parent systems (Wood & Talmon, 1983), there was in this family a great deal of multigenerational ambivalence about both mother's and son's growing up. At times Lena was clearly in charge of David, who often clung to her childishly, but at other times the roles reversed and the son acted like Lena's parent, aligning himself with grandmother to chide or protect his mother. David could not tolerate his mother's involvement with other men and she (a young and strikingly beautiful woman) was not able to act on her needs in this regard. Lena and David's confusion was fueled and amplified by the grandparents, who on one hand told mother and son to be less dependent on them and on each other, and on the other hand acted in ways that denied the possibility of such independence. As the bar mitzvah, the symbol of the boy's impending change, approached, the confused messages that both pressured the system towards movement and kept movement from happening intensified. As David got older (and closer to becoming "a man"), his clinging and Lena's allowing that clinging became less and less acceptable but more and more pronounced.

But if the system was unclear about growing up, it was absolutely clear about both its Jewish identity and about the value of accomplishment and performance. Both in Russia and in America, the family acted to maintain the threads of its Jewish heritage. In Russia, the underground *bris* and the application for a visa (because "what Jews can do was limited in Russia") were two dramatic statements. In America the child was immediately enrolled in a Jewish day school ("to give him the opportunity that I didn't have [to be a knowledgeable Jew]").

That opportunity worked. Not only had David become the most knowledgeable in the family about Jewish culture and religion, but the tradition had become, it seemed, even more important to him than to his mother and grandparents. His desire to be a *Cohen* [of the priestly lineage] like his mother's father was an expression of his identification not only with his grandfather, but also with the Jewish tradition that the family was reclaiming through him.

Both in Russia and in America, the family's valuing of hard work, achievement, and public performance was equally clear. Grandfather's history on the Yiddish stage, both grandparents' intellectual achievements, and mother's striving for a second master's degree were all expressions of this value. The child was expected not only to shine at his bar mitzvah, but also to perform flawlessly at a piano recital a few days earlier and to win a trophy at a karate tournament a day after it.

In contrast to the clandestine *bris*, the bar mitzvah was a very public and momentous occasion. For many in the congregation who had emigrated from the same small town in Russia, this event was a milestone. It was the first bar mitzvah they had ever seen and, for the father, grandfather, and the uncles called to the Torah, it was the first time in their lives that they'd had an *aliyah* [the honor of being called up to bless the Torah]. In a sense this was their bar mitzvah as well as David's.

When it was David's turn to recite the blessing and to chant the *haftorah*, the congregation became silent and completely attentive. David's voice rang out sweetly and unhesitantly. Unlike the previous generations, he had become a literate Jew. Among the women, there was an audible sigh of admiration and everyone was nodding approval. David was "doing good." When it was over, the congregation burst into singing the traditional song of Mazel tov and congratulations.

Once the Torah had been returned to the ark, it was time for the rabbi's sermon. In the absence of an involved father, it was he who drew the connections between the generations and whose speech provided the emotional highlight of the event. Speaking to the extended Russian family and community, the rabbi emphasized the "miracle" of this child's bar mitzvah in America and its meaning in relation to the future of Jewish survival. He reminded everyone of how close they had come in Russia to having lost their culture completely and warned of how easily they could be misled into following the American dream of materialism if they forgot their past and its Jewish values. "David and his family and friends here today are living testimony to the durability of the Jews and the fact that we must not be kept in countries that deprive us of our religious freedom. . . . David, you are here to teach us a lesson. You are here to lead those who came out of the Soviet Union and the future generations who come from them."

The rabbi then turned to the immediate family and spoke in Yiddish. His words were simple words of blessing and congratulations, but their analogic message was profound. In English, he had appealed to the family's intellect and made explicit the international and intergenerational significance of the event. In Yiddish, the language of exile, the rabbi appealed to their hearts.

At the party that night, family and friends reinforced the rabbi's meaning with toasts in Russian that affirmed the importance of the event in all of their lives. Grandfather, for instance, emphasized the uniqueness of his love and went on to talk about his pride in David and the pleasure he'd given him. An old and close friend of the family also made a toast. He told David to "remember this day forever. All the love that is gathered around you on this day of your bar mitzvah and the bar mitzvah itself will give you power. Never forget this day." This speech, by emphasizing the effect of the ritual, reinforced the rabbi's sermon.

The last toast was made by David. Standing on a chair, wine glass held high, David spoke easily, maturely, and extemporaneously to his guests. "I want to thank you all for coming to my bar mitzvah. Especially I want to thank that lady over there (pointing to his mother on the far side of the room). If not for her I would never have had this bar mitzvah and this wonderful party. If not for her, I would never have come to America. If not for her I would never have been born. And also that lady and that man, my grandparents, for helping me so much. And I want to thank my best friend for coming from New Jersey. He has been my best friend since I came to America. I hope I can go to his bar mitzvah next year and that his will be as good as mine." He then added a comic note that spoke precisely to the ambivalence of his development. He ended his speech by turning to his mother and asking if he could stay up past his prearranged bedtime. Everyone laughed as the young man became a little boy again, and the party continued.

Although the feelings of connectedness and accomplishment following the bar mitzvah were intense, they ended abruptly shortly after the weekend when grandmother disclosed a secret she had been keeping from the family. A few weeks prior to the ceremony, she had discovered a potential cancer. Not wanting to "ruin" the bar mitzvah, she did not tell anyone. Fortunately, only minor surgery was ultimately required, but by the time of the three-month interview the bar mitzvah was a thing of the past.

The confusion in roles and expectations, however, was not. Even though Lena was advancing in her career and going on an out-of-town work assignment, and David was going off on a vacation with his father, the developmental issues of moving up and out in this family were still problematic. At this point they were being expressed not only through Lena's ambivalent relationship with her man friend and the conflictual relationship between him and her son, but also through considerable worry on everyone's part about David's upcoming transition from the shelter of the Jewish day school to the "wild world" of public junior high school. "We are afraid," said grandfather, "this changing for him."

HIGHLIGHTS OF THE DEVELOPMENTAL WORK FACILITATED BY THE PROCESS

Four families in western Massachusetts, each planning the bar mitzvah of their first child, were studied. In terms of membership, structure, history, stressors, and level of religious identification, they could hardly have been more different from each other. But from a developmental point of view, these families were all at a very similar "stage" in the life cycle and all were "using" the ritual according to their idiosyncratic needs. For the Steinbergs, it was the adjustment of interpersonal boundaries. For the Goldsteins, it was the adjustment of intergenerational boundaries. For the Hasidic family, it was the anachronistic "transformation" of the child into an adult. And for the Gordovskys, it intensified both cultural connections and the pressure for developmental change.

In general, however, the circular pattern of movement was similar across all of the systems. The child's development, marked by and heightened through the bar mitzvah, pressured for change in the adult subsystem. These changes in turn encouraged further change in the child (which theoretically will pressure for more change, etc.).

Through the bar mitzvah process, Stacy, Ken, and Janet, the three adults in the first family, realigned themselves in relation to each other and to their extended families and so facilitated the child's increasing autonomy and connectedness. During the planning phase and the ceremony, the divorced parents temporarily became closer so that their son would not have to choose between them. This temporary partnership enabled the biological parents to culminate and celebrate the success of their shared custody arrangement and thus "complete" an unclear and protracted divorce process.

Stacy used the process successfully to move closer to and become engaged with her large, extended family. This move potentiated an eventual letting go of her son. For Ken, the bar mitzvah enabled him not only to mourn the loss of his father and the loss of his son's childhood, but, in effect, to ensure the

connection between his son and his father (i.e., his Jewish past) such that
he, also, could begin letting Micah go. That his son be connected to his
Jewish past was especially important to this father, whose new family's
Jewish identity was not at all assured. For Micah, the process intensified his
identification with his father and his culture, while at the same time allowing
him to demonstrate his increasing competence and movement towards greater independence.

Through the bar mitzvah, the parents in the Goldstein family adjusted
the boundaries between themselves and their parents, ultimately enabling
the adjustment of the boundary around their nuclear system such that their
son's movement beyond that boundary became possible. During the preparation period, both Mark and Sandy pushed the hierarchical boundaries
between themselves and their parents, demonstrating *their* increased maturity. Seated on stage, they confirmed their development by vicariously celebrating the bar and bat mitzvahs they had never had. Seated in this way and
in this place, the family was reinforcing the boundary around itself while
simultaneously allowing that boundary to become more permeable.
Through the party, son Seth demonstrated his surprising competence and
readiness to move beyond previous limits.

In the Hasidic family, so "culturally determined" (Quinn et al., 1985, p.
102), the ritual transformed the child into an adult in terms of religious
practice. Secondarily, the event, which was attended by both observant and
secular Jews, reinforced the family's positive sense of themselves and their
world view. In addition, it allowed Yaakov to mourn the loss of his father
and in the process further differentiate from him. Even if this opportunity
had not been taken, however, the ritual's power in this family's context was
so strong that nothing could have interfered with the achievement of the bar
mitzvah's central purpose.

For the Gordovsky family, the process intensified pressure for Lena and
David to change. Both the child's clinging and mother's staying close were
becoming increasingly inappropriate, and the paradoxical messages, increasing in frequency and intensity, were pressuring the entire system. In
addition, the event affirmed the larger significance of the family's immigra-
tion and strengthened the connection between its Jewish past and future.
Through the process, the family demonstrated its success and the importance of its achievement in America, and the child demonstrated his ability
to excel in spite of the system's confused messages about that ability. In light
of the event's enlarged significance, this demonstration becomes more significant also. Through it, the child, undeniably the family's most knowledgeable Jew, becomes the family's leader in reference to the Jewish culture
towards which they are moving. This leadership role creates further impetus
for his increasing maturity.

ON DRAWING CONCLUSIONS

The following conclusions come with no claim to universal truth or scientific validity. Instead, they are presented as the result of an intuitive exploration of highly impressionistic data, more like explicating a poem than performing a scientific experiment.

Metaphorically, the four families were much like poems that the researcher read and tried to understand. The portraits that resulted from the process of fragmenting and regrouping the pieces of each poem (words, images, feelings, etc.) reflect the researcher-as-reader's analysis of that poem in the context of all of the poems. Extending the metaphor, the conclusions drawn from this process were drawn as if the four individual poems had become the stanzas of one larger piece, and the connections within each stanza were related to the connections in all of the others. The "truth" or validity of the conclusions, therefore, is more like the truth derived from poetry than the truth derived from mathematical calculations. Although stated as facts, they are to be read as hypotheses, which, by definition, are constantly evolving.[12]

CONCLUSIONS

1. THE BAR MITZVAH FACILITATES DEVELOPMENTAL CHANGE. Families who choose to mark their first child's 13th birthday with a bar mitzvah "use" the process to *negotiate change in emotional boundaries* within the nuclear system and between that system and its larger context. For the most part, this use is neither explicit nor conscious but a natural consequence of the biological clock's pressure for change and the ritual's classic function of easing transition.

The emergence of the first child's adolescence challenges the system to *change its balance between autonomy and coherence appropriately*. As a ritual of initiation, the bar mitzvah works precisely by increasing the celebrant's *distance* from his parents/family while at the same time increasing his sense of *connectedness* to the larger system of which they and he are a part.

2. THE BAR MITZVAH EFFECTS DEVELOPMENTAL CHANGE DIFFERENTLY IN EACH FAMILY. The bar mitzvah differs in ways that reflect the family's makeup, dynamics, and history.[13] Each family approaches the nodal event with a different set of resources and needs, which determine how the bar mitzvah will look and feel and where in the system the process will have its major impact. Although the "ultimate" outcome is the adolescent's increased autonomy and sense of connectedness, the process differs for each family.

Like all rituals, the bar mitzvah has both *closed and open parts*. In addition to its rigidly defined features, it permits each family to bring to the process its own interpretation and nuance. It can highlight, add, subtract, or modify elements of the performance such that it reflects the family's shape and speaks to its needs.

Although some of these "modifications" are conscious and deliberate, much of the process is out of the family's awareness. It is "simply" how they do what is important to them. For the Goldsteins, the decision to sit together on the stage was a deliberate modification of the traditional performance, but the *idea* of the event as a family project speaks to a different level of shaping. Similarly, for the Steinbergs, Ken's decision to present his son with his father's relics was a deliberate adaptation of the symbolic passing on of the *sacra* [sacred objects or secrets], but at another level it reflects a shaping of father's need to mourn.

3. THE PROCESS BEGINS AND CONTINUES FOR MONTHS BEFORE AND AFTER THE PUBLIC CEREMONY. This phenomenon reflects the fact that *ritual process operates at multiple levels simultaneously*. At one level, ritual participants are in the liminal, transformative stage of the tripartite process only during the public ceremony. At a higher logical level, however, the liminal period encompasses preparation and reintegration as well as performance. At this level, ritual participants are in the liminal state and open to the transformative power of the process long before and long after the actual ceremony.

What is happening in the liminal ceremony is also happening (more diffusely and most subtly) in the pre- and postliminal periods as well. Not just during the ceremony but during the entire extended process, the bar mitzvah operates to synchronize individual and group action through the stimulation of affect and intensity in the context of a safe structure. (This expands Friedman's eloquent notion that "the rite of passage is the year surrounding the event that celebrates it," and that this entire period constitutes "hinges of time" [1980, p. 430] in which the ritual family is most open to change.)

4. IN THE CONTEXT OF THESE MULTIPLE LEVELS, IT IS DURING THE PLANNING PERIOD THAT MUCH OF THE DEVELOPMENTAL WORK IS BEGUN. Because transitional periods require substantive change in families, and because bar mitzvah families are already in the liminal, transitional state as they plan the ritual, it is clear that their actions during this planning period are significant. In this period, the liminal family is "betwixt and between" (Turner, 1982, p. 28), no longer dealing with a child but not yet dealing with someone who has demonstrated his "readiness" (Van Gennep, 1909/1960) to become an adult. It is dealing with someone labeled a "bar mitzvah boy" (Garfiel, 1958, p. 170), a title which (if not itself oxymoronic) accurately captures the paradoxical nature of the age.

It is during this period that the "sacred space" which will cushion and protect the participants' journey begins to be created. The family begins to think of itself as special, to be treated as special, to focus increasingly on the future event, and to actively prevent "defiling" issues or conflicts (e.g., a divorce in the extended family, a medical problem, scheduling changes) from disrupting their concentration or diminishing the likelihood of the event's success.

It is during this planning period that the logistical and emotional pressures build exponentially. As the event approaches, the system increasingly takes on the characteristics of the cybernetic sweatbox (Hoffman, 1981), in which the accumulation of dissonance pressures for a discontinuous leap to a more functional organization. The ritual process (like therapy) heats up the emotional issues inherent in the system and this intensification potentiates the system's transformation.

Preparation for the ritual is part of the ritual itself. It is primarily the parents' part of the ordeal in which they are tested by themselves as well as others. By focusing on the details that are important or difficult for them (e.g., wording of the invitation, seating arrangements, hotel accommodations), the family manages not only the event but also the emotional pressures the event precipitates and brings to the surface. This connection between logistical and emotional tasks explains to some extent the seemingly disproportionate amount of energy that often goes into the planning effort or the seemingly irrational anxiety that often accompanies it. During the planning period the analogic components of the logistical decisions act metaphorically to begin the synchronizing process and prepare the ritual participants for the dramatically emotional process of the symbolic performance.

Even before the first guest arrives, the family has begun to activate connections to past generations, to feel strengthened by those who have demonstrated support, and to feel pride in what they and the child have already been able to do.

5. THE BAR MITZVAH CEREMONY IS THE FAMILY'S PUBLIC STATEMENT OF ITS PRIVATE PROCESS. It is the family's symbolic drama that proclaims, culminates, and amplifies what has already happened and prepares the way for what is yet to come. The drama's "plot" centers on the boy's simultaneous movement away from his parents and towards the larger community. The "subplot" involves the movement of all other principals in relation to the protagonist's journey. The guests, as audience, congregate to acknowledge the movement of the actors, celebrate it, and reinforce it. The effect of this experience is one in which the actors and the audience become joined in a communal feeling of pleasure and satisfaction (Turner's [1969] *communitas*).

Through the use of condensed, multivocal symbols reinforced by the rhythmic stimulation of chants, processionals, oaths, incantations, etc., the drama arouses emotion and conveys messages analogically that cannot be conveyed discursively. In the "hyper affective state" (Wolin & Bennett, 1984, p. 41) induced by this performance, the family's idiosyncratic tensions and conflicts temporarily give way to an overwhelming sense of supportiveness and cooperation. The family's crisis is "brought in to the street" and "the community gathers to mediate, nourish, and absorb" (Slater, 1974, p. 36).

At the micro level, this condensed drama metaphorically recapitulates the more subtle tripartite rite of passage through which the family moves gradually over time. In "scene one," the preliminary prayers set the tone and reinforce the sense of difference between normal everyday action and the special ritual action about to begin. This "corresponds" to the family's growing sense of the difference between its past and its future. In the second scene, the level of affect is heightened and the initiate is called up to accomplish the transforming act. This is the "transcendent synthesis" (Hoffman, 1981), where the family responds to the increasing dislocation between old patterns and new needs by adjusting boundaries and changing patterns that maintain them. In the third and final scene, the level of affect is reduced, as the witnesses confirm and celebrate the initiate's new status and prepare to integrate him into the day-to-day world they are all about to reenter.

6. THE DEVELOPMENTAL WORK BEGUN IN THE TWO EARLIER STAGES OF THE PROCESS CONTINUES DURING THE PERIOD FOLLOWING THE CEREMONY. *Ritual works magically but it does not work magic.* Although ritual resolves existential paradox at a mythic or metaphorical level, it does not provide resolution at the concrete, pragmatic level. *Instead, it helps identify, reinforce, and activate the family's natural ability to work out the practical and emotional solutions over time.*

During the period following the ceremony/weekend, the family is in the process of integrating and assimilating the pragmatic and emotional work of the planning period and the symbolic affect of the ceremonial performance. As ritual participants, the family members are in the process of returning to the profane and ordinary world they had temporarily left. As a cybernetic entity, the family is seeking to reorganize itself at a new level of coherence (Dell, 1982), one which accounts for the perturbations it has just experienced and better meets the demands of its changing field (Hoffman, 1981).

How the family adjusts and what use it makes of the experience depends in large measure on how it "understands" the meaning of what happened (Bogdan, 1984; Quinn et al., 1985). With the exception of the ritually observant families for whom the meaning is highly prescribed, most families "create" the meaning they attach to the experience, a meaning idiosyncratic to each family and generally outside of its awareness. This "meaning" is expressed indirectly in terms of altered emotions, behavioral patterns, self-image, etc.

While on one level the family is sinking back into postliminal normality and allowing the effect of the experience to "sink in," at a higher level the family is still very much in the liminal state of the larger process. In this state, the ceremonial event (and all that led up to it) is experienced as simply more pressure for change in a system that is still in the sweatbox prior to its discontinuous leap (Hoffman, 1981). At this level, the family's continuing struggle with the paradoxical demands of the adolescent's development, as well as its own seemingly regressive behavior, is to be expected (e.g., the Steinbergs' refusal to meet jointly, the Goldsteins' holding on to their daughter, the Gordovskys' ambivalence).

Despite the public proclamations and elaborate performance, the boy is *not* a man and the family members' relationship to him, to each other, and to the larger context is not one of total harmony and clarity. Instead, relationships in the post-ceremonial family are continuing to evolve as small changes begun earlier in the process continue to reverberate through the system over time.

7. THE BAR MITZVAH RITUAL SPEAKS DIRECTLY TO THE DEVELOPMENTAL TASKS OF THE CONTEMPORARY FAMILY WHOSE FIRST CHILD IS BECOMING AN ADOLESCENT. It is a rite of transition perfectly suited to a transitional age in a transitional society. Given the problems associated with the invisibility of the transition into adolescence (McGoldrick & Carter, 1982) in a contemporary culture profoundly confused about how to deal with this stage of life (Elkind, 1981), the bar mitzvah provides for visibility and clarity. It is a dramatic marker that makes change visible, a pacing mechanism that regulates its speed, and an instructional device that attaches positive meaning to the change.

Expressed in terms of the family's primary developmental tasks (Culler, 1987), the ritual promotes the child's autonomy, allows him and his parents to deal with the emotional impact of the separation inherent in the increased autonomy, and allows the parents to begin to focus increasingly on themselves and on their relationship to their own parents. It is a ritual that facilitates the "intercogwheeled tasks" (Golan, 1981, p. 6) of the multigenerational system in the early phase of its middle years, a rite of passage for the entire family.

More specifically, in terms of the *adolescent's needs*, the ritual provides a format in which the child is given a way to show his "readiness" to be treated differently, the parents are given a way both to help him demonstrate this readiness and to mourn the loss it implies, and the rest of the extended family is given a way to support the child and his parents in their new relationship to each other.

Through his "trial by recitation" (Arlow, 1951, p. 358), the child emerges from the "isolation" of study, accepts the frightening challenge of the public ordeal, successfully passes the test, and is embraced by "a loving audience." In the center of the stage and at the center of the family, the child demonstrates his competence and feels his "specialness" and his "power" (Zegans & Zegans, 1979, p. 123). Through this modern version of the "rite in the bushes," the child announces that he is changing and demonstrates that the change is positive. Through this demonstration and the response it evokes from all who are significant to him, the child gains strength for future private ordeals of change.

One source of this strength that has not been mentioned specifically, but of course is obvious, has to do with male bonding. Having successfully endured the "exact same" trial endured by his father and his fathers before him, the bar mitzvah boy claims his place among the males of the tribe; he is ready to be and "deserves" to be identified with his father and grandfather in a way that was not possible before. Similarly, having guided his son through the ordeal that he remembers vividly and having passed on to him the sacra of his past (e.g., Ken with his father's ritual objects and the Hasidic father with his father's blessing), the bar mitzvah father feels closer not only to his son but to his own father as well. The youngest male has been identified as "a man" and in the process the ties among all of the men in the family are strengthened. Although this bonding aspect of the bar mitzvah is most apparent in the Hasidic family, where gender distinctions are reinforced physically and philosophically, it is visible in all cases. (Even in the Russian family where the father played no significant role, the rabbi became the surrogate father and drew the identifying connections between the male generations past and future. Likewise, in the Reform family, where neither father nor grandfather had had a bar mitzvah, the child identified with the male elders by demonstrating his competence as host, a competence both his father and his grandfather were proud to possess.)[14]

8. THE BAR MITZVAH IS A NATURAL COPING MECHANISM FOR FAMILIES FACING THE NORMATIVE CRISES OF ADOLESCENT TRANSITION IN THAT IT POTENTIATES INTERNAL RESOURCES. Just as the child beginning the first of his teenage years with this affirming public event gains strength for the struggles ahead, so too does the family as a whole benefit. Through the private performance (in which the parents, in particular, demonstrate unprecedented maturity and competence, and in which they negotiate changes not only in relation to the child but in relation to themselves and their parents as well), and through the public performance (in which they are literally surrounded by the good will and support of family and friends in a state of trance-like *communitas*), they discover and reinforce resources in both themselves and in their extended systems.

For the family preparing to enter the uncharted (and frightening) territory of the teenage years, this consolidation of strength is natural and timely. It is a way for the family to "take care of itself," which, according to Ackerman (1980, p. 148) is "the best thing it can do for the adolescent" within it. For example, the approval and acceptance of Stacy's Tennessee relatives prepare her for decreased involvement in and support from a nuclear family; feeling and acknowledging their success as childrearing partners prepares the divorced Steinbergs for childrearing changes; maturing in relation to their parents prepares the Reform couple, Sandy and Mark, for the increased maturity of their son and the increased dependency of their parents; publicly affirming a way of life that is often challenged prepares the Hasidic family for the next generation's continuation of that way of life; and enlarging the significance of David's accomplishment prepares the Russian family for his future accomplishments.

9. IT IS THE PARADOXICAL NATURE OF THE BAR MITZVAH THAT ALLOWS FOR ITS POWER TO FACILITATE DEVELOPMENTAL CHANGE. Like all transition rituals, the bar mitzvah resolves existential crises paradoxically. Through its capacity for keeping logical levels both separate and interacting at the same time, the bar mitzvah is able to address the multileveled system's simultaneous need for individuation and connectedness.

The ritual speaks analogically to the basic paradoxical tensions involved in maintaining the health of the family over time. It is both a ritual of transition and a ritual of continuity. In the context of the family, it is a ritual of elevation (i.e., transition), and in the context of the larger system, a ritual of consecration (i.e., continuity). It helps the child's movement away from the nuclear family at the same time that it binds him closer to that family through its larger past; it is a vehicle for separating the parents from the child while simultaneously moving them closer to each other and to their own parents; it celebrates the child's movement while mourning his loss; it strengthens boundaries while making them more flexible.

10. TO THE EXTENT THAT THE FAMILY IS DISCONNECTED FROM ITS CULTURE AND THE MEANING OF ITS RITES AND SYMBOLS, THE FAMILY MODIFIES THOSE RITES AND SYMBOLS, ADDS NEW ONES, AND GENERALLY MAKES THE MEANINGS MORE EXPLICIT. Although I had expected that the effectiveness of the ritual's power to facilitate developmental transformation would be highly correlated to the family's level of connectedness to the tradition and its symbols, such a conclusion could not be drawn from this study.

Although there was no doubt about the ritual's transformative power in the ultra orthodox family, there was no corresponding clarity about the ritual's *lack* of power in the families only marginally connected to their cultural past. Indeed, there was considerable evidence of developmental movement even in the Reform family, the family most emotionally cut off from its religious and cultural past.

What could be observed in this regard, however, was the way in which the families variously disconnected from the original meaning of the rites and symbols tended to modify or add to the ritual in order to enhance its ability to stimulate affect. In those families whose emotional connections to the rites and symbols of the performance were tenuous, new rites were added, old symbols were given more tangible expression, and their meanings were made more explicit. For example, the Steinbergs physically passed the Torah from the grandparents to the parents, and then to the child, and the father literally handed his father's sacred objects to his son. Both the Conservative and the Reform families added a candle lighting ceremony to the party and with it bestowed birthday honors all could readily understand. And for the Russian family, it took the rabbi's explanation for the international and intergenerational significance of David's public accomplishment to be fully understood.

Such innovations allow cultural rituals to change as the participants' relationship to the culture changes. To the extent that the families who needed the innovations included them in their performance, the ritual had affective power and transformative potential.

SUMMARY OF THE PROCESS

To summarize most simply the way in which the bar mitzvah works to facilitate developmental change: The first child's emerging adolescence sends the family into disequilibrium. The tensions mount, old patterns don't work and the family is forced into a new, more functional pattern of organization. The bar mitzvah facilitates this reorganization by both intensifying the stress in the system *and* providing a way to deal with the stress.

Preparation for the bar mitzvah adds a layer of pragmatic stress "on top of" the family's emotional layer of developmental stress. These two layers are connected. The logistical details that emerge as difficult or important reflect those emotional issues that are difficult or important in the family and serve to focus and channel the family's emotional energy.

During the ceremony, the family reinforces and amplifies the emotional work it had begun in the preparation stage by enacting a highly charged, condensed drama that, in effect, publicly proclaims that it has done the work—that the child has begun maturing and is ready for increased responsibilities and privileges, and that the parents are ready to give them to him (and are ready for all of the changes this implies for themselves). This proclamation is heard and reinforced by all who are important to the family.

No matter what else happens afterwards, the family has made the statement. Not only is it more difficult to "go back on" a public statement, but to some extent the very act of stating the change begins the change process (Madanes, 1986). No matter how childishly the boy acts or is treated in the future and no matter what other work the family still needs to do, the boy and his family did accomplish a feat and it was publicly acknowledged. That fact and its repercussions become part of the family's reality, part of how it understands itself.

THERAPEUTIC AND EDUCATIONAL APPLICATIONS

A number of therapeutic and educational possibilities suggest themselves even at this most exploratory stage of investigation.

Therapy

Beyond the obvious use of this material by therapists working with families currently in the process of planning a bar mitzvah, the ritual lends itself to being developed as an *assessment tool* for therapists working with Jewish families. An exploration of what the teenager's (and/or the father's) bar mitzvah was like has obvious diagnostic value. Questions regarding the details of the event (e.g., who planned it and how, what were the invitations like, who came, who didn't, where did they sit, what were they fed, what was the emotional highlight, who in the family was most/least anxious or excited, what would they have changed, etc.) could provide the therapist (and the family) with a great deal of information.

Similarly, the bar mitzvah lends itself to being developed as a *therapeutic intervention*. In Jewish families where the identified patient is a teenager, a depressed father, or a male adult inappropriately involved with his family of origin, etc., the bar mitzvah ritual could be developed by the therapist and the family as a rite of passage marking some necessary change (e.g., "Let's redo the bar mitzvah that didn't work the first time," or "Let's have the bar mitzvah that you missed as a child"). How elaborate or how "public" the event would be, would of course, be a function of the family's needs and circumstances, but, in any case, preparing for the ritual would be a significant part of the therapeutic work.

Education

In terms of education, there is much information in this research which could benefit families beginning to plan for the bar mitzvah of their first child. Given that these transitional families are in what Havinghurst (in

Golan, 1981, p. 15) calls "a teachable moment," where there is "maximum inclination to take on new directions," an educational program built on this material would be timely, and possibly very useful in helping families make the most of the ritual process they have chosen to enter.

Working in consultation with rabbis, teachers, and bar mitzvah families, one could design a set of educational sessions which could go a long way in "coaching" participants towards greater awareness of the developmental significance of the process (without taking the magic out of it by making it too self-conscious an experience), and could help them focus their energies in ways that would enhance the ritual's potential[15] for being what Friedman (1980, p. 437) calls a "golden opportunity for growth."

IMPLICATIONS FOR WORKING WITH OTHER LIFE CYCLE ISSUES AND EVENTS

Although this research focused on the bar mitzvah and its usefulness in terms of adolescent development, the implications for the potential of other rituals for other developmental stages is obvious. Our understanding of the way in which pressure builds and is used in the system long before the public ceremony, of the impact of the symbolic performance, and of the way in which participants integrate the effect of the preparation and ceremony can all be extrapolated and readily applied to our thinking about other multigenerational transitions.

Whether designing a life cycle ritual with families approaching an acknowledged milestone (a marriage, a birth, a death, a divorce) or with families unknowingly stuck in patterns more appropriate to a previous developmental stage, the therapist can do much to enhance the potential of the ceremony. Ritual is both a facilitator of change and a metaphor for that change. To the extent that one can help the family focus on the process of preparation and not simply on the performance, make use of the time preceding and following the ceremony, involve multiple generations, and adapt and incorporate symbols that are meaningful, one can do much to enable ritual's "magic."

NOTES

[1]A Yiddish phrase translated as "Congratulations" or "Thank God!" It is spoken by a person both as an individual and as one implicitly representing the community. It acknowledges that the one spoken to has done something hard or has gone through something dangerous (Rosten, 1970, p. 277).

[2]In modern usage, the term denotes the religious ceremony in the synagogue which marks a 13-year-old boy's attainment of religious majority. More accurately, the word describes the celebrant's adulthood. The word is half Aramaic, half Hebrew. *Bar* is the Aramaic word for son, and *mitzvah*, the Hebrew word for commandments. The bar mitzvah child is therefore a

"son of the commandments." From the point of view of Jewish law, a bar mitzvah is a person who is now able to perform those commandments appropriate to his age and capacity. He is now responsible for his own wrongdoings, able to give witness in court, and able to be counted as one of the minyan [quorum needed to hold a public service].

The actual ceremony varies from congregation to congregation depending on the branch of Judaism with which it is associated and according to local customs. Most contemporary ceremonies, however, include the boy's being called up to bless the Torah (his *aliyah*), the boy's chanting of the prophetic portion of the week (his *haftorah*), and his speech (explicating the readings and/or thanking his family and guests). The ceremony is followed by a feast/party celebrating the event.

Bat mitzvah, a modern innovation, is the female equivalent of bar mitzvah. It was first instituted in the early 1920s and has become widely practiced only since the early 1970s. Prior to this time, there was no public acknowledgment of the young woman's coming of age.

[3]To the extent that they consider it at all, sociologists dismiss the bar mitzvah, among other rituals, as a useless if not regressive remnant of an earlier age, novelists mock it, and much of the lay community sees it as hollow performance at best, and as hypocritical farce at worst. Psychoanalytic theorists explain it as an expression of the oedipal conflict, and few, if any, anthropologists examine it at all. Even professional Jewish educators are conflicted about its value.

[4]The bar mitzvah, dating back at least to the 15th if not the 8th century, is one of the few, if not the only, remaining religious rites of initiation for adolescents in contemporary Western culture. Despite attempts in the Reform movement to eliminate it (in favor of a confirmation ceremony which occurs at age 15 when, it is argued, the child has studied longer and is old enough to make a more conscious choice), and a general decline in ritual practice throughout the culture, the bar mitzvah continues to thrive.

[5]As an educator as well as a student of family therapy, it was my hope that the results of this study would be useful not only for therapists in clinical settings but also for "natural helpers" (clergy, teachers, bar mitzvah tutors, etc.) whose work with "healthy" families can contribute towards keeping them healthy, towards keeping them from "needing" therapy which to some extent has become the modern rite of passage for families with adolescents. (The therapist as secular priest is by now a familiar image and the therapeutic rituals s/he prescribes are logical extensions of this role, if not ironic commentary on contemporary loss of ritual.)

[6]Hasidism is an ultra orthodox movement begun in Poland in the first half of the 18th century. The modern-day bearded, dark-suited Hasidic men and the bewigged, modestly dressed women are distinctive from other orthodox Jews because they believe in a more impassioned, joyous, and mystical expression of Judaism and they adhere to the guidance of a revered spiritual leader, *der Rebbe* (Berger, 1985).

[7]Given that it is generally the first child's development that takes the family over the "growing edge" (Duval in Golan, 1981, p. 33), I delimited the study to families in which the first living child was a son and this was the family's first bar mitzvah. I delimited the study to bar rather than bar and bat mitzvah for two reasons: (1) To simply include girls and bat mitzvah *as if* there had been no gender differences in Jewish tradition (and in society as a whole) would be to further shortchange women; and (2) given the relatively recent advent of bat mitzvah (see footnote 2) it would be much more difficult to find families in which generational similarities and differences could be explored.

[8]For a more complete treatment of this material, the reader is referred to Davis, J., Mazel Tov: A Systems Exploration of Bar Mitzvah as a Multigenerational Ritual of Change and Continuity (1987). Unpublished dissertation, University of Massachusetts.

[9]All names and identifying details have, of course, been changed.

[10]The Lubavitchers are that group of Hasidim who originated in Lubavitch, Poland. They are the largest dynasty surviving Hitler's destruction (Harris, 1985).

[11]"Hasidic children rarely rebel against their parents; they rebel against secular society. The modern goals of innovativeness, independence, and originality that play a role in most adolescent rebellions have no place in this milieu" (Harris, 1985, p. 167).

[12]In addition to the subjectiveness of all such research and the especially impressionistic nature of this specific study, one methodogical problem stands out in particular: That is the self-selective nature of the observed population. Given the level of stress with which families

beginning to plan for their first child's bar mitzvah are coping, it is clear, in retrospect, that families who would agree to be part of this study would be families with a high level of confidence and expectation for success. They would be families who from the beginning felt that they could handle the stress they were facing not only well enough to manage the event, but also well enough to allow themselves to be scrutinized by a researcher who would likely cause even more stress. *Surely the findings and conclusions of this study would have been very different if some of the families had been less well functioning and less resourceful.* Additional research with a more randomly selected population is critical in terms of further developing these hypotheses.

13Given the way in which the bar mitzvah process works differently across systems despite its uniformity of structure and function, it can be likened to Palazzoli's (1986) "invariant prescription." In addition to the fact that the same formal action is prescribed (i.e., divinely "commanded") for all Jewish families, and the fact that the prescription/commandment works analogically rather than discursively, the bar mitzvah is like the invariant prescription in that each family interprets and enacts the ritual differently according to issues and needs most salient at the time.

14It will be interesting to watch the process of gender identification in reference to bat mitzvah girls and their mothers as the bat mitzvah becomes a ceremony shared over generations. Given the fact that relatively few bat mitzvah mothers had bat mitzvahs themselves, it is unlikely that the process works currently in the same ways to deal with issues of gender identification for girls as it does for boys.

It is also unlikely, I suspect, that the process works similarly for girls and boys in reference to gender-identified accomplishment. The bar mitzvah is a male initiation ritual. To the extent that the bat mitzvah girl performs the same ritual as the bar mitzvah boy (i.e., blesses the Torah, chants the *haftorah*, delivers a speech, etc.), she can, in a male-identified religious (and secular) culture, feel accomplished; she can do anything her brother can do. On this level and in this context, her sense of emerging strength and power is reinforced. At the level of a uniquely female sense of accomplishment (K. Turner, 1978, in Doty, 1986, p. 102), however, the currently typical form of bat mitzvah is probably not relevant. Perhaps, though, as the bat mitzvah ritual evolves with the increasing influence of feminist consciousness, the event will be modified such that the similarities and differences between sons of the commandments and daughters of the commandments can be not only recognized but also celebrated.

In light of the emphasis in this footnote on the surmised differences between bar and bat mitzvahs, I need to make clear my sense that in reference to most of the other family dynamics activated by the ritual process, the issues emerging in bar and bat mitzvahs are substantially the same. According to Friedman (1981, p. 55), "The crucial factor determining the emotional intensity of the occasion is not the sex of the child, but the importance of that child to the balance of the parents' marriage, and to the balance of either parent's relationship with his or her own parents."

15For example, it might be suggested to parents that they include in the service a prayer that has been generally abandoned by all but the most orthodox. This prayer, traditionally recited by the father after his son's first *aliyah*, thanks God for making him "no longer responsible for this one." A contemporary adaptation might be to have the parents recite this blessing together and then to have them or the rabbi talk about the adolescent's growing maturity and how it affects the parents' relationship to him, i.e., how they and he are responsible in new ways.

Another suggestion might be that parents and bar mitzvah boy determine together, early in the planning period, what new responsibilities will be expected and what new privileges will be granted after the ritual ceremony. Such tangible symbols of change help concretize the passage.

REFERENCES

Ackerman, N. J. (1980). The family with adolescents. In E. Carter & M. McGoldrick (Eds.). *The family life cycle: A framework for family therapy* (pp. 147–169). New York: Gardner Press.

Arlow, J. A. (1951). A psychoanalytic study of a religious initiation rite: Bar Mitzvah. In R. S. Eissler, A. Freud, H. Hartmann, & E. Kris (Eds.). *Psychoanalytic study of the child: Vol. 6* (pp. 364–374). New York: International Universities Press.
Barron, S. D. (1984, January 15). Reviving the rituals of the debutant. *New York Times Magazine.*
Berger, J. (1985). [Review of E. Harris' *Holy Days*]. Citation unknown.
Bogdan, J. L. (1984). Family organization as an ecology of ideas: An alternative to the reification of family systems. *Family Process, 23,* 375–388.
Culler, E. (1987). Change in the context of stability: The design of therapeutic rituals for families. Unpublished doctoral dissertation, University of Massachusetts, Amherst.
d'Aquili, E. G. & Laughlin, C. D. (1979). The neurobiology of myth and ritual. In E. G. d'Aquili, C. D. Laughlin, & J. McManus (Eds.). *The spectrum of ritual: A biogenetic structural analysis* (pp. 152–182). New York: Columbia University Press.
Dell, P. F. (1982, March). Beyond homeostasis: Toward a concept of coherence. *Family Process, 21*(1), 21–41.
Doty, W. (1986). *Mythography: The study of myths and rituals.* University of Alabama Press.
Elkind, D. (1981). *The hurried child: Growing up too fast, too soon.* Reading, MA: Addison-Wesley.
Forssen, A. (1980). Childhood crises as part of personal development. *Psychiatric Annals, 10*(6), 38–43, 47.
Friedman, E. H. (1980). Systems and ceremonies: A family view of rites of passage. In E. A. Carter & M. McGoldrick, (Eds.). *The family life cycle* (pp. 429–460). New York: Gardner Press.
Friedman, E. H. (1981, Spring). Bar Mitzvah when parents are no longer partners. *Journal of Reform Judaism, 28,* 53–66.
Friedman, E. H. (1985). *Generation to generation: Family process in church and synagogue.* New York: Guilford Press.
Garfiel, E. (1958). *Service of the heart: A guide to the Jewish prayer book.* New York: T. Yoseloff.
Gelcher, E. (1983). Mourning is a family affair. *Family Process, 22,* 501–516.
Golan, N. (1981). *Passing through transitions: A guide for practitioners.* New York: Free Press.
Haley, J. (1973). *Uncommon therapy: the psychiatric techniques of Milton H. Erickson, M.D.* New York: W. W. Norton.
Harris, L. (1985). *Holy days: The world of a Hasidic family.* New York: Summit Books.
Hoffman, L. (1981). *Foundations of family therapy: A conceptual framework for systems change.* New York: Basic Books.
Imber Coppersmith, E. (1982). From hyperactive to normal but naughty: A multi-system partnership in delabeling. *International Journal of Family Psychiatry, 3*(2), 131–144.
Imber Coopersmith, E. (1986). We've got a secret: A non-marital family therapy. In A. Gurman (Ed.). *Case book of marital therapy* (pp. 369–386). New York; London: Guilford Press.
Keeney, B. P. & Morris, J. (1985). Family therapy practice and research: A dialogue. In L. L. Andreozzi & R. F. Levant (Eds.). *Integrating research and clinical practice* (99–107). Rockville, MD: Aspen.
Kimbali, S. (1960). "Introduction" *Rites of passage,* A. Van Gennep. (London, England: Routledge & Kegan Paul, 1909), translated and republished in 1960, Chicago: University of Chicago Press.
Madanes, C. (1986, November). Workshop on "Love and Violence in Family Therapy." Boston, MA.
McGoldrick, M. & Carter, E. A. (1982). The family life cycle. In F. Walsh (Ed.). *Normal family process* (pp. 167–195). New York: Guilford Press.
Quinn, W., Newfield, A., & Protinsky, H. (1985). Rites of passage in families with adolescents. *Family Process, 24,* 101–111.
Rosten, L. (1970). *The joys of Yiddish.* New York: Pocket Books.
Schwartzman, J. (1982, Spring). Symptoms and rituals: Paradoxical modes and social organization. *Ethos, 10,* 3–25.

Selvini Palazzoli, M. (1986). Towards a general model of family games. *Journal of Marital and Family Therapy, 12*(4), 339–349.

Slater, P. (1974). *Earthwalk*. New York: Bantam.

Stevens, A. (1981). Attenuation of the mother-child bond and male initiation into adult life. *Journal of Adolescence, 4*, 131–148.

Tomm, K. (1984a). One perspective on the Milan systemic approach: I: Overview of development, theory, and practice. *Journal of Marital and Family Therapy, 10*, 113–125.

Tomm, K. (1984b). One perspective on the Milan systemic approach: II: Description of session format, interviewing style and interventions. *Journal of Marital and Family Therapy, 10*, 253–271.

Tomm, K. (1985). Circular interviewing: A multifaceted clinical tool. In D. Campbell & R. Draper (Eds.). *Applications of systemic family therapy: The Milan method* (pp. 33–45). Orlando, FL: Grune & Stratton.

Turner, V. W. (1969). *The ritual process: Structure and anti-structure*. Chicago: Aldine Publishing.

Turner, V. W. (1982, October). Are there universals of performance in myth, ritual, and drama? Unpublished paper presented at Smith College, Northampton, Massachusetts.

Van Gennep, A. (1909). *Les rites de passage*. London: Routledge Kegan Paul. (M. B. Uizedom & G. L. Caffee, Trans., republished 1960). Chicago: University of Chicago Press.

Wolin, S. J. & Bennett, L. A. (1984). Family rituals. *Family Process, 23*, 401–420.

Wood, B. & Talmon, M. (1983). Family boundaries in transition: A search for alternatives. *Family Process, 22*, 347–357.

Zegans, S. & Zegans, L. S. (1979). Bar Mitzvah: A rite for a transitional age. *Psychoanalytic Review, 66*(1), 115–132.

III

FACILITATING COMPLEX
FAMILY PROCESSES
THROUGH RITUAL

8

Therapeutic Rituals with Families with Adopted Members

RICHARD A. WHITING

WHEN ONE CONSIDERS all of the "ritualistic" activities and meanings associated with pregnancy and birth, it is very apparent that adoption carries with it a very different set of rituals and meanings. Though there are cultural and class differences, biological parents experience a variety of events, such as feeling baby's first kicks, attending childbirth classes, going to showers and sending birth announcements. These activities tend to "normalize" this developmental process for the couple, relatives, and friends. Having the first child or adding to the family for the adoptive parent or parents is a very different developmental experience. The reasons to adopt are varied: The idea is frequently a viable solution to such difficulties as repeated miscarriages, genetic diseases, sterility, or infertility; for others, humanitarian reasons, such as adopting a handicapped child or a disaster victim, are the primary motivators. Regardless of the reasons, there are few, if any, normalizing rituals associated with adoption. While the non-adoptive parents await the arrival of their child and participate in a variety of rituals, the adoptive parents are being screened and evaluated. Letters of recommendation are required and the potential parent or parents feel they must present themselves in interviews as worthy candidates to the adoption agency representatives. While the gestation period is clear and well defined, the waiting period for the adoptive parents is typically the opposite, especially if the child is from another country.

Upon arrival of the child, the ritual differences between non-adoptive and adoptive families often continue. While the non-adoptive parents have a variety of religious and cultural ceremonies that mark the arrival of the new member to the family, the adoptive parents lack similar markers. Although extended family members, friends, and neighbors may respond ceremoniously with gifts to the arrival of an adopted infant, such ceremony is usually lacking if the child is a toddler or older. When we look at the additional variables of single-parent adoptions or the adoptee being disabled or of a different race or culture, it is apparent that as a society we are underritualized regarding the adoption process. Families are left on their own to define this experience and create their own rituals. Having worked with a number of families with adopted members, I have concluded that therapeutic rituals are a particularly useful way to intervene.

All of the major types of rituals (see Chapter 2) can be utilized in dealing with families where adoption is an explicit or implicit component. The ritual themes — membership, healing, identity, belief negotiation and affirmation/celebration — represent arenas which are frequently marked by confusion and underritualization in adoptive families seeking treatment. For instance, years ago a college student described to me how she was always depressed on her birthday. Her adopted parents celebrated her birthday, but she always wondered — if celebrating her birthday was such a wonderful event, why did her biological parents abandon her? After I encouraged her to talk to her adoptive parents about this, she found out the date she joined the family and they collectively decided to celebrate that anniversary instead of her birthday. This seemingly small intervention helped facilitate a new sense of belonging and self-esteem. In a related case described by Imber-Black (1988), the parents felt they were "bad parents" because of the adopted child's behavior and "bad people" because they were infertile. A celebration ritual facilitated a shift in meaning from shame to joy regarding the adopted son's presence in the family.

Belief negotiation rituals are helpful in shifting meanings, particularly myths surrounding the adoptee's behavior. As Talen and Lehr (1984) reported, the adopted child's biological, social, and cultural history can lead the parents to overfunction or to offer rationales for inappropriate behavior. An odd days/even days ritual was prescribed to the parents of a seven-year-old adopted boy who was stealing. On certain days of the week the parents were to continue their usual behavior of doing nothing but worrying because they knew his biological father had been in trouble with the law and this child "carried his genes." On the other days of the week they were to discipline the child in a manner that was appropriate and similar to their strategies with their biological children. Almost immediately the stealing behavior ceased, as the parents began relating to the child as a boy who needed guidance and advice as opposed to a child whose gene pool was defective.

CASE EXAMPLE: THE WEST FAMILY

The following case describes how rituals were used with a family seen in treatment for an initial assessment, five sessions over a three-month period, a follow-up interview two months after treatment, and a phone call two years later. Adoption was not presented as a problem, but it became a key ingredient in the treatment process.

An employee assistance director suggested to the father, James West, that he call my office for an appointment. When I spoke with Mr. West, he indicated that I was highly recommended and that he and his wife were having a difficult time with their 20-year-old son, Andrew. Andrew was living at home, unemployed, drinking excessively, and coming home during the middle of the night, often bloodied from fighting. When I asked about other children, Mr. West said there was an older daughter, Susan, age 24 and a college graduate, working and living on her own about 20 miles from the family. Andrew's twin brother, William, was two hours away at college, and the youngest daughter, Jennifer, age 18, was an hour away at college (see Figure 1).

When I suggested that everyone attend the session, Mr. West indicated that it would be difficult, if not impossible, for the whole family because of the busy lives of Susan, William and Jennifer. Somewhat reluctantly I agreed to an assessment interview with the parents and Andrew. The day of the interview Mr. West called to report that his wife, Beth, was in bed with "one of her migraines" and a meeting for the following week was scheduled.

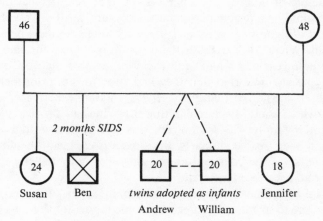

FIGURE 1   The West Family

Assessment Interview

At the beginning of the interview Mr. West let me know how difficult it had been to get Andrew to attend the session. Slumped on the couch, Andrew agreed he had to be dragged in, adding that there were no problems and that he did not have anything to say. As the session progressed, my sense of the family was that their preferred patterns of interaction were characteristic of enmeshment and that the parents vacillated between affection and exasperation, especially with Andrew. The tension and stress in this triad were very intense. A few weeks before the session Mr. West had confronted an intoxicated Andrew at two o'clock in the morning. They shoved and pushed each other and it "ended" when Andrew threw a chair through the parents' bedroom window. Mrs. West reported that almost daily, when she attempted to wake Andrew up so he could begin looking for a job, he would say, "I feel like smacking you." The parents acknowledged that conflicts between them had increased and that, because they had different ideas about how to deal with Andrew, their relationship was being affected negatively. Mr. West advised his wife to stop doing things for Andrew, but she was unable to do so, as she was a "very caring person." Mrs. West reported feeling in the middle. She understood her husband's temper but was upset by the physical confrontations between her husband and son. While the parents were describing their concerns, Andrew was attentive but silent.

When asked if they had had similar struggles with any of the other children, the parents reported that Susan had been rebellious for a short period of time and that it resulted in much less stress on them. Dealing with William was often a struggle, but at least he was in college, though having some academic difficulties. The parents felt that Jennifer had never been and never would be a problem. Somewhat hesitantly, Mrs. West shared that Andrew and William were twins and that they were adopted when they were six days old. When I asked about the decision to adopt, she said that they were adopted a year and a half after the crib death of their two-month-old son, Ben. She also reported that they had filed for adoption before Ben's conception, as she had difficulty conceiving and had experienced a difficult pregnancy with Susan. My comment that the twins had a special place in the history of the family was minimized, and she indicated that all of the children had been treated similarly. Both parents claimed the adoption was not an issue, since the boys had known they were adopted since they were young — it had never been a secret.

My initial assessment impressions went in a variety of theoretical directions according to structural/strategic/systemic models of therapy. For example: (1) the hierarchy was skewed and the parents needed to be put in charge (Minuchin, 1974; Haley, 1980); (2) mother and Andrew were in a cross-generational alliance against father (Minuchin, 1974; Haley, 1980); (3) the parents' solutions were "more of the same wrong solution" (Fisch, Weakland, & Segal, 1982); (4) Andrew's behavior was a solution to the family's dilemma of making the transition from a family with young children to a family with young adults (Tomm, 1984).

At the end of the assessment interview I suggested we meet for five more times and then reevaluate. The parents also agreed with my request to see William and Jennifer with the family while they were home the following month during the Christmas vacation. I explained the use of homework between sessions and planted some seeds by telling them that I might ask them to do some unusual things during the course of treatment. In an attempt to gain some more information, as well as to defuse this triad, I suggested an odd days/even days ritual (Selvini Palazzoli, Boscolo, Cecchin, & Prata, 1977): On Monday, Wednesday, and Friday, Mr. West was to make all decisions regarding Andrew, and on Tuesday, Thursday, and Saturday, Mrs. West would be in charge. The parents were also asked to observe and record the parenting style of the other on their off days. An appointment was scheduled for a week later.

First Session

The following week Mr. and Mrs. West appeared with Andrew, reporting that getting him there had been somewhat of a struggle. They all seemed a little more relaxed and Andrew was more verbal. The parents reported no major confrontations, but their differences regarding Andrew were highlighted as a result of the odd days/even days ritual. The conflict in the marriage was again acknowledged, but Mr. West was very clear that he would decide when he wanted to improve his relationship with his wife. The message was clear that this was not a problem to be dealt with within the context of therapy. Mrs. West somewhat agreed, as she believed that if her husband and son got along she and Mr. West would also. During the session I tried to get more information about the parents' solutions regarding Andrew's behavior—what they had tried, what worked, what failed. Repeatedly they talked about their frustrations controlling Andrew and how they felt helpless and defeated singularly and collectively as a couple. I asked them to continue the odd days/even days ritual and an appointment was set for two weeks.

Second Session

At the next session everyone, including Andrew, reported there had been less stress and no major confrontations. Their explanation for this was that everyone was feeling distant and no one was really speaking; thus, it was not a good solution. There continued to be defiance when either of the parents made a direct request of Andrew to do something—look for a job, take out the trash, bring in the groceries, make his bed, stop drinking, come home on time. The parents continued to feel helpless and began requesting the "answer" from me more directly. Andrew said that he was looking forward to William's and Jennifer's coming home from college, as he would no longer be the focus of the parents' complaints. The parents somewhat agreed, as they felt that William would be a problem while he was home, since they did not have much influence over his behavior. The next session was scheduled for two weeks later and the parents were asked to bring all the children.

Third Session

Susan, the oldest, was planning to attend but at the last minute was called into work. The parents, Andrew, William, and Jennifer came. Although there was less tension in the session, the parents and Jennifer agreed that it had been stressful at home. William showed defiance toward his parents similar to Andrew's, but it was usually briefer and less intense. The pattern of vacillating between affection and exasperation was apparent between mother and father and the adopted twins. Circular questioning (Selvini Palazzoli, Boscolo, Cecchin, & Prata, 1980; Tomm, 1985) focusing on the themes of closeness and distance between members of the family in relationship to the past, present, and hypothetical future comprised most of the interview. The parents were often surprised by the children's responses, especially when they said that they all felt that the parents were, had been, and probably always would be closer to the biological children than to the adopted children. Andrew, William, and Jennifer expressed their opinions in a matter-of-fact, sometimes humorous fashion. Their tone was not angry or hurtful. Mr. and Mrs. West were quite defensive and claimed that they loved all the children equally and that there were no differences between the biological and adopted children. They agreed that presently they felt closer to the daughters because they were good kids and not causing them the pain and sorrow that William and Andrew were inflicting.

Towards the end of the session the parents moved to shift the focus back to Andrew and his defiant, irresponsible behavior. Although Andrew had found part-time employment since the last session, the parents viewed this as insignificant progress. Mrs. West maintained that her husband had not tried to improve his relationship with her and that they were still in conflict about how to deal with Andrew. My sense was that they were beginning to feel frustrated with me, as therapy had not given them much relief.

Therapist Reflections

I felt the session was helpful, as it supported many of my earlier and ongoing assessment hypotheses. In addition, it highlighted some of the difficulties in the family about being different and dealing with differences. The parents' idea of family seemed to mean a very tight, close, loving, loyal unit which emphasized similarity. The more the parents presented this view, the more Andrew and William were defiant, and the more defiant Andrew and William were, the tighter the parents held to their desire for a close family. My attempts to comment on such a pattern were met with reminders from Mr. West that I was to help Andrew. In some ways I was becoming like a child in the family, as the parents felt connected to me, yet exasperated.

Responding to some of the parents' urging me to *do something*, and knowing that William's and Jennifer's vacations were not to be spent in therapy, I invited the family back the following night. They were to come in two cars so that the children could leave the session early. Having some ideas about what I wanted to do the next night, I asked the parents to write separately what each alone wanted to do about Andrew, as well as what steps or solutions would be best for their relationship. Before the next session, I wrote a letter to be used as part of a ritualized prescription.

Fourth Session: Adopting a New Solution

The following night I dismissed the children after they sculpted (Simon, 1972) their image of the parents' view of how they wanted the family to appear. Andrew, William, and Jennifer each showed a close, connected group. Members of the family were placed in close proximity, often holding hands. Jennifer said she thought the parents wanted every day to be like Christmas. After everyone talked about the various sculptures, I thanked the children and told them I would most likely never see them again. Alone with Mr. and Mrs. West, I asked them how they made out with their assignments. What follows is some of the transcript from the remainder of the session.

WHITING: What are some of the ideas you have? What would you like to do?

MRS.:   Sit down, the three of us, and make plans or rules that we can live with, or revise the ones we have and then give Andrew two weeks maximum to start going by the rules with no exceptions. And to also start having consideration and respect for other members of the family, no mouthing off or faces. I realize this is going to take time for him to get over because . . .

WHITING: So that's not within the two weeks or what?

MRS.:   No, that's within the two weeks.

WHITING: OK.

MRS.:   I'm giving him two weeks to break those two habits.

WHITING: OK, if he doesn't? (pause)

MRS.:   Then he'll have to move out. And have him think about drying out not drinking so much, not to go out to the Lantern and get plastered and get in fights.

WHITING: OK.

MRS.:   He might even have to change his friends if that's what it takes.

WHITING: Do you know which ones you want him to change?

MRS.:   Yup.

WHITING: Sounds like the ultimatum, giving him two weeks. What do you think will happen?

MRS.:   If he wants to live at home, he'll change. If he doesn't, he won't.

WHITING: What do you think will happen? What would you bet me right now?

MRS.:   He'll say he's going to change and maybe he'll try for a while, (pause) just like he has before, but then he'll go back to his old ways. But he's going to have to realize this time that the old ways are not coming back.

WHITING: OK. Why is this time different?

MRS.:   Because we're fed up with the way he's been acting. It's about time he grew up.

WHITING: So what do you think will happen? (pause)

MRS.:   About what?

WHITING: Well, do you think on February 1 he'll be looking for a place to stay?

MRS.:   Well, I'm kind of like this—maybe yes, maybe no. Maybe if he really knows we mean it, he won't be, because frankly, he has it soft now and I think he'd like to keep it soft.

WHITING: What else do you have?

MRS.:   That's it on the plan side.

WHITING: What do you have, Jim?

MR.:   I have two plans, one of which I call my immediate plan, which is he has seven days to find a place of his own to live.

WHITING: OK, you gave him less time.

MR.:   That was just . . .

WHITING: That was a plan regardless. He has seven days to find a place.

MR.:   That's, that's if nothing happens. Starting today you have seven days. On the seventh day, I'm going to put your things out in the backyard if you're not out, and you can find your own place. My second plan, which is a more positive plan, says that, from wherever I start, he has 14 days. Within that 14 days he's got to get himself a job, obey all the rules we establish, he's got to start making weekly payments for room and board, start making weekly payments towards his debt, and within 14 days, if he does all this, I'll take it one day at a time. I'm sorry, one week at a time, and if he doesn't do all this within the 14 days, then you're on your own. If he tries for a couple of weeks but then falls back into his old habits, well, OK, one week at a time and if one week at a time doesn't bring anything, um, I'd say give him 30 days to find his own place. The difference being at least he tried and couldn't do it and now we know we aren't going to make it, therefore, give him a little more leeway, give him 30 days to find his own place.

WHITING: OK.

MR.:   Those are sort of my two original alternative plans that I have.

WHITING: OK, how about under the category of what would be best for the two of you?

MRS.:   I just thought of some other things I forgot to write down, I just remembered. Um, have him start going to a local community college, maybe taking one course at night so he can work during the day. Get him started back in his studies. A plan for us that would be best for us would have Andrew move out willingly. Another one that I had thought of would be to have him decide to join some branch of the service. We had talked about it.

WHITING: So you are saying that the idea of some measure where he's not thrown out would probably be best for your relationship.

MRS.:   Uh, uh. (Mr. nodded in agreement.)

WHITING: OK, you both seem to be moving in the direction of "These are the limits and if you cross this line, we've finally had it. If you cross this, this is what is going to happen." But there is still a sense that if that were to happen that probably, in the long run, it wouldn't be best for us. So again, if he could come to this on his own, either go into the service or tell you that he was going to get a place on his own, if that originated inside of him, if he actually did that, that would be good for the two of you.

MR.:   Um. The approach that I had for what would have the best impact on us as I perceived Beth's concerns and Andrew, and I didn't know what she was writing here. So, to give Andrew the rules and behavior patterns, what's expected of him, here are the rules whether it's to make your bed every day before you take your shower, whatever the rules are. If he doesn't comply, uh, we stop doing his laundry, we stop doing his cleaning, we stop letting him use the telephone, we stop letting him use the television. In other words, basically provide a roof and food.

WHITING: OK, OK.

MR.:   Perhaps even going one step further, saying, depending on how these things work out, he can only use the house when we are there. So if we came out tonight to come here, he could not be in the house. He would have to find some place else for the couple of hours we are gone. So, if we go away for a weekend, he's got to find some place to stay for the weekend.

WHITING: Anything you want to ask each other about these?

MR.:   My concern with yours is what are you going to do if he doesn't obey the rules? Didn't you say over here . . .

MRS.:   He has two weeks to go by them. If he doesn't, he moves out.

MR.:   Oh, OK. (pause) Is this all one plan?

MRS.:   Uh, uh.

MR.:   Oh, OK. I guess consider drying out, not drinking so much and getting into fights, and if he doesn't, that's the same thing. Do you think that you can live with that if he moves out?

MRS.:   I don't know.

MR.:   If you read about him in the paper having broke into 30 cars. (pause)

MRS.:   I think I'm going to have to.

WHITING: Could you, Jim? Could you?

MR.:   It would be difficult, yes.

Therapist Reflections

Essentially, Mr. and Mrs. West's solutions were what I had anticipated and hoped. By this I mean that my drafted letter and intervention strategy was based upon belief that their individual solutions would have Andrew complying to their rules, with expulsion being the consequence for non-compliance. I had also hoped that the solutions which would be best for their relationship would include non-expulsion solutions. Therapeutically, I believed that this particular pattern of Andrew's noncompliance and parental threats was problematic. The parents' attitude that "this time we mean business" would only continue to fuel the escalating struggle with Andrew. Since I believe that physical removal is not a healthy launching for either young adults or parents, I had hoped that the parents would suggest solutions that would be the best for their relationship that did not involve expulsion. Pleased with how they had done the assignment, I spent the next several minutes talking about how predictable the parents had become and whether they would be willing to experiment and try a very different solution that would require some creativity in their responses. I suggested that, if they altered their behavior, Andrew's behavior would also change. Essentially I was attempting to motivate them to do something different. After they agreed, I told them that I had a draft of a letter that I wanted their assistance with. The following transcript highlights this discussion.

WHITING: This is where I need your help. One, you're saying all right, we are willing to kick around some things and do something different. What I have here is basically a draft of a letter that I would like some input on. What it sounds like to you. It's not going to be easy to hear, in some ways, I don't think. It might even seem a little outrageous. There are some things I'd like you to do with it, but it is also going to call on you to be pretty creative, I think, in terms of looking at a very different solution. Let me read what I have, maybe sentence by sentence, and ask your thoughts, and then what I would like to do is either go with this or make some revisions that we all could live with, and then for the both of you to write it out in long hand so you will have it. You can keep it and you could make some copies of it and have this available in the home, to post it, to put it up. Let me read the first line: *Although we have had some problems and struggles parenting Susan and very few with Jennifer, our daughters, our children, we have had more problems and struggles trying to be parents for William, and especially for Andrew, whom we think of and love as if you were ours.* Any problems with that line?

MRS.: I never make a distinction and you are making a distinction between the two.

WHITING: That's right.

MRS.: Between the adopted and non-adopted.

WHITING: That's right. There are distinctions. You heard some of them last night. Andrew's made some distinctions. They are saying that they experience the both of you having closer relationships with your own children and that you have a track record, on one hand, that looks better, in terms of your view of how to be parents and how to be a family. It says that you have done a better job with your own children than you have with Andrew and William. I know that there is, well, we'll see where we are going, but all you're doing now is saying I'm on track.

WHITING: (After rereading the first line of the letter) *But we are not your mother and father. We are only your adoptive parents. We have tried parenting you to make you our sons. Our stymied efforts with you, however, have brought us closer to Susan and Jennifer. Although part of us believes we have done a good job as adoptive parents, we have become painfully and depressingly aware of how we have tried to take away your heritage and your loyalty to your natural mother and fa-*

*ther, whom, although you may deny it, do exist somewhere in your
hearts. For this we are truly sorry. We still hope that some day, but now
think neither of you, especially Andrew, will ever forgive our efforts to
make you like our dream of the West family. Probably all we can do is
provide you with food, shelter, clean clothes, and money. Please bear
with us as it will take us some time for us to accept that we can't be
your parents.*

MRS.:   Did you say can or can't?

WHITING: *We can't be your parents.* (pause) *With love, your adoptive
mother and father.* OK, and have this in the house and the next time
you get, the next time and any time you get into any struggles with
Andrew or William, you are to say, "I'm truly sorry I have not been a
good parent" and give him a nickel and turn around and walk away.

MRS.:   A nickel?

WHITING: Yes, because all you can give them is shelter, food, clean
clothes, and money. Just give him a nickel and walk away. Now this is
radically different from a solution of threats, a solution of defeat,
because I think that's what would happen. Because I think it would
escalate, because there is a history of escalation to the point where
people do things to each other, and we all know it doesn't work. But
I'm not sure you are willing to put that to rest for a while and say we
need to do something different. We really want to do something else.
Part of it sounds a little bizarre, but I think there is an element of truth
in it, as well as an element of an attempt to give you something. When
I say I'd like for you to be creative, it would mean that for you to
appear to be painfully depressed and hurt with this information. That
you have not been their parents and that you are upset and that you
have let them down and that you're sorry that you have taken away
some of their own heritage and loyalty to their natural parents and
that's depressing because that's not your picture of the West family.
The picture of the West family is six tight, connected, close, loving
members.

The session ended with Mr. and Mrs. West copying my letter verbatim
and signing both copies and agreeing to post one of them in the bathroom
that night. I told them to make extra copies because they would probably be
destroyed. The parents agreed to make copies, but they said they would not
be needed because the boys would not tear the letter down. After further
discussion, the parents' response to a conflict or struggle with Andrew or
William was expanded. They agreed to give him a nickel, saying, "I'm truly
sorry, I have not been a good parent," and, instead of just walking away, to
call for the spouse and then sit together in the living room and comfort each
other as they pretended to be depressed. It was also suggested, to highlight

their pretended depression and suffering, that they might want to forget to do things deliberately, such as wake Andrew up in the morning. A follow-up interview with only the parents was scheduled in three weeks.

Of importance in this later stage of this interview were my attempts to gain the cooperation of the parents in designing and participating in the ritual. I sought their cooperation with the wording, copying, and posting of the letter and their response to any conflicts that might arise in the immediate future. Although I had written the letter before the session, the idea of the parents' sitting together and pretending to be depressed developed during the session.

The intent of this letter and the prescribed parental response to conflict were aimed at levels of content and process. The specific content of the letter attempted to address the issue of membership and belonging in the family. The idea of differences between the biological children and the adopted children was openly addressed in the interview and the ritual letter. With this challenge to the parents' mythology that there were no differences, the rules in the family could begin to shift from denying differences to addressing them. Such a shift could facilitate openly acknowledging alliance systems, therefore making it possible to make distinctions between members. Being able to make distinctions could serve to make relationships less constrained, as alliances would no longer be concealed and denied.

At the process or interactional level, the intent of both the letter and their response was to prescribe a "one-down" position for the parents. Having them say "I'm truly sorry, I have not been a good parent" and joining together in a pretended state of depression would create a new one-down position that might introduce a difference that would make a difference in the family's symmetrically escalating pattern of interaction. My hope was that if the parents' behavior was altered, a resultant shift would occur in the behavior of other members.

Fifth Session — Feedback

Since I had not heard from the parents since the last session, I was anxious to see what had happened. This next section focuses on the feedback to the ritual.

MR.:   The first thing that happened, two o'clock in the morning, one o'clock in the morning

WHITING: It was Lantern night.

MR.:   Ya, they were both down at the Lantern, right! William came home. He was the one we got the first reaction from. He woke me up, or woke us up, or woke me up.

MRS.:   Both.

MR.:   Both of us, and said something about, "I don't know what that guy told you," something like that. "I don't know what that guy told you." That guy being you. (laughs)

WHITING: Of course.

MR.:   This was two o'clock in the morning. "I don't know what that guy told you, but as far as I'm concerned, you are my real parents," and he seemed kind of emotionally upset at the time.

WHITING: It wasn't so much a positive thing, like . . .

MR.:   "I don't know who that guy is or what he told you, but as far as I'm concerned, you are my real parents."

MRS.:   He was very upset.

MR.:   And he left, he left our room. Um, that was his reaction.

WHITING: What did you folks do?

MR.:   At that point?

WHITING: Yes.

MR.:   Nothing. He left our room and I just thought, huh, at least we struck a chord there.

WHITING: OK.

MR.:   We had talked about trying to not do things for them, or trying to set them up. We found that a little difficult to do, at least you did.

MRS.:   Um.

MR.:   I believe you did.

MRS.:   Huh, huh.

MR.:   But there were occasions when we would screw things up, so to speak, and say, "Ah, I screwed up, I'm sorry. I just don't know how to do things." Oh, the note was torn off the mirror several times and thrown away and we picked it out of the wastebasket, flattened it out and taped it back together again. The next time it was in pieces. (laughs) Remember I told you I wasn't sure. I didn't think they would tear it down, but they did, which meant it had an impact on them.

WHITING: Do you know who did that?

MR.:   I think, well, no, I don't.

MRS.:   We think it was Andrew.

MR.:   Well, I'm not sure. After William went back to school, we put it back up again and it didn't come down the first night. Andrew wrote something on it. Then the second night it came down. So it didn't come down the first night so we really don't know which one was taking it.

WHITING: What was the message to me on this note? What was written on it?

MR.:   Oh, the note had said, this, this had been after a week or so, before William had gone back to school, Andrew wrote on there, "I have already read this."

WHITING: OK, I don't need to hear it anymore.

MR.:   (laughs) And there was something on the bottom about trying, trying or caring or something. What was on the last? Remember? We should have brought it with us.

MRS.:   Was that the one where he wrote . . .

MR.:   I'm just trying to remember. He wrote something on the bottom about you're not trying, you don't care, or something like that.

MRS.:   He got the impression that we don't care about him anymore.

WHITING: OK, so that hurt you.

MRS.:   Yes, I thought, oh no, maybe that's not accomplishing what we wanted.

MR.:   So, anyway, after that we didn't put it back up anymore. He's given us the message that he's got the message. Even before that though, oh, his reaction to the note was to write a note back to us which you might like to read. You remember the original letter? That was the letter he wrote back to us shortly after.

WHITING: (reads letter aloud) *Dear Mom and Dad, I'm writing you this letter to let you know how I feel. You say that you have not been good parents, but I feel that you have done everything feasibly possible to give William and I a good home. We are well-bred, well-educated, and have a wonderful place to live. You have given us love and affection. What more could we ask. Maybe William and I, mostly, have wandered off the beaten path now, but in the future all that you have taught us will be priceless. The way I feel now is that I have lost my real mother and father for the first time and I could live much better knowing that they still love me. I have never known my father to throw in the towel. I hope you won't start now. Love, your son Andrew.* (pause) My father is you.

MR.:   Right. I think he means in there that his real mother and father are us, also, is what he's saying. That's the way I interpret that.

WHITING: OK, so a sense of loss. What did you do with this?

MR.:   Nothing.

WHITING: It hasn't been discussed or talked about?

MR.:   No.

WHITING: Were you kind of wondering about that, or just seeing what, what to do with it? Or just . . .

MR.:   I decided to sit back and wait and see what happened over a period of time. See what his attitude was. I do think what I might do is write him a letter back. Matter of fact, I planned to before this but things happened and I didn't. I was thinking of that mainly because he has trouble sitting down talking without getting emotionally upset.

WHITING: So just sort of going with that as a style of his, going to write back.

MR.:   Well, we wrote to him and he wrote back.

WHITING: Right, right.

MR.:   Well, that was some of the reaction to the letter we wrote to them.

MRS.:   (later) Things have been much calmer around the house.

Therapist Reflections

It was very apparent that the feedback to the letter was immediate. It seemed to have interrupted a pattern of interaction in a dramatic fashion. Just three weeks ago, the parents had been seriously considering Andrew's physical removal from the house. Now the parents appeared more relaxed and were laughing. They acknowledged it had been difficult to *pretend* to be depressed, as they had experienced some genuine sadness about some of their disappointments with the family. However, they said they supported each other and that it had been good. The remainder of the session was spent giving them credit for taking a major risk and encouraging them to continue to use the nickel and to support each other in their real or pretend sadness as they confronted any struggles. The parents agreed to a follow-up interview in two months.

Follow-up — Last Session

When Mr. and Mrs. West greeted me, they said that Andrew told them that he did not want them to get depressed and that they should cancel the session! The following is a brief transcript from our last session.

MR.:   Well, the last time we talked, we talked about continuing on with the depression, but we really haven't had to. I was thinking about that and I think it was the letter that blew things away. It really rattled their cages.

WHITING: Really!

MR.:   And we really haven't had to say much. Well, every once in a while I say, "Well, I screwed up," and (snaps his fingers) and he stops right away. Almost as fast as a snap of the fingers. Does he do that with you?

MRS.:   Yes.

MR.:   As soon as he starts to get uptight, you know, sometimes we start getting uptight, he starts hollering and I start hollering, I just say, "I screwed up."

WHITING: OK.

MR.:   He stops. I don't use it continuously, but I haven't had to go into this mode of depression.

WHITING: So are you saying things are dramatically different, slightly different. . . ?

MR.:   No. Dramatically, dramatically different. (Mrs. nodding and smiling in agreement.)

Follow-up — Phone Call

Two years later I called Mrs. West and indicated that I was interested in hearing how things were going with the family. She reported that things were very well and that Andrew had moved out about a year ago after having graduated from bartending school. He was currently living in New York City and working in a prestigious restaurant as a bartender. She said that she and her husband were pleased with the nature of the contact Andrew had with the family and that he was managing his life appropriately.

Final Reflections

There are a variety of ways to explain the successful use of an intervention which drew upon aspects of membership rituals and the ritualistic action of symptom prescription or absurdity. One explanation could be that the parents began working together effectively as a result of the shift in their affect from anger to sadness. Although they were told to pretend to be depressed, a genuine sense of sadness surfaced. This change united the parents in a fashion that altered the boundaries between the parental and sibling subsystems. Unable to unite previously, the parents now had found a way to support each other genuinely. This process facilitated the evolution of a new organizational structure with new interactional rules.

Another feasible explanation relates to a shift in the meaning of membership in the family. The pattern of the parents trying to convince Andrew and William to change in order to belong reversed itself. The boys were now trying to convince the parents to change. William's immediate response in the parents' bedroom and Andrew's letter represented major changes in the pattern. Previously, the parents had been struggling in their attempts to define the nature of membership in the family. Andrew and William were now acknowledging how they felt about belonging to the family. This change in patterns seemed to allow for the belief that people were members of the family because they wanted to be.

An important consideration in this case was that the content of the letter was not compatible with the parents' belief about membership in the family or their view of themselves as parents. The content made distinctions between the biological and adopted children and said that, "We can't be your parents." At the level of content and belief, those messages did not really fit with the parents' frame of reference. This raises the question of whether the intervention was poorly designed because of this lack of fit. Since the letter dramatically shifted an escalating pattern of conflict within the family, this lack of fit was an effective approach. Perhaps the explanation lies in its fitting at the level of action and not at the level of meaning. I had a great deal of maneuverability as the therapist (Fisch, et al., 1982) because I was highly recommended, the parents wanted me to give them the answer, and they could accept that their attempts were not working. Their willingness to try something different, while simultaneously being pushed by me to do something different, clearly contributed positively to the therapy process. Also at the level of action, one of Mr. West's solutions was to "basically provide a roof and food," which did fit with the content of the letter.

The use of a letter has implications for treating families where direct verbal communication is intense and highly conflicted. I speculate that the intervention would have had less impact or success if the parents had spoken the contents of the letter to Andrew and/or William. Because the written message was not consistent with the parents' ideas, they probably could not have said the words, yet they were able to post the letter. Posting the letter, coupled with the prescribed response to a conflict, allowed the parents to have some emotional distance. This made it easier for them to remain disengaged and increased the possibility of not getting embroiled in the previous pattern. Communicating through the letter also facilitated Andrew's decision to write and to communicate in a fashion that had been previously unavailable.

Finally, having each of the parents copy the drafted letter and add his/her signature was a ritual in itself. In this culture, documents and agreements are not "official" until they have been initialized. In any document-signing process, a shift in the levels of meaning occurs. Adding one's John Hancock ratifies a document in an important psychological fashion. In the case of the West family, the signing of the letter added a level of legitimacy to the contents of the letter and a level of parental commitment to participate in the ritual interventions.

I would also speculate that because Mr. and Mrs. West wrote and signed the letter, thus making it official, Andrew and William interpreted it as a serious and official document. Although Mr. West indicated the letter "really rattled their cages," it is suggested that the ritual rattled, unlocked, and opened the door of the family system cage, offering a greater sense of freedom for all its members.

CONCLUSION: RITUALS WITH ADOPTIVE FAMILIES

Recently, I visited some friends who adopted their first child four years ago after several years of infertility. Within six months after they received their week-old daughter, they discovered to their amazement that the wife was pregnant. In talking about the experience of raising two children, the husband indicated he was especially close to the adopted child because he had shared equally in the bottle feeding of this infant. Because his wife had nursed the other baby, he felt a different sense of closeness with this child. I left feeling optimistic and positive about the family, as the husband was able to make and talk about similarities and differences in his relationships with the children.

In my mind, one of the major tasks facing adoptive families is achieving a balance of similarities and differences between its members. Families with an adopted member or members who seek treatment are typically skewed in the direction of being either too similar or too different. The case example presented in this chapter represented an example of a family where the parents overemphasized similarity and made no distinctions between the adopted and non-adopted children. At the other extreme, the emphasis focuses on differences. Family members report that the adopted children are unlike other family members in every imaginable way.

Because therapeutic rituals deal with belief systems and membership themes, I believe they are an effective intervention for families where adoption is an implicit or explicit concern. Regardless of the ritual theme category utilized, my experience has been that therapeutic rituals yield dramatic shifts in the areas of membership and beliefs by balancing the themes of similarities and differences.

REFERENCES

Fisch, R., Weakland, H. J., & Segal, L. (1982). *The tactics of change: Doing therapy briefly*. San Francisco: Jossey-Bass.

Haley, J. (1980). *Leaving Home: The therapy of disturbed young people*. New York: McGraw-Hill.

Imber-Black, E. (1988). Idiosyncratic life cycle transitions and therapeutic rituals. In B. Carter & M. McGoldrick (Eds.). *The changing family life cycle: A framework for family therapy*. New York: Gardner Press.

Minuchin, S. (1974). *Families & family therapy*. Cambridge, MA: Harvard University Press.

Selvini Palazzoli, M., Boscolo, L., Cecchin, G., & Prata, G. (1977). Family rituals: A powerful tool in family therapy. *Family Process, 16*, 445–453.

Selvini Palazzoli, M., Boscolo, L., Cecchin, G., & Prata, G. (1980). Hypothesizing-Circularity-Neutrality: Three guidelines for the conductor of the session. *Family Process, 19*, 3–12.

Simon, R. (1972). Sculpting the family. *Family Process, 11*, 49–59.

Talen, M. R. & Lehr, M. L. (1984). A structural and developmental analysis of symptomatic adopted children and their families. *Journal of Marital & Family Therapy, 10*, 381–391.

Tomm, K. M. (1984). One perspective on the Milan systemic approach: Part I. Overview of development, theory, and practice. *Journal of Marital & Family Therapy, 10*, 113–125.

Tomm, K. M. (1985). Circular interviewing: A multifaceted clinical tool. In D. Campbell & R. Draper (Eds.). *Applications of systemic family therapy: The Milan approach*. New York: Grune & Stratton.

9

Assessing Family Rituals
in Alcoholic Families

STEVEN J. WOLIN

LINDA A. BENNETT

JANE S. JACOBS

RITUALS CAN TAP deeply into a family's shared sense of identity and affect the behavior of all family members. They clarify family roles, delineate boundaries, and transmit information about family identity across generations. Over the past several years we have studied the role of rituals in the transmission of alcoholism in families. Three successive studies[1] of alcoholic families have led to our identifying specific ritual-related factors which may play a protective role in the subsequent development of alcoholism among adult offspring.

In this chapter we will briefly describe the family rituals we have studied, share the development of our thinking as we conducted each successive research project, and describe the way we use our major research instrument, the Family Ritual Interview. Finally, we will discuss the clinical and research implications of viewing ritual as an important factor in family functioning.

Family rituals were first examined systematically by Bossard and Boll (1950). They documented the rituals as practiced in 186 nonclinical families, observing the important relationship between these shared, repeated symbolic family activities and what they termed the family's level of "integration." They saw rituals as the transmitters of family values, attitudes and goals: the core of family culture (Bossard & Boll, 1950).

David Reiss (1981) has proposed that the perpetuation of a family paradigm, or shared beliefs regarding the world, is a core function of rituals. He identified several types of idiosyncratic family rituals which, through repeated enactment, capture the family's view of the world, reinforce that perspective, and thereby perpetuate the family's paradigm.

The rituals we have studied fall into three groups: celebrations, traditions, and patterned routines. *Family celebrations* include holidays and other occasions practiced widely throughout the culture. Rites of passage, such as weddings, funerals, graduations, and bar mitzvahs; annual religious celebrations, such as Christmas, Easter, and the Passover Seder; and secular holiday observances, such as Thanksgiving dinner or the Fourth of July picnic belong within this category. Such rituals are relatively standardized, often specific to a certain subculture, and contain universal symbols. Rites of passage offer members the opportunity to observe developmental milestones. Through celebration rituals family members can clarify their status, assert a group identity, and signify their connectedness to a wider ethnic, cultural, or religious community. As one woman described,

> Christmas wouldn't be Christmas without certain touches—Frances always helps me bake the Christmas cookies and Pauline drives out to my brother's farm with John to cut down the tree. . . . Lent and Advent in the Christian year really have a theological function of getting ready, and our kids have heard this from us and they've heard it in the church. I think it's become enough a part of the tradition that they may really begin to understand what it really means for your own internal faith, and that's good.[2]

Family traditions are less culture-specific and more idiosyncratic to particular families. Summer vacations, visits with extended family, anniversary and birthday customs, and special parties or family reunions are common examples. While the culture influences the form of these practices (birthday cards and birthday cakes, for example), the family itself chooses the occasions it will emphasize as traditions and often puts its own special stamp on the activities. This family's vacation tradition provides a special limited time for family members to put aside other priorities and to enjoy each other's company:

> We usually try to get to Friendship Beach each summer. We've never taken other children with us. It's a chance for the girls to spend some time together. They don't usually have many interests in common but during that week they really get into the family mode and get along well. They'll go off along the boardwalk and take in the scene. The cottage we rent doesn't have a TV so we'll play games in the evening or get together with another family who's been going there for years.

Patterned routines are the most frequently enacted but least consciously planned of family rituals. Dinner times, bedtime routines with children, and regular leisure time activities on weekends or evenings belong within this category. These patterned routines help to organize daily family life and define members' roles and responsibilities. Symbols underlying such patterned routines provide reinforcement to members' sense of identity in the family and distinguish rituals from simple patterned interactions. In the following example, dinner time serves as an opportunity for contact, use of symbols, and the sharing of experiences:

> Most days we all get together for dinner and we stay after dinner at the table and talk and laugh. The best part is getting into everybody's life, finding out what they're doing. If someone's quiet we don't let them get away with not talking. . . . Julie actually rings a bell to call people to dinner — everyone sits down and we hold hands and say grace together.

Rituals provide a particularly rich and accessible window into the family's private world. Not only do they help to regulate and give meaning to everyday events, but they are also observable and highly memorable components of family life. When asked by clinicians or researchers to characterize their families, both adults and children are likely to describe a meaningful ritual that captures the essence of life in their origin family.

Rituals can also tell us something about family pathology. Dysfunctional families often report severe ritual disruption or disorganization of their ritual activities, suggesting that the stability and consistency of key rituals may provide important information about a family's social and emotional coherence. Low ritualization was evident, for example, in one research family which had been deeply affected by the father's alcoholism and the children's behavior problems. In this family, dinner provided little opportunity for contact or sharing; family members helped themselves to food in the kitchen and watched television in the livingroom or study. Vacations were unpredictable; if the father was drinking heavily, the family did not follow through its original plans and made no substitute arrangements.

Since 1974, we have been studying the role of family rituals in the transmission of alcoholism from one generation to the next. We began with the hypothesis that families which do not allow a parent's alcohol abuse to disrupt important family rituals are less likely to pass severe drinking problems on to their offspring. Many years and three projects later our hypothesis has grown more complex (and longer) and our convictions have deepened. We are impressed by the power of rituals as reflectors of family culture and family pathology. Although we do not yet know whether rituals are the *process* that actually transmits core family values, or whether they are simply excellent *markers* of such values, we are convinced that they can illuminate for clinicians and researchers alike interior qualities of family life and family identity (Wolin & Bennett, 1984).

THREE FAMILY RITUAL STUDIES

Alcoholism Transmission Via Family Ritual (1974–1977)

In our first study we looked only at the relationship between ritual disruption and alcohol transmission. As mentioned above, our hypothesis was that families with more intact rituals would be less likely to transmit alcoholism to the next generation. We defined three levels of ritual disruption, developed an interview to assess each family's degree of ritual disruption, and finally, compared the families' ritual dimension with the rate of alcoholism among adult offspring.

To examine the ritual disruption dimension, we assessed the impact of the alcoholic parent's heaviest drinking behavior on family rituals during the children's growing up years through coding of interview data. In "subsumptive" families, rituals had undergone considerable change, i.e., the alcohol abuse had "subsumed" the rituals and altered their performance and meaning. "Distinctive" families were those whose rituals evidenced relatively little change; the family had kept consequences of the drinking-related behavior "distinct" from its ritual life. "Intermediate subsumptive" families were those having a mix of distinctive and subsumptive rituals, thus not following a clear-cut pattern.

The outcome dimension of this first study concerned the extent of intergenerational transmission of alcoholism. "Nontransmitters" were families that showed no evidence of alcohol problems in the children's generation. "Transmitter" families had one or more children who became alcoholics or problem drinkers, or married alcoholics or problem drinkers (Goodwin et al., 1973). "Intermediate transmitter" families had at least one child who was or had been a heavy drinker. We considered this last category to be indecisive with respect to transmission.

We interviewed 25 middle- and upper-middle-class predominantly white families from Washington, DC; at least one parent in all families met accepted criteria for alcoholic or problem drinker. We also interviewed as many of their grown children (mean age 24.5) as we could contact. We conducted two interviews: an individual personal history of each parent and participating adult offspring, and an individual interview covering the family's traditions when the adult children were growing up (this was the first version of our research instrument, the Ritual Interview). We also held a family "art" session in which the members drew their impressions of the family under the impact of alcoholism. All sessions were held at the Center for Family Research; the first two were audiotaped and the third videotaped. Trained coders who were blind to the family's transmission status coded transcripts of the interview sessions according to the dimensions of degree of ritualization and the extent of ritual change or stability under the impact of parental alcohol abuse behavior. We then examined the relationship between ritual maintenance and alcoholism transmission. When the intermediate transmitter and intermediate subsumptive families were deleted from the analysis, and only the ten families in the extreme categories were examined (see Table 1), the results were significant ($p < .025$ by Fisher's Exact Test), indicating a relationship between substantial change in family rituals and the transmission of the alcoholism into the children's generation (Wolin, Bennett, Noonan, & Teitelbaum, 1980, p. 210).

Alcoholism and Family Heritage (1977–1980)

While these findings were provocative and supported our hypothesis, they also raised new questions. The family ritual type alone (subsumptive vs. distinctive) could not account for why some children within a particular family became alcoholics while others did not. Keeping in mind our focus on ritual loss and ritual continuity, we considered the importance of the adult children's decisions in selecting a spouse and in continuing or rejecting their origin families' ritual traditions.

These concerns led to the second phase of our research, the Alcoholism and Family Heritage Study (1977–1980). At this juncture, we added a second predictor variable, the selection of a family ritual heritage. We reasoned that in negotiating the rules and traditions for his/her new nuclear family, the offspring of an alcoholic family had four options. He/she could maintain his/her own ritual heritage, reject that past and adopt the spouse's origin family legacy, repeat patterns from both origin families, or create an entirely new ritual pattern, one without tradition. We suggested that the degree of risk for transmission depended both on the outcome of rituals practiced during the origin family experience and on the rituals selected to

TABLE 1
Ritual Change Type by Transmission Category
(n = 25 families)

	Transmitter	Intermediate Transmitter	Nontransmitter	Totals
Subsumptive	4	2	1	7
Intermediate Subsumptive	2	2	6	10
Distinctive	0	3	5	8
Totals	6	7	12	25

represent the succeeding generation's family identity. Thus, it was hypothesized that a child from a subsumptive family who retained his or her origin family's rituals would be at higher risk for transmission than an offspring who adopted the spouse's non-alcoholic family heritage.

We interviewed 68 married offspring and their spouses from 30 families with at least one alcoholic parent. This sample was older (mean age 33) than in the first study. At least two offspring and their spouses participated from each family.

Because this study emphasized the couples' negotiation of their own new family traditions, we thought that our Family History and Family Ritual Interviews might be conducted most profitably with the partners together. We could then focus on the offspring's and spouse's individual perceptions of their origin family experience, as well as the couple's *shared* perceptions of their own nuclear family. Before data collection commenced, we weighed the strengths and weaknesses of conjoint rather than individual interviews. We were concerned that one spouse might feel inhibited by the presence of the other and therefore give less information, that the spouses might collude and give a distorted picture, that marital conflicts might be aroused and left unresolved, or that the format might lead the couple to expect a marital therapy session. We also wondered whether the interviewer would have difficulty directing the sessions or handling any marital hostility that was expressed.

We ultimately found that there were several important advantages to a couple interview that outweighed potential disadvantages (Bennett & McAvity, 1985). A main consideration was our conviction that a joint session would enhance the process of data collection and analysis. The joint format gave the couple a chance to discuss issues more thoroughly. Partners were able to challenge each other's perceptions before arriving at a jointly held point of view or acknowledging those areas where they saw things differently. By requesting that couples clarify their agreements or disagreements about their perceptions of family traditions, the interviewer could place responsibility on the couple, rather than on the coder, for determining what constituted the family's shared view of itself.

The results of the study reaffirmed our original hypothesis regarding ritual disruption, in that those offspring from families with distinctive dinner times evidenced less transmission of alcoholism than the others. The most important family heritage variable to emerge from this study was that of the extent of "deliberateness" used by the couple in the formation of their family ritual practices and traditions. Deliberateness represents a family's ability to exert control in the planning and carrying out of rituals. Of the 12 couples with a high level of deliberateness, 75% were nontransmitters; of the 31 couples low on deliberateness, 77% were transmitters (Bennett, Wolin, Reiss, & Teitelbaum, 1987).

*Alcoholic Family Environment: Consequences
to Children (1980–1986)*

In our most recent study we have investigated the relationship between
family ritual factors and childhood disorders in the offspring of alcoholics.
We hypothesized that families with certain ritual characteristics — including
high level of ritualization, high deliberateness in choosing a ritual heritage,
and low ritual disruption in the face of parental drinking (i.e., distinctive
families) — would be less likely to have dysfunctional children.

Again our sample age differed from previous studies. We investigated 82
intact families with parents in their thirties or forties who had at least one
child between the ages of 6 and 18. Thirty-seven alcoholic families and 45
matched non-alcoholic controls underwent multiple assessments. Family
factors included both ritual and non-ritual-related family characteristics;
alcohol and drug patterns over three generations; parental intelligence; and
parental psychopathology. Outcome measures for the 144 children in the
study included indices of behavioral, cognitive, emotional, and social functioning. We conducted a joint Family History Interview during our first
meeting with the parents and covered such topics as family demography,
nuclear and extended family relations, family alcohol history, and structural
and affective qualities of current nuclear family. We used our joint Ritual
Interview in the second session, during which we had family members describe those family ritual areas which they had previously selected as being
most important. This version permitted a more detailed discussion of each
spouse's degree of ritual heritage continuity.

Our analysis of the children's data has demonstrated significant differences between the children of non-alcoholic and alcoholic parents (Bennett
et al., 1987). In the second analytic step we will determine whether or not
ritual-protected, but alcoholic, families produce a less troubled subgroup of
children.

THE FAMILY RITUAL INTERVIEW

As we have refined our notions of ritualization and the continuity of family
heritage, we have revised our Family Ritual Interview for each of the successive studies. In our first study we were primarily concerned with identifying
family ritual areas and determining whether they had been significantly
disrupted by the parent's alcoholism. Consequently we reviewed six areas of
family life during the children's growing up period: dinner, holidays, evenings, weekends, vacations, and visitors in the home. Questions were aimed
at distinguishing "patterned" behavior from rituals. While patterned behavior is repetitive, stable, and continuous, rituals are also characterized by the

family's acceptance of the continuation of the activity over time and the presence of meaningful symbols. The family conveys the message that "this activity says something important about us."

Questions addressed changes in family ritual behavior before and during the period of heaviest parental drinking. These questions covered alcohol use during the family ritual; the response of the family to the parent's intoxication; the change in the alcoholic member's participation in the ritual when intoxicated; the response of the family to that change; and the overall change in the ritual itself during the period of heaviest drinking.

For the second study the "family identity" concept was added to the subsumptive/distinctive variable. In order to investigate ritual heritage continuity, parallel areas were explored in both the origin family interview and the current nuclear family interview. These areas included family demography, nuclear family relations, extended family relations, family alcohol history, the rituals of dinner time and holidays, and family roles. The interviewer asked about origin family traditions and current nuclear family traditions. Specific questions about the family's development of its own traditions, similarities or differences from each spouse's origin family, and the extent of planfulness in the selection from among ritual traditions helped to elaborate the relative predominance of each spouse's family heritage in the new nuclear family.

In our third study we incorporated the notion of deliberateness into our interview format and expanded the focus on current ritual activities. The couple selected two nuclear family and two extra-nuclear family rituals for a discussion of their emotional and symbolic meaning, as well as their structure and continuity. The interviewer then addressed whether each selected ritual represented a continuation or a change from either origin family heritage and the degree to which this was a deliberate act. Finally, in alcoholic families, disruption due to the alcoholic parent's behavior was explored for each ritual.

In the ritual interview we systematically explored four aspects of these key family activities (see Table 2). First we examined the *level of ritualization*: We were interested in the consistency of the ritual behavior over time; the extent to which each family member played a specific role; the degree of affect and symbolism associated with the event; and how much investment family members had in maintaining the ritual. Secondly, we assessed *change and development of the ritual* over the history of the family. Starting with the early performance of the ritual, we inquired about any events, such as alcohol use, that might have altered or disrupted the ritual in significant ways.

The third important aspect of each ritual was its *similarity to rituals in each partner's origin family*. We were interested in whether each marital

TABLE 2
Ritual Interview Format
(Second Couple Interview)

Four family life areas — two that are carried out mainly by members of the immediate family and two involving relatives, friends or other associates — are selected on the basis of information collected during the first couple interview. At the start of this session, we ask the parents to agree upon the two most important areas of family life in each of these categories. The following topics are covered in an open-ended interview procedure regarding family members' perceptions in each of these four areas:

I. *Level of Ritualization*

    A. Overall description: basic pattern and variation
    B. Roles that various family members typically take
    C. Positive and negative aspects

II. *Evidence of Developmental Changes*

    A. Current performance
    B. Experience early in marriage
    C. If an alcoholic family, change that occurred during the heaviest drinking period
    D. Degree of stability over the years of marriage
    E. Other disrupting influences upon this activity

III. *Comparison to Same Events in Origin Families*

    A. Similarity to or difference from wife's family
    B. Similarity to or difference from husband's family

IV. *Role of Drinking*

    A. Whether the family is alcoholic or not, the emphasis upon drinking alcoholic beverages in carrying out this activity
    B. Changes in the role of alcohol over the years

partner had continued his or her origin family practice or had adopted a new set of traditions from the spouse's family or from another source. For adult children of alcoholics, we see this as an important choice point in reducing the power of their family alcoholism heritage. We also tried to understand whether such choices were deliberate or simply happened as the result of circumstances. Finally we explored the *role of drinking behavior in the ritual*, regardless of whether the family was alcoholic.

THE CODING OF FAMILY IDENTITY AND RITUAL DIMENSIONS

After the families responded to all the questions in the Family History Interview and the Ritual Interview, a transcript was produced from the audiotaped sessions. This transcript became the basis for the decisions made about family ritual dimensions by two coders, a psychologist and an anthropologist. A coding manual was developed to provide guidelines for the coding process. Coders read and coded three family record sets at a time. Following a random order listing of families, they alternated alcoholic and non-alcoholic families in the coding process.

The 14 questions encompassed in the coding procedure (see Table 3) were divided into two general subgroups, eight of which pertained to the family's overarching attitudes and behaviors regarding ritual continuity (called the Family Identity Section), and six of which specifically addressed the current family's ritual complex (called the Family Ritual Section). Since there were multiple sections in each of the general questions, and since we selected four rituals for analysis in this study, the total number of questions posed was 24.

For each question, the coder determined whether the family was high, moderate, or low on that dimension. The coding manual[3] provided an extensive description of each possible choice for each of the 14 questions. Key words were also provided, alerting the coder to frequently-used phrases which would indicate a high, medium, or low response. Because we were interested in a shared family view, coders were asked to arrive at the score which best reflected a family consensus. The coding manual also provided guidelines as to which questions in the ritual or family history interview should be referred to for each answer. Finally, examples illustrated typical couple responses.

The Family Identity Section

The eight questions in this section cover family ties, family heritage, and other aspects of family identity. Questions 1, 2, and 3 cover three related issues: the family's current level of *ethnicity, religiosity*, and their *attention to family history*. For each we asked the coder to determine the family's level. For example, with regard to ethnicity, the manual instructs the coder to select a "low" level of ethnicity if

> the family barely knows about their ethnic heritage, and if they do, it is simply taken as information with little meaning to the value system of behavior of the family. They may describe themselves as just Americans. What they do know is downplayed in their talk about the family as well as in their family activities. Some may be embarrassed to talk about it, or think it is a highly boring subject. In such families the children don't tend to ask questions about ethnic heritage, and the parents don't have much to tell them.

In contrast, a "moderate" level of religiosity is determined when a family shows some, but not a lot, of affiliation to a religious group, and a family

TABLE 3
Ritual-Related Questions

1. Assess level of ethnicity for:
   a. Wife's origin family
   b. Husband's origin family
   c. Current nuclear family

2. Assess level of religiosity for:
   a. Wife's origin family
   b. Husband's origin family
   c. Current nuclear family

3. Assess degree of emphasis placed upon family history for:
   a. Wife's origin family
   b. Husband's origin family
   c. Current nuclear family

4. How much has this current nuclear family evidenced physical proximity, social contact, and emotional connectedness to the:
   a. Wife's origin family
   b. Husband's origin family

5. Early in the couple's marriage, to what extent did they think about and discuss their intentions for developing a family identity (including rituals, interactional patterns, and family organization) that was similar to or different from either of their origin families?

6. Over the history of this nuclear family, to what extent has the couple and their children charted an explicit course with respect to their rituals, family interactional patterns, and family organization?

7. To what degree are the nuclear family's ties to people and/or organizations outside the immediate and extended family developed in this generation?

8. In the alcoholic families, how much have members confronted the drinking behavior of the alcoholic parents?

9. At what level is the specific ritual ritualized?
   a. Ritual 1
   b. Ritual 2
   c. Ritual 3
   d. Ritual 4

10. Which is the more important nuclear family ritual?
    a. Ritual 1
    b. Ritual 2

11. Which is the more important extra-nuclear family ritual?
    a. Ritual 3
    b. Ritual 4

12. With respect to each ritual, to what extent has the wife's origin family heritage been carried over into the current family's observation of the ritual?
    a. Ritual 1

TABLE 3
(*continued*)

   b. Ritual 2
   c. Ritual 3
   d. Ritual 4

13. With respect to each ritual, to what extent has the husband's origin family heritage been carried over into the current family's observation of the ritual?
   a. Ritual 1
   b. Ritual 2
   c. Ritual 3
   d. Ritual 4

14. In the alcoholic families, how much has each ritual changed due to the impact of the parental drinking?
   a. Ritual 1
   b. Ritual 2
   c. Ritual 3
   d. Ritual 4

with a "high" level of attention to family history amply demonstrates its commitment to the family's past. The manual gives this description for a "high" level of attention to family history:

> [k]nowing about and valuing family history is a core part of the family's identity. Outsiders quickly come to know these families' relatives because they are prominently displayed in the house and talked about frequently. There is often pride, even about unsavory characters from the family's past. Stories are told with enthusiasm and flair. Children are taught the stories, especially focusing upon prior generations. Migration history for the family can be important in such high family history families. Current characteristics of family members are often attributed to events and personalities in the past.

Question 4 examines the *social and emotional connectedness* that the current family maintains with both origin families. We include the frequency of contacts, the kinds of activities which bring the two generations together, the emotional bond or felt ties experienced across generations, and the overall importance placed on the maintenance of strong connections across generations. Connectedness is evaluated separately for the wife's and the husband's families of origin, since it is possible for them to hold different levels of attachment to these two families. An example of our description of a "moderate" level of connectedness includes the following:

> "Selective connectedness" is probably the most apt phrase to describe these families. They recognize their relationship to the origin family, while not organizing their family life around that relationship to a great degree. . . . Ties to certain

family members may be more highly valued and developed than to others, but there are at least some that the family feels a sense of closeness to. By and large the extended family is less important in their social life than are friends, co-workers or neighbors. At the same time they keep the family up-to-date on major happenings. . . . Rituals do not typically revolve around these members and their presence or absence.

Questions 5 and 6 probe the couple's level of planning and carrying out an explicit family identity. We consider it important that some young couples pay a high level of attention to the kind of family identity they establish. Other couples are quite adrift about their subsequent family identity, exercising little control over that area of their life. We have captured this difference by two questions; the first focusing on the level of the couple's expectations, and the second on the subsequent course of family development.

In Question 5 coders consider the period of courtship and early years of marriage. *Early expectations for family identity* concern the extent to which the couple thought about and talked over what kind of family they wished to develop. This includes how much of their origin families' style they wished to continue or leave behind, and how much they spoke specifically of their new family. Were they aware of possibilities, the advantages of some and the limitations of others? Was there agreement between spouses about their ideal plans? How different did they wish it to be from their origin families? Some key words included in the manual to describe a couple "high" on this quality of deliberate planning are the following: "Purposeful, motivated, explicit, intentional, directed, determined, proactive, deliberate." Maureen and Roy Bishop,[4] one couple from our sample, were determined not to repeat their own family experiences when they got married; Maureen's mother was an alcoholic and both of Roy's parents were "remote and relatively uninterested in family life." Roy's description constitutes a "high level of deliberateness":

> I think our dreams for our family were shaped to a great extent by what our own family background was. I remember each of us talking about what our born-into family was like and that we didn't want it to be that way in most cases.

For Question 6 we turn to the *actual course that family identity development took*. We are concerned here with behavior rather than aspirations. Was there a clear-cut plan and could the spouses take control of their lives to carry it out? Key words for a family "low" on this characteristic are: surprise, unpredictable, inconsistent, frustration, resignation, disappointment. An example used in the manual for such a low rated family: "Try as we might, we can't get things organized at home. It is just a lot of coming and going, each of us doing his own things. We hate to have people stop by since the house is such a wreck. We don't want it that way but no plan seems to change things." In contrast, a family rated "high" on this dimension might say, "Even though we have encountered some potential setbacks in taking our two vacations a year as breaks for the family, we have managed to pull them off every year. It does require being flexible about other things, such as school attendance and sports. But they learn so much by these breaks that we think they take priority."

Question 7 concerns the level of attachment the current generation has to the nonfamily social network. *Ties to nonfamily* include participation in community activities as well as the family's friendship network. While families low on this scale are described as "cut off, isolated and detached," families highly connected in their community are described in the manual as "outgoing, socially engaged, and joiners." Once again, mid-range families are intermediate in their level of connectedness, intermittently and selectively involved.

> The Chaits are a family low in nonfamily ties. In describing their children's participation, Caroline Chait said, "For a while they were in some sports. Then they said they didn't want to do it anymore, and they stopped. There really isn't any group around where we are." Caroline and John don't encourage them to rejoin because it simply isn't a priority.

The final question in this first section pertains to only the alcoholic families and was coded only for them. We want to know the *level of confrontation of the alcoholic parent* exhibited by the family as a group. How active were the non-alcoholic family members in directly addressing the abusive drinking behavior? We consider this question central to our family identity/family ritual model because families who actively protect their rituals are to be distinguished from those who do not. As we have shown in a prior study (Wolin et al., 1980), confrontation of the alcoholic is one important way that families without an alcoholic identity protect their cherished non-alcoholic rituals. Consequently, we wish to establish each family's level of confrontation.

The family was rated "low" if members ignored the alcoholic's drinking problem and discouraged active discussion of the issue. In the "moderate" range, individual family members might try to influence the alcoholic, but these attempts were intermittent and lacked the force of a concerted family effort. In families with a "high" rating, "at least one family member has taken verbal, and then effective action, and has been backed by the rest of the family." While the drinking may not have stopped, "the alcoholic has been put on the spot and the family has gone on record saying that they would not permit the drinking to continue in the same way."

Bob Trueheart's wife and sons have made intermittent, isolated, and ultimately unsuccessful attempts to confront his drinking. "I've confronted him verbally," says Ann Trueheart, "but I've also covered for him, and made excuses. John (her son) got angry at Bob last year and let him have it, but it didn't do him any good so he just avoids him now."

This family would receive a moderate score.

The Family Ritual Section

The six questions in this section examine aspects of the family's actual ritual observation. Each family had chosen two nuclear family rituals and two extra-nuclear family rituals; these became the basis on which the remaining assessments were made. In the interviews we explored the ways in which couples arrived at a shared perspective, and we asked the coder to choose a code that reflected a family-level consensus about the ritual activity.

Question 9 covers the family's *level of ritualization*. The coders determined this by considering six dimensions of the rituals selected by the family: the designation of roles to family members in carrying out the ritual; the routine and timing of the event; attendance of family members; affect surrounding the ritual; the importance of continuing the ritual over time; and the attribution of special meaning and symbolism to the event.

The manual instructs the coder to select a "low" level of ritualization if there is uncertainty and considerable flexibility in the way the ritual is carried out. The low ritual family does not give significant meaning or priority to the ritual and it is quite vulnerable to internal and external changes in the family, such as parents' work schedules and children's extracurricular activities. The ritual has a functional rather than a symbolic meaning to the group.

A "moderate" level of ritualization is selected if the family places some priority on carrying out the ritual, but there is considerable fluctuation with regard to the family members who attend, the roles they perform, and the form the ritual takes. The family enjoys the ritual event but expects that it may change significantly or die out as the family develops. Cue words for this category include "moderately variable, waxes and wanes, and intermediate affect."

In contrast, highly ritualized family events are characterized by their stability and predictability, and by the special value the family places upon them. The ritual is often memorable because of special practices the family always includes as part of the activity. From the manual: "Roles are clearly assigned, the absence of regular attenders is not taken lightly, and changes in routine tend to be discussed and resolved in advance. The ritual contains special symbols and brings out strong feelings, although these feelings are not always positive. The family intends to preserve this ritual into the future." An example from the study of a "high" level of ritualization:

> Because our families live so far away from us, we have made a point to hold a family reunion every year. It's really a fun time. We do the cooking and preparation as a family, and we really stress the children's role. After everyone leaves, the children always have lots of questions about who did what when we were kids.

Important to the "high" category is the ability of the ritual to bring out a strong sense of family identity.

Questions 10 and 11 deal with the *relative importance of the rituals*. Using the six criteria considered for determining the level of ritualization, the coders decided which of the two nuclear family rituals and which of the two extra-nuclear family rituals are of greater value to the family. Once again, the rituals which were most stable and most associated with strong family affect were coded as more important. These questions are designed to categorize families regarding their focus on ritual practices, i.e., within or outside the nuclear family.

Questions 12 and 13 address the *carry-over of origin heritages into the current observation of the ritual*. Considering each spouse separately, the coders again used the six criteria to evaluate the extent to which the four ritual areas constitute a continuation of family-of-origin traditions. For a "low" carry-over of origin heritage, the coders looked for "virtually no resemblance to the current ritual observation. The couple may have made an explicit effort to do things differently around this ritual or to create a new one where one did not previously exist."

A "moderate" degree of carry-over was selected when similarities to the previous generation's observation is more accidental than planful. There are generally more differences than similarities, and the families show some evidence of making the ritual "their own thing." An example: "When we were growing up we didn't have enough money for presents, so we got a card and my Mom would bake us a cake. Now we give the kids a gift and we usually try to take them out for a meal that they like."

In the case of "high" carry-over, the previous generation's ritual is clearly the model for the current family. The manual notes that, while the particulars of the event are rarely identical, the couple is "immediately able to identify and describe where there are similarities. The sentiment and symbolic value surrounding the ritual are the same, and great importance is placed upon continuity with the previous generation.

In Question 14 we consider the degree of *ritual change under the impact of parental drinking*. For the alcoholic families only, we assess whether the ritual has retained its original character over the family life cycle or has been substantially disrupted or destroyed. When "considerable change" has occurred, "the ritual-related events have changed permanently or fluctuate so much from time to time that it appears that the alcohol abuse has subsumed the ritual. Roles, routines, and attendance have changed in a notable way. Any positive affect has eroded, and the family may avoid holding the ritual to avoid negative feelings." In the case of the "moderate" change, the family has adapted some elements of the ritual to include the intoxicated parent's behavior, but the ritual still bears a significant resemblance to the way it was observed in earlier years. The family spends a good deal of energy keeping the drinking at bay, and the long-term preservation of the ritual seems uncertain. When a family is coded as "slight change or none at all," the essence of the ritual has been maintained despite occasional disruptions by the alcoholic parent. Key words in the "distinctive" category include: constant, intact, and stable. The following vignette illustrates the "distinctive" category:

> Charles and Ruth Woodson and their children have been going to a music camp for two weeks every August for the past 10 years. Charles plays the oboe, his son, Bobby, plays the flute, and the other family members enthusiastically attend their concerts every afternoon. As Ruth's drinking has gotten worse she often falls asleep on the couch of their cabin by concert time. After many instances of trying to wake her, they have settled on putting a blanket around her and going on without her. Even though Ruth doesn't attend, the family members have retained much of the enjoyment of their shared concerts.

DISCUSSION

After conducting these three research projects, we are much closer to an interview format for the assessment of rituals within families, which we hope will be useful to clinicians and researchers alike. Although confirmation of this instrument must necessarily await reliability and validation studies currently in progress, some conclusions regarding family rituals can be drawn. In this concluding section we will review our current thinking about ritual, offer suggestions for the clinical use of these concepts, and point to several areas where additional clarifications would be helpful.

Characteristics of Family Rituals Which Make Them Helpful to Researchers and Clinicians

First, rituals are *universally found* in families of all types. Because family life takes form by repetitious, patterned and symbolic activities, rituals are inherent to families. We have been struck by most families' use of ritual, across the three categories of ceremonies, traditions, and patterned routines. Regardless of the stage of family development, the ethnic orientation of the family, or its composition and structure, ritual is easily defined as a family activity. Because rituals are so ubiquitous, they permit us to *compare* families who at first glance appear very different. Rituals around mealtime, around rites of passage, and around leisure time activities, for example, make all families sound more alike than different.

Second, family rituals contain, better than any other aspect of family life, the myths, history, and identity of the family. A group level ritual conveys and teaches family *identity* to all its members. There is no better route into the themes of particular families than to interview its members about their cherished (or despised) rituals. "The way we do Thanksgiving," one man reported, "with all our repeated stories, our recurrent fights, our great traditions and our petty disputes, the day is really us. It's really our family!"

Third, ritual is largely *a conscious activity*, one that families can, and usually want to, talk about to outsiders. In our experience families become charged up at the prospect of talking about their ritual activities, whether they concern this generation or those of the past. This common response is quite different from the reaction we often get when talking to a family about such issues as "closeness" or "intimacy," which for many family members are more abstract and more difficult to describe.

Fourth, rituals can be *taught* to families who don't have them, *changed* in families who are so inclined, and *dropped* in families who collectively make such decisions. There are few tools that we, as clinicians, can use so easily with families to educate and shape their lives. As group behaviors, rituals are *preemptive*—when instituted they take precedence over alternative activities, when removed they allow for the development of new family events. In our view family rituals are a largely unappreciated, potentially powerful force in the clinician's repertoire.

Clinical Range of Families on Core Ritual Dimensions

LEVEL OF RITUALIZATION. Families vary considerably on their ritual level. Some families, high in ritual, have many group events. They exercise considerable planning and organization in their lives, pay close attention to the past way of doing things, and issue strong directives to insure consistency and control. Symbolism abounds in such highly ritualized families, and great meaning is found in relatively small events. For the members who take comfort in such structures, high ritualization may feel right and appropriate. For other members, however, these activities may be hollow and constraining. The ritual may have lost its meaning; what is left may only be the command to perform and the shell of what once was.

Families low in ritual, on the other hand, place much less emphasis on role and hierarchy in their collective lives. When compared with families high in ritualization, such families are more egalitarian, more present-oriented, and less organized in the activities of daily life. For these families ritual plays only a small role in their lives; they feel little need or derive little benefit from ritual, sensing quickly the constraints posed by order and the pressures posed by family expectation. On the other hand, members of low ritual families who need more than such families offer will feel a marked emptiness and lack of values. We speculate that the children in such families will find order and meaning elsewhere, often in destructive behaviors outside the family.

FAMILY OF HERITAGE. As we noted earlier, families vary on the source of their ritual. Briefly, some base their ritual form on one or the other origin family, while other couples have amalgamated new rituals from both origin families. Families in a fourth group have divested themselves of the traditions and patterns of both origin family legacies and adopted totally new rituals or taken on virtually none at all. While we cannot say which of these possibilities produces either the healthiest or the most dysfunctional situation, there are some suggestive trends. Usually one family's ritual heritage predominates; because our culture encourages "kin-keeping" activities by the wife, typically her origin family ritual patterns prevail. This works well except when the balance has shifted too far and the husband feels neglected or heritage-deprived. Some integration of both families' past seems proper, particularly when there has been a clear decision for such an adaptation.

When the rituals of both origin families have been dropped in the new generation, and the couple develops strong community ties, we see a viable alternative to the carrying over of past rituals. However, when the new family is very low on ritual and struggles for a meaningful identity *without structure*, we are pessimistic. Such families, we propose, are quite vulnerable to chaotic response when the unexpected strikes, because they have few supports both inside and out to assist them. From our perspective these families, low in ritual and low in heritage, are in a most precarious status.

DELIBERATENESS. We see a considerable range of differences as we watch young couples negotiating the development of their own family ritual traditions. Families high in deliberateness think in a conscious way and make purposeful decisions about their own rituals and family traditions. Throughout the life cycle of the family, in the wake of ordinary changes and of major crises, family members maintain their commitment to important traditions. At the other extreme, families with a low degree of deliberateness exhibit a passive attitude towards the creation and maintenance of a shared ritual identity. The young couple may just slip into a continuation of one or both of their origin families' traditions without any discussion of the shared values which might motivate them to make this decision. These rituals then become devoid of any special meaning for the new nuclear family.

We have been impressed by the observation of children from alcoholic families who select prospective spouses who have grown up in highly ritualized, non-alcoholic family traditions. Making a deliberate decision to discard the alcoholism-related rituals in one's own family and to adopt one's spouse's non-alcoholic traditions in the new nuclear family seems to provide some protection for the adult child of an alcoholic. In such an arrangement the new nuclear family rituals may be almost identical to the spouse's origin family heritage or may incorporate changes developed by the new couple. While the protective effect of this choice is compelling, the spouse from the alcoholic family may initially feel overwhelmed by the intensity and intimacy of the non-alcoholic ritual practices. If the differences seem too great and too difficult to manage, at first the spouse may resist the changes or withdraw.

SUBSUMPTIVENESS/DISTINCTIVENESS. Families vary widely in their ability to maintain their important traditions in the face of severe parental drinking. Some families persist with unswerving commitment, as in the case of one of our research families where the wife and children literally carried the inebriated father into the back seat of the family car so that they could start their summer vacation on schedule. Subsumptive families permit the drinking behavior to alter the ritual substantially, so that it is robbed of its original meaning or, in some cases, ceases altogether. One spouse from a research family described the changes that had taken place in the dinnertime ritual, which had once been the cornerstone of family life. "It seems like a shadow of what it once was, a ghost. Ed stands in the corner of the dining room with a drink in his hand while the rest of us eat. We're afraid to say anything that might set him off."

Families that can keep their rituals distinctive despite the drinking behavior show an ability to *disengage* from the alcoholism in a healthy way. Optimally, such families are able to continue with important priorities without getting sidetracked by the alcoholism, yet without totally rejecting the alcoholic. These family members can remember and carry with them the positive elements of their origin family life, while selectively disengaging from the damaging alcohol-related ones. The dilemma for these offspring often comes when they are establishing and deepening their own nuclear family commitments; the disengagement style which proved so helpful in facilitating their separation from their alcoholic family may make it more difficult for them to form successful intimate bonds with their marital partner and children.

Areas for Future Ritual Research

Two aspects of ritual—the family's adaptability in the use of ritual and the family's use of symbols in performing ritual—appear important in the assessment of individual families.

ADAPTABILITY. Over the family life cycle family needs around ritual change considerably. Young couples without children frequently eschew rituals from their origin families, especially when their practice involves lengthy commitment back in the arms of the past. They may forcefully reject their past during this phase of their marriage, only to find renewed meaning in rituals as time passes.

Children typically elicit parental desires for ritual establishment. This may come about as decisions are made for religious identity reasons or as parents sense their child's need for structure and family. Children themselves may demand the institution of family rituals, from regular bedtime storytelling to annual celebrations commemorating all sorts of anniversaries. Here the family's ability to *flexibly devise appropriate rituals* will first be demonstrated. Some families will leap at the opportunity to dust off well worn rituals from the prior generation. The process usually goes smoothly. Other parents, who never had such traditions or whose celebrations are remembered with pain and disapproval, will invest rituals to meet their family's needs—another healthy adaptation. On the other hand, some couples, because they disagree about the proper way to proceed, or are set against all structure and formality in their lives, or are insensitive to the request at the moment, never create the traditions. Dinner time may not be elevated as an important hour for regular family interaction. Birthdays may be forgotten or discounted. Religious celebrations may be avoided or rejected. In each of these situations, we would suggest that families can benefit from introducing rituals into their lives. The family incapable of sifting through all the possibilities, we believe, is nonadaptive and will in time suffer.

Later on in the family life cycle a similar need for flexibility around ritual use occurs. Ritual is often a prime target for disapproval and rejection during adolescent rebellion. Teenagers are too busy with their peers to bring out the old traditions once more. They may feel that standard family celebrations fail to carry meaning for them, so they refuse to attend. The flexible family, we propose, adjusts its use of ritual to meet the needs of this phase of family development. Hollow rituals are dropped or altered to make use of current interests. Membership is adjusted as appropriate to include important new friends. Some rituals are maintained in spite of protests and, perhaps, without the protesting family members. They will be encouraged, without pressure, to return next year, when their attitude may very well have changed. If the ritual works its spell they will likely return.

Thus, we find adaptability of ritual across the life cycle an important, but as yet untapped, dimension in evaluating family resources. Whether families are basically high or low on the level of ritualization they will benefit from a flexible approach. The low ritual family should institute some ritual observances to meet their small children's needs, especially around holidays, birthdays celebrations, and daily routines. The highly ritualized family should be prepared to adjust, modify, and even discard rituals which are no longer effective or relevant. With such adaptability, high ritual families stand the best chance of motivating their children to transmit these important events into the succeeding generations.

SYMBOLISM. Similarly, it is our impression that families will vary considerably and in important ways around their use of symbols and symbolism during ritual celebrations. In some families symbols of the past, both of the current generation as well of their origin families, play an important role in ritual observance. Heirlooms may be brought out for annual holiday celebrations, such as Thanksgiving dinner. In these families, who are high on a symbolism scale, special foods will be cooked, familiar music will be played or sung, and traditional clothing will be worn to capture meaning through symbolic objects. The power of the ritual feeling is enhanced when such objects are used; consequently, families high in ritualization typically use many objects of symbolic importance when they practice their traditions, celebrations, and even daily ritualized routines.

By contrast, some families appear studiously to avoid symbolic behaviors and symbols themselves. They may even renounce the use of objects which represent the past, trying to erase memory as if it had power over them. Families who can find only negativity and pain in their roots may be incapable of reproducing that past with its symbolic representatives. Other families may reject such symbols as religious relics or traditional meals, seeing them as constraining, meaningless devices. We suspect that such symbol-absent families have gone too far in ridding themselves of ritual symbols, just as the symbol-rich family may be inciting rebellion by strangling creativity in ritual observance.

With both these dimensions of ritual—adaptability and symbol use—we predict a relationship between mid-range adherence and family health. However, because these are untested hypotheses, any conclusions as to their importance must await future studies.

Clinical Applications of the Family Ritual Dimension

Clinicians can make use of these ideas by viewing family ritual activities as a source of important information about family dynamics, as well as a potential area for powerful interventions. As part of making a family assessment, a therapist might ask a family to describe important family rituals. Family members' responses may be viewed as a window into that family's core themes, symbols, and values. In making a systematic clinical assessment of family rituals, the clinician might consider the following areas.

LEVEL OF RITUALIZATION. The therapist can ask the family to describe one or two important rituals, including the details of the events themselves, the participants, and any changes in the rituals over the years. Of particular interest is the symbolic meaning to family members of special objects or activities, as well as the "pull" of the rituals — their power to preempt compelling events in the family's life.

FAMILY HERITAGE. The therapist can ask about the process by which these rituals were passed — or not — from the spouses' origin families to their own nuclear family. The family can reflect on which origin family heritage predominates in the current family, and on whether this choice represents an adoption by one of the spouses of a healthier family pattern.

DELIBERATENESS. This area is related to the previous one and addresses the current family's degree of purposefulness in establishing its ritual traditions. The clinician focuses on the early phase of the family's life cycle, when the couple was developing its own unique identity and values. The therapist elicits information about the spouses' awareness of family traditions they wanted to keep or discard, their ability to develop and plan a set of meaningful rituals for their family, and their capacity to maintain the important rituals over the lifetime of the family.

ADAPTABILITY. The therapist can assess the ability of the family to make necessary changes in the key ritual areas as children get older, work and school schedules change, and new individual and family priorities emerge. The clinician is interested in the extent to which the family can strike a middle ground between ritual continuity and respect for the individuality of family members.

MAINTENANCE OF RITUALS. This area enables the therapist to assess the ability of alcoholic families to continue with the rituals they have described when parental drinking threatens to disrupt them. The clinician can ask what family members actually do when the drinking becomes severe. Of importance here is the ability of the family to sustain the special meanings and feelings inherent in the rituals while disengaging from the alcoholic family member in a respectful way.

We also recommend that therapists consider the power of rituals in planning treatment interventions. Because rituals can embody core family symbols and values, a therapist may be able to help family members mobilize a sense of shared meaning and purpose by assisting them in constructing a relevant ritual.

We have described elsewhere (Bennett, Wolin, & McAvity, 1988) five possible interventions for clinicians who have assessed the role of rituals in a family. Among the interventions are *constructing* a ritual which has never been there, *reinstating* a ritual that was once highly valued, and *redirecting* a ritual which has undergone destructive changes due to an enduring problem in the family's life.

Brief Example — Recovering Intimacy Through Rituals

Joshua, 25, had been on his own for eight years when he met Sarah, also 25. As the second oldest son in a family with an alcoholic father, Joshua had watched his mother try unsuccessfully to bring a sense of normality to the family's daily routines. Joshua's father frequently broke into rages when drinking, frightening all four children and causing Joshua to spend most of his time at his best friend's house. One of the reasons Joshua was attracted to Sarah was that she came from a close, loving family with many valued traditions and rituals.

Joshua and Sarah were married and soon had a son and a daughter. Joshua was delighted to adopt the rituals practiced by Sarah in her origin family, with some minor changes. Joshua sometimes had a few too many social drinks, but Sarah helped by kindly but firmly letting him know he had had too much.

The world of this family changed irrevocably when at age 32 Sarah discovered that she had breast cancer. She had breast surgery, but during the long recovery process Joshua began to drink heavily. The long family dinners and the regular weekend family excursions disappeared, as neither parent could take responsibility. Finally Sarah's physical strength returned, but for three years Joshua continued to get drunk every night.

When Sarah threatened to leave, Joshua agreed to go into therapy. At that point Sarah and Joshua were not speaking to each other and were providing only the most basic level of care for their children. Information that needed to be conveyed from one parent to the other was communicated through the children.

Before dealing directly with the events of the past three years and the feelings they had engendered, the therapist attempted to restore a basic predictable family structure. Appealing to the parents' concern for their children, he helped them put together a plan for a family breakfast routine (*a ritual constructed*). Although the negotiations were painfully slow, they eventually set up a workable routine. Sharing responsibility for the meal and providing a reliable shared time for the children eased a little of the tension.

Next the couple worked on restoring a dinner time routine (*a ritual reinstated*). The therapist learned that during dinner times before the illness, family members had sat and talked about their day at work or school. He helped them start this ritual again. Through this activity the parents and children started again to share personal experiences with each other. It helped them recall the closeness of the family before Sarah's illness, although they were still very far from that point.

When Joshua and Sarah had achieved some success in restoring a limited degree of stability and contact among family members, the therapist began to help them with the difficult work of dealing with the catastrophic events of the past three years. Over the next few months the presence of these mealtime rituals helped to provide an underpinning of stability for the family as the couple went through the gradual, painful process of repairing their relationship. After much work, when Sarah and Joshua had finally recovered much of their capacity to talk with and trust each other, the therapist helped them to institute new vacation rituals. Their vacations had become filled with Joshua's intoxicated binges; now they were geared toward the interests of the two children, who helped to plan them (*a ritual redirected*).

A therapist can also *modify* a ritual which does not represent an acceptable form to the couple due to family heritage or cultural differences. Both partners may have brought elements of their respective origin family rituals into the new nuclear family but without being able to address important differences or to bring the disparate pieces together to form a coherent whole. In this situation, the therapist can help the family *integrate* the separate components into an event that has genuine meaning for everyone.

Brief Example — A Christmas Dilemma

Evelyn and Joseph Laudry sought the services of a therapist because they were "not communicating." They frequently disagreed about how to bring up their children. Through extensive questioning, the therapist discovered that Evelyn grew up in a well-to-do urban Protestant family, while Joseph grew up in an Irish Catholic family from a smaller community and more modest means. While Evelyn and Joseph had many intellectual interests in common, they had been unable to deal with the differences in their origin family values and practices.

The differences were reflected in many ways. One example was the different practices each origin family had evolved in celebrating the Christmas holiday. In Evelyn's family Christmas was a joyous celebration of generosity and good fellowship. These values were expressed through giving thoughtful presents to all family members and by gracious and generous entertaining of extended family and friends during the holiday. For Joseph's family Christmas represented the expression of deep religious convictions. The family studied the religious meaning of Christmas during the weeks before the holiday, always attended mass on Christmas Eve, and spent the actual day only with the immediate family. A special grace at the Christmas day dinner symbolized the central spiritual meaning of the holiday.

The therapist helped the spouses to see these differences as a natural outgrowth of their diverse cultures, rather than as "right" or "wrong" ways to conduct family business. She encouraged each partner to reflect on the most meaningful elements for them in the origin family ritual practices. When each spouse understood the essence of the ritual's meaning, the therapist helped the couple to construct a Christmas ritual which incorporated each partner's core values in a coherent way.

The couple planned a series of family religious activities in the weeks before the holiday, which culminated in family attendance of mass. In the past Evelyn had thought Joseph's emphasis on Bible readings and church was insensitive to her. Reframing the issue in terms of two family cultures helped Evelyn to understand her husband's commitment to the practices, as well as to be clearer about which practices she could join and support.

Joseph continued for a while to feel uncomfortable with the notion of Christmas as a social event. However, once he felt satisfied that his spiritual values were being respected, he was able to plan an annual gathering on Christmas day for extended family and special friends (*a ritual both modified and integrative*). Through extensive discussion and careful attention to each spouse's core values, the ritual eventually became a coherent and meaningful family event.

CONCLUSION

In summary, experience conducting successive research projects has convinced us that family rituals provide accessible and valuable information about core family traditions and values. Our Ritual Interview is the primary assessment tool for tapping this dimension of family life. Currently, we are using this interview with both alcoholic and non-alcoholic populations in order to refine our understanding of just what family rituals tell us about the family and to test rituals' power as predictors of subsequent psychological functioning.

NOTES

[1]The research on which this paper is based was supported by grants from the National Institute on Alcohol Abuse and Alcoholism (2R01AA04784) and from the Still Water Foundation.

[2]Case vignettes are condensed from actual interview transcripts, with identifying features changed.

[3]Available upon request from the authors.

[4]Names used are fictional.

REFERENCES

Bennett, L. A. & McAvity, K. (1985). Family research: A case for interviewing couples. In G. Handel (Ed.). *The psychosocial interior of the family, (3rd Ed.)*. New York: Aldine Press.

Bennett, L. A., Wolin, S. J., & McAvity, K. (1988). Family identity, ritual & myth: A cultural perspective on life cycle transitions. In C. Falicov (Ed.). *Family transitions: continuity and change over the life cycle*. New York: Guilford Press.

Bennett, L. A., Wolin, S. J., Reiss, D., & Teitelbaum, M. (1987). Couples at risk for transmission of alcoholism: Protective influences. *Family Process, 26*: 111–129.

Bossard, J. & Boll, E. (1950). *Ritual in family living*. Philadelphia: University of Pennsylvania Press.

Goodwin, D. W., Schulsinger, F., Hermansen, L., Guze, S. B., & Winokur, G. (1973). Alcohol problems in adoptess raised apart from alcoholic biologic parents. *Archives of General Psychiatry, 28*: 238–243.

Reiss, D. (1981). *The family's construction of reality*, Cambridge, MA: Harvard University Press.

Wolin, S. J., Bennett, L. A., Noonan, D., & Teitelbaum, M. (1980). Disrupted family rituals: A factor in the intergenerational transmission of alcoholism. *Journal of Studies on Alcohol, 41*(3), 199–214.

Wolin, S. J. & Bennett, L. A. (1984). Family Rituals. *Family Process, 23*, 401–420.

10

Systemic Rituals in Sexual Therapy

GARY L. SANDERS

THERE ARE FEW HUMAN concerns that arise so frequently and yet are so shrouded in mythology as human sexuality. Sexual ideas, expectations, and activities vary greatly from culture to culture, from one geographic location to another, among religious denominations, from community to community, and from one family to another. Human sexuality is further complicated by expectations that it will fulfill a variety of personally felt cultural and social needs. These can include reproduction, fulfillment of duty and commitment, expressions of interpersonal intimacy and uniqueness, and interpersonal bonding. With such complex demands being made of our sexuality, it is not surprising that we in North American cultures, who all too often appear preoccupied with issues of sexuality and yet, paradoxically, remain highly constrained by social and family sexual taboos, end up having sexual symptoms and dysfunctions. These symptoms and dysfunctions are frequently brought to health care professionals by those hoping to find a satisfactory resolution through therapy.

This chapter will examine the nature and use of systemic rituals as applied to the sexual aspect of interpersonal relationships. A clinical case and the discussion of its treatment will be used as the foundation from which an elaboration of the methodology and use of systemic rituals will be offered. In addition, a brief description of a recursive model of intervening in sexual concerns will be offered.

STATE OF THE ART

Before reviewing systemic rituals and their clinical application in sexual therapy, a word of caution is in order. Since it is known that many over-the-counter medications (including alcohol and tobacco), numerous prescribed medications, and a large number of medical illnesses and physical traumas can severely affect physiologic capability for sexual functioning, the clinician should first evaluate areas of biologic concern and treat them where indicated.

Many advances have been made, particularly in the last 15 years, in the biologic understanding and treatment of sexual problems. The work of Masters and Johnson (1970) filled in many of the gaps about the physiologic and anatomic basis to sexual activity, and other researchers have carried on their work (Hoon, Hoon, & Wincze, 1976; Hoon, Wincze, & Hoon, 1977; LoPiccolo, 1980). Until the more recent interest in medical management (Morales, Surridge, & Marshall, 1981; Morales, Surridge, Marshall, & Fenmore, 1982), specific sexually oriented biologic interventions have focused almost exclusively on surgical methods for either the implantation of erectile prostheses or the creation of artificial vaginas. Although these interventions are beyond the professional scope of most therapists working with sexual concerns, the assessment of the need for biologic interventions is not.

In all cases of sexual concern an adequate assessment of the biophysiologic functioning of the individuals involved should be completed before one moves on to assume that the most useful method of intervening would be through nonorganic interventions. For instance, a series of direct investigative questions used to explore a patient's sexual response cycle could be:

- "Are there *ever* occasions when you feel sexually desirous, whether or not you act on them?" "Have you noticed that these have increased or decreased over the last few months?" (*desire phase*)
- "On an occasion when you do feel sexually desirous *and* you choose to act sexually, whether with self or another, are you able to increase your sense of arousal through the sexual actions you engage in?" "Do you have physical changes such as (for males) erection, etc., or (for females) vaginal wetness and pelvic fullness, etc., that accompany arousal?" "Are you usually able to maintain your arousal for the sexual purposes you want?" (*excitement/arousal phase*)
- "Do you get to a point where you feel the urge to release your arousal through a rapid rhythmic release usually called orgasm?" For females, "Are you able to be orgasmic most often when you want to be?" For males, "Are you able to influence the timing of your ejaculation?" (*orgasm phase*)
- "About how long does it take for your body to return to normal after you have been sexually active—minutes, hours, or days?" (*resolution phase*)
- "Do you find sexual activity to be as pleasurable or enjoyable as you would want it to be?" (*pleasure/evaluation phase*)

Given that the individual experiences sexual desire (i.e., a sense of sexual urgency, not just sexual curiosity) on some occasions and that within some of these occasions she/he is able to have a complete sexual response, including physical indications of arousal and resolution, the likelihood of organic abnormalities accounting for the symptoms is extremely low. That is, if the neurological, vascular, and muscular reflexes involved in the physiologic sexual response operate on some occasions (whether interpersonally or self stimulatory) when the individual is desirous, the sexual physiology is sufficiently intact for the response cycle to potentially operate in other contexts.

The other questions assess the ability of an individual to modify his/her sexual response for interpersonal reasons. The ability of a man to influence the timing of his ejaculation or the ability of a woman to reach orgasm is a learned modification of the ordinary physical sexual response capabilities. The appropriateness of learning these events depends on the sociocultural context of the sexual activity. For instance, in North America and Europe, it is expected that men will influence timing of their ejaculation during sexual intercourse to enable a more mutual sexual event for each partner. In other cultures, such as Arabic countries (Katchadourian, 1985), this may not be an expectation. Cultures are not static in their expectations of appropriate sexual activity. Our own culture has only recently added the expectation that sexual contact between a couple be a mutual bonding and arousal opportunity. Indeed, it is only recently that we have added the expectation of female orgasm to interpersonal sexual activity.

If an organic abnormality is suspected because of a global inability (i.e., inability in *any* context, including masturbation, dreams, as a simple reflex, as well as interpersonal sexual activity) to achieve a physical sexual response, evaluation by a physician competent in sexual assessment is indicated. On the other hand, if the above series of questions rules out a significant organic component by uncovering at least occasional full physical response, the therapist may confidently move on to work psychotherapeutically.

To date, most sex therapy interventions have focused on common sense, psychoanalytic, behavioral, or simple interactional solutions. The application of systemic principles (by which the author means second-order cybernetic principles such as applied in Milan therapy[1]) to sexual issues is a relatively undeveloped area in the literature (Sanders, 1986). Yet, since some concerns remain difficult to treat with traditional sex therapy techniques, the adoption of systemic principles has brought another useful tool to the treatment of sexual issues.

As an example, I have clinically observed that once vaginismus is resolved, the partner often develops erectile dysfunction. Another example is the belief that a disorder of sexual desire resides in the individual presenting with lower desire for sexual intercourse or activity than the partner; this is most often labeled *inhibited sexual desire (ISD)* (Kaplan, 1979). I prefer to understand the symptom as indicative of a *discrepancy* in sexual desire between the two. This alternative understanding orients the therapist towards an interpersonal view of sexual desire rather than a linear view of something being "broken" within the individual.

Such clinical symptoms may be understood not only within the domain of the couple's sexual or marital relationship, but also, perhaps, within some other domain, including rules about sex from the family of origin, the couple's past history, subcultural or gender-based beliefs, popular sexual myths, or even more deeply ingrained cultural and historical myths. When a larger and more connected understanding of the symptoms is indicated, one may profitably turn to systemic methods, adding them to established sex therapy principles. Common bonds between the more usual directive sex therapies and sex therapy conducted systemically include a behavioral orientation, the use of active prescriptive interventions, a focus on context construction, and the use of positive connotation (usually termed successive patient successes in traditional sex therapy).

There are also differences between the directive sex therapies and sex therapy from a systemic perspective. First, of course, one is using a cybernetic or circular understanding in systemic therapy. Secondly, even when rituals are used, systemic therapy is nondirective in its intent, while traditional sex therapies are highly directional. Traditionally, when a task is prescribed, the intent is "practice makes perfect," but in systemic therapies rituals are prescribed with the intent of providing information that will make a difference in the couple's problem-solving abilities. The therapist's intent often determines his/her response to the patients' subsequent actions. For instance, the patients could be seen by the therapist as "failing" to practice toward perfection; this may result in the therapist's taking an unintended blaming posture toward them. On the other hand, it is almost impossible for the actions of the patients not to provide the therapist with *information*; consequently, this approach enables the therapist and the patients to avoid a blameful or pejorative stance. Thirdly, systemic therapy is seen as nonexpert; that is, the therapist does not assume greater or better knowledge than the sex partners about their experiences, their understandings of those experiences, or how they should feel and act in the future. This conveys the therapist's respect for the autonomy of the patients. Finally, the attribution of change is quite different. From a systemic understanding, the partners and their significant system are seen as responsible for determining any change that occurs. The therapist is responsible for his/her own actions and the potential effects of those actions (and statements) on the patients, but not for the actions of the patients themselves. In more traditional sex therapies, either the therapist or therapy itself is seen as the responsible "change agent." When the therapist views his responsibility as the potential interpersonal effect of his own actions, he has more options for acting differently (and helpfully) in the therapeutic process than if he focuses on the actions of the patients.

Often the simple provision of information is all that is necessary to "kick start" patients' own problem-solving mechanisms. For example, a remarried couple in their forties was referred because of escalating fights over their unsatisfactory sexual relationship. Since the beginning of their sexual activity with each other three years prior to referral, the woman had been unable to achieve orgasm during sexual intercourse. She had never experienced coital orgasm in her previous relationships and did not consider it a major problem. Her new husband, however, felt that he would end up losing her, as had the other men in her life, unless he could *give* her an orgasm. The fact that the difference in genital anatomy between the sexes is important for achieving mutual sexual satisfaction was discussed. It was pointed out that females have a separate reproductive (vagina, uterus, fallopian tubes, ovaries) and sexual (clitoris, mons pubis, breasts, and other sensual areas) systems, whereas men have both their sexual and reproductive systems in one genital structure (penis, testicles, scrotum). It was also pointed out that women do not need a sexual response for reproduction but men do (in order to deposit the semen where it will do the most reproductive good). The information that sexual intercourse does not promote an equal sexual opportunity for men and women (even though it is an equal reproductive opportunity) helped this couple to refocus their sexual efforts toward mutual sexual pleasure regardless of *how* it was obtained.

Other times, resolution of biophysiological interference provides the physical freedom to create a useful and mutually satisfying sexual relationship. This may come about through simply allowing "nature to take its course" (e.g., healing after surgery or accident) or through the help of trained medical professionals for treatment of illness.

Frequently, directive therapeutic strategies can provide patients with enough impetus to find solutions to their symptoms. However, there are occasions when these strategies are not sufficient. Here the judicious use of creative and personally tailored systemic questions, opinions, and rituals may be applied to sexual relationships. Once the individuals appear better able to use the available resources, more directive or informational therapy may again be indicated. Using what I term a *recursive model of intervention*, the therapist changes levels of understanding by moving from one level of conceptual abstraction to a more complex and comprehensive one when needed. This might entail moving from a biologic conceptualization through an informative one, then to a behavioral understanding, on to an interactional one, and then to a systemic formulation (see Table 1).

One indicator for the need to move between levels of conceptual compre-

TABLE 1
A Recursive Model of Intervention

	Indications to Move Up a Level of Conceptual Abstraction	Indications to Move Down a Level of Conceptual Abstraction
SYSTEMIC THERAPY		— Lack of available resources (information, finances, etc.) — Once again able to use available resources
DIRECTIVE SEX THERAPY	— Inadequate use of available resources — Therapy becomes "stuck" or regresses — No or minimal response to usual therapeutic methods	— Sexual responses are independent of the context (i.e., global dysfunction) — Onset of significant bodily illness — Long — term use of medications
BIOLOGICAL INTERVENTIONS	— Individual patient responses to questions about physical functioning reveal episodes of context — sensitive symptoms — Patients won't cooperate with treatment	

hensiveness is the degree of *compliance* with therapist instructions. If there seems to be "resistance" to the current level of therapist conceptualization and treatment, it is time to move to a more complex or comprehensive level of understanding. On the other hand, *useful* compliance with therapist suggestions and directions is a good sign that more directive or informational interventions will be effective.

Another indicator for level shift deals with *utilization of resources*. If a *lack of resources* available to the patients is perceived, it may be best for the therapist to move towards a more directive, informative, or biologic understanding of the symptoms. If, on the other hand, *inadequate use of available resources* is observed, then it may be best to move to a more complex frame of understanding and subsequent intervention in which the *positive* systemic function of such inadequate use may be understood.

One can see, therefore, that within any interview situation this model of intervention becomes a recursive interaction between various levels of therapist understanding and patient actions. The specific use of rituals in sexual therapy can become an important addition to such a recursive model of intervention.

SYSTEMIC RITUALS

In order to orient the reader to the application of systemic rituals in sex therapy, a case example will be presented. It deals with a long-term history of primary (i.e., total) vaginismus. However, before going on to describe the case itself, let me set the clinical context.

Clinical Setting

The Human Sexuality Programme (HSP), Department of Psychiatry, Faculty of Medicine, is a small professional training program that operates within the auspices of the Family Therapy Program at the University of Calgary. Patient referrals come through family physicians, specialist physicians, mental health professionals in the community and nearby hospital institutions, and from the Family Therapy Program itself. Professionals involved are fulltime family therapists, psychiatrists, psychologists, social workers, and medical residents. Since there is no out-of-pocket user fee, the costs being covered by Alberta's universal medicare program, the patients referred are often those who are unable or unwilling to pay for non-medicare-funded private practice sex therapy provided by other professionals in the community. Because there are so few publicly funded therapeutic resources for sexual concerns, by the time most patients are first seen they have often been waiting anywhere from two to six months since requesting referral from a physician or mental health professional.

Since one of the program's primary goals is to advance the training of allied mental health professionals in the area of human sexuality, all patients are initially made aware that other professionals may be involved, usually on a team basis. It is explained to them that, although members of the team are often professional trainees with respect to understanding clinical issues of human sexuality, they are all advanced medical or mental health professionals. The team is presented as an added resource of multiple minds. Additionally, couples are asked to permit videotaping for the purpose of clinical review and professional training. However, as with all patients who come through the Family Therapy and Human Sexuality Programs at the University of Calgary, couples are given free choice to agree or not to videotaping and observation, without detriment to their treatment. This also occurs with respect to observation through one-way mirrors.

Usually patients are seen as couples only, for one or two initial assessment sessions, during which time biophysiologic information and resource assessments are completed. This may include completion of a Derogatis Sexual Functioning Inventory and a modified Lock Wallace Marital Adjustment Inventory.[2]

Case History

Sheila and Ted, a couple in their mid thirties, had been adolescent sweet-hearts who married when Ted was 22 and Sheila 20 (see Figure 1). Referred by their family physician, they presented with the complaint of not having children. By the time they were seen at the program, both were quite hope-less about any solution being found quickly, but interestingly, both were highly motivated to continue seeking one. Through questioning, a concern of primary vaginismus was uncovered. For the entire 13 years of their sexual relationship they had cooperatively tried once or twice a week to effect vaginal penetration, with not one success. The sexual ritual they had devel-oped consisted of Sheila's notifying Ted of her willingness to try sexual activity by prolonging a hug or caress or sexually teasing him by making requests to be "caught" in a game resembling hide and seek. They would then permit personal arousal to the point where Sheila would motion for Ted to mount her in the missionary position (male superior). Ted would then try inserting his penis into Sheila's vagina and carefully watch her facial expres-sion. As soon as her expression of discomfort turned to one of pain, as evidenced by her showing her teeth as she tried to subdue the pain, he would withdraw.

They had a number of variations on the ritual, depending on their general marital relationship state. If there had been tension or anger during the preceding few days, they would often make blameful recriminations toward each other—she that Ted didn't persist long enough, he that she didn't try hard enough to relax. If they were at peace with one another, they would go on to complete their sexual activity in some other way. They had developed

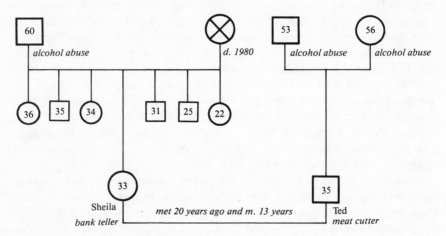

FIGURE 1   Sheila and Ted

an alternative sexual style that included oral sex to orgasm for either or both, manual stimulation to orgasm, and interfemoral (between the thighs) intercourse.

These activities seemed to meet most of their individual sexual needs, but both felt they were somehow inadequate as both spouses and individuals for not being able to have sexual intercourse. Now that age was prompting a more discerning look at forming a family, this sense of incompleteness and inadequacy became sufficient to prompt looking for outside help. Although the spouses agreed that they were most concerned with not having children because of vaginismus, they also reported increased marital arguing and less enjoyable times together over the last few months.

Initial Treatment

After initial successes with Sheila and Ted using a more traditional informative and directive therapy involving sensate focus exercises[3] for the couple and preparing Sheila to learn how to "accommodate" objects intravaginally, a sudden setback in therapy developed (see Table 2). The spouses complained of increasing arguments and irritability; they did not complete their homework assignments and instead called them "tests." At this point in therapy, the therapist, noticing that he perceived "resistance" to doing the prescribed tasks, moved from a directive therapeutic method to a systemic inquiry into the process of therapy.

Ted admitted that he wished things had remained as they were before the couple started their "tests," because at least then he knew where he stood with respect to Sheila. Sheila spoke about her fears of losing Ted's affection to a new baby if they had children in the future. The domain of parenting and spousal commitment was explored in depth using circular questioning, and specific systemic interventions were then elaborated.

Theory

As has been stated earlier in this book, rituals describe prescriptive behavioral events of multiple meanings which express, and therefore permit definition of, social realities (Imber-Black, 1986). They are specific tasks given to the patient system, carefully prescribed with respect to details and the sequence of actions and usually offered as an experiment, trial or symbolic gesture, or a transient rite. Rituals are often prescribed as temporary, without any implications that they are, in fact, the way things should be. In this light they are quite different from the more usual sexual therapy "tasks," such as sensate focus. Rituals are an attempt to introduce something new, unusual, or unexpected.

TABLE 2
Clinical Case Summary

SESSION	INTERVAL	MAJOR INTERVENTIONS
1.	3 wks	sensate focus (hands, head, or feet)
2.	4 wks	sensate focus (partial body) and self-exam
3.	3 wks	time out, sensate focus (full body without genitals), accommodation exercises
4.	4 wks	time out and sensate focus including genitals, repeat accommodation exercises
5.	4 wks	systemic split opinion
6.	4 wks	systemic opinion and list task of past events
7.	4 wks	burning ritual of past events
8.	1 wk	burying ritual of past
Follow-up	6 wks	"go slow"

When working with rituals, the interviewing principles outlined by the original Milan associates are particularly important. Of the three original guidelines — hypothesizing, circularity, and neutrality — perhaps that of neutrality is most important when dealing with issues of sexuality. Neutrality is not intended as a strategic stance that can be used to increase the likelihood of the therapist's will being done, but rather as a direction of interpersonal perception that is perceived by the patients as nonjudgmental, nonfavoring, and nonexpectational. The goal of systemic interventions, including rituals, therefore, is quite different from what we usually think of as outcome goals. As opposed to a specific behavioral outcome, the goal is to enhance the patient system's ability to create nonsymptomatic solutions as it continues on its path of evolution through the life cycle. This comes about, we hope, through a shift in the way couples are able to change (see Tomm, 1984a, b, for a more complete discussion of systemic theory and its clinical application).

The purpose of rituals as applied to sexual issues can be seen as the provision of increased opportunity for mutually satisfying and need-fulfilling couple sexual activity, without defining what the sexual activity per se will be. When a therapist intends to use therapeutic rituals, I believe it is necessary to examine the larger social context in which we as therapists are working in order to avoid unintentionally promoting other problems or symptoms. Nowhere is this examination more necessary than in our definition and expectations of sexual activities.

Interestingly, in order for individuals to experience what our society calls *good* sex, a number of different conditions or contexts must be met. First, personal physical and emotional arousal must occur in a context of one's partner being nearly, or equally, as aroused emotionally and physically. Second, the opportunity to experience one's own arousal without having to monitor the partner's arousal must be present. Finally, an interpersonal context of emotional and physical vulnerability along with sufficient trust that the vulnerability will not be abused (that is, intimacy) must exist. If all these conditions are met, the experience is considered to be a sexually meaningful one.

A pragmatic definition of sex according to the North American meta context is: *the personally felt experience of sexual arousal in an interpersonal context of mutual emotional and physical vulnerability and trust (i.e., intimacy) occurring within socially permitted relationships.* Anything other than this our society deems something other than sexual. For instance, if one person is sexually aroused and the partner is not and this state occurs within a context of violence, society deems this activity as sexual assault. If, on the other hand, only one partner is aroused and the other is not, then we deem the activity duty or taking care of one's needs. Whether or not both partners are sexually aroused, if the context is one of child-adult, society considers this to be sexual abuse.

Rituals are designed, therefore, to enhance the likelihood of a couple's having sexual experiences that will meet the individual, interpersonal, and societal needs of what is culturally defined as "good sex." The design and potential enactment of a ritual may in itself be an enhanced method of sexual satisfaction over the couple's usual practices. However, the *intent* of the ritualized alternative is to provide information about *any* alternative to the usual, more symptomatic sexual behaviors, not just that of the ritualized behaviors.

Indications for Use of Systemic Rituals

Systemic interventions and rituals in sex therapy can be useful with a number of groups: couples who have somehow continued to make inadequate use of available social and interpersonal resources; couples who show a high degree of confusion with respect to the nature of their problems; people who are likely to express their concerns nonverbally; and those who have had numerous other forms of therapy and not found them useful (i.e., "therapy wise" persons). Members of cultures embedded in a larger one (for instance, orientals in an urban Chinatown or North American native people living on reserves) may find rituals oriented towards their own culture more helpful in accessing their personal sexual feelings than those oriented to the dominant culture.

Using Systemic Sexual Rituals

Therapeutic rituals create an emotional and physical experience that is an alternative to that which supports the patients' symptoms and thereby produce news of a difference (Keeney, 1983). Based on the spouses' reported history of their own life experiences, ritual details are generated. This accounts for rituals' being unique to one, and only one, specific patient system. Although the ideas or concepts behind different rituals can be used repeatedly with different cases, the exact ritual itself happens only once.

In setting up sexual rituals, a number of areas outside the usual sexual assessment need to be reviewed. The interpersonal context of the couple's being sexual and the actual methods of sexual activity should be examined as to whether or not the current ritual activities appear underritualized, rigidly ritualized, skewed to one member's family of origin, flexible in creating and perhaps amplifying rituals, or empty and hollow without an interpersonally meaningful experience (Wolin & Bennett, 1984; also see Chapter 9).

For instance, the rituals involved in managing time for sex and other activities must be evaluated. Many couples want to be sexual without providing time to access sensual and sexual experiences. It is almost as if some couples expect the biophysiologic reflex of sexual arousal to be turned on or off as easily as their television set, and hope that somehow they will be able to manage a quick interpersonal bonding during a commercial break. Additionally, couples seem to get caught up in deeming other life events as more important than the spousal relationship. Many young couples consistently put their children's needs or the family's financial needs ahead of their own couple needs. Couples who do not make time for themselves often have sexual troubles, since the sexual contacts often become rigidly ritualized attempts to meet otherwise unattended intimacy needs.

Couples' ability to differentiate between affection and sexuality is another useful area of exploration. Many couples appear to have elaborated rituals that do not take this distinction into account. I define *physical affection* as those physical activities between individuals that have as their primary intent a message of caring, with any sexual feeling or display as secondary. In *sexuality*, on the other hand, the intent of shared physical arousal and its experience in an intimate context is primary and the affective display is secondary. As Zilbergeld (1978) has pointed out, males and females in our society have great difficulty differentiating between affective display and sexual actions. From an early age both women and men struggle with the expectation that if a man is physical then he is sexual. When he becomes involved in an affective relationship and displays his feelings physically, he and his mate may understand them as a sexual request rather than simply as an expression of deep feeling. Frequently, women complain that their men seem to want only genital sex. The men, on the other hand, state that their women appear to want only affection. When the man approaches the woman with what he intends as an affectional display but does so with a sexual behavior, she often withdraws, thinking him only after intercourse. On the occasions when she may be aroused and approaches her man with an affectionate behavior that she intends to lead to sex, he may not respond for fear of being seen as only after sex.

As we return to Sheila and Ted, we should remember that, if, indeed, there is a hypothesis that some of the sexual symptomatology may be related to other, often more encompassing, interpersonal events, but somehow the spouses cannot be oriented towards resolving them more easily, devising a clarifying therapeutic ritual may provide them with the opportunity to "discover" the issue and resolve it. Ritual construction does require that the ritual fit with the systemic hypothesis. Rituals, as one form of systemic intervention, must also fit in with other methods of intervening systemically. Nevertheless, in order to elaborate a systemic hypothesis it is best to temporarily abandon nonsystemic ideas and understandings.

Sheila and Ted's therapist used the perception of resistance as a cue to move into a more complex conceptual posture. The first step after the therapist noticed his experiencing the patients as "resistant" was to inquire about the process of therapy from a systemic perspective. This changed the nature of the therapy. The patients' reaction was one of renewed curiosity about their own experiences, with subsequent reengagement in the process of therapy. Part of this reaction could probably be attributed to the increased neutrality of the therapist, who became actively engaged in a genuinely curious reformulation of the couple's behaviors and statements from a systemic perspective. The newness and novelty of therapist's actions could also have played a part in the patients' response.

Initially, the therapist used systemic opinions that split his understanding of how best to comprehend the "slowing down" in therapy. The spouses were asked to help the therapist understand whether the upset in therapy was simply one of those ordinary events where things slow for a while or whether it was indicative of the therapist's making an error in using sex therapy when in fact their "real" problems were more to do with becoming a family. Their response was to come back to the next appointment and discuss their fear of parenting and of losing each other. This appeared anchored in the early formation of their relationship and was alluded to by Sheila as an early event that she "could never discuss and never forget."

At this point in therapy, the therapist gave an opinion that put them together as victims of the *idea* of marriage, in that when they married in

their youth they appeared to give up being lovers. A ritual was then prescribed: They were asked to come up with individual lists of the most important past events, either as individuals or as a couple, that were interfering
with their being a couple as they wanted to be in the present. They were
asked to jot down as many things as they could think of as soon as they left
the session, but to also keep the list available at all waking times for other
events that came to mind. They were told not to preoccupy themselves with
trying to fill up the list, but rather to alternate between times when the list
would be on one's mind and times when other events of life would take
precedence. Each was also asked to research the listed items to determine
how important they were in interfering with the present. This research could
take the form of casually conversing with the people involved, discussing the
event either openly or covertly with friends or family, or reviewing what
acquaintances might think in a similar circumstance. Before coming to the
next therapy session, each was to choose a quiet, private place where she/he
could sit down in the evening and order the listed items from least to most
important in their interfering effect on the present relationship. This ritual
of making and ordering a list of past events that each believed were continuing to interfere with the present relationship was designed to enable Sheila
and Ted to take an observer perspective with respect to their own contributions to the current symptoms. It included in its design and delivery such
notions of ritual construction as alternations among thinking of and researching the listed items, ordering relationally interfering past events, and
acting "spontaneously"; repetitively evaluating the relative importance of
each remembered event; the prescription of a time and place for the ritualized behaviors to occur; and the use of very specific instructions on how to
do the ritual, yet open instructions on what events would be ritualized (see
also Chapter 3 for further discussion on ritual design).

When Sheila and Ted returned to the next session with lists in hand I
implemented an in-session ritual. They were invited to read the lists to
themselves, to intrapsychically recreate the emotional tone that accompanied the original event, and then to say good-bye to the event as an active
influence in their current lives. They readily agreed to my "invitation." If
they had shown reluctance or had not completed the listing ritual, I would
have responded by accepting whatever was presented and using that as the
information on which my next therapeutic action would be based. I would
not insist or constrain them to do what I had intended. Upon completing the
intrapsychic recreation, I then suggested they burn the memories one at a
time. This appeared more difficult for Sheila to do. She began crying and,
by the time she came to the item she had chosen as most influential in
disturbing her current life, she found it difficult to burn. Finally, with an air
of bravado, she tossed the paper into the fire and the act was completed. The

burning of these "events" was intended to create a marker in time for each spouse; that is, each would have the option of escaping the paradox of the past, present, and future appearing collapsed in his/her experience of time. The rituals provided an occasion to demarcate the past from the present and the present from the future. I chose an in-session ritual for a number of reasons: to utilize surprise, since I had not used in-session tasks or activities before; to engage the couple through the use of novel therapeutic events; and to enable me to fill the role of "witness" to the "putting of the past in its place."

The next session, one week later, included a burying ritual. The couple was instructed to bring a container that symbolized their relationship to date yet could also be given up. This was done in order to use a couple-specific object of familiar symbolism. Interestingly, this couple, who could be hypothesized as having difficulty "consummating" their relationship, brought the container that originally held their wedding rings. The ashes from the burning session were then "interred" in the box. Sheila and Ted were told to find a private burial site for these past events that were being "given up" and to "lay the memories to rest." A brief discussion of potential emotional reactions to grief ensued and the couple was scheduled to be seen in six weeks. The therapeutic intent here was to use a familiar and socially acceptable symbolic act to create an opportunity for a way of interacting as a couple different from their usual "more of the same wrong solution" (the reader is referred to Luckhurst's (1985) article, "Resistance and the 'New' Epistemology"). The intent was *not* to truly "put the past in its place" through the enactment of the ritual.

When they returned, they appeared almost transformed. Sheila stated that she had to take a week off work following the burial since she would unexpectedly break into tears. During the week's leave, she found herself thinking almost constantly about the past. She recalled that one day, about two weeks following the burial, she suddenly brightened and began planning her future. Ted described a different experience. He said that at first he believed the sessions of burning and burying were ridiculous. However, about two weeks after the couple had buried their wedding ring box filled with ashes, he found himself becoming increasingly angry at nothing in particular. After an occasion at work where he cut himself on one of his butcher knives, he suddenly realized that he was dwelling on the past and began speaking with Sheila about how their relationship would be in the future if they had children. Subsequent to this, Sheila decided to persist in her vaginal accommodation exercises, only to find them much easier than before. When asked how their sexual life had been over the last six weeks, they sheepishly admitted to having sexual intercourse on a number of occasions. This had occurred in a context of mutual pleasure and with relative ease. At first, in fact, Sheila could not believe Ted had actually entered her.

Interestingly though, they stated that intercourse was not all they had expected it to be. Both agreed that their previous sexual activities (oral and mutual caressing) were more enjoyable. They asked the therapist if it would be all right if they continued having sexual intercourse in order to try for a pregnancy. The therapist suggested instead that they go slow and practice mostly what they knew best.

On an eight-month follow-up (the couple kept postponing their appointments), Sheila and Ted had not had a pregnancy and had initiated adoption proceedings. They stated they were occasionally having intercourse but relied most heavily on their usual sexual practices. Sheila had received a promotion at work and Ted had left his job to go to school for computer technician training.

Case Discussion

In reflecting on the treatment of Sheila and Ted, a number of inferences about the therapy can be made. It appears that at a point when they were having great difficulty in utilizing directive sex therapy, the interpretation of this "resistance" as an event in the therapeutic relationship, and not a property of the individuals involved, led to different actions and understandings on the part of the therapist. This may then have freed both the therapist and the patients from the constraint of each trying to get the other "to see it my way." This freedom could then be acted on by the therapist in creating novel interpersonal opportunities for the patients that relied more on a systemic view of events than on the more usual cause and effect perspective. The rituals themselves could be seen as providing concrete events that permitted these opportunities. Through the making and ordering of lists, the notion of separating in time their experiences of past, present and expected future could be indirectly and experientially examined. Through the burning and burying of these written symbols of past emotional events, both Sheila and Ted had an opportunity to demarcate time experienced personally in a more interpersonal manner. With the increased interpersonal permissiveness generated from such novel distinctions, the behavioral and experiential options of the couple increased. New experiences could be coherently understood, while past events were still personally experienced.

SEX THERAPY AND THERAPEUTIC RITUALS

There are a large number of potential rituals related to sexual issues. They are limited only by the therapist's creativity and the ritual's social appropriateness.

Action rituals, such as actually freezing a relational symbol when the introduction of time is thought to be needed, can be useful. Each spouse is instructed to remove the object and let it defrost when he or she perceives events to be getting out of control (arguments, sexual expectations, etc.). They are instructed to not continue the behavior being interrupted during the defrosting period, but rather to reflect or act upon a systemic distinction that the therapist sees as potentially useful (for example, to think about whether the arguments are in service more of affectional or sexual needs). After the object has defrosted, it is suggested that the spouses go on with their lives until time needs to be introduced again (see Chapter 4). The burning and burying rituals used with Sheila and Ted are also action rituals.

Many sexuality rituals fall into the action category. Even sensate focus exercises can be used ritualistically (as opposed to the practice makes perfect notion of a task) to highlight the distinction between a self-sensual focus and an other-person-performance focus. Other forms of rituals that can be used to describe the distinction between sexuality (as a sensually based event) and performance (of self, of other, of genitals, etc.) can include what are usually thought of as sex therapy tasks. Some of these are: role playing orgasm, first privately and later in the presence of her mate, for the pre-orgasmic woman; prescribed sexual intercourse alternating with intercourse occurring only when both mutually desire it for spouses with a discrepancy in desire for intercourse; and the use of prescribed self-stimulation in the accepting presence of a mate as an alternative to duty-bound taking of responsibility for the partner's orgasm. The intent of the therapist, as well as his/her consequent enactment of the ritual, distinguishes ritualized events from simple tasks.

Thought and feeling rituals, such as the prescription of odd days/even days to examine the experience of a relationship event as being either more in the service of personal and couple intimacy needs or more in the service of personal and couple sexual needs can be used along with prescribed "be spontaneous" times of acting naturally. The ritual with Sheila and Ted of listing important events from the past that were deemed as negatively influencing the present is an example of a thought ritual.

Context rituals promote opportunities to meaningfully distinguish different contexts and respond more appropriately. For instance, the prescription of *time outs* involves one partner's finding of an activity he or she would potentially enjoy and arranging to do it. The other partner then accompanies in an "obligatory" manner. The outing time is limited and the events restricted to those that do not require the participation of the partner for the first person's enjoyment (e.g., dancing and playing cards are out, but eating dinner and going for a walk are not). The "task" for the choosing partner is to enjoy himself/herself as fully as the event permits. The "task" for the other is to observe the enjoyment of the first. For the next time out, the partners reverse roles. Time out rituals and others, such as celebration rituals, help to distinguish contexts of personal opportunity from duty to others, gender roles from couple events, and so on.

Mixed rituals mix the intended distinctions, say, between action and context, such as a sensual dinner or sensual bath ritual. In a sensual dinner ritual, the opportunity for co-creating an intended context through specific actions is prescribed. The partners are told to negotiate a menu for a special dinner. When the menu is decided upon, they are instructed to go together to the grocery store and shop for the ingredients. Once supplies are purchased, they are to prepare the meal together, even if one acts as the "lead hand" and the other as "chef" in the kitchen. They are instructed to eat the meal in an unusual place compared to their everyday meals. Finally, they are told to not use utensils or feed themselves, instead relying on their partner to feed them. Further suggestions can be made, depending on the intent of the therapist and the needs of the specific couple, such as a directive against any verbal communication. Rituals of this type can help couples construct an interpersonal language of sensuality and fun as distinct from performance and duty.

NOTES

[1]The use of the term *systemic* throughout this chapter refers to the collection of ideas and theories alternatively referred to as Milan, ecosystemic, or second-order cybernetic. The common theoretic thread among all these views is a circular pattern view of interpersonal process. This is in contradistinction to the more physicalistic view of systems that has been promoted within general systems theory and the views that have been built on its original physical epistemology of force and power. For a more detailed discussion of these points the reader is referred to Bradford Keeney's book, *The Aesthetics of Change* (1983).

[2]The Derogatis Sexual Functioning Inventory is a fairly lengthy multiple choice questionnaire. It asks about sexual knowledge, attitudes, values, behaviors, fantasies, body image, general psychological symptomatology, and sexual relatedness. Normative data are available from the original publisher.

The Lock Wallace Marital Adjustment Inventory is a brief fill-in-the blank questionnaire that examines couples' marital relationship from interactive and role perspectives. The author uses this particular questionnaire to compare one spouse's response to that of the other. I have also modified the questionnaire to include live-in relationships and to be less sexist in its wording.

[3]Sensate focus exercises were popularized by Masters and Johnson in 1970 and have formed one of the basic tenets of sex therapy ever since. These exercises are a prescribed couple session of sensual caressing and touching focusing on sensual information as opposed to sensual or sexual performance. Overt sexual activity such as intercourse is usually "banned" from occurring during these sessions. The intent is to reduce or remove performance expectations while creating a setting in which the couple can practice the basis of sexual arousal — the ability to focus sensually on one's own bodily feelings.

REFERENCES

Hoon, E. F., Hoon, P. W., & Wincze, J. (1976). "The SAI: An inventory for the measurement of female arousal." *Archives of Sexual Behavior, 5,* 208–215.

Hoon, P. W., Wincze, J., & Hoon, E. F. (1977). "A test of reciprocal inhibition: Are anxiety and sexual arousal in women mutually inhibitory", *Journal of Abnormal Psychology*, *86*, 65–74.

Imber-Black, E. (1986). "Toward a resource model in systemic family therapy" in M. Karpel (Ed.). *Family Resources*, New York: Guilford Press.

Kaplan, H. S. (1979). *Disorders of sexual desire and other new concepts and techniques in sex therapy*. New York: Brunner/Mazel.

Katchadourian, H. A. (1985). *Fundamentals of human sexuality* 4th Edition, New York: C.B.S. Publications.

Keeney, Bradford P. (1983) *The aesthetics of change*. New York: Guilford Press.

LoPiccolo, L. (1980). "Low sexual desire" In S. Lieblum & L. Pervin (Eds.). *Principles and practice of sex therapy*. New York: Guilford Press.

Luckhurst, P. (1985). Resistance and the "new" epistemology. *Journal of Strategic and Systemic Therapies*, *4*, 1–12.

Masters, W. H. & Johnson, V. E. (1970). *Human sexual inadequacy*. Boston: Little, Brown.

Morales, A., Surridge, D. H. C., Marshall, P. G., & Fenmore, J. (1982). Nonhormonal pharmacological treatment of organic impotence. *Journal of Urology*, *128*, 45–47.

Morales, A., Surridge, D. H. C., & Marshall, P. G. (1981). Yohimbine treatment of impotence in diabetes. *New England Journal of Medicine*, *305*, 1221.

Sanders, G. L. (1986). The interview as intervention in sexual therapy. *Journal of Strategic and Systemic Therapy*, *5*(1,2), 50–63.

Selvini Palazzoli, M., Boscolo, L., Cecchin, G., & Prata, G. (1978). *Paradox and counterparadox*. New York: Jason Aaronson.

Selvini Palazzoli, M., Boscolo, L., Cecchin, G., & Prata, G. (1980). Hypothesizing-Circularity-Neutrality: Three guidelines for the conductor of the session. *Family Process*, *19*, 3–12.

Tomm, K. M. (1987). Interventive interviewing: Part II. Reflexive questioning as a means to enable self healing. *Family Process*, *26*(2), 153–183.

Tomm, K. M. (1984a). One perspective on the Milan systemic approach: Part I. Overview of development, theory and practice. *Journal of Marital and Family Therapy*, *10*, 113–125.

Tomm, K. M. (1984b). One perspective on the Milan systemic approach: Part II. Description of session format, interviewing style and interventions. *Journal of Marital and Family Therapy*, *10*, 253–271.

Wolin, S. J. & Bennett, L. A. (1984). Family Rituals. *Family Process*, *23*(3), 401–420.

Zilbergeld, B. (1978). *Male Sexuality: A Guide to Sexual Fulfillment*. New York: Little, Brown.

11

Creation of Family Identity Through Ritual Performance in Early Remarriage

MARY F. WHITESIDE

The first part of the summer was sort of fractured, with my boys going to California with their dad, and his son here, then away. But we all pulled together after the family camping trip. My former husband has custody of the tent, and when we opened it up it was missing the two center poles. It was a comedy . . . in the middle of nowhere . . . Bob's antics as he engineered setting up this tent with everyone contributing wildly impractical suggestions . . . we still laugh when we think of planning another vacation.

— Kay, describing her first summer in a remarried family.

The first camping trip we went on as a family was a disaster! We made the mistake of going to a spot which had been a favorite in my first marriage. Memories kept interfering, nothing seemed to work right. Sam and I got into our first big fight. Our kids refused to sleep together in the pup tent, so we ended up with his daughter in the tent with us. . . . It was weeks before we recovered from that experience.

— Andrea, describing her first summer in a remarried family.

TYPICAL OF REMARRIED FAMILIES, each of these families was faced with a small crisis in which both positive and negative legacies from previous marriages were embedded in a novel experience for the new family grouping. In the first years of a remarriage, families face numerous situations in which formerly well-established patterns do not work. Successful experiments can

In the examples used throughout the chapter, names and other identifying details have been changed to protect confidentiality.

become the beginnings of the new family's ritual bonding. Ritual performances from the level of everyday patterned interactions through highly formalized rites of passage become opportunities to redefine family membership, to revise, honor, or desecrate memories from first marriages, and to establish patterns of family organization which have lasting impact. The shape and emotional tone of these solutions both reflect and influence the developing family organization.

In the initial stage of a remarriage the process of integrating the wife's and husband's heritages is similar to that of early first marriage, except that, rather than negotiations between two adults, there are negotiations between two strongly bonded subgroups of adults and children. This makes differences more visible and more difficult to accommodate. In addition, many of the usual rules of family living are based upon the nuclear family and are no longer helpful or appropriate. These rules order a family unit which resides in one household, with both adults biologically related to and totally responsible for the children, and with two sets of extended family networks. Remarried families have members living in several different households. Financial, legal, biological, and emotional ties extend across household boundaries, and kinship networks spread to as many as six or more extended families. As yet there are few societal guidelines for organizing families in remarried kinship systems and few models for normal step- or former-relationship roles. There are few formalized patterns for remarried families going through the usual family life transitions. Moreover, there are no traditional ceremonies for the developmental transitions unique to the remarried family.

Because of this evolving, nontraditional, complex and interdependent nature of the remarried family system, attention to ritual performance is critical in the therapy situation. In the early stages of remarriage the creation of feelings of belonging, cohesion, and normality is an ongoing problem. Most authors note the absence of societal support for stepfamily roles (Papernow, 1984; Sager, Brown, Crohn, Engel, Rodstein, & Walker, 1983; Visher & Visher, 1979). They suggest that an important task of the stepfamily is to develop new rituals for the consolidation of the new family. New rituals are to be constructed so that some old ways are maintained and some irrevocably changed. However, there is little exploration of the process through which families proceed or suggestions for family therapists which might be useful in treatment at different stages of remarriage development.

It is my opinion that in the stage of early remarriage attention to developing family ceremonies and traditions can be a powerful preventive intervention in maintaining family stability and in minimizing the degree of psychological stress experienced by individual family members. The introduction of the remarried family structure into formalized rituals uses the impact of tradition to give legitimacy to this new family form. Special occasions give the opportunity for public enactment of desired family connections and values. The conscious repetition of everyday routines can help to develop a sense of normality within and across households. On the other hand, each of these times can also be used to create distance, to demonstrate undying struggle, and to consolidate splits within and between subgroupings of the remarried family. In this chapter examples are drawn from clinical and nonclinical families to illustrate the role of ritual performance as it facilitates and impedes the creation and integration of remarried family organization.

DEFINITION OF RITUAL

Family Identity

The definition of ritual used in this chapter is that proposed by Wolin and Bennett (1984):

> a symbolic form of communication that, owing to the satisfaction that family members experience through its repetition, is acted out in a systematic fashion over time. Through their special meaning and their repetitive nature, rituals contribute significantly to the establishment and preservation of a family's collective sense of itself, which we have termed the "family identity." (p. 401)

The development of a satisfying sense of family identity for a remarried family is a key struggle in its first few years; in fact, many families do not succeed. In observing the "past embedded in the present" (Wolin & Bennett, 1984, p. 402) we may see residues not only of families of origin, but also of first marriages and of years spent as a single-parent unit. Remarried families struggle over how many of the former and step relationships to include in the notion of family, while at the same time trying to preserve an integrated sense of home. In addition, the definition of "home" and of "immediate family" is different for different members of the household. A woman with children from a former marriage has familial transactions with her current spouse and children and with her former spouse and children. Her spouse, with no previous marriages, confines his family to their household. Her children from the first marriage have their mother's and father's households, plus two stepparents and their families. Lacking neatly defined family membership boundaries, a concept of family identity needs to be constructed which includes and normalizes a highly complex network of kinship relationships. It must acknowledge the fact that divorce and remarriage change the nature of previous relationships, but do not terminate them.

Family Celebrations

Wolin and Bennett (1984; also see Chapter 9) describe three categories of family rituals, each of which implies special challenges for the remarried family in the construction of family identity. *Family celebrations* are described as the celebration of holidays or rites of passage in ways which "assert the larger group identity for the nuclear family" (p. 404). For the remarried family these celebrations are as important as for first marriage; yet, they must be restructured in a manner consonant with the unique role requirements of families stretching across more than one household. They must accommodate many more threads of ritual inheritance, as the extended family now includes step and former relationships.

Rites of passage "help to define the membership list of the family" (Wolin & Bennett, 1984, p. 405). They continue to do so in a remarried family, but the membership lists now include new relationships and role definitions which do not fit easily into standard formulas for heavily ritualized occasions. Where do one's children fit in a marriage ceremony? How does one accommodate four parents with two tickets to a graduation? Who presents the bar mitzvah boy to the rabbi? Who is in the reception line for a daughter's wedding? Children's rites of passage are relevant to the extended family of both parents and stepparents, but there may not be a consensus among family members as to who belongs in the family and who does not.

The remarriage wedding ceremony is the formalized marker of the commitment to the stepfamily. The manner in which it is carried out makes a statement about membership in the extended family network, as well as about ideals concerning the shape of the stepfamily unit. Generally, all family celebrations become opportunities to dramatize continuing conflict, to act publicly on intentions to exclude particular family members, or to creatively redefine family relationships in an inclusive, yet differentiated form.

Family Traditions

Family traditions which "symbolically represent a family" (Wolin & Bennett, 1984, p. 404), imply traditions developed by a nuclear family within a household unit. For events which involve children, the remarried family can develop traditions which stretch across households and acknowledge the fact that children have primary relationships in at least two places. For some families the symbolic statement becomes we are a "binuclear family" rather than a "nuclear family." In other families a tight boundary is drawn around the stepfamily, with the message given to the children that "we are a 'normal family' again with two parents in the same household." Yet this message contradicts the reality of a difference in quality of relationship between step and biological dyads—a difference which often becomes more marked the older a child is. This message denies the past life in the first marriage and devalues the importance to the child of his/her continuing contact with the parent in the other household. It fuels the feelings of anger and denigration in the nonhousehold biological parent.

On the other hand, while acknowledging the reality of cross-household ties, the stepfamily must develop traditions which reinforce a boundary around the stepfamily subgroup of the family and which integrate the husband's and the wife's family subsystems. These traditions may need to flexibly accommodate the comings and goings of varying numbers of household members. In early remarriage many of these traditions are in flux and experimental, even though the developmental stage of the family according to the age of the children may be well advanced.

Patterned Family Interactions

Finally, *patterned family interactions* "help to define member's roles and responsibilities; are a means of organizing daily life" and "through these commonplace activities, families will express their shared beliefs and common identity" (Wolin & Bennett, 1984, p. 406). In early stages of a remarriage there is not yet a shared belief and common identity. Thus, confusion, struggle, and tension are played out in the commonplace. What once was invisible and automatic becomes explicit and endlessly negotiated. Struggles over beliefs about parenting and being a sibling, as well as all the other "right ways to live together," do not necessarily reflect only the common pains of a new social grouping sharing the same space. They also reflect the reality that nuclear family beliefs are not smoothly transplanted to stepfamilies. Many rules of everyday life must be reinvented—and this upsets each family member's sense of social stability and personal and family identity.

It should be noted at this point that an integrative model of the remarried family system is emphasized in this chapter. An integrative model is one in which both biological parents are considered to be emotionally significant and are encouraged to remain actively involved with their children—even when one parent may reside at a distance from the other. In addition, cross-linkages within the extended family are supported and clarified. (These are, for example, relationships between mother and stepmother, between father and former mother-in-law, and the like). This bias comes from my belief that therapists, as well as other societally sanctioned helpers, can have a strong preventive impact on family structure through their vision of "normality." The problems of children in remarried families are typically exacerbated by absentee noncustodial parents and overburdened stepparents. If therapeutic interventions are conducted with the expectation that all the adults in a child's life must be attended to, if a repertoire of courteous and respectful patterns of co-parenting exchanges is conceivable, and if children's biological and emotional bonds across households are encouraged, more often than not a new, more resilient structure can be developed.

SAMPLE OF REMARRIED FAMILIES

The examples for this chapter are drawn from three sources of data. First, I am in the process of completing an intensive exploratory study of the development of ritual in remarried families with adolescent children in the first year following their remarriage. These families were obtained by word of mouth when I told friends, colleagues, and lecture audiences locally that I was looking for remarried families who were "doing well." To date material is available from three families, interviewed in their homes for one and a half hours monthly for a 12-month period.

The second source of data represents an attempt to use clinical material in a more focused, cross-sectional manner. I asked each of the 12 staff members of the Ann Arbor Center for the Family to take one remarried family in their practice and track with remarried family members the holiday celebrations in which they participated during the month of December, 1985, and the months of November and December, 1986. I then interviewed the staff members about their observations during the following month. The Ann Arbor Center for the Family is a private outpatient clinic whose staff members are established family therapists from the disciplines of social work, psychology, and psychiatry. Because a sliding fee scale is used, the center's client population represents a broad range of socioeconomic strata, as well as a range of ethnic backgrounds typical of southeastern Michigan (Polish, Italian, Arabic, Hispanic, Greek, Dutch and German among others, as well as both Black and White Southerners whose parents emigrated to work in the automobile factories, and a nationally and internationally varied family and student university population). This study resulted in anecdotal descriptions from 16 remarried families whose marriages ranged from 4 months to 12 years (mean=4.4 years).

The third source of data is my own general clinical practice in family therapy.

DEFINITION OF THE REMARRIED FAMILY
WITHIN THE EXTENDED FAMILY NETWORK

The definition of the "family" which results from a remarriage with children is more inclusive than that of the "nuclear" family. Family membership includes the wide network of people and relationships created through the divorce and remarriage. These ties include blood, in-law, former in-law, and step relationships. One initial task is the formulation of a view of extended family which can in some way include all these people. Within this definition each member then must define the degree of closeness or distance for former in-laws, new in-laws, and step extended family.

Furstenberg and Spanier (1984) suggest that "relations acquired by marriage are automatically eligible to be relatives . . . but may not be considered as kin unless there is some intimate contact over an extended period" (p. 133). They also observed that for adults in-laws are replaceable and substitutable, while for children extended kin are augmented and expanded through a parent's remarriage. Johnson and Barer (1985) note the role of women as the "kinkeepers," carrying the primary responsibility for interaction. They describe several patterns of grandparenting relationships after divorce and remarriage, ranging from "contracting kinship network," where former in-law relationships are distant and formal, through "expanding kinship systems," which include close relationships throughout complex two-generational divorce and remarriage chains.

When remarried families give their versions of what a family "should be," their plans illustrate the diversity of organizational structures possible for satisfying integration. One family viewed their remarried extended family as a series of concentric circles (the couple with their biological child, then this group plus stepchildren, finally extending through the former spouse and in-law relatives). Their holiday plans included a variety of events, with varying membership, all seen as integral parts of a complicated whole. Another family conscientiously supported the children's inclusion in celebrations of extended family for each household, accommodating schedules and providing transportation as needed; nevertheless, they kept a careful distance between the households. The children moved between two separately organized, minimally overlapping household organizations.

This process of new family definition involves complex choices about acceptance of relationship in the new grouping. If one accepts family relatedness, how much responsibility and commitment does that entail? A stepparent has to figure out a way of being an adult member of an intimate family without taking on full parental responsibility. A new spouse and a former spouse have no societally defined relationship, yet they may find themselves sharing decision-making around important child-rearing issues (see Ahrons & Perlmutter, 1982, for a discussion of various patterns found for these relationships). Grandparents must deal with seeing their grandchildren, even when the children spend a majority of their time with their mother, the grandparents' former daughter-in-law (Johnson & Barer, 1985). Within such a complicated kinship network it is impossible to come up with neat guidelines for family boundaries. However, ritual occasions provide opportunities both to increase clarity and to promote feelings of closeness.

Brief Example — The Bernsteins

David and Barbara Bernstein are a nonclinic couple whose immediate family includes Barbara's two children from her first marriage, and David's three children from his first marriage (see Figure 1). Barbara's former husband lives on the opposite coast. The children see him on vacations. David's former wife lives one hour away and has primary custody of all three children. The oldest child is going to college in the same town as David; the younger two are scheduled to stay with him every other weekend. Barbara's family and former in-laws all live near her former husband.

The Bernstein's believe in an inclusive family network for their children and have made conscious efforts to support connections between the children and the former in-laws as well as creating step-connections. Andy C., Barbara's 13-year-old son, describes the scene at the airport when he goes to stay with his father. "When I get off the plane, they're all there — my Dad, his parents, my Mom's parents. They all hug me, we talk a few minutes, then we go home separately. I see my Mom's parents again later in the week when they have us and my Dad for dinner." Andy is equally included by David's parents. "After the Thanksgiving dinner we had at their house, my step-grandmother sent me a bag of pistachio nuts — I don't particularly like them, but she sends them to all her grandchildren."

In both clinic and nonclinic populations, couples gave examples of the power of the grandparental generation in lending support to the new family unit or in adding to the burden. Mrs. Bernstein's mother had gone to great

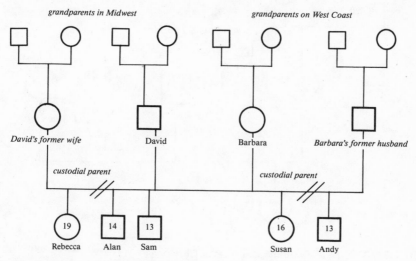

FIGURE 1   The Bernstein Family

lengths since the divorce to maintain connections with the children's father and his parents. The result was an ease about the time spent by the children with their father, and a sense for them that they encountered supportive relatives wherever they went.

Brief Examples

In a clinic family (see Figure 2) in which the six-year-old daughter, Heidi, had been referred for enuresis, the mother's parents, who were Heidi's major babysitters, disapproved of Heidi's father and his new wife. Heidi felt torn apart as she moved from one household to the other. She had great difficulty acknowledging her positive feelings for her stepmother. At Christmas time, there were major blowups, as each part of the family competed for Heidi's presence at their key holiday celebrations. In addition, Heidi's father acutely felt the loss of contact with his former brother-in-law. It would cause friction to see him independently, even away from the family celebrations.

In contrast, in a nonclinic family, Bob Anderson feels that the relationship his former wife had developed with his family should be preserved. Therefore, he uses what he calls "strategic absence." At Christmas time when she comes to pick up their daughter from his parents' house, Bob leaves for a long walk, allowing them "connecting time."

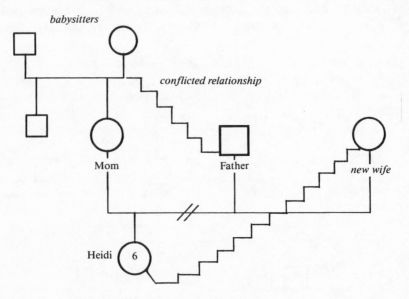

FIGURE 2   Heidi's Family: Conflicts at Christmas

In the clinic research sample a subgroup of four families who had been remarried for several years (average=8.1 years) had abandoned the attempt to integrate their stepfamily into the families of origin. For the December holidays each parent and biological children went separately to family-of-origin celebrations and made no attempt to carry out holiday celebrations together. That these couples were seeking treatment and were on the verge of marital separation is likely symbolized by their inability to create rituals that both transformed and stabilized their new unit within an integrated kinship system. In the following example, the Smith family's therapist hoped to reverse this destructive trend.

Brief Example—The Smith Family

Dwayne and Carol Smith (see Figure 3) came to the clinic with concerns about Dwayne's 16-year-old daughter's running away from home, sexual involvement, and school failure. As Thanksgiving approached, conflict between Dwayne and his former wife accelerated and the daughter, Shanna, announced she had made plans to work all day and didn't care what anyone else did. During a family meeting, their therapist encouraged them to work out an explicit plan for the day, giving each person a chance to state what he or she wished to do. Initially, Dwayne angrily insisted that the girls had to drive with him to see their grandmother. Shanna angrily countered that she was going to work because she needed the extra money so she could move out of the house sooner. Carol threatened to walk out unless they stopped yelling at one another.

With the support of the therapist, Dwayne was able to tell his daughters directly that the source of his concern was his worry that his mother was too ill to survive another year. It was very important to him that they made use of the little time left for them to be with their grandmother. Shanna was able to say that she worried that she would not fit in, that her father's family regarded her as a slut, and that she would be humiliated. Besides, she argued, they had never spent Thanksgiving this way in years past. Carol was able to sympathize with her, saying that she too worried about Dwayne's family's opinion of her. But for her, in contrast with Shanna's mother, Dwayne's contact with his family was important.

Once Shanna heard her father's real concern, she was willing to agree to a plan in which the whole family attended dinner. Dwayne was willing to agree to let her return to work after dinner. Once this was clear, Dwayne was able to give a direct message to his former wife about their plans, which she accepted. They reported later, with much surprise and pleasure, that the dinner had been very enjoyable. Shanna had discovered new friendships with her cousins. Carol felt that Dwayne had supported her, including her in

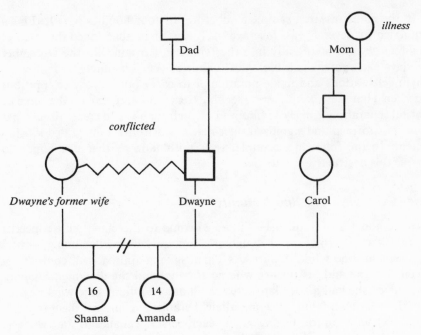

FIGURE 3   The Smith Family: Planning Thanksgiving

conversations rather than abandoning her while he watched TV with his brother.

Extended family relationship choices, changes, and possibilities can be fruitfully explored in therapy interviews. The anticipation of ceremonial occasions where contact is inevitable allows family members to be clear about what relationship statement they wish to enact. This process involves hearing a family member's discomfort about too much closeness ("I'll go to your son's graduation, but I'll never stay overnight at your former in-law's house!"), as well as encouragement around breaking new territory ("We were the only ones to introduce all four of us as Josh's parents at the basketball banquet, even though many of the other boys have stepmothers and stepfathers"). When a ceremonial occasion has been successfully navigated, there can be a marked decrease in the sense of strain and anxiety, as well as an increase in feelings of normality. However, all too often noncustodial parents, former in-laws, or half-siblings in other households are either intentionally or inadvertently excluded from central family rites of passage. If they do not participate meaningfully in an emotionally important ceremony, feelings of estrangement and alienation increase, endangering everyday relationship continuity.

A unique opportunity for formalized definition of stepfamily identity within the broader family network is that offered by the events surrounding the wedding ceremony.

THE WEDDING CEREMONY

The wedding ceremony is the formalized public marker of the beginning of the remarriage. Einstein (1982) suggests that remarriage wedding ceremonies give the couple a chance to "use the ceremony to symbolize brave and powerful statements" and that generally rites of passage "give stepfamilies a chance to enlighten friends and community as well as to show how old relationships can fit into the scheme of new ones" (p. 33). As a transformational event, the wedding can also be an opportunity for a cohesive experience for all new members, marking new boundaries, describing the outlines of the new structure. Alternatively, a remarriage can be a difficult, complicated event, symbolizing failure and providing embarrassment to children and family.

Brief Example—Off to a Bad Start

Linda's first wedding had been a large, formal ceremony, held in the Catholic church with all the traditional trappings. When her husband left her for another woman eight years later, she felt her whole world and sense of identity disintegrating. She went into a severe depression. Her romance with

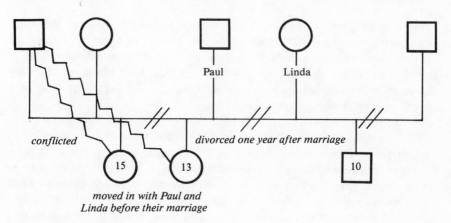

FIGURE 4   The Adams Family

Paul swept her off her feet and made her feel, for the first time since her divorce, that her dream of a happy family was again possible. Paul's teen-aged daughters also latched onto the dream, precipitously deciding to move in with Paul and Linda to escape a conflictful relationship with their stepfather.

As tension developed between Linda and Paul about their differing views of parenting and as ambivalence about a long-term commitment surfaced, they decided that marriage would settle down the household. Knowing that Linda's son would be upset by the decision, they planned the ceremony for a weekend he would be spending with his father. Denying the importance of Linda's religious tradition, and unable to reconcile her beliefs with Paul's vehement rejection of formalized religion, they decided to be married in the judge's chambers, with a minimum of ceremony.

They followed the marriage ceremony with a party of friends. Paul's brother was the only family member included. Paul spent the evening drinking heavily, finally passing out in the bedroom. Linda felt abandoned, depressed, and furious at Paul for his performance in front of her friends. She ended up cleaning up the house the next day, with no help from Paul or his girls, feeling as if she had made a serious mistake.

Their myth that the nuclear family structure could be recreated, their pattern of avoidance of conflict, and denial of difference left the family no options for constructing a new vision. The differences in bonding and in authority between biological and step parent-child dyads could not be acknowledged without threatening the couple's commitment to one another. Without support from extended family, they had no relief from child responsibilities, and thus, little time together as a couple. One year later their marriage ended in divorce.

In describing wedding rites across cultures, the anthropologist Van Gennep (1960) illustrates three themes in the wedding ceremonies: rites of union with the new couple, rites of incorporation into the new extended family, and rites of separation from family of origin. He describes these marriage processes in many cultures as proceeding over a long period of time with various segments performed serially.

Established wedding ceremonies tend to be geared toward the ritual needs of first marriages. For the person marrying for a second time, attention to each of these themes is more complex. If a couple in treatment is moving toward marriage, explicit discussion of symbolic actions of union, incorporation, and separation can be quite profitable. Although the central rite of union remains similar to first marriages, second marriages carry the added agenda of being compared to the first rather than created in their own right

(Furstenberg & Spanier, 1984). In addition, the union means not only dreams for the adult partnership but also immediate childcare responsibilities. As a couple plans their marriage ceremony, values about marital versus child-centered priorities surface and can be made explicit in their public statements. They can make vows about their union and about the incorporation of children into the new family.

Incorporation of Children Into the New Marriage

A study by Morgan (1984) reported that, for college students whose parents had remarried, attendance at the wedding was related to the student's attitude toward the remarriage. Of course, it is likely that the more favorably disposed the child is to the marriage the more likely he/she is to attend. On the other hand, when a child is defined as a family member from the beginning of the stepfamily, even though he or she may not reside with the couple, a basis for future bonding has been established. Some families design their ceremonies to reflect different levels of kinship with those attending. They may choose to treat the children from both families equally and to give them a central role in the ceremony. Surrounding the children are other family members, then a group of friends and more distant relatives. The symbols are circles: all joining hands for a benediction, chairs placed in concentric rings, a small group in the rabbi's study, followed by a large open house.

Brief Example — An Intentional Matrimony

Bob and Kay Anderson announced their "intention to commit matrimony" with a letter to all their close friends and extended families which began with a picture of Bob, Kay, and both sets of children, introducing each person with humor and a few details about his/her history. They planned their ceremony with the minister of the church they had been attending together, making clear to him that they had several statements they wanted to make. They purposefully reversed tradition by standing at the door of the chapel, greeting their guests as they arrived. Yet, they honored the past by including a statement in memory of Bob's mother, who had died the previous year. In addition to their marital vows, they had their children each make a statement agreeing to accept the others as "brother (sister) and friend." All felt the experience to have had strong positive impact. They felt warmly supported by their friends and family who attended. It was an opportunity for new in-laws to meet one another and to connect with friends and some relatives from years past.

It should be noted that suggestions for public demonstrations of inclusive remarried family models meet with disagreement from other, commonly stated, public opinions. Westoff (1978) observes, "most remarriages avoid all the problems of who is in which pew or how to get two former families together for the occasion . . . by skipping all the formal trapping. They marry in a courthouse or a friend's home and usually ask their own children and a few best friends to attend. They don't include people they don't want and who don't want to come, and they often don't include parents" (p. 64) The message is that this is a complicated and difficult occasion. Hurt feelings are to be avoided; the importance of the ceremony is to be downplayed. For couples married in 1950, Hollingshead (1952) found that, if the wedding was the woman's second, the wedding trip cost less and there were fewer showers. The partners were less likely to have a formal or a church wedding, there were fewer guests, and they were less likely to have a reception. The consequence, thus, is that less material and network support is offered to the couple. One couple married under these conditions ended up feeling alone, isolated, pulled in different directions by families with no interconnections. They sometimes wondered if they were "really married." They still have to face these complicated and difficult situations — but with less help.

Connection to the Past

While first marriages symbolize separation from the families of origin, second marriages sometimes signal a reconnection in a positive way to families of origin. The theme of separation becomes more salient in relation to the first marriage. Clinical material suggests that an important preparation is a direct communication with the former spouse about the decision to remarry. In this way there is explicit acknowledgment of the meaning of another stage in the break between them and a chance to say good-bye in a new way. Because the ceremony marks a life transition, it brings back the experience of the loss of the first marriage and a resurgence of memories and emotion. These feelings, coming just at the time of an expected joyous new start, are tremendously disconcerting. For example, one woman described the day when she and her fiancé went for their blood tests. She suddenly felt tremendously sad and missed her first husband acutely. Confused, she ended up arguing with her fiancé and suddenly doubted the wisdom of "marrying too soon."

Attention to the past in the formal ceremony can be a loaded issue. It elicits themes of loss, guilt, and the possibility of continuing conflict with former spouses. Nevertheless, two of the nonclinic research families made explicit reference to previous marriages. They explained in the interview that they wanted to use the wedding as an opportunity to "redirect energy in a positive way." They also agreed that it was important for the children to have their ongoing ties with their other parents clearly acknowledged. In one family each made a marital vow to support the new spouse and the parent outside the household in their parenting decisions.

In clinical work it is useful to note that the degree to which the wedding ceremony can be used as a transforming experience depends in part on the extent to which the partners can think and talk together about the type of family they want to create, the amount of agreement—or willingness to confront disagreement—they show, and their sense that they can control this process. Each of the three nonclinic research couples expressed a high degree of control, intentionality, and pleasure over their marriage ceremonies. They commented, "We were in charge," "You have the opportunity second time around to do it more the way you want," "We turned things upside down."

If a couple comes in after the marriage, asking for the story of the ceremony becomes a useful intervention. If a positive story is told, it helps the couple reexperience a time of good feeling and to reflect on their expectations. A negative story can illustrate a denial of the importance of the remarriage and a lack of kinship support. For these families the task of constructing an event which will declare publicly their commitment to the marriage will frequently bring to the surface a host of central issues to be resolved. If these are satisfactorily confronted, the spouses may gain a great deal of pleasure and support from constructing a new ceremony for themselves which symbolizes real commitment and which provides opportunities for revised kinship connections.

Although the marriage ceremony may be a public statement of a bold new vision of family structure, the years that follow are filled with a series of experiments and experiences which forge the real outline of the family. Particularly complicated and contradictory are the issues which surround the co-parenting of children across households.

DEFINITION OF THE REMARRIED FAMILY ACROSS HOUSEHOLDS—THE BINUCLEAR FAMILY

Ahrons (1979) has described the concept of the "binuclear family" as follows:

> The reorganization of the nuclear family through divorce frequently results in the establishment of two households, maternal and paternal. These two interrelated households, or nuclei of the child's family of orientation, form one family system—a BINUCLEAR FAMILY SYSTEM. . . . Some families make very distinct divisions between the child's primary and secondary homes, whereas in other families these distinctions may be blurred and both homes have primary importance. Hence, the term BINUCLEAR FAMILY indicates a family system with

two nuclear households, whether or not the households have equal importance in the child's life experience. (p. 500)

At the time of remarriage there is usually an established pattern of rules defining when and how each parent has continued to relate to the children and defining the pattern of relationship between former spouses. If the new marital relationship begins to involve collaborative discussion and decision-making about schedules, money, and childrearing issues, the nature of the cross-household co-parenting relationship has to change. This may evolve into a three- or four-way co-parenting collaborative "executive team"; it may remain a biological parent primary team with the additional, background support of the stepparent; or it may become an embattled triangle with the remarried parent caught in a cross fire of possessiveness, jealousy, and defensiveness. Whatever pattern evolves, there is clear interdependence between the different households as long as both biological parents remain involved with their children (Ahrons & Rodgers, 1987). Key interactions defining the pattern of this interdependence are spelled out around ritual performances on all levels.

Occasions which require cross-household participation have very little societal support for a co-parenting model, yet are critical in preventing the disruption of ritual continuity for children. A workable co-parenting model is necessary not only for the traditional holidays with extended families, but also for the many encounters in public where messages are sent both to family members and to outsiders. These relationship messages have strong impact on feelings about self and family identity.

Brief Example

Adam finally was able to tell his parents that he didn't care that they did not sit near each other at his hockey games. What he wanted was for them to say a few words directly to one another when they exchanged him. He knew they had trouble agreeing on most things surrounding him and was coming to terms with that. However, he was continually mortified at their public demonstration of distance in front of his teammates and their parents.

Susan became very upset around parent nights at school. These were occasions at which mother and stepmother vied with one over who was the more loving parent. If she dressed at her mother's house her stepmother criticized her and her mother for being sloppy. If she forgot her lines, her mother accused father and stepmother of putting too much pressure on her. After a performance her anxiety increased. If she went first to her mother, she was criticized by her father. If she went first to her father, her mother's feelings were hurt. In her normal schedule Susan could avoid confrontation.

When all were together in public she found it impossible to please everyone at the same time.

At a minimum, a commitment to the extended family model requires public performances of courtesy and civility, even when one has no positive feeling toward the other parent. In therapy interviews families can anticipate and rehearse scenes at school, at former in-law's homes, at graduations, and the like. Parents can decide how close or distant they care to be with a former spouse, and children can express what makes a difference for them. Acting out a desired pattern demonstrates its possibility and makes true relationship change more likely.

When this does not happen destructive intrusion into ceremonial occasions may occur.

Brief Example – The Millers

Jim and Betty Miller, a couple who came to the clinic for marital counseling, described the disruptive effects of their ongoing battle with Jim's former wife over care of the children. For Thanksgiving Jim and Betty's dinner celebration included their two-year-old son, Ben, Jim's 14-year-old son, Steve, his 10-year-old daughter, Karen, and Jim's brother and family (see Figure 5). Earlier in the day, while Jim was working in his study, Betty had confronted Steve over his refusal to cooperate with her. Although they agreed to drop the dispute, they were not speaking to one another during dinner. To add to the tension, in the middle of dinner Jim's former wife

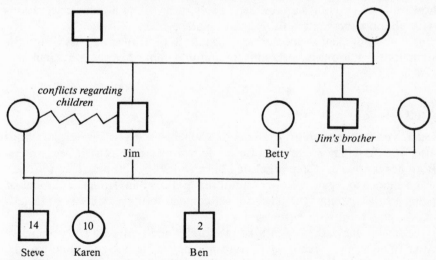

FIGURE 5   The Miller Family: A Conflicted Thanksgiving

called, demanding to speak with the children. Jim answered the phone, then hung up on her. This sequence was repeated four times, until he left the phone off the hook. Karen lost her appetite and struggled to hold back tears. Steve remained sullen. Betty worried that she was developing an ulcer. Jim had to restrain himself from leaving the table and retreating to his study. Jim's brother commiserated with Betty, agreeing that the children's mother was an impossible person to deal with. Steve muttered to himself that no matter where he is, the other parent is being torn apart. For all of them the chronically unresolved battle from the first marriage was being allowed to interfere with the times critical for building stepfamily cohesion.

If a family cannot devise a working model independently, the therapist can provide an important function by offering his/her office as a neutral place for co-parent executive meetings. This includes all the adults in both households negotiating concrete plans which involve the children. Stepparents in these meetings are coached to offer relevant information, but to avoid the "white knight" role of protecting the spouse from conflict with the former spouse. Sometimes they are moved physically to a stance behind the spouse, giving support but not interfering. Stepparents in this format offer a strong motivating force for the implementation of a cooperative co-parenting model. They see clearly the drain on their current marriage from ongoing tension from the former marriage. In addition, if the stepparent can openly support the parents in the other household and if the biological parent can assume responsibility for the child, the relief in tension between stepparent and child is usually marked. Once a productive mode of cross-household discussion is established, a way of handling holiday celebrations which honors these relationships will usually evolve.

Acknowledgment of the heritage from both biological parents within the stepfamily traditions is important for children even when the other parent is absent.

Brief Example—A Lost Ritual

Leah, a college sophomore, described to her therapist very upsetting feelings after the first Christmas celebration following her mother's remarriage. Both her mother and stepfather had been widowed. The marriage for them was a chance to regain a sense of adult fun and freedom from the burdens of being a single parent. They had not yet come to terms with a way of including the past within this new vision.

Following her father's death Leah's family had evolved a Christmas Eve ritual of creating a wreath out of holly and placing it around a picture of the family as a whole, including her father. This continued their feeling of being a part of a warm, close family happily gathered together for holidays. After the remarriage the picture had disappeared from the mantle. On Christmas Eve Leah had no support for the continuation of the ritual. She felt hollow, out of joint. "It didn't seem like Christmas."

One can imagine on such an occasion the modification of this ritual to honor the memories of both Leah's father and her stepfather's former wife. It would be a painful ritual, to be sure, but one with a healing impact. Unable to do this, the marital couple was faced with the cost for Leah, which included increasingly hostile rejection of her stepfather as well as a diminution of support from her siblings.

In sum, ritual disruption is most likely to occur when there are ongoing disputes between parents, competitive struggles over who is to be the best parent, or denial of painful history. Coparenting patterns around holidays can range from heated battles which make any kind of celebration impossible, through avoidance of one side of the family, to tense but civilized joint participation.

In marked contrast are celebrations which acknowledge the complexity of relationship and are flexibly adapted to reflect this. For example, in the Miller family (see Figure 5), Betty, as stepmother, actively tried to include her husband's children as full members of her extended family. One of the traditions of her family of origin was that all family members over age 12 participated in a drawing of names for the gift exchange. This year Steve was included in the drawing, even though he spent Christmas Day with his mother. He missed the Christmas Day gift exchange, but was included by exchanging gifts with her family at a special dinner when he returned.

When experiments such as this are successful, the feeling for all members is confirming and the interaction may over time become ritualized. Despite the great changes in family structure, each person can feel normal, part of a supportive and respected family. Just as a respectful co-parenting model allows space for the stepfamily unit, developing cohesion from successful stepfamily experiences can allow parents to be more relaxed and flexible about their dealings with other households.

A SENSE OF "HOME": BUILDING THE STEPFAMILY UNIT THROUGH DAILY RITUALS

The development of cohesion within the stepfamily has its own special challenges. Attention to everyday patterns as well as to the development of new traditions can be critical in the formation of a workable family identity. While negotiating connections within the broad family network, the stepfamily is consolidating its own internal organization. For the nuclear family boundaries around the basic family unit are clear. Everyone knows where home is and whether or not he/she belongs to the family. For the remarried family the rhythm of everyday life, the emerging family coalitions, and the sense of "home base" for the children are determined by their highly structured schedule of divided time between households. In a family with joint custody agreements for both sets of children, one boy expressed a feeling of home in both houses. Yet for his stepbrother, who spent less time in the household, the schedule resulted in his always arriving a day later. He never felt quite as much part of the family because it appeared to him that much had gone on between stepsibs and parents before he arrived.

For the children who spend most of their time in one household, this is referred to as "home" and considered to be the most influential in shaping their identity. For children who are there less frequently, the stepfamily task becomes the creation of a feeling of home as their second household. One important ingredient needed to create this atmosphere is a sense of joint endeavor and a mutually respecting and trusting couple relationship. Some couples give a sense of "our house" and "our family structure" which exists alongside the acknowledgment of the tighter biological subsystems and differing opportunities for inclusion. The planning is joint, but the enforcement goes along biological lines.

Brief Example — "Home" for the Bernsteins

When David and Barbara Bernstein (see Figure 1) moved into their first house together, they made sure that all the children were present for the first night spent in the house, even though Barbara's children were to have it for a primary residence and David's children were not. Despite these efforts, each of the children has a different feeling about where "home" is. Andy says "home is where your parent is." However, his stepbrothers, Alan and Sam, feel that "home" is their mother's house. Andy's sister, Susan C., age 16, is clear that "home" is with her mother, but she is ambivalent about just who belongs in her immediate family. She likes her stepsiblings, but feels she needs an explicit invitation to be included in their special events. She is comfortable with her stepfather, but it is her father's opinion, not her stepfather's, which has an impact on her school performance.

A primary technique for building a sense of home is to rely on repetition and routinization of relatively neutral everyday events. Within the constraints of scheduling, a family can make explicit efforts to create regular times when all the persons considered "immediate family" are doing something together. This is perhaps the most conscious attempt to define family in the traditional sense of nuclear family. The success of these times carries much weight for the couple regarding their feelings of progress and accomplishment. For many families "immediate family" seemed to include all members who live in the household at any time during the month. Older children who live independently were welcome to join (sometimes they were explicitly invited), but were seen as being in control of their own schedules. They would call or drop in on irregular schedules, appearing to be working out for themselves an acceptable form of family membership. The adults felt they had little control over these children's comings and goings, and expressed some irritation over having to accommodate. For the children still living at home there were clear messages about which events were "required attendance" and which were "optional."

Brief Example — The Johnsons

For the Johnson family (see Figure 6), a nonclinic family, the central organizing event of the daily schedule was a highly ritualized evening meal with a blessing at beginning and end, permission needed for leaving the table, and the exclusion of outsiders. For Gregory and Alice Johnson the commitment to come together as a family unit was worth the effort in organizing their day around this meal. For Alice's children, however, the commitment was less clear. They had loyalties to both their mother and their father and felt a continuing need to keep the image of their old family alive. As their mother's household became more organized, they felt torn. For months they refused to carry on a conversation with their stepfather during dinner, even though they participated in the form of the ritual. All their comments were directed towards their mother.

Over time the repetition and firm commitment on the part of the adults were effective. There was an increasing sense of calm around daily schedules

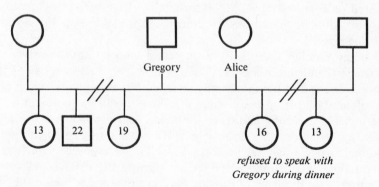

*refused to speak with
Gregory during dinner*

FIGURE 6   The Johnson Family: The Evening Meal

and less struggle. Eight months after initiating their dinner routine, Gregory and Alice reported with delight that they had left the children home alone for dinner and the girls had sung grace just as if their stepfather were there. The ritual had begun to have a life of its own.

For many clinic families an important focus of treatment is the struggle to develop a vision for their unique combination of family members and households, and to translate this vision into everyday routines which work. It is important to keep in focus during this time that the children in particular will resist even the best laid plans of the adults. Even though the nonclinic research families reported many successfully cohesive stepfamily experiences, each family also reported continual struggles. Visiting children forgot their decent clothes, knowing that the family was going out. Plans with friends always seemed to interfere with family plans. No matter how many different options were offered for breakfast, someone always was not pleased. Needless to say, nuclear families with adolescents report struggling with teenagers' resistance to routines which define them as children. There also is a normally increasing disengagement from family times as competing interests with friends, work, and school activities draw them away. The usual adolescent struggle reflects the need for flexibility within family rituals to accommodate developmental changes. This process occurs within the context of long established and unquestioned family patterns. For the stepfamily the resistance is related not only to normal adolescent concerns (which are clearly present) but also to the implications of incorporation into a new, basically different, family pattern.

In addition, in both clinic and nonclinic families everyday events offer dramatic opportunities for refusal of relationship, for defining oneself as an outsider. For example, one boy refused to sit near his stepmother at church. A teenage girl received weekly letters from her stepmother which she never answered or acknowledged. Mr. Bernstein's college-aged daughter consistently turned down invitations for dinner, but would appear just as dessert was being served.

In many families there will be one child who is more reactive to the remarriage than the others. This child will be particularly resistant to attempts to define him/her as a family member. For example, the child will be more often absent from the evening meal and less likely to attend a group gathering. This is a combination of the child's resisting inclusion by defining him/herself as an outsider and the parent's not wanting to go through the emotional struggle required to force inclusion. This process can lead to a compounding interaction: when feeling outside the child is reluctant to participate; then by virtue of missing out, he/she becomes even more on the outside.

Creating a Heritage of Differing Values

Most difficult in the stepfamily unit is the resolution of the clashes of everyday patterns which embody conceptions of identity highly valued in each family. All newly married couples have certain areas of difference which become symbolic of their family-of-origin identities. Normally the couple will struggle, experiment, and come to some compromise, accommodation or transformation. This is no different for the newly remarried couples. However, for these families the working-out of differing values takes on a new dimension because the children's identities are involved. Value differences impinge on rules for acceptance in the household, on the relationship between households of former spouses, and on the relationship between stepparents and children.

Brief Example — Whose Time?

In the Bernstein family (see Figure 1) time has a very different meaning for the two families. For Barbara's family to be on time, to plan ahead, means to be responsible, to be in charge, and to be able to work out a way to achieve what is important for one. For David's family holding off commitment to the last moment, going with the flow, means to be flexible, maximizes individual options, avoids intentionally hurting others' feelings, and maximizes the opportunities for being able to seize what one wants when it occurs and not be left out of a good thing. As a married couple David and Barbara have been able to accommodate their differences. However, both sets of children and David's former wife do not accommodate so well. Each feels confused and struggles to make sense out of the everyday family interactions which used to hang together in a coherent manner. For David's children to plan ahead puts them directly in a loyalty struggle between their parents, even when they privately agree with the value of one parent's position.

Thus, differences which normally are contained within a marital dyad as the couple constructs its own value system become played out in complicated ways throughout the system. This makes the construction of a common family identity unusually difficult.

In a clinic setting it is important to de-escalate and depathologize the uproar over such arguments by placing them in context. The therapist needs to note that the explicit examination of such basic assumptions of everyday living is unsettling but necessary. One might suggest that neither family should change too rapidly. It is only when both traditions are kept alive that a higher level of integration can occur. Family meetings are excellent arenas for discussions of any everyday matter which causes tension. To dramatize the importance of maintaining patterns from both families, a variation of the odd days/even days ritual can be used (Boscolo, Cecchin, Selvini Palazzoli, & Prata, 1978). Once the differences between families are made explicit, the therapist can give them the task of alternating weeks following each family's routine, with each spouse enforcing the other's rules with his/her children.

NEW STEPFAMILY TRADITIONS

Throughout the first few years of the remarriage, family traditions are constructed from several different sources. Some emerge from the successful navigation of novel and/or upsetting situations together. Some traditions are taken over from one side of the family or the other. Others represent a creative solution to the clash of competing heritages.

Mastery of the Novel Experience

Many families see vacations spent together, in a new place, as important consolidating experiences. Time spent away from usual routines offers a wealth of opportunities for a negotiating and defining new relationships. Thus, there are discussions about who sits where in the car, who rides with whom if there are too many for one car, how it is decided who sleeps on the floor, or in the small tent, or on the couch, and so on. They are confronted with the task of setting up a tent, in the rain, when the poles have been left behind. When a solution is reached by pooling everyone's ideas and cracking a few very funny jokes, all members of the group feel closer and more trusting. In the process of making these decisions, new family values become evident. For example, "There will be no favorites — we'll draw straws for the comfortable bed." "We'll rent a van for vacation so there will be room for everyone." "There are new groupings in this family by age — younger children in one car and older children in the other." "When you are injured and your mother is far away, your stepmother can care for you."

Direct Incorporation of Old Rituals

One way of handling a holiday event is to continue one family's tradition without challenging the old ways and without creating serious tension in the stepfamily unit. This solution is likely to occur when one spouse carries with him/her highly organized and ritualized traditions and the new spouse does not.

For example, in the Bernstein's family, Barbara has learned to cook the dishes in her mother-in-law's style and now reads the service from a book in which her name is written over the crossed-out name of the previous spouse. Since her family placed very little importance on the Passover celebration, she has enjoyed the opportunity to adopt traditions she felt her family had neglected. The basic pattern of the Passover ritual has not been altered by Mr. Bernstein's remarriage. The old structure continues with replaceable actors.

However, many stepfamily celebrations are carefully accommodated to children's holiday schedules, which were worked out painfully in the highly emotional postdivorce years. A common feeling is that they do not want to rock the boat and so are willing to begin to build household cohesion within that framework.

The Integration of New and Old

Some household celebrations evolved a mixture of small traditions from both households in a nice blend of new and old. The Johnson family, for instance, adapted a series of events from both families into their Christmas celebration. Alice's family added a special new ornament each year as they decorated the tree. This year Gregory's oldest daughter sent an ornament, even though she was not going to be with them. Gregory's family lit candles in the Advent wreath before Sunday dinner. In the remarried family they added to the candle lighting a time when each person spoke a few words about something personally important. In this way the form of an old ritual was used to enable the new family members to know one another more intimately.

THERAPEUTIC IMPLICATIONS

In therapy with remarried families, attention to the ritual process on all three levels can suggest a wide variety of interventions. The stance suggested here is not one in which the therapist invents a ritual as a therapeutic tool. Rather it is one in which the therapist encourages the family members in their creation of their own rituals. The therapist places the topic of rituals and ceremonies in the area of explicit discussion and facilitates opportunities for ritual to develop. Particularly important is the therapist's view of the transitional nature of the family's structure and his/her vision of the goals for the family. The therapeutic moves can reinforce a creatively flexible, evolving family organization, or they can add weight to unattainable myths of the idealized nuclear family. In the absence of established societal guidance for or sanction of stepfamily roles and patterns, the therapist can serve as a societal representative, offering suggestions for models and encouraging innovation.

When families describe chaotic lives with low cohesion and attachment, attention to the everyday routines is valuable for giving some sense of control and creating opportunities to build a sense of relatedness. Techniques commonly used by stepfamilies are the expectation that all family members be together for at least one meal per week and/or the expectation of attendance at family meetings to discuss household issues. Other everyday routines may honor interactions from the single-parent time within the context of the new family.

For example, 12-year-old Eleanor complained that she never has time alone with her father since he remarried. In previous years their most enjoyable time together was planning their weekend meals, shopping, and going back to his apartment to cook dinner. Once she was able to say this to him, they were able to work out a plan in which the two of them shopped for the whole family. Normally, Eleanor's stepmother felt excluded by Eleanor and her father. However, this plan fit everyone's needs.

For children with shifting schedules a routinization of the transition times can be useful. One stepmother noted, "Susan always becomes irritable on Sunday afternoon before her mother picks her up. We have learned not to bring up any disciplinary issues at that time and to schedule a low key, pleasant activity. When she arrives on Friday afternoon we expect her to go to her room and unpack her suitcase. We hope that having her clothes in drawers makes her feel more at home."

Most remarried families experience tension and anxiety as major holidays approach and they face the necessity of reconciling competing holiday organizations. This may be played out in heated debates over the details of the celebrations themselves or reflected in an upsurge of tension in other areas. In one clinic family a battle over finances left no energy to plan for a combined Hanukkah/Christmas celebration with returning adult children and obscured other important differences, too threatening to discuss. In another family planning for the household celebration was lost in the furor of renewed court action, as father and former wife battled over the amount of time their son would spend with each on his holiday break from school. Therapists report difficulty helping many families negotiate holiday celebrations which mesh competing traditions because an upsurge of serious tension and conflict threatens the very fabric of the marital relationship and/or the stepfamily.

It is possible that attention in the therapy to the construction of a positive household celebration might well have dealt with feared differences in a manageable way, while at the same time creating a new source of cohesion. This intervention does not eliminate the very difficult sources of trouble for these families, but it can de-escalate the intensity of feeling and can provide strength in moving ahead. For most families, however, the feelings do not accelerate to the point of destruction of all tradition. Instead, the holiday debates allow for an exchange of family histories as well as the articulation of varying plans of what the hoped-for remarried structure will be. The emotional push for resolution—because family members do care for one another—adds power to any symbolic solution which works.

Finally, major rites of passage which involve public, formalized rituals involving extended family can be seen as critical events in a family's history, with the potential for major structural and psychological impact. Anticipation of these events, discussion of how to handle the diplomatic complexities so that adaptive messages are conveyed, exploration of the emotional issues raised, and support and acknowledgment of the difficulty of these events are all important.

In sum, therapeutic attention to the process of identity formation for a remarried binuclear family involves families in explicit exploration of complex choices about values, of preconceptions about kinship patterns, of commitments to family responsibilities, and of the results of innovative experiments in everyday living. In both the clinic and the nonclinic families we interviewed, there were opportunities for establishing the beginnings of family rituals which worked and those which did not. The clinic families were more likely to have very difficult former spouse relationships, and a few had no times in which the family members could come together without friction. Although all the nonclinic families had examples of very successful celebrations, each also had times when household tensions or difficulties with former spouses interfered. Knowing that the early years of a remarriage are times when a family is forced to reexamine patterns at every level of interaction, therapists can be supportive of the seemingly endless period in which "nothing feels right." By forestalling a rush into too early consolidation into patterns which deny the reality of the stepfamily complexity, they can encourage the development of a new structure which allows for confirmation of all members and leaves space for growth of real relationships. With explicit planning and careful negotiation, room can be made in formal ceremonies and informal traditions for all emotionally important family members. Particularly when connections through children provide a larger common relationship, ritual occasions become a vehicle for expressing change—there has been a divorce and a remarriage—and at the same time expressing continuity—the family continues and the coming of age traditions are strong. Under such circumstances both children and adults can experience a sense of belonging, with both a secure connection to the past and permission to explore the possibilities of the future.

REFERENCES

Ahrons, C. R. (1979). The binuclear family: Two households, one family. *Alternative Lifestyles, 2*, 499–515.

Ahrons, C. R., & Perlmutter, M. S. (1982). The relationship between former spouses: A fundamental subsystem in the remarriage family. In L. Messinger (Ed.). *Therapy with remarriage families* (31–46). Rockville, MD: Aspen.

Ahrons, C. R., & Rodgers, R. H. (1987). *Divorced families: A multidisciplinary developmental view*. New York: Norton.

Einstein, E. (1982). *The stepfamily*. New York: MacMillan.

Furstenberg, F. F., Jr., & Spanier, G. B. (1984). *Recycling the family*. Beverly Hills, CA: Sage.

Van Gennep, A. (1960). *The rites of passage*. London: Routledge and Kegan Paul.

Hollingshead, A. B. (1952). Marital status and wedding behavior. *Marriage and Family Living*, 308–311.

Johnson, C. L., & Barer, B. M. (1985). Marital instability and the changing kinship networks. Presented at the annual meetings of the Gerontological Society of America, New Orleans, LA.

Morgan, A. (1984). Stepparent wedding. *Stepfamily Bulletin*, Spring.

Papernow, P. L. (1984). The stepfamily cycle: An experimental model of stepfamily development. *Family Relations, 33*, 355–363.

Sager, C., Brown, H. S., Crohn, H., Engel, T., Rodstein, E., & Walker, L. (1983). *Treating the remarried family*. New York: Brunner/Mazel.

Selvini Palazzoli, M., Boscolo, L., Cecchin, G., & Prata, G. (1978). Ritualized prescriptions in family therapy: Odd and even days. *Journal of Marriage and Family Counseling, 4*, 3–9.

Visher, E. B., & Visher, J. S. (1979). *Stepfamilies: A guide to working with stepparents and stepchildren*. New York: Brunner/Mazel.

Westoff, L. A. (1978). *The second time around: Remarriage in America*. New York: Penguin Books.

Wolin, S. J., & Bennett, L. A. (1984). Family rituals. *Family Process, 23*, 401–420.

IV

RITUALS, FAMILIES,
AND THE WIDER
SOCIAL CONTEXT

12

Use of Ritual in "Redocumenting" Psychiatric History

JANINE ROBERTS

"ALEXANDRA"

"JULIUS"[1]

ALEXANDRA WAS DIAGNOSED as "schizophrenic" 20 years ago when she was an inpatient at a prestigious psychiatric hospital. Several years later, upon admission to another hospital, she was diagnosed as "chronic, undifferentiated schizophrenic." In individual therapy some 10 years after that, Alexandra was given the diagnosis of "schizoid personality." Recently, in another psychiatric evaluation, she was described as having a "martyr complex." Meanwhile, the various labels attached to Alexandra had the effect of: (1) distancing her and her husband from the substantial resources they had to offer each other, because "surely the experts knew better"; (2) making Alexandra more dependent on outside helpers; (3) causing the two children to be wary of their Mom's "condition" and how to help her; (4) masking how Alexandra's symptomatic behavior seemed to be linked to very serious concerns of the family, including medical problems, their son's alcohol and drug abuse, divorces of the two children, etc.; and (5) putting Alexandra in a bind where she could not draw upon her own considerable intelligence about her difficulties. As she said, "Since I was sick, how could my judgment about my 'illness' be trusted?" Ultimately, the labels added a deep level of concern to this family that Alexandra would never be well.

MEDICAL MODEL: THE LABELING PROCESS

The medical model of psychological illness has had far-reaching implications for the mental health disciplines in terms both of how therapist-client relationships are defined and of how problems are identified. For instance, the method by which insurance payments are made is based on a taxonomy of identifiable diseases *within* a person (*DSM-III*). Use of this type of classification system (which is built upon the medical model) ignores the social context of mental health difficulties on two levels.

First, diagnosis is done with the idea that disease is housed within the boundary of one person. Second, *DSM-III* does not acknowledge that its diagnostic categories are constructed and exist within a larger social context in which labels and meaning given to labels vary over time and across cultures. Working with social labeling theory, Waxler (1981) has explained how the outcomes of different mental illnesses are often congruent with cultural expectations:

> A five year follow-up of diagnosed "schizophrenics" (quotes mine) living in Sri Lanka shows that social adjustment and clinical state at the end of five years is remarkably good. The findings for Sri Lankan patients are consistent with similar individuals in other traditional societies such as Nigeria and India and consistently different from outcome for schizophrenia in patients followed in industrial societies. For example, the proportion of individuals labeled "schizophrenic" who have no further episodes of illness after the first one ranges from 58% in Nigeria, 51% in India, 40% in Sri Lanka, to 7% in USSR and 6% in Denmark. These large and consistent differences suggest that industrial societies process psychiatric patients such that large proportions are alienated from their normal roles and continue to have symptoms. In contrast, beliefs and practices in nonindustrial societies encourage short-term illness and quick return to normality. *Cultural differences in prognosis, then, may be the result of culturally based labeling and delabeling processes.* (p. 300)

Besides the cultural context of labeling having impact on how someone views mental illness, the labeling process has consequences for how the relationship between client and helper is defined. With its roots in the medical model of illness, diagnosis in psychiatry traditionally defines a hierarchical model where an expert makes a static analysis which connotes several things. First is the notion that the psychiatrist knows best and the patient should follow his/her more expert view. Second, the diagnosis implies a notion of discoverable causes with a regime of treatment that the expert can outline and the client can follow (Robitscher, 1980). Third, the problem is usually seen as internal to the person presenting symptomatic behavior, reifying "illness" as somehow existing within and not looking at the multiple levels of interaction regarding the problematic behavior.

Yet, as Michael Glenn (1984) has thoughtfully documented, diagnosis in medicine and psychiatry is a more trial-and-error process than is usually acknowledged. Further, events in the history of the development of the American Psychiatric Association's classification system illustrate how diagnostic categories are not "truth" but exist in a relative cultural context. Homosexuality, which was listed for years in *DSM-III* as a subcategory of personality disorders, was changed in 1973 to "sexual orientation disturbance (homosexuality)." Homosexuality was now only viewed as a disease if a person expressed distress over it. This is a new criterion for disorders (Robitscher, 1980). The open debates in APA about whether or not homosexuality was a diagnostic category of dysfunction, and the emerging consensus that it should be presented as described above, demonstrated the shift in views of society about homosexuality. Throughout the five year-process of creating the *DSM-III* manual, the fact that diagnosis is a constructed reality was exposed in differences over whether to add caffeinism as a diagnostic category, drop hysteria, change neuroses to anxiety disorders, etc.

"Diagnosis is a social event" (Glenn, 1984, p. xxiii). Meaning is created in the diagnostic process between the helping person and the client as to etiology of the illness, how it will be "cured," and what long-term impact it will have. Glenn speaks of the need for diagnosis to be a more collaborative, descriptive process, rather than static, mysterious labeling.

RITUALS AND THE THERAPY PROCESS

Some 20 years after her first diagnosis, Alexandra entered family therapy with her husband, Julius. This chapter is written by the therapist who worked with them in conjunction with both Alexandra and Julius. In it, we examine family therapy treatment over nine months, as well as how the process of traditional diagnosis affected the family in prior interventions. Three rituals were used to access more of the family resources and to delabel Alexandra.

Alexandra had a particular identity defined by the larger systems as a mentally ill person. Other aspects of the self can become less important when a labeling occurs, and the constraints of labels often make people imagine themselves as markedly different from others. In this case, we used an identity-redefinition ritual to (1) realign the relationships between the family and outside "expert" helpers, (2) remove some of the stigma of previous labels, and (3) achieve new relationship choices within the family that highlighted and balanced the strengths of both members of the couple. In addition, two out-of-session rituals helped to move the family out of therapy and to highlight the importance of family connections, as opposed to the connections between Alexandra and outside "experts."

A final document written with the family and ritually signed with the team moved from labeling in treatment to a collaborative descriptive summary of family difficulties and strengths. Follow-up data over three years are presented.

ENTERING TREATMENT

Hopefully this family story does not assign roles of heroes or villians to family members, but is simply about people sharing their fears and hopes, strengths and weaknesses, successes and failures. St. Paul wrote about the church when he said, "If one member suffers, all suffer together, if one member is honored, all rejoice together." Families are like that, too.

Alexandra and Julius

A wife and her husband in their mid and late sixties, respectively, were referred to our family team by a neighborhood emergency service agency. The wife, Alexandra, was in a respite placement for several days after she had tried to seek admittance to a private psychiatric hospital and was refused; after that she had tried to go to a public state mental hospital. Alexandra complained of being depressed (since the age of 12) and of having a fear of suicide—a fear that sometime she might be depressed enough to want to commit suicide, although she felt that she had not reached that point yet. She had had two hospitalizations in 1966 and 1972, during which she had acquired the labels first of "schizophrenic" and then of "chronic undifferentiated schizophrenic." She had also been in individual therapy for some time, where she was diagnosed as "schizoid personality." (See Figure 1.)

Alexandra described the impact of the diagnoses as follows:

Time and effort can be wasted arguing about the correctness of a label attached to a person that can be better spent addressing the real issue of its effect on the labeled person. The effect of a "bad medical record" can be disastrous. In my case, the labeling had a devastating effect on how I felt about myself. I cannot deny having displayed ominous symptoms, while feeling that no allowance was made for emotional and physical strains that accompanied these unfortunate episodes, as well as my inability to take medications without dangerous allergic side effects. The labeling resulted in a deep fear that I was psychotic and might some day kill myself. But this labeling might have served another purpose, protecting an institution after a particularly disastrous intervention took place. When I first entered the prestigious institute that ultimately labeled me as "schizophrenic," I calmly signed myself in, secure in my belief that I was going to get the best treatment available. Instead, I was put on a ward called "The Hole" and dosed with massive amounts of mind-altering drugs by a young doctor. Within six weeks I was transferred out on a medical emergency to a hospital where I was treated with steroids for acute drug poisoning due to allergic reactions. In addition, the

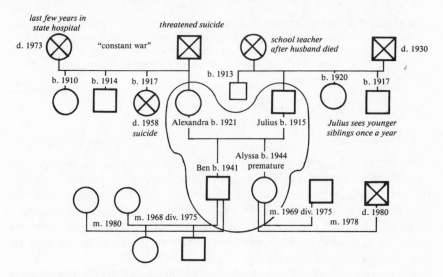

FIGURE 1   Alexandra and Julius

labeling put me in a classic double-bind because, by challenging its validity, I could in fact appear to be reinforcing its accuracy by this act of resistance.

Words indeed do have power and may be used for either enlightenment or obfuscation. They may be used to help another, or to protect oneself. Words that cut like a sword into the patient may be a sturdy shield for the doctor. In my case, I felt as though I had been handed an examination paper marked with an "F" in advance. Julius was frightened and intimidated by the psychiatric labels which threatened his own self-confidence.

The couple was semi-retired, with Julius still working a few hours a day outside the home. Some of the precipitants for the wife's seeking the current hospitalization seemed to include a falling out with her adult daughter as well as with her pastoral counselor. Alexandra felt quite close to the pastoral counselor and had been seeking help from him for over a year. When he felt unable to help her further, he said to her, "You should see a psychiatrist." Julius and Alexandra were themselves requesting couples treatment at this point. Alexandra felt that the past hospitalizations and some of the individual work had not really been helpful to her. Understandably, Julius was skeptical of the therapy process; as Alexandra later commented, "I wasn't much of an advertisement for it."

With the notable exception of the one time when the individual therapist met with Julius and me (when I was attracted to a mutual friend of ours), Julius was left out of all other interventions. He was forced into a passive role of quiet miserable suffering because of my misguided reliance on so-called experts (a lesson I learned well in my work over the years in law offices), and also by the ethics of traditional methods of therapy which seemed to require that treatment take place in a vacuum.

— Alexandra

Clinical Setting

This couple and family were treated in an outpatient clinic where I worked on a team with Dr. Sandy Blount, Dr. Stuart Golan, and Lynn Hoffman. We were working primarily with a Milan approach, although, as has been described elsewhere (Roberts, 1986), I was also particularly interested in tapping and working with the family's own resources. This might sometimes mean incorporating other family system models which fit better with the family's own style of help-seeking.

I was working in front of the mirror with the family. At the beginning of the first session, when the couple responded to my question about meeting the rest of the team by saying "yes," the team came into the room to be introduced. Stuart, Sandy, and Lynn were promptly dubbed by Alexandra as "the boys and girls behind the mirror" (from the song Marlene Deitrich used to sing, "What will the boys in the backroom have?"). The "boys and girls" stayed behind the mirror until the last session.

Overview of Treatment

There were three distinct phases of treatment over the nine months that we worked with the family. The phases break down into roughly three sessions in each phase (nine sessions altogether).

In the *first phase*, creating a systemic picture, we were gathering background data and doing some *life review*. We also brought in the adult children to see how they viewed the current crisis and to see how they might be able to help.

In the *second phase*, as we moved into some changes (many of which were initiated by the spouses themselves or instigated by the circular questioning process), we were primarily focused on anchoring the changes throughout different parts of the system.

In the *last phase*, we moved away from the centrality of our therapy process in the room and looked at therapeutic process outside of the therapy room. Alexandra's past diagnoses were relabeled. The three rituals that will be described were used in the second and third phases.

FIRST PHASE OF THERAPY:
LAYING THE GROUNDWORK

The first three sessions were focused on gathering enough background information to understand why Alexandra had been designated as the "patient" for at least several decades in this family and to build a foundation from which to view her symptoms more systematically. We also wanted to assess any current worry about her or anyone else's safety in the family, as well as look at the dynamics of the family beyond just the couple, including their two adult children and outside helpers.

In working with the important people in the system over the first three meetings, a striking polarity emerged. Julius was "the lump," as Alexandra put it, quite untalkative compared to her and more content to be alone. Yet there was a solidness and generosity of spirit about him that she really seemed to appreciate, especially in the early years of their marriage. Alexandra was viewed by Julius as "bright and sparkly," as smarter than he, as talkative, social, and someone who liked being with people. These two different styles of being in the world were strongly reflected in different ways Julius and Alexandra parented, coped with stress, and interacted with "outsiders."

Alexandra was much more involved with parenting and, as the children had experienced difficulty over the years with alcohol and drug abuse, two divorces and the death of a spouse, she was much likely to be pulled into the difficulties and become agitated about them. Under stress, she was unable to sleep and was anxious. She would increase her demands for contact, particularly wanting to talk with Julius. Julius' usual pattern of coping was to withdraw from people more and become a "sleeping bear." As Alexandra found her husband unavailable to her, she would tend to go outside of the family to engage counselors, friends, or the child with whom they were not currently experiencing problems (the children seemed to alternate somewhat with their symptomatic behavior). Apparently, escalation then occurred both within the system and without, as Julius was compared unfavorably to these outside helpers. As Alexandra said several times, "I had to pay someone to listen to me." Things appeared to become even more problematic and escalate out of hand when one of the outside helpers (a close male friend, individual therapist, pastoral counselor, or Alyssa, the daughter) became more distant or was not available for some reason. Alexandra would then look even further outside of the family for support. New helpers would quickly be brought in by some dramatic behavior and hospitals would get involved. This outward spiral further amplified the distance between her and Julius.

Family history also began to give us some sense of the potency of each parent's style and Alexandra's special role. In Julius' family, he was the oldest sibling in the home when his father died unexpectedly after an inappropriate medical intervention led to his bleeding to death in his bed at home. Suddenly Julius, in his mid teens, had to put aside many of his own needs, wants and desires to help his mother take care of the family. As Julius put it, "I was taught to shoulder burdens and keep them inside." One effect of his taking on this responsibility, of his "doing what had to be done," appeared to be a cutoff with his younger siblings; even though they lived in the area, he saw them only once a year.

Alexandra came from a more volatile family, with a lot of fighting, a father who threatened to commit suicide, and a sister, just next in age to Alexandra, who had in fact committed suicide some 30 years earlier. Alexandra also knew that she was an "unwanted child" (she was not "planned"), and as she stated, "I learned in second grade to go outside of the family for help." Also, Alexandra's mother spent the last several years of her life in a state hospital, having deteriorated rapidly after her husband's death of natural causes.

In the first session, as we gathered pieces of the above data, we also focused on whether anyone was currently at risk in the family. What emerged was not a concern that Alexandra was going to commit suicide, but a pervasive fear that at some point she might experience *suicidal feelings*. We were also aware of several comments that Alexandra, in particular, made about how repetitive it was to go over this data again, along with innuendos that, since I (the therapist) was younger, I might not understand.

We left the family after the first session with the following message:

> You have worked very hard with these issues for a number of years. We need time to gather all of that data and to look carefully at all you have tried so that we are not asking you to do the same things you have already worked on.
>
> We would like to ask Alyssa and Ben to come to the next session to understand more their view of things and what seems like their tradeoffs in the past when one was having problems and then the other.
>
> Also, we wanted to let you know that we were struck by the twists of the concern in whether Alexandra would hurt herself or not. It seemed like the biggest fear was the fear of feelings about suicide — a fear of having them, not a concern that Alexandra would actually commit suicide.
>
> Alexandra, I have a message to you from the team. Alexandra, you would not understate the danger if you thought it would protect someone else.

This message reflects the team's hypothesis that perhaps in Alexandra's cries for help with outside systems she was asking for help for other family members. They wondered if in fact she was protecting someone else.

Alexandra's response was, "That's right, I would try to protect someone else. I never thought my sister would kill herself." Julius and Alexandra were also very attentive to the differences noted between fear of suicidal feelings and actually committing suicide. They seemed glad to invite the children in and began immediately to make plans to invite them.

In the second session, the children came in with their parents and we asked circular questions regarding the two different styles of the parents. Alexandra and Julius were still doing a lot of parenting, given that both children were in their forties. The daughter, Alyssa, had just moved out of the family home again. Ben had been back and forth, living with them after a stint in the service and the dissolution of his first marriage. To some extent, the continued parental involvement seemed related to the fact that much care had been required when both children were little—Alyssa was premature and Ben developed numerous allergies and skin rashes. Therefore, both children were in and out of doctors' offices, with extra attention needing to be paid to their diet, medications, night feedings, etc.

In addition, Alyssa had pituitary gland failure, which led to her being very small in size (wearing size 2 clothing when she was six, for example). She also had arrested secondary sexual development; her parents described her as appearing much younger than her years during adolescence. Because of the physical difficulties, the markers were not clear as to when she moved from being a child to an adolescent to a young adult.

In the first years of family life, Dad worked long (12–13-hour) night shifts and the family was quite poor. Julius said that he stayed on the periphery of educating and working with the children as they grew older because he thought Alexandra was brighter and better at doing things. Over time, Alexandra had come to resent this, as Julius was always slower to become concerned about things. During the children's teenage years, for instance, she did not feel supported by Julius when the children were dating, breaking curfew, and experimenting with alcohol.

We also asked a number of questions about Dad and his retirement, how he was experiencing these last several decades of his life and what worries other family members had about him. Reflexive questions were asked about how much longer the children might be needing the parents and when the parents might need the children—stressing the theme that Alyssa and Ben were now adults who, in fact, might need to think about how and when they might need to be available to their parents.

At the end of this session, we thanked Alyssa and Ben for coming to help their parents and cautioned them all about making too many changes too fast (the couple had reported that they were talking much more and were appreciating the strengths of their two different styles, and Alexandra said she was feeling much better). We also mentioned how the fear of suicidal thoughts seemed to help in slowing things down.

In the third session, we asked more about Dad's experiences growing up and in the marriage, as it always seemed easier to get data from Alexandra, the "talker" in the family. What started to emerge was a sense that Julius had been scared off by Alexandra's psychiatric treatment—a process in which he had never been involved. Given his view of himself as a person not as smart and capable as Alexandra and the seriousness of the problem that the diagnosis seemed to imply, his stance was: "Let the experts work with her. I do not know how to help her. They must know. If they can't help her, how can I?" The more he took on this stance, of course, the more Alexandra was upset by his distance and the more she pushed for outside intervention.

SECOND PHASE: CHANGES

In the next three sessions, the couple continued to report a lot of changes. Alexandra was sleeping, eating, and feeling better. Alexandra and Julius were talking. Julius had moved in more to help with interactions with the children, and they were supporting each other in drawing some boundaries with them. (For instance, when Alyssa showed up fairly regularly at mealtimes, they began to wait it out and not serve meals until she went home. As they said, "This finally had its effect.") During this phase, the couple took a trip to Europe. They had wanted to do this all their lives (this was their first big trip), but Alexandra had been worried that she would be too depressed to go. They had a marvelous time as a twosome, with no worries about the children. They sent us several postcards at the clinic. Some of the comments were:

> We're having such a glorious time I can't remember what I was worrying about!! This is a real upper! Just wish we'd done it before! Better late than never, tho— right? Best to the guys and gals in the "backroom"!

When they came back, they brought Swiss chocolate for us all.

The goal during this phase of treatment was to slow them down, anchor in the changes, and continue to carve out a more systemic view for all of the family of how Alexandra called for help. By the fifth session, they were not reporting any more day-to-day problems, but said they wanted help with the fears about suicide, fear that at some point Alexandra *might* feel suicidal. In our intervention for this session, we presented them with our therapeutic dilemma. First, we positively connoted the joint decision-making style that Julius and Alexandra had described, where they stated their positions about things that needed to be decided, monitored the level of tension between them if their positions were different, and over time came to some consensus. Then we said we were in a dilemma: "We can work with you to rid you of the fear of suicide, yet that fear is something that has seemed to work well in the past as a calling out for help — and help came for the family before Alexandra ever got to the point of feeling suicidal. If we took this away from the family, what would replace it? Also, what would we work on in therapy if we did not work on this, as you are presenting no day-to-day problems?" Finally, we left the couple with a team split, saying that we felt that Alexandra still wanted very much to be in therapy, that other things had somehow not been addressed, while Julius was more distant from the process. "Alexandra, the women on the team think you are more ready to stay in therapy and the men think that you, Julius, are more ready to leave." We recessed them for a month to think about our dilemma and their different positions and to use their shared problem-solving style to work it out.

They came into the sixth session with Alexandra saying that she had thought and thought about why the women had the idea she had other things to work on in therapy (her interpretation of our message) and that she realized she needed to face up to something. She had talked with Julius about it many times and they had come up with a plan; it had been in place for the last three weeks and had been working well for them. What the couple then presented was that, when Alexandra was under stress or depressed, her tolerance for alcohol was very low, which only compounded the sleeping problems and her overall agitation. Alexandra called the drinking her "secret agenda" because she had not shared it in her previous therapies and also because for years, she had used it to see covertly whether Julius really cared for her. In the past, they had worked out a system where liquor was to be kept only in a refrigerator in the basement; Julius was to keep it padlocked and not allow Alexandra access to the key. Inevitably, this system would break down, with the refrigerator not being locked or the key being left out. Alexandra would then say to herself, "See, he doesn't really care about me; I can get into the alcohol again."

In the new system, which they put into place between the fifth and sixth sessions, they decided to keep no liquor in the house so that the game could not be played. They were within walking distance of a neighborhood restaurant and bar where Julius could easily get his occasional beer.

We were very impressed with how the spouses problem-solved this issue on their own. They were still not presenting any day-to-day issues that they could not solve. They were, however, talking about fear of future problems that they might have with their two children.

The team felt as if Julius and Alexandra were ready to keep distancing more from therapy, to access their own resources, yet we wanted to help them do it in a structured way that connected some of their positive experiences in therapy to their time outside of sessions. We also wanted to build on the new connection between the couple and their children, rather than re-connecting Alexandra with therapists, which was the predominant pattern over the last 20 years.

Out-of-Session Rituals: Transitions and Reversals

In the session, we had talked a lot about warning signals that things were starting to unbalance and noted that these signals were usually more dramat-ic for Alexandra than they were for Julius. Some of the signals were: Julius sleeping more, Alexandra sleeping less; Alexandra and Julius not talking with one another; Alexandra starting to drink and Julius leaving liquor in the house; problems with the kids and their not supporting each other; and disappointments in other close relationships. We decided to work with these warning signals (what we dubbed the Very Early Warning System or VEWS) with two out-of-session rituals. We chose out-of-session rituals because we felt that in the past, Alexandra had become too joined with helpers and we wanted to link the spouses together. We also wanted to acknowledge the tremendous strengths they had (for instance, the work they had just done in regard to the drinking).

In the first ritual, intended to begin the transition out of therapy, we asked the couple to meet every Friday at 1:30 (the time and day we had always met in therapy) for the next two months. They should choose the same comfortable place to do this—to sit down, have tea or something, and make it a pleasant coming together. During this time, they should talk about the VEWS (sleep patterns, alcohol, communication, etc.) and decide togeth-er if any of these areas that signaled imbalance were getting out of hand. If they felt an area or areas were becoming problematic, they were then to decide as a couple what they needed to do to bring their daily interactions back into line. Could they handle it themselves? Did they need to bring their children in to help? Mother's individual therapist? Us? They were to decide how to work with the problem.

We also asked them to have a meeting with the two children that included role reversals. They would practice asking the children for help. In this family, the rules seemed to be that it was OK for the children to ask the parents to help, particularly the mother. She had been the caretaker for over 40 years. Yet, as parents grow older, caretaking has to gradually shift, so that children are independent and in fact show that they can take on the responsi-bilities of helping their parents if need be. This had not happened in this family.

As a beginning shift, we wanted Julius and Alexandra, who were with very good reason proud of their own abilities to be independent, not to ask for help, but to *practice* asking the children for help. We wanted to have them experience what it meant to need someone else in the family, rather than to the needed person. We asked Julius to call this meeting, as a symbolic action representing his increased involvement in relation to the children.

We chose these out-of-session rituals to mark the movement out of therapy, as well as the developmental shift for the family necessitated by the parents' aging. By having the spouses meet outside of therapy but at the therapy time and on the therapy day, they were both in therapy and not in therapy at the same time. We had requested Alexandra and Julius to meet to discuss certain topics, yet they were meeting without us. Here we drew upon common elements in traditional cultural transition rites. The persons going through the changes are "betwixt and between" statuses (Turner, 1969). For instance, when a bride and groom become engaged, they are neither unmarried nor married yet, forming a separate unit from their families. In puberty rites, the novice is both child and adult at the same time. In bat and bar mitzvahs, the adolescent chants the sacred Haftorah of that sabbath for the whole congregation like an adult, but when she or he is done, often little bags of candy, a symbol of childhood, are thrown.

With the second ritual, we were looking for a role reversal of helper and helpee in this family. This role shift is a common element in cultural rituals utilizing reversal. For instance, in some Bantu tribes, one day a year women do the men's jobs (such as milking the cows) and wear men's clothing (van der Hart, 1981). In the United States children are often expected to nurture and care for their mother on Mother's Day.

Van Gennep (1960), in studying rites of passage across cultures, found three common stages: separation, transitional, and incorporation, where people are reintegrated into society in their new status. With this family, we moved into the separation phase by raising the issue of continuing to stay in treatment or not, as well as by outlining to the couple our therapeutic dilemma of whether to work with them around the fear that suicidal feelings might come. With each of these interventions, both therapist and client were separated from clear status definitions of who was the helper and who needed help.

With the out-of-session rituals we moved into the transitional phase. They were out of treatment with us for two months, but in treatment on their own and with their two children. Some of the parts of these out-of-session rituals were quite closed. For instance, the Friday meetings were to be on the same day, at the same time and in the same chosen place. This was to highlight the connection to the therapy time. Other parts were much more open—for instance, their choosing how to deal with any problems they had, and when and where Julius would call the children together. In designing the two out-of-session rituals for the transitional phase, we used the family language and themes that had been brought up as signaling difficulty (sleeping-nonsleeping, access to alcohol, etc.).

We also left them with a very open-ended remark directed at Alexandra, "You have a way of finding how things can work for you. You may have to find another 'secret agenda' that can help you test the threshold of response, as you did with the drinking."

The couple came back two months later, having met very faithfully on Fridays as well as many other days. They kept close watch on the VEWS and felt that none of those behaviors had become unbalanced. They also met with each of the kids separately and adapted our notion of practicing calling upon them for help to their own values and needs.

> We did not ask the children for help in the ordinary sense of the word but made every effort to encourage them to give us time and space to be together and to work on our own relationship with each other, without being constantly pressured into doing things for them or listening to their troubles. We feel that we have devoted enough of our lives to parenting and only want the kids to reciprocate by giving us time for ourselves.
>
> —Alexandra and Julius

Alexandra was intrigued by the comment on how secret agendas work for her. As she and Julius talked in their meetings, she decided that she needed to face up to her diagnosis of mental illness and what people were saying about her in medical reports that had remained secret and were never seen by them. Julius and Alexandra did an amazing thing in their two months of work. Alexandra, first on her own and then with Julius, went to the places where she had psychiatric records. They requested copies of the records and tried to piece together how Alexandra had been diagnosed and labeled.

> This was a frightening thing to do but my desire to find some logic and consistency as well as some reasonable explanation of the past impelled me to move in this direction. Old insurance records were studied (for diagnoses); laws relating to release of records were checked; my individual therapist and the State Hospital were contacted. In every case the first response was one of reluctance to respond, but citing of the law and assurance that no harm would result brought forth the requested information.
>
> —Alexandra

Alexandra also brought in a two-page letter of corrections to her psychiatric history, which she had written to her individual therapist. She opened it with:

> Thank you for reviewing my records with me today. I know that many people

check with credit rating bureaus to verify the information recorded there, and it seems equally important to me that my health records be as accurate as possible.

She then went on to make several major corrections in her record, such as that there were mistakes in how long she had been hospitalized (five weeks instead of eight or nine months), that she did not "run down the street naked," and that her mother never threatened to kill her father in front of the children. As she said in the session, "Their saying I ran bare down the street was a bare-faced lie!"

The letter concludes with some comments about her current view of herself and her husband and family:

> I cannot deny having had psychotic episodes. These have been brought on by long periods of stress as well as serious physical problems requiring surgery. All of this adds up to the fact that I will always have to be very careful in periods of stress. Thankfully, family therapy is building a good basis for the family to help me.
>
> There is a long history of marital problems which cannot be dismissed, mostly stemming from the fact that I married much too young when I was emotionally immature. Does anyone ever really know what they are doing when they get married?! It would be a mistake, though, to say that our marriage has been a complete failure. We have had a great deal of happiness too, but sometimes painful memories blot out the good ones. I know that there is real love between us in spite of our differences. Julius has gained as much from the family therapy as I have, and I agree with you that we should have taken this step many, many years ago.
>
> I will always have to be careful in times of stress, as I said before. I have to watch my sleep patterns very carefully, because this is an early warning signal of trouble ahead. My balance between conscious/unconscious is like a razor's edge — always has been and probably always will be. It is terribly dangerous, I know, but it can be interesting!

Alexandra and Julius had again demonstrated remarkable strengths in facing issues. They had introduced, in a most thorough manner, the possibility of working with the labels in past treatment. This was not something we had dealt with extensively in the family therapy. Nor was it something for which we had the earliest psychiatric records (from the individual therapist we had records going back only to 1972).

Alexandra, in writing about the process of researching her records, said that the "unsettling mistakes shook me, particularly the ones in the record of my individual therapist because I had always believed that she understood my case so well. Glaring discrepancies indicated otherwise." However, in doing the summary of the mistakes in her psychiatric history, "The chore that started with such trepidation ended with a greater sense of power over my own life." She was starting to define herself as the expert about her own life.

The groundwork was set for an identity redefinition ritual, as we now had: (1) the full naming of all the psychiatric labels that had been given (previous identification); (2) a broader picture created in family therapy as to how various family difficulties were interrelated (shift to a new identification); and (3) clear delineation of family strengths (to anchor in the new identity).

Identity redefinition rituals focus on relabeling and on establishing new roles. There is a distinction made between old labels that are self-imposed, imposed from outside the family (schools, courts, etc.), or given in therapy, and new roles. For instance, a family presented for treatment with an 11-year-old girl labeled "hyperactive" by the school, family, and pediatrician (Imber-Coppersmith, 1983). She had been on Ritalin for several years but the medication was not seen as very effective at this point. In therapy, as the girl's identity shifted from hyperactive to normal but naughty, a burial ritual was designed to throw out the Ritalin and the label it implied, thereby highlighting the child's new identity.

As we were moving out of therapy, the couple introduced another theme. How could we move beyond past treatment experiences and the static nature of labeling, which had left the couple feeling betrayed, worried about prognosis, and powerless? Since we thought the labels attached to Alexandra were not at all descriptive of the complex processes which led to her difficulties, we wanted to throw the weight of our expert opinion behind a more precise discussion of past problems and current resources. At the same time, we did not want to contribute to another one-up/one-down relationship by ending treatment without allowing Alexandra and Julius to see our case notes.

We decided to write an official summary report collaboratively with the couple. This would address not only our and the family's work together, but also their previous work with helpers. The intent was to place the other documents in a different light by clearly defining the old identity and then marking the new identity that had emerged out of our treatment. We would also be continuing the transition out of therapy as we worked together as colleagues.

THIRD PHASE: EXAMINING THERAPEUTIC PROCESS BOTH PAST AND PRESENT

This decision moved us into the third phase of the therapy and the final ritual, which was primarily in-session but included an out-of-session component. In co-creating this summary document, we purposefully did not call it a termination summary, because the work, in a sense, was not complete.[2] Rather, it would be ongoing along with the document, as the couple took it and used it. At the end of the seventh session, we outlined how we saw the process of the document proceeding. First, we pulled together a rough description of how we currently saw things. Then we asked for input from the couple. They ended up going off and writing up long sections about particular clusters of stresses in the past that had led to therapeutic intervention. We then combined our writings and reviewed the final document.

Our ninth and final meeting was an in-session ritual of signing the document. This marked the shift from therapy to everyday life, as well as the couple's new identity as a unit that did not contain a psychiatric patient. The summary statement was typed up with a signature page at the end with all six of our names in (four team members and the couple). The first part of the session was spent going over the document with Alexandra and Julius to get their final approval. Questions were also asked about what the most useful parts of therapy were ("having the kids come in"); least helpful ("going over the family history"); and advice they would give to other families with similar problems ("go to family therapy with a team"). Then, the team was asked to join us in the therapy room, providing some symmetry between the first and last session, as the team had come into the session nine months earlier to be introduced. As the three-member team entered, Alexandra said, "Ah, the boys and girls from behind the mirror." The team (all over 40) laughed, and Sandy Blount said, "I like the description."

After handshakes and reintroductions, we all sat down in a circle and had a ritual signing of two copies of the six-page document — one for the couple and one for the clinic. As I said, "We should have a nice gold pen," Lynn Hoffman came up with a fancy pen, saying, "It feels like the Declaration of Independence." Each person signed the document in turn, beginning with Alexandra and Julius, and the couple was told, "We trust you implicitly, with all of your strengths and resources that you demonstrated here on your work with the drinking, your problems of interaction, and previous labels attached to Alexandra, to know how to use this document should you ever start to get into difficulties again. You also know how to use, so well, the Very Early Warning System. Please put this statement in your safe deposit box and if you ever get involved with outside systems again you will have it as a resource."

Alexandra then said, "I can always tell when I'm feeling better. I'm doing a lot of work with pastels, trying new styles of painting that I never worked with before. Julius has been doing all kinds of creative things too. We probably have the only wall-papered door in Montague. And he made me a big bulletin board to hang all my things on while I'm painting."

The therapist commented that they should have brought some of the things they were working on to share at the session, like a gallery opening. And Lynn Hoffman said to the couple, "One of the things we don't always get hold of is the wonderful talents of people because that is not why they come here. So we don't get to know the best parts."

We then shared apple pie (brought in by the therapist as it was a symbol for the couple of when things were going well between them) and tea and coffee and talked of Julius' paintings of birches and renovations on their house. Alexandra promised to make a painting for us. (It now hangs in the same therapy room where we worked with them.) The couple also asked for a copy of the tape of the session with their two children, as there were some promises that the children made on the tape that they wanted to go over.

We ended the session out of therapy. We were now together as a social group, eating, talking of everyday things, not as family, therapist and team. As Julius and Alexandra stated,

> The concluding ritual was sort of a "graduation." The solemnity of the occasion was appropriately symbolized by the signing of the document, followed by a delightful sharing of refreshments that symbolized that Janine and the team had actually been family members, in a sense, throughout the therapy.
>
> The traditional moment of "going forth" was a poignant one for us and we like to think that Janine and the team shared a similar feeling. Bill Cosby wrote that his father asked for his house key right after he graduated, indicating that he took the "going forth" very seriously, but Janine and the team mercifully left a little crack in the door by reassuring us of their continuing interest in our progress.
>
> The use of ritual during family therapy was especially meaningful to us because of our familiarity with its use in the liturgy of the church, where ritual is used to mark every great transitional period in an individual's life.

Together we had renamed and reclaimed history that highlighted the family resources. In the feedback from Alexandra and Julius over the next several years, you can see how they made use of their strengths.

FEEDBACK FROM THE FAMILY OVER THE THREE YEARS AFTER TERMINATION

I have continued to get written feedback from the family over the last couple of years, as well as verbal feedback from a few times that I have run into them in town. It gives some sense of the impact of the therapy process upon this couple. In fact, as I am writing this, I just received a postcard from the couple on a trip down south. They say, "We still think fondly of the team."

The first letter was received some four months after treatment ended. It begins:

Dear Janine:
   Julius was so excited when he came home the other noon and said "Guess who I saw at school this a.m.?" I have been so very grateful that the two of you have

such a nice relationship. He never really had much faith in "therapy" and I can't blame him because I wasn't much of an advertisement for it, but our experience together with you and team certainly turned a lot of things around.

He told you about our coming trip to Crete. We are so excited about it, and have been having a wonderful time getting ready. One of the things we have been doing is walking all over Montague, up and down hills, etc., to get in shape for sightseeing. Sometimes we have walked two hours and it has just seemed like minutes — you wouldn't believe the great conversations we have. And you must tell the team I don't do all the talking anymore (at least not always!). I think Julius must have been a "sleeping giant" as far as being a conversationalist was concerned.

But this is what I am working up to, because it was such a wonderful experience I have to share it with you. Early this week, I wakened in the night and felt the early signs of my annual spring depression knocking on the door of my consciousness. Just like the first robin, it seems like it always comes. Anyway, it was all the worse because I was so sure that by taking our trip I was going to be able to circumvent it. The disappointment I felt reduced me to almost despairing panic. Naturally, I thought, "I wonder if I should call Janine." Then, while Julius and I went for our walk, I spilled out all the fears and tears and discouragement, and he just kept holding my hand and telling me to get it all out. Fortunately, we walked in the wide-open spaces because no one could see or hear me. Suddenly, I realized that it was possible to find the help I needed with my "present" family and I felt so different. It was the best therapy session I have ever had, and it was because I trusted Julius to help me. Wow! Breakthrough! I had to tell you about this.

I have not forgotten that I promised you another drawing. When we are in Crete I will take a picture or draw a sketch to work from with you in mind.

If you want to share this letter with the team that is fine because they certainly all shared in "bringing up Alexandra."

With love,
Alexandra

A year after treatment ended, a card was received at Thanksgiving for "Janine & Co." In it, Alexandra wrote:

Just a note to say that one of the things that Julius and I will be very grateful for this Thanksgiving is all the help we received from you and the team. (I think of the old parable about *giving* a man a fish vs. teaching him *how* to fish.) Julius is so happy to know that we can work together and that he can really help with his good, solid common sense. Every time we have a good result, his confidence, and mine, grows.

. . . It was so kind of you to make our last session such a memorable one. And it was fun to see the rest of the team who have had to sit and freeze all that time. It costs me a tear just to think about it!! Julius sends his very best wishes, along with mine.

Two and one half years later at Christmas, I received a card in which Alexandra wrote:

Hi! Julius and I remember you and team very often. You helped us so very much and we are grateful. We have had many opportunities to practice team-work and (pardon if it sounds like boasting!!) I think we are becoming quite adept. Both of us, especially Julius, have gained a lot of confidence. We don't have a set day or hour, but just go right into action like a regular session as things come up. Julius has super inner guidance now that he listens! We are getting along better than ever, so I guess you can write "mission accomplished" on our file. Working together beats looking in the yellow pages for help.

Alexandra's correspondence with me once or twice a year indicated to me that the therapy still remained with her and Julius in important ways. I did not see it as an indicator that they remained dependent on therapy, since the content of the letters was so clear and positive about what they were doing for themselves.

IMPLICATIONS FROM THIS CASE FOR USE OF RITUALS WITH OTHER FAMILIES

There are three rituals used in this case that can be adapted to other situations—in a sense, "generic" rituals. First, making the report-writing an open, ritualized process in the mental health professions has implications for cases where (1) reports are filed about individuals or families, and (2) labels are attached to people. Co-creating a document with clients and then giving them a copy to keep in a "safe" place is very different from the therapist's writing a report that is never seen by or shared with clients. In cases where there is social service, welfare or court involvement, this can be a way to empower clients to work with the system. It can also be an important way for therapists to define clearly where they stand on social control issues (Imber-Black, 1988).

For instance, where there has been child abuse, rather than the therapist going to the courts with recommendations unknown to the parents as to whether she or he thinks it is safe for the child to go back to the family, the family and therapist together report on the work, changes, and current issues in the house. This moves the therapist out of the social control arena. The therapist says to the family, "I can work with you in these areas and together we will make a report, and *the court* can appropriately make the social control decisions."

Open access to written records can also move the therapist out of the bind of knowing about agendas of other agencies that are hidden from families. For instance, a community mental health agency, in making a referral to an intake team at a residential treatment team, may recommend a "parentectomy" (separation of the adolescent from the parents with no plans to return him or her home). Since the family will more than likely sense that such recommendations are being made, and the intake worker is immediately caught in a triangle with the family and referring agency.

In cases where people have been psychiatrically labeled, the process of "redocumenting" their experience through a joint report can provide the force of the written work, which is more powerful than a verbal reframe of prior experience. For instance, in this case, having four "expert" family therapists sign and verify this document was important, I think, to counteract all the previous experts who had given their diagnoses. The document also allows both clients and therapist to step outside of the convoluted circle that is created when a therapist labels, for instance, saying to someone, "You are paranoid." The client can respond by saying, "I am not! How can you think that?" The more the client resists, the more his protestations are given as evidence for his problems. Alexandra, in fact, commented upon this bind in her case, stating that the more she questioned the diagnoses over the years in her own head, the more she said to herself, "Well, how can you know if you are sane or not because if you are "sick" then you are not capable of judging yourself." In the final session, Alexandra ultimately found her way out of this circle by saying with a good hearty laugh, "I know I'm not crazy. I read *Catcher in the Rye* and I know I'm not like that."

The importance of dialogue about diagnoses, which acknowledges that diagnosis is a social event, is highlighted in a study of psychiatric hospitals by Waxler (1981). "The psychiatric patients who feel that they are 'back to normal' one month after their first hospitalization are no different, diagnostically, from the 'still sick' group, instead, their better clinical outcome can be explained by the greater power certain hospitals give patients to renegotiate their legal status, treatment plans and diagnoses with hospital staff" (summarized in Waxler, 1981, p. 283).

Important elements to consider in creating a documenting ritual beyond the guidelines highlighted in Chapter 3 include (1) examining what ways the process of co-creating the documenting is an empowering one; (2) making sure you have enough data on previous labels and documents to "redocument" them; and (3) thinking carefully about placement of documents, where they will be kept, who has access to them, and so forth.

Traditional rites of passage transmit key cultural and mythological traditions in three main ways (Turner, 1967):

1. The demonstration — "what is shown" (through relics, masks, statues);
2. Action — "what is done";
3. Instruction — "what is said."

These may be important elements to consider in the construction of this kind of identity redefinition ritual. In looking at the in-session ritual from this perspective, the report itself becomes what is shown. It contains within it the newly created cultural traditions. The actions of the ceremony included the signing of the report, with the witnessing by the previously hidden team, and the eating and talking together out of therapy. The instructions were to put the report in a safe place in case it ever needed to be used again.

The second "generic" ritual in this case is the idea of gathering adult children together to help their parents. Here we adapted the pretend techniques of Madanes (1984) for adults by using the terminology of practice (instead of pretend), which was more age-appropriate, and by emphasizing with reflexive and circular questions that, in fact, in the future this reversal really will need to take place.

As the "greying" of America continues and there is less stigma attached to therapy for this generation of elders, this type of ritual may be needed more often. Many families' day-to-day interactions are rigidly ritualized around parents' helping children. With this kind of "practice" ritual, who is to help whom in families can be reversed. Also, just as when someone "pretends" to have a symptom (Madanes, 1981, 1984), the distinction between what is real and not real — what is possible and not possible — begins to break down.

Indications for using this kind of role reversal include times when families are not acknowledging that the parents are moving into their last developmental stages, when there is a history of child-focused problems with little time and space for the adults, and finally, when children seem unsure of how to help parents. Some particular things to consider in creating it are: (1) a clear rationale for why you are asking them to "practice"; (2) who will call the children together — how can it be best done to shift helping patterns; and (3) in what areas the children can practice providing help.

The third type of "generic" ritual that emerges from this case is the termination ceremony where *in* session you move *out* of session. For instance, when team members come into the room, this physically breaks the boundary of the one-way mirror, putting everyone in the same space and level. Interacting with team members face to face also allows closure, saying good-bye to real people rather than leaving the team as an unknown. Another important component is asking the clients questions about the therapy, therapist and team. (If they could change one thing about the therapy, what would it be? What advice would they give to the therapist, the team, etc.?) This puts the family outside of therapy and meta to the process. Talking about day-to-day events instead of therapeutic issues can also mark the boundary that therapy is finished, as can "breaking bread" together, something you do not normally do in treatment.

A final important element to consider in termination ceremonies is the exchanging with or giving to the family of any symbolic gifts or statements. This can be a unique way to highlight family strengths, as well as to give something back to the family members for all that they have given to you. The relationship is shifted from helper/helpee to a more reciprocal one.

Areas to think about in designing this kind of termination ritual are (1) asking circular questions about the therapy process; (2) timing (when do you want the team to come out, to move away from "therapy"); and (3) what symbols from the therapy process can be given to the family members to validate their own strengths.

CONCLUSION

This case illustrates differences in treatment between a traditional hierarchical model where diagnosis is a hidden agenda and a collaborative model where diagnosis is recognized as a socially constructed process:

Hierarchical Model	*Collaborative Model*
1. Case reports written by clinician. Not read by clients.	1. Case reports written by clinician and clients together.
2. Diagnoses given by clinician. Not shared directly with clients.	2. "Diagnoses" decided upon collaboratively.
3. Supervisor/team remain unknown.	3. Supervisor/team come into room; team process observed.
4. Interventions presented with a focus on the doing of the task, not the process.	4. Process of the interventions seen as important as the actual intervention.
5. Co-creative process not seen as crucial.	5. Co-creative process seen as essential.

The use of collaborative rituals created during the therapy process is emphasized rather than the rigidly set rituals of the mental health establishment. As Alexandra wrote:

> I try to remember that life is always in motion and will never be free from storms; the striving must then aim for equilibrium at the center. Julius and I wish all families Godspeed along their journeys.

NOTES

[1] I particularly want to thank "Alexandra" and "Julius" for their willingness to share their views of the therapy process in this chapter. I continued to learn from them in the collaborative writing of this chapter as I learned from them throughout treatment. I also appreciate very much the work done by the team, Alexander Blount, Stuart Golann, and Lynn Hoffman. — J. R.

2As Alexandra noted in working on this chapter, she is still healing from the inside out, like a puncture wound.

REFERENCES

Glenn, M. (1984). *On diagnosis: A systemic approach*. New York: Brunner/Mazel.

Imber-Black, E. (1988). *Families and larger systems*. New York: Guilford Press.

Imber-Coppersmith, E. (1983). From hyperactive to normal but naughty: A multisystem partnership in delabeling. *International Journal of Family Psychiatry* (3/2), 131–144.

Madanes, C. (1981). *Strategic family therapy*. San Francisco: Jossey-Bass.

Madanes, C. (1984). *Behind the one-way mirror*. San Francisco: Jossey-Bass.

Roberts, J. (1986). An evolving model: Links between the Milan approach and strategic models of family therapy. In Don Efron (Ed.). *Journeys: Expansion of the strategic-systemic therapies* (150–173). New York: Brunner/Mazel.

Robitscher, J. (1980). *The powers of psychiatry*. Boston: Houghton Mifflin.

Turner, V. (1967). *The forest of symbols: Aspects of Ndembu ritual*. Ithaca, NY: Cornell University Press.

Turner, V. (1969). *The ritual process*. Chicago: Aldine Press.

van der Hart, O. (1983). *Rituals in psychotherapy: Transition and continuity*. New York: Irvington.

Van Gennep, A. (1960). *The rites of passage*. Chicago: University of Chicago Press.

Waxler, N. E. (1981). The social labeling perspective on illness and medical practice. In L. Eisenberg & A. Kleinman (Eds.). *The relevance of social science for medicine* (283–306). Boston: D. Reidel Publishing Co.

Women and Ritual
in Family Therapy

JOAN LAIRD

> Once upon a time, many ages ago, in the land of the Mundurucu, in Brazil, the sacred trumpets of the tribe were all owned by the women. These women kept the golden trumpets in the forest, where they convened secretly to play them. But, alas, the women devoted so much time to playing the trumpets that they eventually abandoned their husbands and their household duties. The women, as possessors of the trumpets, had thereby gained ascendancy over the men. The men had to carry firewood and fetch water, and they also had to make manioc bread. . . . But the men still hunted and this angered them for it was necessary to feed meat to the trumpets. . . . So one of the men suggested that they take the trumpets from the women. This they did, forcing the women to return to the dwelling houses and to remain subservient to the men. Subsequently the people were taught that the women should not be permitted to meddle in the affairs of men, or take part in the secret male rites when the sacred musical instruments were played. The woman who would violate this prohibition stands condemned to death, and any man who shows the instruments or reveals the secret laws to a woman will be obliged to kill himself or be killed by his fellow man.
>
> (Myth constructed from text and quotations in Bamberger, 1974, p. 273)

THE GOLDEN TRUMPETS ARE, of course, symbols of sexual and political power. Speculation to the contrary, to date there exists little firm evidence that women, in any time or in any society, have actually owned the secret symbols of authority. Furthermore, the Mundurucu myth suggests that women do not know how to handle public power and responsibility. It warns us of the risks women take and the dangers they face if, indeed, they are allowed access to the idols of the tribe or to the central rites that express the society's cultural code. It tells us that, in Mundurucu society at least, it is gender that is central in the very definition of culture and of power. This is no less the case in our own world.

Sex, at birth a biological given, must be distinguished from gender, a social construction, defined and shaped over time in particular historical, political, and sociocultural contexts. In turn, social constructions of gender identity and role, as they are expressed and shaped in the family and in other social groups, are powerful determinants of individual identity and activity. In recent years, as the feminist critique has spread to family therapy, the field has, at times painfully, begun to examine the social constructions and normative gender prescriptions implicit in major family theories and models and their underlying assumptions about mental health.[1] At the same time, family therapists and other mental health professionals have been questioning the central organismic, mechanistic, and sociological metaphors that have dominated model-building, as well as the languages that not only express but also create and recreate our world views.[2]

In recent years some have moved toward the adoption of a sociocultural metaphor, emphasizing the social and individual construction of meaning. Such a stance calls for a different view of reality and of normative behavior and leads to the adoption of new metaphors for practice. Family therapists have redefined therapy as story (Hartman & Laird, 1987) or as conversation (Hoffman, 1985), implying a recursive, co-evolving process between therapist and client in which each is changed as a new "story" or construction of reality unfolds. If the sociocultural metaphor indicates a search for meaning, then it becomes clear that therapists must search for the important sources of meaning, for the ways that families build and make sense of their worlds and hand down their values and traditions. Thus, family therapists have become increasingly interested in many of the categories long familiar to anthropologists in the study of small societies, such as language and metaphor, world view, folklore and myth, belief and spirituality, religion and ritual.

In the last few years this last category, ritual, long ignored in the family therapy field, has attracted considerable attention from both researchers and clinicians; the present volume is clearly an expression of that interest. What has not been addressed, however, is the very powerful relationship between gender and ritual. This chapter offers a beginning look at that relationship, particularly as it pertains to women's lives and to women in therapy. The notion of gender as a cultural construction is introduced, followed by an overview of women's ritual lives, both in other societies and in our own. This material is followed by a discussion of women and ritual in family therapy. A number of case examples are presented, illustrating the use of ritual in family systems therapy with women, as individuals and in families.

A CULTURAL CONSTRUCTION OF GENDER

Ritual is probably the most potent socialization mechanism available to kin and other groupings for preparing individual members to understand the group's meanings, carry on its traditions, and perform those social roles considered essential to its continuation. Through ritual, as males and females, we learn who we are to be, what words we may speak to whom and on what occasions, what we can and will do and how we shall do it, with whom we are to be, to what we can aspire. Our identities are not only reflected in the rituals we perform, but also reinforced, changed in some way, and created anew in each action. Ritual *implies* action and performance. Furthermore, no two such performances are ever identical, nor are the contexts in which they occur (Moore & Myerhoff, 1977). As Kenneth Burke once phrased it, "Ritual is dancing an attitude" (quoted in Myerhoff, 1983).

Anthropologists Gregory Bateson and Margaret Mead were among the first to attend to the cultural worlds of women and to suggest a cultural conceptualization of gender, a conceptualization that emerged largely from their studies of ritual in traditional societies. Bateson, in his effort to interpret the *Naven* ritual, demonstrated that the analysis of such a complex ceremonial required multidimensional perspectives on ritual, culture, and mind. To understand a single ritual, or a series of rituals, in even the least complex of societies requires not only an exploration of the ritual in terms of the society's ecology, its economy, its psychology and sociology, its sexual politics, its world view and symbolic system, but also a vision of "how such partial modes of understanding can be fitted together in a coherent process of explanation" (Keesing, 1982, p. 17). Keesing warns that "bridge building between partial explanations itself entails further dangers. We are likely to be left with nothing more than an ever more complex functionalist matrix of interconnection, ultimately static and circular: 'the system' endlessly reinforcing and perpetuating itself" (1982, p. 33). Careful attention to the societal construction of gender and the relationships between the sexes is an essential part of that vision.

It is clear that many rituals, particularly initiation rites and other rites of passage, are very directly concerned with definitions of power and status as well as definitions of gender identity and social role. In traditional anthropological analysis, from Durkheim (1915) to the present, rituals have been seen as taming chaos and imposing order, as reinforcing social integration and celebrating society itself. More recently, however, Keesing (1982), reviewing anthropological studies of the Eastern Highlands of New Guinea, observed that boys' initiation and other central social rituals celebrate the unity and power of *men*. As he points out:

They celebrate and reinforce male dominance in the face of women's visible power to create and sustain life, and in the face of the bonds between boys and their mothers which must be broken to sustain male solidarity and dominance. Women's physical control over reproductive processes and emotional control over their sons must be overcome by politics, secrecy, ideology, and dramatized male power. (p. 23)

Male initiation rites in the Highlands not only transform boys into men, but are transformations in which the senior men define themselves as special in relation to women and to uninitiated boys. Langness (1974) argues that "the social solidarity [expressed in ritual] rests upon a power structure entirely in the hands of males, a power structure supported where necessary by a variety of acts that are magical, pure and simple, and designed to keep power in the hands of males" (p. 19). Such power is obtained through maintaining a clear sexual polarization in the world of economic production and through controlling women's productive and reproductive powers, as men or male-dominated kinship groups exchange women and bridewealth. Since male power, status, and prestige are dependent in large part on women's labor, "it is ties with women that pose the greatest threat, from both within and without. The bond between mothers and sons could keep boys from becoming men: it must be broken dramatically and traumatically" (Keesing, 1982, p. 24). Men's shared secrets of ritual contribute to the maintenance of a supercommunity in which women are either excluded from the central society rituals or play roles complementary and subordinate to those of men, "as spectators and fringe participants in male-dominated ritual pageantry and politics" (Keesing, 1982, pp. 24–25).

While the Eastern Highlands of New Guinea may afford a dramatic illustration of these themes, in general male rituals throughout the world tend to be more public and more central to societal cosmology than female ones. Women's rituals are usually less dramatic or colorful, less important in terms of power definitions, and tend to define women's domain as domestic. What rituals exist tend to celebrate woman's role as nurturer or caretaker and her assignment to a particular lineage and a particular male. Rituals that portray and thus bestow great power and authority, as well as the respect that comes from the accumulation of such power, are not generally available to women. Whatever contributions women make to public life are rarely made explicit; their social personae are usually defined by virtue of their relationships to men.

While the above interpretations and generalizations emerge from the study of less complex and diverse societies than our own, societies in which ritual experiences rather than written words or abstract concepts are the primary sources of learning, nevertheless they draw attention to some of the issues of power and definitions of gender implicit in American ritual. A few observations about our own cultural rituals may be made and briefly illustrated.

1. Women's rituals in the United States are less central and less definitional in terms of national values than those of men.
2. National rituals tend to define and confirm the assignment of the public domain (and thus greater power and prestige) to men, the domestic domain to women.
3. Many rituals, both societal and familial, continue to define women's deference and subordination to men.
4. Women's power, in this society, continues to be feared by men; thus, as in many traditional societies, women are seen as dangerous and polluting and must undergo elaborate purification rituals.

Power and Authority

In this country, our most colorful national pageants, which send powerful messages concerning what is to be most celebrated and valued, are associated with the military and with male-dominated spectator sports, particularly football and baseball. In these public enactments, it is the corporate-military complex as well as characteristics associated with males, such as aggressiveness and physical prowess, that are celebrated. Women tend to play subordinate and supportive roles in these dramatic pageants, cheering on the real actors in the drama. There are no rituals equivalent in visibility or drama which celebrate female symbols, roles, or characteristics. The public domains (and thus the public rituals) that are associated with power in this society, those of politics, the military, banking, the corporation, and even academe, remain largely under the control of men. It is difficult for women to see themselves reflected in or to know how to participate in such rituals.

Question may be raised as to whether even those rituals in our society highly identified with women clearly celebrate women's lives and contributions or are under women's control. Reproduction provides one example. In pre-industrial societies, argue Paige and Paige (1981), the rituals of reproduction are essentially political, a means by which men control the reproductive powers of women in order to gain political and economic power. Rich (1986) vividly describes how birthing in our own society was stripped from the control of women, becoming an experience in which women were isolated from the support and comfort of other women. Women were encouraged to relinquish breast-feeding, which became an isolated, embarrassing, and somehow "primitive" practice. In spite of what appears to be a contemporary reclaiming of birthing on the part of women, Paige and Paige argue that the male-dominated medical profession still controls the processes of childbirth; the "natural childbirth" movement has offered only minor modification and, in fact, its major innovation is paternal participation in delivery, a practice they see as a new form of couvade. Furthermore, while some women may have assumed more control over their own rituals of birth, it is men who dominate the legislative and judicial bodies which will ultimately decide whether women can make decisions to terminate pregnancy, to whom and under what conditions birth control will be available, to whom custody will be granted, and so on.

In Levi-Strauss's theory of kinship, marriage was seen as "the most basic form of gift exchange, in which it is women who are the most precious of gifts" (Rubin, 1975, p. 173). Rubin argues that "kinship and marriage are always parts of total social systems, and are always tied into economic and political arrangements" (p. 207). The marriage contract and kinship obligations serve as charters for bestowing or limiting rights in person and property. In Rubin's view, if in pre-capitalist society women were kept in their place by men's cults, secret initiations, and so on, "capitalism has taken over, and rewired, notions of male and female which predate it by centuries" (p. 163). The notion of the exchange of women is still enacted in the traditional American marriage ceremony, in which the daughter is "given" to the groom by her father and in the process exchanges the name of one male for another. It will be argued that in our society the powerful symbolism and language in this rite lack the literal meanings of ownership and connotations of women as property found in many traditional societies. Nevertheless, such words and symbols create recursive worlds of meaning which continue to tell women who they are and what they may become. Women must make conscious and unusual decisions to modify these symbols and rules of relationship and, in fact, in many marriages it is clear that what has been purchased is women's domestic labor.

The notions of exchange of and control over women by men through marriage and kinship alliances have other, very concrete applications in American marriage and family patterns. For example, men continue to earn far more money than their working or nonworking wives and, as sociologist Pepper Schwartz (1987) points out, in marriage as well as in the larger society, "money talks." Her research has demonstrated that money or earning power buys the right in marriage to make decisions — decisions concerning whether to stay or leave, what the family shall purchase, where they shall live, how the children shall be educated, whether therapy shall be paid for, whether father will attend, and so on. Furthermore, in many cases money buys the right of men to bind women to unhappy marriages and in some families to rituals of violence and humiliation, since many women lack the resources to live independently or the skills to compete in the public world.

Public : Male = Domestic : Female

Male rituals everywhere celebrate men's entry into and participation in public life. Female rituals everywhere celebrate and define women's entry into and participation in domestic life. Rosaldo (1974), whose own field work was done among the Ilongot in the Philippines, points out that in many societies there are radical divisions between the lives of men and the lives of the domestic group. Such arrangements leave men free to design rituals of authority that define themselves as superior, as special, and as separate. These rituals increase the distance between men and their families, creating barriers to the demands for intimacy which family life implies. She argues that "because men can be separate, they can be 'sacred'; and by avoiding certain sorts of intimacy and immediate involvement, they can develop an image and mantle of integrity and worth" (p. 27). An analogy may be made to American society, for it is clear that even in dual career families women continue to carry much greater responsibility for the care of the children and the maintenance of the home. It is much more difficult for women, even those who work outside of the home, to construct or control public images of authority, since they are weighted down with the demands of caretaking and the burdens of domestic life. In public life, men are the authors, women the helpers; in domestic life the reverse is the case. For Rosaldo, as for many feminist scholars, the distribution of work roles is key to issues of gender equality and distribution of power.

Women's Rites of Passage

In our own society, no clearly defined or universal initiation rites of passage exist, a phenomenon which contributes to the difficulties young men and women face in leaving home and defining adulthood. The period of adolescence is prolonged and poorly marked. For many the high school graduation serves as a diffuse transition rite, for others entry in the military, for still others marriage.

Those rituals that do exist for the young female in our society carry confusing and ambiguous messages that fail to ready her for public life, that continue to define her in relation to and contingent upon males. The imagery from the "sweet sixteen" party and the debutante's "coming out" party emphasize beauty, femininity, and grace — and the availability of young women for potential husbands. These messages are most powerfully portrayed and best exemplified in the national Miss America pageant, that male-directed annual rite of fall in which women parade their bodies in a ritual somewhat reminiscent of the slave or cattle auction.

There are few rites, at least rites for which cultural material is available to the individual family (with the exception of the wedding, the birthday, and her own funeral), that help women mark *any* of the major transitions in their lives. The married woman's life is most clearly marked by family rites that celebrate the movement through life of her children; the single woman lacks even these. While childbirth may bring special privileges and recognition for the new mother, it often lacks symbolically rich rites of passage which help women incorporate the new status of motherhood. It is her reproduction (product) that is celebrated. Similarly, the transition to post childrearing is inadequately honored as the loss of children is mourned. The fact that these transitions are so poorly marked through ritual may contribute to the common occurrence of depression during both of these life phases. Women never "retire" from their domestic jobs, while the family's movement in time marked by the husband's career, the birth of grandchildren, and so on. There are no widely sanctioned rituals that celebrate or help her incorporate public roles, that move her into the company of senior women, that venerate her achievements and wisdom as she moves to old age. Since rites of passage are important facilitators in the definition of self in relation to society, there is clearly a need for women to reclaim, redesign, or create anew rituals that will facilitate life transitions and allow more meaningful and clear incorporation of both familial and public roles.

While women have made substantial inroads into many male-defined and male-dominated professions and occupations and thus into the public domain, the risks are often heavy and some gains are achieved with substantial costs in ritual degradation and humiliation. The contemporary heroine is often criticized and ridiculed by both men and women in a male-controlled myth-making process, which reminds us all continually that the public sphere belongs to men. For example, Eleanor Roosevelt was villified repeatedly, her appearance and her mothering held up for public approbation. More recently, the attack on Margaret Mead's work by Derek Freeman (1983) excited the media for many months, while the occasion of Mary Catherine Bateson's (1984) loving and eloquent memoir of her parents gave male reviewers license to disparage not only Mead's contributions to social science but her abilities as wife and mother. The caveat to all American women was clear: Women who try to gain the golden trumpets will fail in both the public and domestic domains.

We are also reminded that women in the public eye, no matter how successful, are chained to their husbands' choices. While Gerald Ford does not seem to have been brought down by Betty's drinking, Geraldine Ferraro did not fare as well in relation to her husband's financial decisions. And recently, Elizabeth Dole, the only woman in President Reagan's cabinet, resigned to devote her energy to her husband's presidential campaign, sending one and all a very powerful message concerning whose career comes first.

In the field of family therapy, perhaps Virginia Satir is the only genuine female folk heroine, although others are emerging. Satir's contributions to the field are increasingly unremarked as the history of the family therapy is constructed and reconstructed during the field's major rituals, that is, its conferences and organizational meetings, those places where its traditions are defined and transmitted. Women need to monitor the myth-making processes in the profession's central rituals, as women's ideas and contributions are frequently ridiculed, overlooked, or trivialized.

Dominance and Submission

Another theme repeatedly enacted in both domestic and public ritual is one of dominance and subordination, as women perform in ritual roles that define their supportive and ancillary positions in relation to men. In many societies, women's deference to men is demonstrated symbolically by, for example, walking several paces behind their husbands, covering their faces in the presence of men, keeping their eyes downcast, or sleeping at the feet of men (Bamberger, 1974). In our own society, the images are no less powerful nor the messages less clear. For example, in hospital rituals, (usually) female nurses hand over the tools of the trade to (usually) male surgeons. Nurses and female doctors are often called by their first names, while male doctors are addressed by their professional titles, actions that not only symbolize but also confer authority and prestige. In many American families, men sit at the head of the table, are waited on and often served first by their wives, and are usually offered the choicest part of the meal.

Purity and Danger

A final set of symbols common to many rituals throughout the world identifies women with notions of sexual pollution and danger. Women everywhere are, on the one hand, portrayed as virginal and pure and, on the other, as sexually dangerous and polluting. In this paradoxical position, women are identified with and seen as closer to "nature," men to "culture," a false but useful dichotomizing process in the world of sexual politics (Ortner, 1974). Women are the "other," a marked category in relation to the generic, unmarked category of "self," which is owned by the male.

In many societies, women undergo elaborate purification rites at particular times, such as after childbirth or menstruation. While such cleansing rites carry multiple layers of meaning, they can be used, according to anthropologist Mary Douglas (1966), to assert male superiority, to claim separate social spheres for men and women, or to blame male failure on women's transgressions. Purification rituals, argues Douglas, both mirror and reinforce existing cosmologies, social structures, and balances of power, binding men and women to their prescribed social roles. In her view, where social systems are stable and well-articulated, such purification rites may be largely unnecessary, but where the social structure is poorly articulated and gender roles and relationships are highly ambiguous or changing, those who would challenge the established hegemony represent danger and must be defined as polluting.

While few clearly-defined purification rites exist in our society, we are subjected to a discourse and to a set of diffuse rituals that define women as unclean and as sexually dangerous. The onset of menstruation provides one example.

> The lord said to Moses and Aaron. . . . "When a woman has a discharge of blood which is her regular discharge from her body, she shall be in her impurity for seven days, and whoever touches her shall be unclean until the evening. And everything upon which she lies during her impurity shall be unclean; everything also upon which she sits shall be unclean. And whoever touches her bed shall wash his clothes and bathe himself in water, and be unclean until the evening . . . "
>
> (Leviticus 15:1, 19–24)

In some societies, for example among the Navajo, menarche is an occasion of joy and celebration. The Kinaalda ceremony "ushers the girl into society, invokes positive blessings on her, insures her health, prosperity, and well-being, and protects her from potential misfortune" (Weigle, 1982, p. 180). In most traditional societies, however, the onset of menstruation is an ambiguous occurrence, celebrated and feared. Says Washburn:

> This explains why the rituals appear to fall into two categories, a cause for dancing and a cause for seclusion of the girls. In either case, the ritual marks an understanding that the girl needs a symbolic, interpretive framework as she negotiates her first life crisis and redefines herself as a mature female. These rituals also express an understanding that discovering our identity as women is not to be a solitary struggle but is to be worked out within the context of the community. In each primitive ritual a form of self-transformation is expressed through trials, symbolic acts, and words which promote healing and integrate the forces at play. The girls and the community move into a new identity *through* the crisis.
>
> (Washburn, 1977, p. 9)

In our society, the onset of menstruation for the young girl has often been a solitary, secretive, and shameful experience, marked only by a furtive trip to the drugstore, and perhaps by her first pelvic examination, often a ritual of humiliation. The event is not, as Washburn says, *recognized* in a way that provides the young girl "with a symbolic framework within which to find resources for her questions of meaning" (1977, pp. 12–13). She does not usually, in our society, emerge from this crisis with an increased sense of pride in her own body or sense of worth and integrity as an individual. Furthermore, the well-documented tabooing of sexual relations during menstruation, pregnancy, and in the postpartum period, in spite of an absence of evidence of health hazard, "clearly suggests that the widespread notion of sexual pollution is shared by Americans" (Paige & Paige, 1981, p. 276).

If menstruation is associated with impurity and uncleanliness, it is also linked with notions of power. Weigle (1982) accumulates a rich cross-cultural sample of ritual, myth, and folklore demonstrating that the menstruating woman is seen as dangerous, as emitting a *mana* or supernatural power. Not only must men protect themselves from contamination, but in some societies male rites symbolize the taking over of the reproductive powers that menstruation implies, as in *couvade* rituals or in the ritual cutting of male genitals in circumcision or supercision. In fact, women's sexuality in general is seen as powerful and potentially dangerous, a vision handed down from ancient mythology and still expressed today in myth and ritual. If in traditional societies men must refrain from sex before a hunt or a raid, in our own society some athletes must observe similar sexual taboos. For example, "during summer training camp—a liminal period prior to the start of the football season—professional players are isolated from their wives or other women. Both college and professional players are also expected to abstain from sex on the night before a game" (Arens, 1976, quoted in Kottak, 1978, p. 513).

If in some societies the menstruating female is seen as powerful and dangerous to self and others and thus must be isolated, in our own society a form of isolation is accomplished through defining her as "sick" and in need of time-out or a rest. In both cases she removes herself from the public world and the company of men. Furthermore, it is ironic that, at a time when our society seems to be moving toward sexual liberation and equality for women, many young women are literally starving themselves and ritually gorging and emitting food. The latter theme, not unlike the theme of fasting or starving during menstruation seen in the mythologies of various traditional societies, may express the female's shame over her own body image and bodily processes, denying her sexuality and conforming to male-defined stereotypes of beauty.

WOMEN AND RITUAL IN FAMILY THERAPY

Ritual permeates family life and thus provides the therapist and family together with rich sources for understanding issues of gender as they affect women, as well as powerful sources for change. The family therapist should develop skill in understanding and interpreting the meanings and prescriptions embedded in existing family rituals, in assisting women and families in preserving rituals important to individual identity and family coherence, in reclaiming those that may have been passed over or now exist in truncated, outdated, or destructive forms, and in sharing in the construction of new rituals. Ritual form and content can be drawn upon to help underritualized families to more meaningfully order their lives, to help newly joined couples to creatively forge new rituals, and to incorporate traditions from both heritages (tasks often made more complex because of remarriage or ethnic or religious difference), to help families master crises and expected life transitions, or to disrupt rigid, destructive, or humiliating rituals (Laird, 1984).

Interpreting Ritual

First of all, family therapists need to listen for the ways in which gender role and identity are being shaped in the central rituals of the client's life. Questions to be explored include:

1. How are women and women's roles portrayed and performed in major family celebrations and in everyday ritual interaction?
2. What messages do such rituals send concerning how women are defined and define themselves?
3. How are relationships between men and women portrayed and defined?
4. How and for what reasons are women's contributions valued and celebrated?
5. How are such definitions enforced? What rewards and punishments are sanctioned in ritual?
6. How are these meanings interpreted by women themselves and others in their interpersonal networks?
7. What impact do these messages have upon the family dance and upon women's lives and self-images?

The therapist needs to be sensitive to the family's rituals as they involve women and to the other rituals interwoven throughout the fabric of women's lives, in their relationships with work, recreation, religion and spirituality, in fact throughout their social and cultural networks. Much understanding of ritual occurs on an analogic level and is not consciously interpreted by the participant. Furthermore, participation in ritual often stimulates deeply felt emotions as it orders life in particular ways and is a powerful reinforcer of the behaviors enacted or performed. Thus, most of us are unaware of the ways in which our participation in ritual orders our social and emotional functioning and creates and recreates our self-images. Often women are aware of feeling sad, resentful, or discontented without connecting these feelings to the powerful rituals in which they participate. The therapist needs to be sensitive to the events and the discourse surrounding daily interaction rituals and to the ways women participate in periodic or intermittent rituals such as family vacations or situations of pain or illness. Further, the family therapist should be alert to the normative and idiosyncratic life transitions of individuals and the family as a whole, as well as to the religious and secular holiday patterns in families. All of these ritual events are in some way relevant to a woman's identity and to her well-being. Inasmuch as possible and, of course, determined by the purposes for which therapy is undertaken, these events need to be "unpacked," the family's symbolism and layers of meaning interpreted. The interpretation of ritual is risky business; each of us will see different meanings in family symbolism and action, influenced by our own gender, our ethnic heritages, our political ideologies, our family experiences, and many other factors. Thus, the therapist needs to be wary of "editing" any family ritual without understanding how such ritual fits into the family's larger cultural context and meaning system.

In the following example, a typical holiday festival is explored for its potential meanings in relation to women's lives. Each of us will see different arrangements of color and symbol in this kaleidoscope. The composite portrait is based on the stories of many women, colleagues, friends, students, and clients, here presented as the reminiscences of a daughter and focused primarily on her vision of her mother during this festival.

A Christmas Carol

My mother began preparations for Christmas months in advance, shopping for and wrapping gifts, making new decorations for the house, and addressing cards. She began preparing and freezing some of our family's traditional dishes weeks ahead of time, plum pudding, the pumpkin and mince pies, her collection of cookies, the jams, sauces, and candies, the vegetable casseroles. Since she worked fulltime as an administrative assistant, as Christmas approached she often stayed up late at night wrapping gifts, getting my father to sign the tags for the gifts she had purchased for his parents, siblings and other family members. Mom still tries to make at least one gift for each person in the family, fussing when she can't get them all finished and sighing that she's glad Christmas comes but once a year. Every year she said, and still does, she will be relieved when it is over.

Christmas seems to have always been almost entirely her responsibility, even though all of us have helped in small ways. My sister and I used to help decorate the cookies when we were children, and now we help with last minute dinner preparations and with the cleanup. One of my father's jobs is to get the tree into the house and properly secured, but he refuses to become involved with the decorating. I remember he would sit reading his newspaper, occasionally criticizing the placement of an ornament or the way we were hanging the tinsel. My mother would struggle with the lights, always complaining that she got the worst job, while my sister and brother and I would unwrap each special ornament with great pleasure as we rediscovered old favorites. The lights would finally be lit, and after a moment for admiration, my mother would begin to try to tame the chaos in the living room.

While we sometimes had friends or relatives over for dinner or visiting on Christmas eve, Christmas morning was of course very special when we were children. I know now, as I prepare them for my own children, that the Christmas stockings, perhaps the most exciting tradition I remember, required a great deal of thought and work. My mother always cooked a special breakfast on Christmas morning, after which we were allowed to go into the living room. My father, of course, assumed the role of Santa and presided over the distribution of gifts until he grew bored, at which point we would all share that role. Mother would rush in and out of the living room, trying not to miss anything while cleaning up the breakfast dishes, stuffing the turkey, and getting the rest of the dinner ready in time for the arrival of other family members.

Although now that we children are married and spend Christmas morning in our own homes, the rest of the holiday hasn't changed very much over the years. We all gather at my parents' house about 1:00 p.m. After a half-hour or so of family greetings and conversation, the men usually retire to the family room to watch television, the children play, and the women help my mother get the feast to the table. When we are all seated, my mother, with considerable ceremony, places the bird at my father's place at the head of the table. After the suitable "ohs" and "ahs" he raises his polished and sharpened carving knife and with a dramatic flourish makes the first cut. My mother never sits for very long, running back and forth from dining room to kitchen for much of the meal, keeping the bowls filled and beginning the next course. We all complain about this, to no avail.

There are parts of the holiday I dread. For as long as I can remember, there has been some sort of painful argument at dinner, in the earlier years almost always a fight between my brother and me. Someone usually gets a migraine headache, and my mother ends up in tears at least once during the day, making all of us feel guilty and irritated, because she is overburdened and we know it. On the other hand, it seems a source of pride to her to "do it all" and she often refuses help.

After dinner the males retreat, some to play cards or watch more television and some to nap, while the women and older female children begin the long and tedious business of cleaning up, and my brother puts another log on the fire. This is the time I tend to experience the most resentment, for even though I enjoy this special time for talking and sharing with the women in the family, I would like nothing better than to sneak upstairs for a little nap, to play cards, to watch football, to call for a beer.

I try to carry on most of the same traditions, even though I have a very demanding job. It just doesn't seem like Christmas if anything is skipped. My husband, who helps some and who tells me he doesn't want a "traditional" wife nevertheless seems to, like me, want a "traditional" life! It is difficult to understand why this special day, looked forward to all year long, usually leaves me exhausted, depleted, experiencing a sense of relief, of loss, but already thinking about next year.

Caplow et al. (1982) have suggested that the symbolism and activities of American holiday festivals celebrate the role of woman as caretaker and nurturer, particularly in relation to her job of childrearing. In their view, the family is the institution most at risk in our society, at least in its traditional form, as well as an institution undergoing change, conflict, and contradiction. The secular part of the Christmas ritual "glorifies the hearth and home, and the housekeeper most of all" (p. 235). Wives and mothers are rewarded with gifts and praise, with respect and admiration from relatives, friends, and neighbors for a job well done, while father's role is recognized in the Santa Claus symbolism. Santa, like father, tends to drop off the toys (the paycheck), "bringing good things into the family from the harsh outside world" (p. 235), but thereafter plays only a minor role; it is mother who transforms the gifts/money into wonder and excitement, who affirms and symbolizes the family's complex social ties, each gift symbolizing and defining a particular social relationship. In their view, as more and more women have migrated to the marketplace, Christmas has played an increasingly important role in reminding the community of the dangers to the family. "By glorifying the raising of children and insisting on its importance, the symbols of the festival cycle quell any doubts that parents may have and shore up the emotional conviction that sacrifices for children are worthwhile" (p. 244).

If the above interpretation has merit, paradoxically (for rituals can mask the paradoxes in women's lives), it is women who must perform the difficult and exhausting tasks which are said to culminate in their own praise and reward. While some women who work outside of the home report that their husbands "help," the family Christmas ritual has not in general been modified to reflect the changes in many women's lives and can represent an enormous burden in time and anxiety. The ritual also reflects women's position as subordinate to that of men. One and all are reminded that women "serve" men, and it is the male who sits at the "head" of the table or in the comfortable armchair. Just as man the hunter is feted after bringing home the kill (the tree, the roast, the gifts), the American husband is celebrated through the carving rite and festival games. His mate has the tasks of cooking, serving, and cleaning up after him and their progeny, even though in our society it may have been she who brought home the bacon.

Many women in therapy report exhaustion and resentment around such family celebrations. Often angry at their husbands, they remember feeling sorry for their mothers and resentful toward their brothers. Many women complain that they "give" a great deal at such times, while their husbands may fail even to remember their birthdays. Yet such rituals are very difficult to change because they have been performed in similar ways for many generations; each gender knows the proper steps to the dance. If men have been reluctant to serve, to toil on the domestic front, women are reluctant to give up their centrality in the family, the satisfaction and praise that accompany the success of the ritual, the gratification that comes from nurturing and giving, and the power that comes with orchestrating social relationships.

USING RITUAL FOR CHANGE

The therapist who would draw on the power of ritual for change has two choices. First, she may design and prescribe a ritual to be enacted by an individual or family members without necessarily calling upon their interpretations, meanings, or cognitive understandings of their own ritual life. Based on the therapist's understanding of a dysfunctional, symptom-maintaining pattern, the family may be directed to perform a new set of ritualistic behaviors with little understanding of why such a request is made. This kind of intervention, central in structural, strategic, and systemic therapies, is a hallmark of Mara Selvini Palazzoli's work. She and her colleagues maximize the ritual form of therapy itself with their skillful use of time, team, secrecy, and so on, and have pioneered the use of ritualized prescriptions as well as elaborate ritual enactments (1974). In recent years she has experimented with the "invariant prescription," actually a series of ritualized prescriptions designed to alter the family's interactional patterns and its system of meanings and beliefs (Pirrotta, 1984; Viaro & Leonardi, 1986).

In more cognitively-oriented family therapies, particularly those devoted to growth and differentiation rather than symptom relief or structural change, or those that draw upon the "story" or "conversation" metaphor, the therapist may engage women and families in exploring and interpreting their own ritual lives, designing changes that reflect their desired meanings.

The family therapist, for example, can help women and families consider, as they participate in such family celebrations, what meanings are being expressed, to claim and perhaps enhance or intensify those they wish to preserve, and to discard or transform those that no longer express their desired lives or identities. In this approach, the therapist takes the stance of the "stranger" or "ethnographer" who wishes as completely as possible to learn about the culture of the "other," to learn the native's point of view, her meanings, her interpretations. However, unlike the anthropologist, the therapist has the responsibility to provide a context in which change can occur. She may reflect back her own interpretations and ideas, some of which may fit with the family's system of meaning. Individual women or women in groups may be coached to develop strategies to negotiate such changes in their marriages or families. Couples and families may be invited to consider what meanings their central family rituals convey for males and females, and what they would like to preserve or change. In the examples below, it is the ethnographic stance in the therapeutic use of ritual that is illustrated.

Mastering Women's Transitions

It has been argued that few meaningful rituals exist in our society to mark or celebrate the young girl's movement through the life cycle, to help her shape her own identity as a female. Birth and death have become male-medical affairs, with women playing peripheral roles in these most universal of phenomena. Girls' puberty rites, for example, which may have very powerful meanings closely integrated with social and kinship structures and the cosmologies of more traditional societies, are in our society truncated. As alluded to earlier, in our society the onset of menarche often has been a joyless occasion, unmarked by celebration and accompanied by shame, secrecy, confusion, and a sense of uncleanliness. Menarche might be embraced as an event that defines new possibilities and welcomes the young girl into a new world of power and fulfillment, linking her to the larger context and to men and women in new ways. Rarely do families endow this event with the deeper and more lasting meanings that ritual potentiates. Family therapists can help families and their daughters incorporate this experience in new ways, helping them consider the implications of this transition for their individual and familial lives, as in the following illustration.

Brief Example: Becoming a Woman

The Riggs family includes Reverend Donald Riggs, a Congregational minister, his wife Maggie, a legal assistant, and their three daughters, Bonnie, 17, Trudie, 12, and Diane, 10 (see Figure 1). The family had originally come for help in relation to Bonnie, a high school senior who seemed consistently

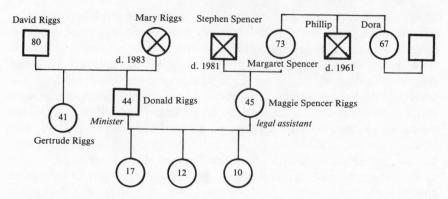

FIGURE 1   The Riggs Family

depressed. A high achiever academically and a very serious and responsible eldest, Bonnie could not decide where to go to college, seemed to be increasingly anxious as high school graduation approached, and was experiencing long bouts of weeping. It was hypothesized that Bonnie, strongly identified with her mother, who had never dealt with her sorrows and disappointments in her own family of origin, was both weeping for her mother and reluctant to leave her with her sadness. Initially, the family therapist argued that young women matured at different rates, were not necessarily prepared to leave home at 17 or 18, and that Bonnie should get a job and remain at home for at least a year. This prescription was linked to a recommendation that Maggie, with the help of the therapist, work on resolving some of the unfinished business with her own family. These interventions unleashed Bonnie's sense of humor and preparations for college, and Maggie's sharing with her daughters for the first time some of the "real" events in her own family, including a history of secret alcoholism on the part of her father. The therapist, however, was more concerned about the highly rebellious Trudie, the family joker, overly intense and thin, potentially anorexic, and full of scorn for both mother and older sister. Trudie envisioned moving to Australia and becoming a famous actress or writer, as soon as she was 18.

The onset of Trudie's menstruation, an event "spilled" in a session with mother and daughters by a giggling Diane, which occasioned much blushing and anger on Trudie's part, created an opportunity for the therapist to inquire about how the family had reacted to this event. She asked, for example, how Bonnie's menstruation had been handled and what meanings menstruation held for females in the family. Maggie, with some embarrassment, talked about how the subjects of sex and maturation had never been discussed in her family. Her mother had handed her a box of sanitary napkins and had said something about "the curse." She remembered feeling ashamed and humiliated, somehow tarnished, as well as feeling conspicuous; something about her was different — "everyone would know." Her menstrual periods were painful and embarrassing and it was several years before she was able to make a connection between menstruation and childbirth. While she had tried to be more open and positive with Bonnie, she had been very uncomfortable talking about menstruation, and Bonnie reported feeling confused and ignorant about the meanings of the event. Maggie reported that Trudie, earlier in the week, had said, "I know all about it, I don't need you to tell me," when she had tried to talk with her.

The therapist suggested that the family members talk about their ideas about menstruation and what meanings it had for each of them. This discussion revealed that even Maggie had little understanding of female biology or could allow herself to feel proud of her female reproductive abilities or sexuality. Bonnie, buried in her studies and sadness, had little pride in her femininity, while Trudie expressed disgust with the whole discussion, announcing she planned never to marry or have children anyway. Diane, the youngest, said that she had many questions but no one wanted to tell her anything. No one expressed joy or pleasure or pride. Donald seemed the least uncomfortable member of the family. For him it signaled the fact that his daughters were maturing and perhaps more "vulnerable." He indicated that he would not feel embarrassed to talk with his daughters about menstruation, but everyone in the family felt this was a female issue, an area in which they did not want father to assume family leadership. The therapist suggested that perhaps what was needed was instruction in and celebration of the ways of women by women, since in this family the girls' natural curiosity and opportunities for pride and self-valuing had been frustrated.

With father's consent, over the next several weeks, in a part of the therapy defined as "woman time," the family women and therapist worked together teaching and learning about becoming women and celebrating the beginning of Trudie's biological womanhood. Maggie, for the first time, was able to talk to her daughters about her own disappointments, her struggles to define herself as woman, wife, and mother, a contribution that seemed particularly meaningful and freeing for Bonnie. After a period of "education," during which time the girls were invited to ask questions and to contribute their ideas about what becoming a "woman" would mean and what they wanted it to mean in their family, in school, in church, and in the community, a final celebration was planned, drawing upon ancient customs and the family's own symbols. This rite took place over a two-week period of time. The therapist had suggested that first Trudie needed to say goodbye to a phase of her childhood. She was to spend some time alone each day for a week, thinking very carefully about what she was giving up and leaving behind and what she thought ought to be changed in the family to recognize her maturing. At the end of the week, she and Diane were to have a special time alone. Trudie would pass on to Diane that childhood possession she thought Diane might most cherish. Trudie wrote and dedicated to Diane a very beautiful poem about a young girl's last joys of childhood, reading it to her aloud and giving her a locket Trudie said was a little young for her.

In a second assignment, Maggie was to preside over a family meeting, during which Trudie would describe for the family those changes she felt would appropriately define her new status. Trudie, for the first time without anger, was able to present her case for not attending church every Saturday and Sunday, taking further instruction, and so on. She agreed to attend once a month and to discontinue a series of antics in church which had been highly embarrassing for her parents. Her parents agreed to give her more autonomy in choosing her own clothes (her tastes were far more flamboyant and androgynous than the family norm), and to allow her to participate in school and community plays, an activity that had been discouraged.

The two weeks ended with a family celebration, to which Maggie's mother and aunt and Donald's father and sister were invited. These family members were told the nature of the occasion and asked to bring a gift for Trudie, while Donald and his father, both skilled cooks, were asked to ready a celebratory dinner. The gift that Trudie most valued came from her grandmother, a lovely gold ring that had belonged to her great-grandmother. Interestingly, the grandmother also presented Maggie and Bonnie with family heirlooms, a beautiful quilt made by her mother for Maggie and a carved crystal bowl for Bonnie, connecting these young women to the generations of women who had preceded them. Donald composed a special blessing honoring his daughter's uniquely maturing self and her special gifts to the family of laughter and creativity, Diane read her poem, and the celebration ended with a toast to the family's newest young woman.

After a few more family sessions, during which time Bonnie, who had long since ceased her weeping, made the decision to attend a college in a nearby community and Maggie and Trudie greatly improved their relationship, Maggie contracted for ongoing individual family-of-origin work.

In this example, a normative life transition which happens to occur during the family's therapy is not ignored but becomes material for change and growth. Existing rituals and their definitions are examined, the family's meanings are explored, and the family is encouraged to ritualize the transition in a way that positively links the young girl to a wider world of pride and meaning. Other events may provide similar opportunities. For example, in our society women have "showers" when they are about to be married or to bear a child. No richly constructed rituals exist on the societal level to celebrate the movement to a new status of a young woman who is not

marrying or bearing a child, aside from the high school or college graduation, and these rituals often celebrate a completion but leave indistinct,
particularly for young women, what the implications are for a new status in
family and community.

Family therapists may explore with families what the moving away from
home means to both family and young person and what the terms of the new
independence may be. Some families have created "independence" celebrations complete with party and gifts. In these situations, it is particularly
important to help the family consider how the parents' roles will change,
particularly the mother's role, to also define, mark, and celebrate her new
status as her children leave. This latter point needs emphasis, since much of
the field seems to have given more attention to extricating children from
their "overinvolved" mothers than helping mothers define what these leavings mean for their self-definitions and their place in society.

Reshaping Women's Self-Images Through Ritual

Women may also be helped to consider how they are mirrored and recreated
in the family's daily and intermittent rituals. For example, a woman may
seem sad or depressed during the holiday season, after the birth of a child,
or after a family reunion. In these situations, family and therapist together
need to explore the meanings implicit in the symbols, language, and actions
performed throughout the transition and in the celebratory enactment.

1. How are women defined? How is this different from the way males
   are defined?
2. What images of women are projected, what roles performed?
3. How are male-female relationships enacted?
4. Do these definitions and enactments reflect what the woman and
   her family want for themselves?
5. Do they fit in terms of the contemporary individual and familial
   needs and the family's relationships with the larger society?
6. Are there elements that place the woman in a deferring, subordinate
   position?
7. How do family rituals tie her to the past and what do they predict
   for the future?
8. What does she/they wish to preserve to reclaim from the past and
   alter for the future?

Therapists can help families frame these questions for themselves and
negotiate altered designs for family celebrations, designs that preserve precious traditions from the past but reflect modern conditions.

For women in our society the birthday is often a traumatic event, since much of women's self-worth may be dependent upon cultural messages which eulogize youth and beauty. In the following example, a woman in "family-of-origin" treatment is facing many of the typical changes associated with middle age.

Brief Example — A Mid-life Celebration

Janice (see Figure 2) was approaching her 50th birthday, a date she "dreaded." Divorced several years earlier, she had adjusted well to living alone and enjoyed her work as a human services worker. Her son was about to graduate from a local college and would attend graduate school in another state. Her parents, to whom she was quite tied in a conflicted, anxiety-producing relationship and whose approval she continued to seek, had recently moved to California. One of the decisions Janice had made in treatment was to apply to a graduate school of public health, in part because she recognized the need to continue to define herself apart from her roles as wife, mother, and daughter and to replace her losses with something new and challenging. She was, however, feeling that she was too old and that she might not be able to compete with younger students; moreover, she was feeling quite abandoned. Most of these events were expressed in relation to her approaching 50th birthday, which she seemed to see as an "ending" rather than a "beginning"; in fact, she seemed surrounded with "endings."

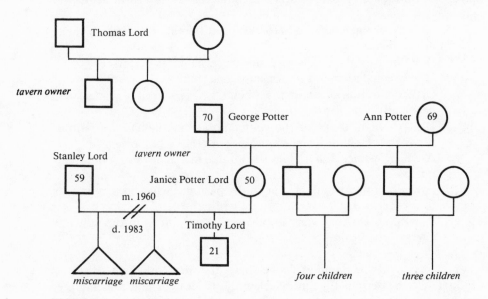

FIGURE 2   Janice

The therapist suggested that perhaps Jan needed to think about this birthday in a very special way, as a chance to continue to come to terms with the past, to reflect on the many changes that had and would be happening, and to more clearly define her future. As these questions were examined and as Jan considered what she wanted "becoming 50" to be for her, she began, with the therapist's support, to construct a very special celebration. First, she decided to invite 55 people, one for each year of her life and one for each decade to come, since she had decided to define her life as only half over. These guests included family members and both old friends and new acquaintances whom she wished to know better.

In several ways the symbols and actions of the party reflected her past life, but with a difference; she decided, instead of rehashing old grievances, to express some of the positives. For example, the menu consisted of two dishes that had been a specialty of hers from her married days. She hired a small steel band, a reminiscence from earlier vacations to the Caribbean with her husband, and the music she planned traversed some three decades of her life. Jan's father had been in the restaurant business and she had spent her teenage years working, often resentfully, after school and weekends serving ice cream. For her party, much to the delight of her guests and the amusement of her parents, she created a small ice cream stand with various kinds of cones and sundaes, in honor of the family business. Her mother and father helped with this part of the celebration, and her son helped to tend bar, positively linking him with his grandfather and great-grandfather, who had owned taverns.

Leaving Home at Last

Leaving home, physically or psychologically, for many young people a protracted and difficult enterprise in our society, seems particularly difficult for women who choose not to marry, or who marry late, as is the case in the following example.

Brief Example — Lorraine, a Spiritual Seeker

Lorraine, 33, daughter of a nonobservant Jewish father and a mother who had converted to Judaism at marriage (see Figure 3), reported that she still felt like "a little girl." Although she had lived independently for several years, through college and graduate school, her parents worried constantly about her, whether she was eating right, whom she was dating, whether she kept her apartment properly heated, and so on. A recent graduate of a doctoral program in psychology, she felt an intense pull back to the city in which her parents lived, and had difficulty both in committing herself to

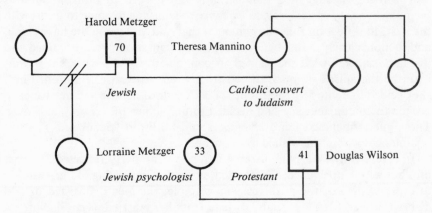

FIGURE 3   Lorraine Metzger

constructive relationships with men and in separating when relationships became unfulfilling. Exceptionally bright and talented, she undervalued her own abilities and was willing to take few risks professionally. She expressed feeling periodically depressed and wanted to become less dependent emotionally on her family.

Lorraine's therapy, focused on resolution of family-of-origin issues, took place in individual therapy sessions, in a professional development group, and in extended family interviews which included her parents. At one point several sessions were conducted with her and a man with whom she had been involved for three years. The use of ritual entered the work in a number of significant ways, some of which will be summarized here. One event in particular, an adult female initiation rite which she designed herself, will be described in some detail.

Much of intergenerational family systems therapy consists of changing one's steps in the ritualistic family dance, of altering communications or other kinds of actions in order to initiate new patterns of interaction in which the client may perform more proactively and autonomously. Many such interventions were planned and carried out successfully throughout Lorraine's therapy. Lorraine learned how to be an adult with adult parents, to see her parents more frequently and with less conflict, to understand their lives and issues with more empathy, to shift dysfunctional family coalitions, to bridge cutoffs, and so on. Many of the most powerful of these interventions occurred during family rites, her birthday, graduation, the Seder, and eventually, her wedding.

One theme that permeated much of this activity was her search for religious and spiritual meaning. Her Jewish identity was extremely important to her yet in many ways an area of conflict, particularly since she felt she could not fully claim a Jewish heritage. This meant that she had to work harder for acceptance and authenticity in local Jewish organizations and in her work on behalf of Jewish causes. A feminist, she found herself angry at the longstanding patriarchal hegemony in Judaism and the continuing differences in the ways that males and females were being defined and allowed to practice their faith in the local synagogues.

On the family level Lorraine was able to make significant changes. A sudent of Jewish ritual and profoundly interested in religious and spiritual issues, she in a sense became the family rabbi for this generation, learning what her father and mother could teach her but in many ways going beyond their teachings to new interpretations. It was she who began to infuse the family Seder with new traditions and new importance, planning, organizing, and assigning roles on the basis not of gender but of skill and interest, which meant that she herself performed the central readings. This work also performed a function in helping to heal strain and conflict in her relationship with her father, who had long expressed contempt for Jewish practices and who had been largely excluded from the coalition between Lorraine and her mother. Her interest in and respect for Jewish tradition, her wish to draw upon his knowledge and to discuss issues, seemed not only to bring them closer together but also to play a role in renewing his own pride in his Jewish identity. At the same time, Lorraine used these important ritual occasions to introduce her male friend, from a different faith and different ethnic heritage, to her family and to her tradition of meaning, testing the incorporative potential of her family, whom the therapist and she suspected would not let her go easily.

Some two years into the therapy, Lorraine announced that she wanted to do something to recognize and celebrate her adult womanhood, her Jewish womanhood, the woman she now felt she had become. She thought she might draw upon the *mikvah* or ritual bath which women participate in after birth or menstruation. At first her therapist, a gentile, was surprised, since the bath, in earlier times required for both sexes and in modern times, at least in the orthodox tradition, required only for women, seemed to associate women with uncleanliness and impurity. But Lorraine had a vision of how she might reclaim this rite as a feminist, Jewish woman and a developing interpretation of ways in which the symbolism could express a set of meanings significant for her own process of growth.

Her preparation for this event took place over a number of months. It included interviewing rabbis and selecting the rabbi she wanted to perform the rite, choosing who would participate and in what ways, what actions she wished to perform as part of the *mikvah*, and a careful consideration of how she could best prepare herself for this significant transition.

As part of her preparation, Lorraine intuitively recognized that she needed in some way to separate from the old, a "time out of time," a liminal period in which she would no longer be child but not yet adult woman. She decided to go to a woman's retreat, a special place where women might meditate, read, walk, be alone or with other women, talk or not talk about their individual and collective meanings. Her preparation for this special time was most thoughtful; a selection of readings which symbolized ties to her past and hopes for her future, a plan for how she would spend her time there, and preparation for how she would communicate or not communicate with her family during this period.

The *mikvah*, part of the traditional Jewish conversion, symbolizes a rebirth, for Lorraine a way ceremonially to separate one part of her life from another. It also represented a way for her to formally convert to and to reaffirm her place in Judaism, according to Conservative tradition. She prepared for the *mikvah* in the same way that Jewish women have done since ancient times, carefully cleansing her body in readiness for the three sequential immersions. Subsequently, Lorraine took a new, untraditional Hebrew name in a ceremony in the local synagogue.

A year after this event, Lorraine was married to the man she had been seeing for three years, in a very moving and meaningful ceremony which combined and preserved valued traditions from each of their religious heritages, reinterpreted and reclaimed in ways appropriate for their definitions of self and the meaning of the intermarriage. In Lorraine's own interpretation, the *mikvah* and name-changing rituals freed her from having to continually "prove" her Judaism, and allowed her to begin to follow her own path with less guilt. This meant that she could resign from her role as "super Jew" (her expression) in her family, and could marry a non-Jew without feeling that her Jewish identity was at stake. In her words, she is still exploring "what it means to me to be Jewish and to be a spiritual seeker, which often leads outside the boundaries of Judaism."

Rituals for Innovative Families

In the above example, the form and content of existing rituals are altered and reshaped in creative ways, and the meanings of ritual actions reinterpreted. However, there are some central life experiences for which our society offers virtually no culturally sanctioned rites; women and families must rely on their own innovations. When these experiences are not celebrated, women are often left with a sense of disappointment, emptiness, guilt, or incompletion. In some cases this occurs because there is cultural ambivalence or lack of approval about the event or transition, as in the case of divorce or abortion, in others because the event is relatively idiosyncratic or uncommon, as in the case of adoption, entering or leaving an institution of some kind, or leaving for or returning from war. In still others the loss or other impact is insufficiently appreciated or there is a wish to avoid or deny, as sometimes happens in the case of miscarriage or stillbirth or the onset of menopause for some women. In such situations the family therapist may help women and families to examine the meanings of the experience and the impact of the changes, to explore the symbolism and other family or cultural material available for ritual use, and to design the ritual itself in a way that fits with the experience and the family's culture.

Furthermore, much of the material in our national rituals assumes a family setting and the traditional family form; the lives of women in other contexts may be underritualized, lacking ritual richness and significance. The family therapist can help the single woman, the single-parent family, and the lesbian couple with or without children to reclaim interrupted rituals and to reshape family rituals to fit their circumstances. In this work, the symbols and actions available in cultural material and family tradition can be drawn upon but often need reclaiming and recreating in ways that fit new contexts and altered meanings. In the example below this process is traced over the course of work with a family in which the presenting problems and subsystems in therapy altered over time.

Brief Example — Julie and Donna (Figure 4)

Originally, David, his new wife Jennifer, and David's 17-year-old daughter Julie were seen in various groupings, primarily around the difficulties in forming a stepfamily and Julie's "dropping out" issues, since she was failing to make clear choices for either college or career. David was a prominent educator and a member of a wealthy family in the small college town in which the family resided. Many of these issues were resolved over the course of therapy, as the stepfamily gradually defined itself, separating from but also incorporating parts of the past, and as Julie came to terms with the loss of her mother, the acceptance of Jennifer, and a clearer definition of her own issues.

Some two years later, the family sought help again, this time because Julie had announced to the family that she was a lesbian. David was quite upset over his daughter's news, but his wife and her sister both urged family meetings in which the impact of the daughter's "coming out" on family relationships could be addressed. A brief series of family meetings was held, a process in which the therapist helped absolve the father of guilt, some mourning occurred, but also new possibilities were defined, culminating in David's reserved but loving acceptance of his daughter's choice.

Again, some two years after the above work, the family sought help. This time Julie came to see the therapist with her lover/partner Donna. The

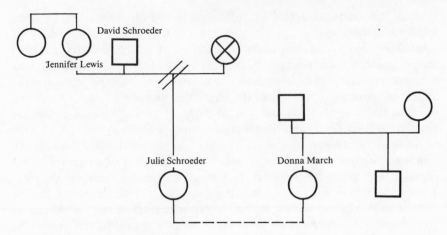

FIGURE 4   Julie and Donna

women, who had been living together for several months, were experiencing conflict in their relationship, much of which had to do with difficulty in the relationships with families of origin and with the lack of any public sanction of their coupling. Donna's parents, to whom she was quite tied in ambivalent and negative ways, refused to define or recognize Donna's lesbianism or her relationship with Julie. This meant that they could visit and were accepted by Julie's family, but Julie could not visit Donna's family nor did her family visit them. This resulted in their often being separated from each other during important family rituals, such as Christmas and Thanksgiving. Donna's family was also terrified that others might know about the lesbian issue, which led to other restrictions in the women's social lives, since Donna would not attend social gatherings in which she could be identified as Julie's partner. Julie, naturally gregarious, resented the lack of definition and the enforced isolation. She wanted a marriage that could be accepted and validated by both families and, inasmuch as possible, a wider context of social and professional relationships.

In the course of work with the couple, Donna's family agreed to come in with her for one session. In that session, it became clear that her parents, for whatever reasons, would not sanction her choice. Her father announced, "I would rather see her dead," while her mother, who seemed less threatened, could not bring herself to disagree with her husband. Donna expressed a great deal of sadness over their lack of tolerance, but also was able for the first time to make clear that she needed to be in charge of her own identity and her own choices. She was forming a new family and she wanted to remain connected to her parents, but if both were not possible, she would have to choose Julie.

Over the course of the next several months, Donna began to take more risks, recognizing that the social isolation would negatively affect the potential for survival as a couple. Donna and Julie began to develop their own family rituals, bringing in traditions from both families but incorporating a network of friends as well, and they participated in Julie's family rituals, times that were both pleasurable and difficult for Donna, since she missed what had been special times with her own family. In therapy, Donna continued to work on enriching her understanding of herself in relation to her family, and to initiate communication with various parts of the family in new ways, a process which is continuing and which she understands will be slow and will require considerable patience.

About a year after the work with the couple began, the therapist was invited to a marriage ceremony, written by Donna and Julie and planned with the help of Julie's family, the therapist, and the minister, a ceremony which incorporated some of the symbols and words of the traditional rite, reclaimed for their particular situation. The music of Holly Near and other women's music was central. The marriage costumes reflected each woman's sense of personal style; Julie wore an elegant off-white satin pants suit, Donna a beautifully designed print caftan. It was a large and joyous occasion, attended by all of Julie's relatives and friends of her family as well as many people from the couple's growing social network. From Donna's family came her brother and two cousins, a small but significant beginning in healing the kinship network.

Reparative Rituals: The Underritualized Event

Another situation to which the family therapist must be alert is the incompletely mastered transition in a woman's life. For example, the onset of puberty may be ignored, a marriage may be performed in hasty and secretive fashion, a loss may be incompletely mourned, or the move toward independence on the part of a young person may be inadequately defined or celebrated. This may mean a woman is left with doubts about her autonomy and a sense of ambivalence or irresolution concerning her personhood. Such a situation arose in the following case, in which a 57-year-old woman still expressed anger and uncontrollable sadness about her grandmother's death, which occurred when she was 10 years old.

Brief Example—A Long Overdue Memorial Service

Barbara, in a family-of-origin group for professionals, would weep whenever she talked of her grandmother, and would repeat her anger at her parents for not helping her with this loss. Barbara had been away at summer camp, and unexpectedly was sent home with the mumps. When she arrived, her grandmother, who lived in her home, was not there and her things were gone. Barbara remembers wandering about the house looking for her grandmother and trying to obtain an explanation, but her parents would tell her nothing. A day or two later she overheard her father on the telephone, telling a family friend about the grandmother's death. This Jewish family did not sit shiva, or if they did, Barbara was not included, nor was she allowed to attend a service and indeed does not know if there was one. Her mother spent much of the rest of her life in a mental hospital, dying when Barbara was 18, and her father, whom Barbara remembers as cold and secretive, also died at a young age, so that Barbara had had little opportunity to resolve her issues with her parents.

Barbara's relationship with her own daughter was a very difficult one, most distressing to her. Terrified of separation, she had been unable to confront the serious difficulties in her marriage, including her husband's distancing and his series of affairs over a number of years. Both had been in individual treatment for many years and on two occasions had pursued marital therapy. While she felt she had grown personally in her own treatment, she did not feel the marriage had improved.

Barbara had done some productive family-of-origin work with her one sibling, a sister, and had reinitiated contact with an elderly aunt, a beginning in reconstructing and interpreting the meanings of her family experiences for her own life. From her work in the group came the suggestion that over a period of time Barbara consider planning a memorial service for her grandmother. She was very excited about this idea, and with the group's help began planning. Barbara chose a synagogue that she felt her grandmother might have been comfortable in and she, the family therapist, and a friend met with the rabbi. The rabbi at first was quite puzzled and skeptical about the efficacy of a memorial service for someone who had died almost 50 years earlier, but after Barbara, with occasional help from the therapist, articulated her purpose and the meaning such a service would hold for her, he began to support the idea and made a number of helpful suggestions.

Barbara and the rabbi planned the memorial very carefully and thoughtfully—what readings would be included, the content of the rabbi's contribution, whom she wanted to attend, and what she herself would contribute to the service. The group, Barbara's sister and daughter, her husband, and several of her friends attended this most moving memorial to the woman whom she had experienced as the only warm and loving person in her early life and with whom she was so closely identified. Barbara read a very poignant letter to her grandmother, expressing not only her caring, her disappointments, and her loss, but also thanking her grandmother for the many gifts she had given her, gifts of wisdom and womanhood.

Subsequent to this event, Barbara seemed far less depressed in the group, made a number of important changes in her interactions with her daughter, and made the decision to separate at least temporarily from her husband, since she had recently discovered that he had been having yet another affair.

CONCLUSION

Family therapists have just begun to explore the richness and power of ritual life and its potential for therapeutic change, particularly in relation to issues of gender identity and relationships. In this chapter an effort has been made to identify some of the common themes and issues that emerge when the relationships between ritual and women are explored. Certainly the focus on women's ritual lives and an accounting of some of the personal and social costs of women's rituals generates questions concerning the ritual lives of men. If male-controlled public rituals often are accomplished by power and prestige, men's work rituals can be accompanied by humiliation and drudgery. Furthermore, men may be excluded from meaningful participation in many of the important rituals of family life. Public and domestic rituals clearly carry both rewards and costs for both sexes.

We need not only to learn more about American national and family rituals and how to begin the difficult task of interpretation, but also to understand men's and women's ritual lives in the larger sociocultural and political contexts of gender relationships. It is our responsibility as family therapists to understand our role in contemporary ritual life and to consider how we may be participating in the social construction of gender definitions and relationships.

NOTES

[1]See, for example, Goldner, 1985; Hare-Mustin, 1987.
[2]See Fraser, 1984; Hoffman, 1985.

REFERENCES

Arens, W. (1976). Professional football: An American symbol and ritual. In W. Arens & S. P. Montague (Eds.). *The American dimension: Cultural myths and social realities* (3–14). Port Washington, NY: Alfred.

Bamberger, J. (1974). The myth of matriarchy: Why men rule in primitive society. In M. Rosaldo & L. Lamphere (Eds.). *Woman, culture, and society*. Stanford, CA: Stanford University Press.

Bateson, M. C. (1984). *With a daughter's eye: A memoir of Margaret Mead and Gregory Bateson*. New York: William Morrow.

Caplow, T., Bahr, H., Chadwick, B. A., Hill, R., & Holmes, M. (1982). Family symbolism in festivals. In *Middletown families: Fifty years of change and continuity*. Minneapolis: University of Minnesota Press.

Douglas, M. (1966). *Purity and danger: An analysis of concepts of pollution and taboo*. New York: Praeger.

Durkheim, E. (1915). *The elementary forms of religious life*. New York: Free Press (1965 reprint).

Fraser, J. (1984). Process level integration: Corrective vision for a binocular view. *The Journal of Strategic and Systemic Therapies, 3*(3), 43–57.

Freeman, Derek. (1983). *Margaret Mead and Samoa: The making and unmaking of an anthropological myth*. Cambridge, MA: Harvard University Press.

Goldner, V. (1985). Feminism and family therapy. *Family Process, 24*, 31–47.

Hare-Mustin, R. (1987). The problem of gender in family therapy theory. *Family Process, 26*, 15–27.

Hartman, A. & Laird, J. (1987, April). *Migration and family folklore*. Plenary paper, Ninth Annual Meeting, American Family Therapy Association, Chicago, IL.

Hoffman, L. (1985). Beyond power and control: Toward a "second order" family systems therapy. *Family Systems Medicine, 3*(4), 381–396.

Keesing, R. (1982). Introduction. In G. H. Herdt (Ed.). *Rituals of manhood: Male initiation in Papua New Guinea* (1–43). Berkeley, CA: University of California Press.

Kottak, C. (1978). *Anthropology: The exploration of human diversity*. New York: Random House.

Laird, J. (1984). Sorcerers, shamans, and social workers: The use of ritual in social work practice. *Social Work, 29*, 123–129.

Langness, L. L. (1974). Ritual power and male domination in the New Guinea highlands. *Ethos, 2*, 189–212.

Levi-Strauss, C. (1969). *The elementary structures of kinship*. Boston: Beacon Press.

Moore, S. & Myerhoff, B. (1977). Introduction: Secular Ritual: Forms and Meanings. In S. Moore & B. Myerhoff (Eds.). *Secular ritual* (3–24). Amsterdam, The Netherlands: Van Gorcum.

Myerhoff, B. (1983, November). *Rites of passage*. Plenary speech, National Symposium, National Association of Social Workers, Washington, DC.

Ortner, S. (1974). Is female to male as nature is to culture? In M. Rosaldo & L. Lamphere (Eds.). *Woman, culture, and society* (67–87). Stanford, CA: Stanford University Press.

Pirrotta, S. (1984). Milan revisited: A comparison of the two Milan models. *Journal of Strategic and Systemic Therapies, 3*(4), 3–15.

Paige, K. & Paige, M. (1981). *The politics of reproductive ritual*. Berkeley: University of California Press.

Rich, A. (1986). *Of woman born: Motherhood as experience and institution*. (10th Anniversary Edition) New York: Norton.

Rosaldo, M. A. (1974). Woman, culture, and society: A theoretical overview. In M. A. Rosaldo and L. Lamphere (Eds.). *Woman, culture, and society* (17–42). Stanford, CA: Stanford University Press.

Rubin, G. (1975). The traffic in women: Notes on the "political economy." In R. Reiter (Ed.). *Toward an anthropology of women* (157–210). New York: Monthly Review Press.

Schwartz, P. (1987). *American couples: The intimate struggle for power*. Plenary paper, Ninth Annual Meeting, American Family Therapy Association, Chicago, IL.

Selvini Palazzoli, M., Boscolo, L., Cecchin, G., & Prata, G. (1974). The treatment of children through brief therapy of their parents. *Family Process, 13*(4), 429–442.

Viaro, M. & Leonardi, P. (1986). The evolution of the interview technique: A comparison between former and present strategy. *Journal of Strategic and Systemic Therapies, 5*, 1 and 2, 14–30.

Washburn, P. (1977). *Becoming woman: The quest for wholeness in female experience*. New York: Harper & Row.

Weigle, M. (1982). *Spiders & spinsters: Women and mythology*. Albuquerque, NM: University of New Mexico Press.

14

Political Traumas, Oppression, and Rituals

CECILIA KOHEN

> The Armed Forces responded to terrorist crimes with an infinitely greater terrorism than the one they fought against, because after March 24, 1976, they had the might and the impunity of the Absolute State while they abducted, tortured, murdered thousands of human beings. . . . We are certain that the military dictatorship produced the greatest and most savage tragedy of our history . . . because the fight against "subversives" had turned into a deranged and generalized repression.
>
> CONADEP (Commission for the Investigation
> of the Disappearance of People), 1986

> The members of the first three military juntas of the so-called Process for National Reorganization, who usurped power by means of a coup d'etat on March 24, 1976, have been brought to trial in Argentina, accused of the most terrible violations of human rights. This event can already be considered of historical significance and without precedent in Latin America. . . . The National Commission for the Investigation of the Disappearance of People, the CONADEP, inquired into the abduction, the forceful detention in clandestine centers, the torture and the murder of Argentine and foreign citizens. . . . In many cases the crime committed had been just that of thinking.
>
> Camarasa, Felice, & Gonzalez, 1985

THIS CHAPTER WILL discuss the use of therapeutic rituals and the appearance of new rituals in families under extreme political oppression. A case study of a family reunion, and the use of rituals during the process of therapy designed for the parents' reacquisition of their parental function, which had been forcefully taken away from them, will illustrate this issue. The role of the therapist and his/her own involvement in rituals shared with the families treated will be discussed.

The family as a social unit is articulated in a particular context and clearly influenced by it. Stable surroundings are obviously different from highly unstable ones for family life. In Argentina, highly unstable circumstances profoundly altered the organization, values, and functioning of family life during the 14-year period of 1970–1984.

One such area was the economic one, which was turbulent, unpredictable and where monthly inflation went up to 30% or more. Families suffered extreme economic ups and downs as the country tumbled into an economic disaster.

Another extremely violent and dangerous area was the sociopolitical one, which profoundly affected family life and family rituals. Families became either over- or underritualized, maintained rituals empty of meaning, or were subject to coercive rituals. Some of these families later turned to therapy. Many of these families had been actively militant or had terrorist members; some were free-thinkers, and others suffered severe repression by mistake or "just in case."

GENERAL BACKGROUND

Argentina had a brutally repressive military dictatorship that inflicted nothing less than state terrorism on the people of the country. Before this, from 1973 to 1976, ultra-leftist and right-wing nationalist groups also operated paramilitary forces and death squads with total impunity.

During those years, thousands of people "disappeared." They were "Chupados" (in Argentine slang, "sucked," abducted by paramilitary task forces for political reasons), brutally dragged from their homes or their workplaces, or picked up in the street, sometimes in broad daylight. Most were never heard from again, casualties of the so-called "dirty war." A few were luckier, freed after a few years or, luckier still, after a few weeks.

The families of these people suffered unbearable pain, while searching for their relatives through different channels, knocking on official doors only to be faced with silence. For most, the search has been fruitless. All these families who have been the object of severe repression have had their ritual life systematically damaged. Effective family functioning was harmed. Normative rituals lost their significance, became empty of meaning, or proved to be impossible to perform since significant members were not there, due to abduction, needing to hide, or exile.

THE APPEARANCE OF NEW RITUALS IN FAMILIES UNDER EXTREME POLITICAL OPPRESSION

New rituals appeared in families who had been victims of the extreme repression of state terrorism. Usually, these families had suffered the loss of one or more relatives during Argentina's "dirty war."

In many of these families a "maybe" construction of reality was observed, as family members believed and behaved as if "those who disappeared will reappear." In one case, parents kept their two boys' room exactly as it had been, ritualistically cleaning it everyday. Their place was also set at the dinner table. In line with the ideas of structural invariance, Crescini and Droeven (1985) consider this a mythical invariant. This structural invariance is accompanied by a chronological time-arrest phenomenon for the families involved, and a crystallization of a pattern of the possible ways of organization. They refer to Morin (1984), who has offered a description of the occurrence of a new event in a system which has experienced catastrophe and trauma.

In other cases there were mythical constructions of the "she/he is alive in another place" type. In other words, "those who vanished are not really disappeared and dead." Families developed ritualized behaviors around this myth, as in the case cited by Crescini and Droeven (1986) of a grandmother and three girls who ritually repeated for nine years that the mother had gone to another city, 30 miles south of the capital, Buenos Aires, and was too busy working there as a nurse to come back. They did not admit her disappearance or death, and wanted to consider her alive and well. They also systematically informed the school, hospitals, friends, and the rest of the family accordingly, as a ritualized verbal communication to protect/maintain the myth they had constructed. The father, who in the meantime had exiled himself in Europe and had already been living with someone else for six years, still wore the wedding band of his former marriage. Obviously, he had not completed the process of accepting the disappearance/death of his first wife either. Furthermore, his new wife was not recognized by any of the family members, even when they moved back to Argentina with their new baby.

Clinical observation has also demonstrated that, in many of these families, the impact of traumatic loss through terrorism is so devastating that it destroys certain previous paradigms. New beliefs or meta-rules are thus born and then crystallize (Bateson, 1972; Ritterman, 1985). An example is that of a father who, after the death "in action" of his guerrilla son (the son had received orders from his superiors in the guerrilla movement not to carry out that specific attack because it was tantamount to suicide), stopped talking to his adult daughter because she had not lived up to the "necessary standards of behavior" as the son had done. She was a leftist thinker, not a guerrilla, and had not "lived and died as one should." The father adopted a new paradigm. He built up the significance and value of his son's death and constructed a new attitude in life. This crystallized and, in fact, he was then left with two deaths: a real one, that of his son, and a symbolic one, that of his daughter whom he had rejected. Old family rituals were abandoned, the daughter was no longer available to participate in family rituals, and a new one appeared, the grieving of the son's death anniversary.

GENERAL CONSIDERATIONS
FOR THERAPY WITH FAMILIES
WHO HAVE EXPERIENCED TERROR

During the dictatorship, families and family rituals were systematically attacked by violence from the social context. Thus, the use of rituals in the process of therapy helps the family to reacquire affective ritualized behaviors. Rituals provide models, sanction transitions, and aid in the expression of emotions. Some rituals give family members the possibility of exploring themselves deeply, providing meaning to their lives, and giving them a feeling of belonging and a sense of commitment. They allow individual freedom, while preserving intimacy and bonds. As social terrorism and repression attack all these aspects of human life, the healing value of rituals in therapy is considerable.

Healing rituals also permit the expression of deeply rooted emotions such as pain, desperation, grief, "madness." Since after a "disappearance," many families had to hide or flee, and since public expression of those feelings was condemned and forbidden for such a long time, the emotional impact was catastrophic. It affected all family members. Wilson (1957) spoke of rituals for misfortune as similar to healing rituals. They constitute a group within the transition rituals, but tend to be less standardized than these last ones. They are specifically directed to solve specific transitional problems, detentions or damages. They aim to change disturbed relations and provide the opportunity for expressing emotions (van der Hart, 1983). The need in Argentina was to heal a severe misfortune.

There are families that may have a specific need to go through all the steps of a special death ritual (kidnapping, disappearance, torture, death, and burial of the corpse) and grieve. The difficulty lies in the fact that the body of the missing person may never have appeared, or he/she may never have been officially declared dead, and so the family cannot accept him/her as dead. There is no corpse over which to mourn, no tomb to place the dead, no burial, NOTHING. These families must be able to "bury their dead" and not continue to keep them "alive" or in limbo. In these cases, a clear farewell rite might be included in therapy.

During the process of therapy with severely politically repressed human beings, there also appears the phenomena of spontaneously performed rituals, that is, rituals not thought of by the therapist but done by the person or persons. Such was the case of a couple who had lost their two sons in the "dirty war." They originally came from another state. For one session somebody phoned for them saying they wouldn't be present for their appointment. At their next interview they said they had suddenly decided to go to their town and there they retraced and reenacted all of their life together, from their day of meeting, their courtship, falling in love, their marriage. They went to the places where they worked and lived at the time. They relived the birth and the growth of each son and the final migration to Buenos Aires. This journey led them to deep memories and emotions, until they "walked up" to the disappearance and later death-acceptance period. They were facing their pain, but were more serene.

When designing the type of therapy and the use of rituals with families who are victims of political repression, one must not fall into the misconception that only the social context was violent. Although state terrorism was, indeed, indiscriminate, there were many family members who were actively engaged in political violence and who practiced and believed in the value of armed terrorist struggle to attain their goals. So if therapeutic rituals are to be considered adequate, it is important that this issue—violence and terrorism within the family structure—be taken into account. I personally believe that since violence or passive complicity was such a terrible issue in our country, it must be taken into our therapeutic lens.

Here, there is also the delicate question for the therapist regarding what subjects to touch, whether or not certain sensitive issues should be broached again and again, and how far to go. This is a common problem in therapeutic practice in general and it is especially present in the treatment of families involved in extreme situations. Should a certain subject be mentioned? How? In a family setting or with the couple alone? What, for instance, should one do with grandparents consulting over the functioning in their new family situation, with their three small grandchildren living with them since both the mother and the father disappeared? And what if the therapist discovers, as it happened to me, that the father in the family is an active paramilitary torturer, and his wife and children "ignore" it? And what does the therapist do if the family members sitting in the hospital consultation room are speaking of small Peter's learning problem while father's handbag under his chair holds an electrical torture instrument inside? Obviously, the therapist's ideology is poignantly present.

There is also the question of how detailed the information given to children—especially small children—should be, and how much they can tolerate in terms of description of events, panic, intensities of pain and humiliations suffered. Timing is a very important factor, too, and the therapist has to take into special consideration the different wishes expressed by the families regarding the management of these issues. Different therapists have reported enormous differences between families: those who lied to children, those who said a simplified truth, others who "spilled out" everything.

There are no adequate statistics yet, and maybe there will never be, but mental health professionals working with families that have fallen victim to repression commonly report several coincident observations. Families that have come to terms with their reality and have accepted their true situation rather than continue living a hopeful lie have adjusted better in their lives. Also, those families who have made active contact with others—civil rights organizations, for example—are psychologically better off than those who kept to themselves in Argentina or in isolated exile. The general criteria used for "psychologically better off" are less symptom appearance, participation in a clear mourning process, and continued life cycle unfolding. Therapeutic rituals can powerfully promote these developments.

A CASE STUDY

Political Context of the Case

This case concerns the difficulties experienced by parents in their reunion with their children and the reaffirmation of their parental function, which they had been forced to relinquish when they were abducted during the dictatorship.

In 1983, when this case was seen, Argentina was going through its tenth year of political upheaval, with terrorist activity and an extremely repressive military dictatorship. It was clear to everyone, however, that general elections would be held at the end of the year and that a democratically elected government would take over.

Initial Call and Therapist's Doubts

The mother, Esther, phoned my office sounding very agitated, saying that she was very depressed and asking for an urgent interview. She said that she was very unhappy, could not bear the way she felt any longer, and was totally overwhelmed by her circumstances. I told her that if I agreed to take on the case, I would need to see the whole family. They were to call me if the answer was affirmative, and I would, in the meantime, consider my own possibilities. The case was extremely complicated right from the start. Living under state terrorism necessitated each therapist's considering the danger certain cases presented. Obviously this included the constant review of the therapist's sociopolitical ideas and beliefs. The possibility of being available also varied enormously for each therapist. Many professionals did not accept cases with any kind of sociopolitical commitment since it meant life-risk.

The decision to see the family was difficult, since as their therapist my life might be endangered. Professional services given to free-thinkers or leftist thinkers by lawyers, physicians, psychotherapists, etc., had resulted in innumerable cases of professionals abducted, tortured, and killed. The whole family on the father's side was now legally accused of handling the investment of some money for the leftist guerrilla movement. The mother and father, as well as the grandfathers on both sides, had been kidnapped, tortured, imprisoned for years, and then released. The case had been widely publicized, and their name was stigmatized.

I had to consider several aspects in this case. On the one hand, they had been freed, and there was a court case going on to decide their guilt or innocence. The legalization of their existence and official recognition rendered a "secure zone" to work with them. On the other hand, I could not subject myself to repression, stigmatization, and blind fear. During the whole dictatorship, one was faced continually with the issue of how much to endanger oneself. On the other hand, there is a limit to which one can live like a turtle, always protecting oneself in one's own house. Also, I did not feel comfortable in the role of "judge" deciding that "I wouldn't work with these people." All of these factors made me decide to take the case. I knew a case like this would force me to work "secretly" in a style different from the common professional confidentiality. Here secrecy provided a benefit for both the therapist and the client.

Some Background Notes on the Family

The family consisted of the father, Gabriel, the mother, Esther, and the three children, Roberto, 16, Jaime, 13, and Ana, 10 (see Figure 1). The father came from a strongly work-oriented Jewish family, working in finance. Members were aggressive with each other. The mother's family, also Jewish, was more highly educated and the members expressed more tenderness toward each other. Neither of the families was religious or traditional.

In 1976, the father and, shortly afterwards, the mother, were kidnapped by a paramilitary task force. A group of heavily armed, masked men entered the home, shouting, pushing and hitting. They noisily broke and stole many things. The little girl was asleep when this happened, while the boys were awakened. Both grandfathers were also picked up at their respective homes. Twice, each time after one of his parents' abduction occurred in his presence, Jaime attempted suicide by throwing himself off a third-story balcony at school. After the second suicide attempt, the school asked the maternal grandmother to remove the child from school.

For five years after these events took place, the children were left in the care of this grandmother. After two years, the maternal grandfather was freed. The paternal grandfather was released after four years.

When Esther and Gabriel were taken away, nobody knew whether they were alive and had been tortured or had already been killed. Two months later, the lawyers and the family found out that they were in separate pris-

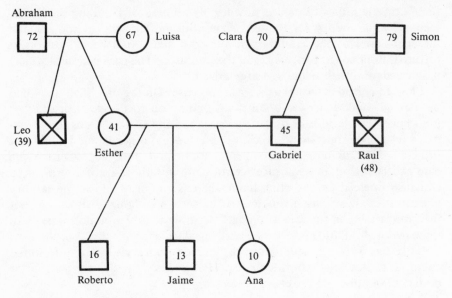

FIGURE 1   Political Oppression

ons. They were being transferred often and could not receive any visits. Having been officially recognized as prisoners, their safety was relatively guaranteed. Approximately ten months after their abduction, the children were allowed to visit them, but only one at a time and always accompanied by their grandmother. First, they could talk to them only through a glass panel, and only much later were permitted in the same room, where they listened to the parents' stories about the different jails in which they had been placed.

Gabriel and Esther were in relatively good physical condition, and although they had been tortured, it had happened some time before. Once, for example, Esther spoke about "rats in the cells, all over us." Gabriel did not tell the children such things. On one occasion, while Ana was visiting her father and paternal grandfather, who was also in jail at the time, she asked to go to the toilet. Her grandfather took her to a small bathroom inside, through a back door in the visiting room, and along a "horrible corridor" where she saw the prisoners in cells, behind bars, looking, just looking, and saying hello to her. Although it was really forbidden, the guards let her go there on the grandfather's suggestion. Ana later said she would never in her life forget that hideous scene with all the men in those horrible prison clothes, calling her from behind the bars.

During the last two years of their imprisonment, Esther and Gabriel were allowed to write to each other by means of censored letters. Finally, she was released, and a few months later, so was he. "And they all lived happily together again." This may sound ironical or incomprehensible if we don't place it in the context of this family's reunion being the exception. In the majority of cases, "picked" people never reappeared. No complete family reunion was ever possible. The majority never "got together" again.

A First Look at the Family

They came for consultation a year and a half after they were freed, so some time had elapsed before the family sought psychological help. They had, by then, accomplished quite a bit by themselves. They had traveled a long way already in their "reunion." But this, somehow, was not enough.

The boundaries defining the family were unclear. They themselves considered the family to be the five people present, but every time a real problematic issue was discussed, the maternal grandparents were mentioned. Esther appeared anxious and depressed and regarded many family situations as out of control. A much more detached Gabriel worried about their finances and an important pending lawsuit. Both were worried about "different symptoms" the children presented. The older boy, Roberto — a "parental" child — was rebellious and bad-mannered, gave orders, and did not want to be present to participate in the session. Jaime, the second boy, repeatedly tried to take center stage: He started the conversation, pointed out the problems, interrupted the others, or spoke for them. Though he was at the right level for his age in school, he was performing very badly. He had always been helped by private tutors and, all throughout primary school, he would just lie in bed while his tutor finished homework for him. At the time of consultation, he was seriously behind in his schoolwork and in danger of failing his grades. Six or seven years before, he had developed the habit of constantly chewing on his jacket. He asked for help continually for every minor thing. Physically, he was behind in his development. He was short and looked like a 10-year-old. The youngest child, Ana, gave the impression of being a very sweet child, but her brothers said she was "spoiled and cried about anything." For the past four or five years, she had had frequent terrifying nightmares.

The family members' adaptive resources were exhausted and they didn't easily resolve small problems. Any small stimulus might constitute an unbalancing problem for them. My hypothesis was that, during the period in which the children lived with grandmother, there was a "parental child," Roberto, a second child, Jaime, who was considered by everyone in the family as the identified patient, in a very tight bond with the grandmother, and the girl, Ana, whose function seemed to have been the "pet" or the "sweetie pie." Although the family was reunited, this structure remained unchanged.

The Use of "Prison Bars" in Therapy

Two or three times, Esther had mentioned that, in prison, she was much more secure and that things were really easier for her there. In that sense, she missed prison, where others controlled her, and "now I am always uncontrollable, and feel miserable, I can't control myself." As therapist, I tried to augment the presence and pressure of "prison bars" upon and around them, to see if Esther and Gabriel fought to take them off, since Gabriel agreed, "it is very difficult," or just sat silently conceding. If they did not really want to be free, our task was blocked. A graphic metaphor, "prison bars," permitted my therapeutic movement between the extremes of confinement and freedom. This metaphor also clearly permitted me to touch the absurd. The differences of being behind prison bars or without prison bars were framed as:

- In prison, behind bars—"Ah! So you are still behind bars!" or "We can quickly put the bars around you again!"—mentioned in a light humorous way.
- Out of prison, without bars—"One of the difficult things about being without bars is you have more responsibilities and commitments. Maybe you can get yourself back in there again so you don't have responsibilities."

We worked with "future" fantasies: How much more time, many more years, did each of them think they would have the "prison bars" around them? They each thought about where they felt the bars in relation to their bodies: around their bodies, against them, without elbow space, or lower prison bars, maybe in front of their legs so they could not move, or all around, or inside the head, and so on.

During one session, Esther took a big cushion and covered her head with it. Immediately, Gabriel said to her: "You have the jail on top of you." Use of this metaphor in the session led to an at-home ritualized prescription. Every two days, they were to form a small cave around themselves (a prison) with pillows and cushions, and stay there for five minutes each time, in silence, thinking about prison period, both at the same time but without looking at each other. They were to do this for two weeks. It had a profoundly shocking effect on both of them; while they spoke little about it, they referred to it as being incredibly moving. Esther grew increasingly angry at "having to be in prison," and said, "Why can't I choose liberty?" Gabriel found himself crying twice beneath the cushions. Several times they stayed together for a time crying and talking to each other.

After this session, the "prison" metaphor was seldom used again in our meetings, but its graphic impact functioned as a turning point in therapy. Esther said: "I now want to leave that horror behind." This ritualized use of "prison bars" involved two sessions of therapy with just the couple.

Esther always appeared more fragile and confined than Gabriel. Prison had been a long process of disintegration for her, and she came out destroyed. Gabriel, on the other hand, felt much more enraged and had built a "wall" to protect himself from what he strongly believed was the cruelty of the strongly anti-semitic attacks of the country's power structure. Since they were totally innocent, he believed that they had been unjustly picked up and stigmatized simply because they were Jewish.

I worked with the positive aspects these two different attitudes had in their present relationship. Esther helped Gabriel to get in touch with his feelings and his inner world. Her "weakness" helped him by feeding his strength. He had to get strong, more aggressive, and be a fighter against the hostile environment. In turn, she began to be "more on her feet."

Some Setbacks

Two months later, an incident occurred that brought the couple to the verge of a very serious disruption. Gabriel's father had a violent outburst and made very insulting remarks about Esther's father to her. As a result, she refused to receive him at home or see him at the office. Gabriel made excuses for his father as being an old and violent man.

To make things worse, the same week the court announced a preliminary verdict against them, and their case became widely publicized again. The lawyers decided to appeal. These incidents menaced the stability of the family's loyalties and affections. Jaime started worsening again, bothering everyone, asking for assistance for any minor thing, and not concentrating on his studies. Ana cried constantly. Esther was saying again that she could not bear the situation any longer. Gabriel began having ulcer symptoms. In short, the family was in acute distress, everyone's coping mechanisms taxed to the limit. These emergencies might easily develop into a new shattering crisis, pushing the system to disorganization. As Reiss (1981) would put it, this family was in danger of going into a new critical process in which their own reality would again be subordinated to that of a larger, more powerful, social (legal) community. In this situation, their basic paradigms, their attitude towards life, would run the risk of being sacrificed again to the stronger structure. Both the family and I believed that therapy would help them overcome this looming crisis.

The Debt-Gratitude Issue

During earlier therapy sessions, Esther had insisted that she had an "eternal debt" with her parents, especially with her mother, "one of those debts in life which can never be repaid," because her mother had fully taken care of her children during the imprisonment. Gabriel agreed that they had a debt, but did not put it as strongly as that. This "eternal debt" feeling augmented the closeness of mother-grandmother bond.

I worked with this debt-gratitude issue in the following manner:

1. With a humorous approach and using the absurd and other paradoxical interventions, I increased the image of *big-great-immense-infinite-eternal* debt.
2. After that, in a very casual way, I started playing with the concepts of "debt" and "gratitude." A debt leaves you indebted, you have to pay it back. Gratitude is different. And so is love.

The goal was to sow a seed that would shake her belief and make it more flexible and amenable to intervention. I asked the parents' permission to talk about this and other matters with the grandparents. When they agreed, we held a special session with the family and both sets of grandparents, in order to discuss the issue with all its deep emotional aspects, as well as the different attitudes of the family members.

During this meeting Jaime was clearly aligned with his mother and maternal grandmother, and said so, tentatively holding the grandmother's hand most of the time, until I changed the seating arrangement. They brought up different issues, but mainly, and most importantly, they discussed and voted on what each thought of Esther and Gabriel's finally taking over the leadership of the family. All four grandparents clearly agreed that the parents not only could but should be in complete charge of the children. There was no question about this for them.

We discussed this issue for four sessions. In order to facilitate the desired changes, I designed a "separation ritual."

A Preparatory Phase: The "Separation Ritual"

This ritual was aimed at reestablishing and enhancing parental functioning. It also involved redistribution of the roles of the individual members of the family. In this area I expected to achieve at least two major changes: for Roberto to modify his "parental" role; and for Jaime to diminish his "bad" behavior, while increasing his learning abilities. I did not expect any changes in Ana's behavior then. I had not yet found where or how the nightmares fit in with the rest of the picture, and I did not think the nightmares would disappear by altering this family pattern. She was expected to act like a pretty doll, sweet as candy, and she obliged them by always smiling back. This would have to change too, but it was not an immediate goal.

The ritual was also aimed at facilitating the couple's cohesion and intimacy. After so many years in prison leading separate lives, they were out of sync as a couple. Finally, I hoped to rebalance the grandparents' bonds with the children and reframe the debt-gratitude-love issue.

During the next session I spoke of an "honor" or "thank-you celebration" for the grandparents, or perhaps a dinner for them, as they had taken such good care of the children for several years. The family decided to ask them to a special dinner at home. Gabriel would be the one to formally invite the grandparents, stating that it was in their honor and that they were to be special guests. They would all dress up, put flowers around the house, and take photographs. A picture of the nuclear family, one they already had, would be framed, dedicated by each family member, and offered as a present to the grandparents. After this dinner, mother was to ask maternal grandmother's advice on an issue once a week.

I was surprised when, later that same session, Esther brought up the idea of speaking with Gabriel to see if they could think of some new activity for her mother to assume. I interpreted this as a positive indicator of change.

The separation ritual was to serve as a context marker for "inside/outside" and a time marker for "before/after." A formal recognition of the separation of the grandparents from the parents and children, both in a direct way (a clear thank-you and celebration) and in an indirect way (the message that the previous situation was clearly ending), was expected.

The party took place as planned. Gabriel invited the grandparents with a clear explanation. Esther had some difficulties and got very anxious about the menu. She started expressing to Gabriel her doubts about being able to prepare such a dinner. So they both thought about the food they'd like to serve. Roberto had begun giving orders, but the parents said they would take care of the issue. They prepared themselves with liveliness, though Jaime was troublesome and demanding before the grandparents arrived.

During the dinner Jaime's difficult conduct went on, so father called him away and he calmed down. Grandmother cried near the end of the dinner, and so did mother. As mother put it: "It was *so* much that has happened to all of us!" Afterwards, father told Roberto to present the grandparents with the photograph. As a surprise, father offered champagne and a toast "to the future."

Some Positive Changes

In the first session three weeks after the separation ritual, mother and father told me of better functioning in the family. On one occasion, coming out of a restaurant, Roberto, the eldest, had roughly pushed his mother "because she was nervous" and had treated her with remarkable rudeness. She started to shout at him in the middle of the street, but Gabriel intervened, stopped him firmly, and told him off. For the first time, the father had taken charge of things and had put Roberto in his place. Roberto responded well.

Also, the parents decided that Jaime had to change schools, and together with him they picked another one — further evidence of their new position as parents able to exercise authority and responsibility.

Gabriel continued, nevertheless, to be uninvolved in many everyday situations, which Esther resolved by herself as she could. Sometimes she insisted on discussing issues with Gabriel and they did so. Esther still saw her mother almost every day despite her tight schedule. She had asked for advice three times. She continued to feel overburdened and frequently felt out of control.

Both the father and the mother continued to state that they still felt they had no real control over many family situations. They said they wanted to improve their own relationship and have a better understanding with their children. They had been discussing matters and they were tired of the fact that the children did not help at all around the house, but instead relied on them for every little thing. They also wanted to put a stop to the children's coming in their bedroom anytime they felt like it.

I decided a second ritual, a ritual of transition, was needed.

A Rite of Passage: "The Transition Ritual"

THE PLANNING OF THE CEREMONY. The ritual consisted of a very special ceremony, involving a document reestablishing the parents' position in the family. For the actual planning of it, several steps were taken. I introduced Gabriel and Esther to an attorney who met all the necessary requirements set by me. It had to be someone outside and distant from the therapeutic system, since I wanted a figure who clearly represented the external wide society; a male, as I am a woman; a gentile, as both the family and myself are Jewish.

The lawyer was important here because he represented secondary groups and symbolized the law of the community in general. I had not chosen their own criminal attorney, who was defending them publicly in their court case, as an authority figure for the ceremony. Maybe my own limitations or fears at the time led me not to do so. In a country of indiscriminate sociopolitical repression, being perceived as having a commitment with their group could certainly be dangerous for me. I was willing to run the risk of working with them, but I had to set certain limits. If my limits were too rigid, I would consider myself a coward. I could take, as part of my personal/professional self-image, being afraid. I could not take being a coward. On the other hand, I would not take unnecessary life/death risks. Furthermore, he was not a family lawyer, and I needed one here.

We agreed that both the mother and the father would be present and participate in this ritual with their children. The main targets of this ceremony were the parents as active agents, but it was also designed to affect the other family members present.

There were a few points I was doubtful about, for example, what words should be directed at the children. I decided to go through the parents, reestablishing the generational line that had been broken, and not give the children an especially active place in the ceremony. The children were not asked to sign the certificate. Gabriel and Esther discussed the possibility of inviting somebody else to the occasion, but they decided they preferred to be there just with their three children, thus drawing a boundary around their nuclear family. The oral delivery of the document would be in the hands of the lawyer; the introductions, the positioning of those present, and the closing words were in the therapist's charge.

While our everyday mode of communication was by the "tuteo" (the familiar form of address in second person singular), the use of the formal mode was decided upon because of the solemnity of the occasion. This change is significant, since it clearly accentuated the importance and seriousness of the event. We established from the beginning that it would take place at our next session and, as it was to be a very special day, I set a date a month in advance. This time, contrary to our normal procedure, we made the next appointment before we started our session that day.

THE RITUAL CEREMONY. On the prearranged date, we all met: Gabriel, Esther, their children, the attorney and I. The ritual ceremony took place in a formal room with a desk next to which the attorney and I stood, while both parents stood in front, with their children sitting to one side of the room. The following is the text of the certificate we read and signed:

In Buenos Aires, the 16th day of June of 1983, with the presence of Dr. X. X., attorney-at-law, expert in family law, and of Cecilia Kohen, clinical psychologist, expert in family development; and with the agreement of the elders, and the community, represented by the law of this country; we are here gathered to give full recognition to the parental rights and duties of Gabriel and Esther; being the parents of the youngsters Roberto, aged 16, Jaime, aged 13, and Ana, aged 10; and having always exercised their parental function with its rights and duties, their love and authority, their dedication and decision, their responsibility and enjoyment, their difficulties and problems, since the birth of each child, except when forcibly prevented for five years from carrying out their everyday functions as parents for reasons beyond their own control and free will; we now solemnly and finally declare them in full charge of their family functions, with the confirmation of Argentine law; this being the only natural and just outcome in recognition of the fact that parents do their best for their children, although they may go through periods of greater stress during which they may need to help each other in their function. Therefore, we now place the three children in the total care of the mother, Esther, and of the father, Gabriel, so that they may fully exercise their functions of parenthood and their ability to: love and take care of their children, guide and counsel them, help and aid them, lead them in their knowledge of the world, protect them from its dangers, teach them to take care of themselves as they grow older, be together and have fun, limit their mistakes, let them be themselves, permit them to explore their own possibilities, help them in hard times, comfort them in their pain, set limits to their excesses, correct them in their mistakes. We now ask each of the people present if they have clearly understood this statement, and proceed to sign this document that certifies this ceremony.

Starting with the father, all four adults, including the couple, the attorney, and myself, signed the document.

While he was listening, Jaime started chewing on his clothes, but in the middle of the ceremony he suddenly stopped. Roberto sat sideways in his chair and did not pay much attention at the beginning, but later he got closer and looked on attentively. Ana was very concentrated and watched the ceremony with amazement.

Towards the end of the ceremony, congratulations were included. The attorney and I congratulated Gabriel and Esther. They embraced each other, and then each of them, one at a time, with their own timing and space, embraced the three children while the rest looked on. Finally, at my instruction, they all left the office without further comments.

Discussion

This ritual was intended as a very strong "push forward" to enhance parental performance and function. It marked a turning point from one period to another. It was designed to lead to an improvement in family relationships. In Van Gennep's words (1960), a ritual should be an act of going through more than steps. It should work as a model of and a model for.

With this ritual, we covered most of the idiosyncratic, situational, and cultural factors involved. Also, the alliances and coalitions, distances and hierarchies within the family system were realigned. Both this ritual and the earlier separation ritual were planned as a parallel to the current social and political context of change: the handing over of the country's command to its natural leaders. The country was to hold general elections soon. A democratically elected government — our legal constitutional political system — was to direct and guide our republic. So, the therapist's action, designed to bring about a change within the area of the therapeutic system, was isomorphically reinforced on a broader level. The ritual was given a meta significance from the wider context.

The ceremony, per se, was designed to have:

- a special time and space;
- a sociopolitical frame;
- a recapturing of old times for the family;
- a reference to the parents' period of absence, highlighting that the lack of parental practical functioning did not imply a cessation of their love;
- inclusion of complete handing over of "command" to the parents;
- a legal aspect reaffirming parental rights and functions, especially since the couple still had a pending lawsuit of "The Country" against them and they were socially stigmatized;
- elements pointing towards the success of the parents in their enhanced functioning;
- a confirmation that the three children really "understood."

Since they had been immersed in a confused and violent social context, with a total absence of legality and respect for the individual, culminating in their specific personal stigmatization, a socially symbolic ritual was especially useful for this family. The solemnity of the cultural ceremony, in a format isomorphic to a marriage ceremony, provided powerful symbolic action especially in Argentina, where there was no legal divorce and where marriage had a legal implication of indissoluble bonds. The bonds of parents and children were highlighted in this ritual as similarly indissoluble.

This ritual was designed in accordance with the values and beliefs of both the family and the elders in the family. With this ceremony, we contributed to the sanctioning and perpetuation of the specific social system of the nuclear family and its functioning (van der Hart, 1983).

The ritual also proved to be healing for me, as the family's therapist, as it enabled me to function for the well-being of others in ways that the years of political oppression had often prevented.

The Next Session

The family came for their next session a month later. The ritual proved to be an effective catalyst towards reordering hierarchical and affective functioning. Certain feelings became more accessible for them. The parents said things were more peaceful. Mother was still asking the grandmother for advice once a week, as planned. I suggested now that father remind mother to ask for this advice once a week and that he become involved in knowing what the questions and the answers were. Roberto was in a better mood and more fun to be around. Jaime was doing much better at school and in all his other activities. He still chewed on his clothes, but he listened to his mother much more.

Everyone had been very moved by the ceremony of the previous session. I noticed that, while we were talking, Ana was fidgeting and getting more and more upset, until finally she broke down in tears. The mother tried to comfort her and eventually got her to speak. She cried and cried while she said: "The worst, really the worst thing of all is how I could have had fun sometimes, when mother and father were in prison. I even remember being happy sometimes, playing with my friends." She wept with a feeling of profound sorrow and guilt. With the boys looking on in a total silence, the mother and father also wept, and I wept with them. The despair felt by the girl overwhelmed everybody in the room, touching many deep emotions we all felt in this suffering country. Ana was in her mother's arms, and the father told her firmly and kindly that in jail it was a comfort for him to know that the children were well taken care of and growing up fine. He said that both the mother and he were happy that Ana had been able to play and relax. Esther kept caressing the girl and approving Gabriel's words, while she also cried, and for the first time in a session, the father held the mother's arm and hand.

Family restructuring and a new handling of emotions emerged after the ritual, in a family in which members had said they "didn't want to reopen their luggage."

Follow-Up

After this interview, Ana's nightmares disappeared. At one-year follow-up, there were no nightmares. Jaime's clothes-chewing habit was dealt with in the process of therapy in a paradoxical manner. It diminished but did not disappear completely.

Soon after this session the parents went on a weekend holiday, just by themselves. It was the first time they had left the children since their release from prison. Since so much time of being together as a whole family had been lost during those years, they had been making up for this, always doing things together as a group during their free time. A process of change was working here, too, for not only did Esther and Gabriel make space for themselves alone, but they also decided not to place the children in the total care of the grandparents while they were away. With this spontaneous move, one of my goals was achieved, which was to facilitate the couple's cohesion and intimacy.

After two more monthly sessions, they said they wanted to manage more by themselves. I believed that this family would come to consultation if they had any important problem.

Later, in 1985, almost two years after the therapeutic process had been ended, they were legally exonerated of all responsibility in the trial, and their possessions—those that had not been stolen during their ordeal—were returned to them. This was a very positive factor in their development. While scars certainly remained, the parents continued functioning better and feeling more in control of the direction of their family's life.

THE THERAPIST AND HER OWN INVOLVEMENT IN RITUALS WHEN WORKING IN A SITUATION OF EXTREME SOCIOPOLITICAL VIOLENCE— RITUALS FOR AN INTERNAL EXILE

The therapist working in a severely repressed sociopolitical context has to consider her own survival and other ethical and functional issues. Some of these issues are quite clear and evident, such as: "If I work with these people, will that put me in a life-risk?" Some other points may leak much more inadvertently into the therapist's style of intervention. As a small example, *after* the transition ritual had been celebrated, I thought that perhaps it would have been important to have had the ceremony take place at the attorney's office to emphasize the legal aspect. I am sure I did not even think of it before, just because I was too afraid of."moving around" with the family, and in consequence, being perceived by "others" as "having something to do" with them and becoming a possible target of paramilitary forces. I want now to accentuate that my fear was present, manifested in what I did not think of. That kind of fear makes one a "not thinker," a "mutilated creator."

Aside from the therapeutic rituals discussed so far, one must also consider the possible ritualistic adjustments made—sometimes unwittingly—by the therapist, to survive in a situation of personal risk. Certain protective ritualized behaviors were adopted during work with sociopolitically repressed families, such as looking around when leaving a building, keeping no record of the therapy session, making no notes in the date book, or sometimes meeting at different locations. The need for secrecy was absolute, and these precautions became a "magical" life-ensuring tool for the therapist. Another was the burning of "compromising" books. All of this ritualized behavior typified the transition towards a state of "internal exile" in this country.

When we look at the therapeutic interviews, we find that another ritualized form of behavior developed by therapists was to ask too many questions, way beyond what can be considered necessary and sufficient information, about the traumatic events that took place. Aside from a certain degree of morbid curiosity on the part of the therapist, this seemed to represent a sharing of a ritual with a particular family, where both the family and the therapist carried out the ceremonial aspects of excessively reviewing and examining the facts and events related to the repression suffered. Such ritual-ized behavior does not function as a model or a stimulus for a positive transformation within the family structure. To the contrary, it ritualizes a state of permanent trauma and can lead to a worsening or congealment of the condition. Thus, the therapeutic process may develop into a "ritual of crystallization," obviously resulting in a serious failure. This is exactly the opposite of the therapeutic process as a rite of passage or as a rite of transition (Kobak & Waters, 1984).

Another form of ritualized behavior for the therapist was the immediate interruption of the therapeutic treatment of compromised persons, such as political activists or simply free-thinkers, as well as of innocent victims picked by mistake or denounced by other interested parties. Since the perse-cution of free-thinkers and innocent victims certainly occurred, this attitude on the part of the therapist, resulting in a cutoff, was part of the adaptation to a generalized extreme repression. We have seen clients with a traumatic experience in relation to these interruptions on the therapist's part. We have also seen patients who woke up one morning and went to their appointment to suddenly discover that their therapist had been abducted or killed or had abruptly fled the country.

Some therapists left the country because of patients' sociopolitical com-mitments. Extremist groups might have attacked them, and in many situa-tions that was the case. Other therapists engaged in a ritual of silence or a ritual of avoidance. Regrettably, many therapists systematically avoided all discussion of or attention to issues brought by people in relation to the sociopolitical aspects of life. Sometimes this was done inadvertently by the therapist. Other times it was a deliberate choice to remain uninvolved. Ter-rorism, severe political repression, indiscriminate oppressive attacks, power-fully affected the person of the therapist and the practice of therapy.

For us as human beings and as systemic therapists to fall into such rituals is to have let cowardice enter our hearts, our bodies, our being. In the work described here, I have tried in my own way to overcome the negative rituals attendant to political oppression, and to share positive, life-giving rituals with my clients.

REFERENCES

Bateson, G. (1972). *Steps to an ecology of mind*. New York: Ballantine.
Camarasa, J., Felice, R., & Gonzalez, D. (1985). *El juicio: Proceso al horror: de la recupera-cion demoratica a la sentencia*. Buenos Aires: Ed. Sudamericana-Planeta.
CONADEP (1986). *Nunca mas*. Buenos Aires: Editorial Universitaria de Buenos Aires.
Crescini, S., & Droeven, J. (1985). *La familia con miembros desaparecidos. Impacto de la violencia represiva en la familia*. Presentation at the Family Therapy Congress of Buenos Aires.
Kobak, R., Waters, D. (1984). Family therapy as a rite of passage. *Family Process, 23*, 89–100.

Morin, E. (1984). Personal communication.
Reiss, D. (1981). *The family's construction of reality*. Cambridge, MA: Harvard University Press.
Ritterman, M. (1985). Symptoms, social justice and personal freedom. *Journal of Strategic and Systemic Therapies, 4*(2).
van der Hart, O. (1983). *Rituals in psychotherapy: Transition and continuity*. New York: Irvington Publishers.
Van Gennep, A. (1960). *The rites of passage*. Chicago: Aldine Press.
Wilson, M. (1957). *Rituals of kinship among the Nyakyusa*. London: Oxford University Press.

V

RITUALS AND
FAMILY THERAPY TRAINING

15

Rituals and Trainees

JANINE ROBERTS

THE MANY TRANSITIONS and shifts in training can be richly marked by the conscious use of ritual in the learning process. In addition, as trainees articulate and understand their use of ritual in both their family of origin and current life, they gain a more careful appreciation of the role it has played in their own lives, helping them to see potential uses and areas of difficulty in doing ritual work with families in treatment.

TRAINING SETTINGS

Early Stages of Training

For groups that meet on a regular basis, whether in academic classrooms, classes in freestanding clinics, or supervision groups, rituals can be used to mark the various phases of the group. In my classes, I frequently start out with a *naming ritual*, passed down through the grapevine of family therapy training exercises (originator unknown). All group members share what they know about their names: what they mean; how they have changed over time with migration, marriage, religious conversions; who they are named after; who named them; what the ethnic and cultural significance of their name is; and what name they want to be called in the class. People begin to name their identity within the group while sharing the evolution of past changes in their lives. For instance, Tom Wise noted that his name had been shortened from Wisegarten at Ellis Island when his grandfather immigrated from

Russia and that at 31 he was still trying to get his family to call him Tom. They still called him by his boyhood name of Tommy. Tom was thinking of changing his name back to Wisegarten to reclaim his Jewish identity.

As each person concludes with the name he wants to be called in the group, he reaffirms the names of all the people that have gone before him by looking at each person and saying his name. After everyone has introduced himself, I go around the entire circle saying each person's name and welcoming him or her. This ritual begins to introduce the family context for each person in the group to the class, validates the importance of each person, and provides a beginning for people to start to know one another.

Early in the group's formation, I have also asked people to write short response papers *assessing their own family of origin's use of ritual.* After talking in class about the typology of family rituals found in Chapter 1 (underritualized, rigidly ritualized, flexibility to adapt rituals over time, etc.), students examine their own families. One female student in her early thirties wrote:

> I first and most simply placed my family within the hollow ritual category. The descriptive words certainly mirrored my experiences of rituals within my family of origin. Following protocol rather than a creation of and working with meaning characterized our family events. Form rather than feeling or meaning were the organizing factors. Elaborate beautiful tables filled with feast food and of course the mandatory turkey made for Thanksgivings that were beautiful enough to be photographed for any magazine cover, and yet did not distract anyone sufficiently from the pervading mood of gloom, tension, and insufficiently disguised sadness, as each year, each person was left to privately re-experience the discrepancy between form and feeling. Everything looked right, and yet there was no connection, no shared meaning. It was an attempt to recreate somebody else's ritual, and each year it left its participants lonely in the midst of many, waiting for it to be over.
>
> Yet, these hollow rituals within my family only really begin to make sense when I examine them within the context of the next category, that of ritual process interrupted or unable to be experienced openly. My parents, aunts, uncles, great aunts and uncles experienced a world torn apart, relatives and friends murdered, community and culture destroyed (in the Holocaust)—loss of a magnitude that I still find difficult to comprehend. Yet this tremendous loss was not mourned, not ritualized, not openly experienced and shared, but rather it was denied, made private, and hidden. At first this was because there was too much to do, survival came first, then beginning a new life in a new place, and later when there was time and physical safety enough to allow for some expression of grief, it was already too buried, too frightening, and too mystified. So my family did not mourn its losses, did not create rituals around these terrible and terribly important transitions. Without the mourning of deaths, can there be a real celebration of births? With the denial of the meaning of major transitions, can a family with meaning mark other transitions, or do these rituals of transition then need to be carefully contained so that they do not lead too dangerously close to thoughts and feelings of other times of change, to those who are not there, and to feelings that have not been allowed?

A divorced man in his forties described how he adapted holiday rituals with his three children, as well as how he has continued a ritual from his family of origin:

> In preparation for Christmas, a live tree is purchased in North Orange where my children live. The tree is decorated on the last Sunday the children are with me before Christmas. My children mark Christmas with their mother on Christmas eve, and I pick them up Christmas morning for a vacation with me until January 2nd. The tree remains in the home until the first of the year at which time it is planted. The tree planting ritual started the year of my divorce and involves preparing the earth in late fall, before the ground freezes.
>
> In January of every year, I have a bonfire to burn the brush left over from last year's work on the land. Metaphorically it represents a transition to the New Year and is a tradition going back to my grandparents on both sides of the family who were farmers and loggers.

Another student, David, described his rigidly ritualized bedtime exchange with his mother when he was a child.

> Every evening before bed, Rachel repeated the same words to each child, after which we were expected to repeat the same phrase. Rachel, "I love you, David." David, "I love you, Mom."

He went on to describe how vestiges of this ritual remain in the Sunday morning phone calls that he has each week with his family. His mother always says to him, "I love you, David," and he feels compelled to repeat the same phrase back.

After I respond to these papers with written comments and questions, the students, in dyads, exchange what they have written, read the assessments, and discuss the following questions:

1. How do you think your experience with ritual in your family of origin impacts you in your work with ritual in family therapy?
2. What are the implications of the use of ritual in your family of origin for ritual patterns in your current family?
3. If you were going to intervene in the families of origin described in the paper in regards to their ritual use, what might be one or two small steps that you could take?

Students then meet all together and share (if they wish) any parts of what they were working on with the class. For instance, one young man in his thirties, Michael, commented on how in his large extended Lebanese family he experienced rituals as fairly set and predetermined and so he had not really thought of them as a resource to bring into the arena of family therapy. As he began to see the possibility of flexibility in ritual process and the process of preparing for ritual events as being an important marker of family dynamics, he got in touch with typical gender roles around Christmas which he was inadvertently passing on from his family of origin to his current family. In Michael's family, the women bought the gifts for Christmas. In his family, even though his wife was Jewish and Christmas was not particularly her holiday, she was expected to buy the gifts. Michael decided that for the Christmas coming up he would buy the gifts; he later found that his wife became much more interested and open about celebrating Christmas with his family.

Another way to start a group is by having members bring a *food from their family of origin*[1] that shares something about their ethnic traditions. People share with the group the significance of the dish that they brought as a way of introducing themselves in their family context. Foods are very symbolic and provide a view of family that is much richer than mere words. For instance, one woman, Sue, brought an elaborate decorated chocolate cake that she had begun to bake at 10:30 the night before. Sue, describing her alcoholic family, stated that she could have brought either spam sandwiches or the cake, that they symbolized the two extremes of caretaking in her family. She said that she finally decided to bring the cake because it represented for her the times when the family was functioning better and she was trying to pass that heritage along to her own current family. Another woman, Chinwe, brought foo-foo,[2] soup and chi-chi's from her native Nigeria. She explained how foo-foo is one of the mainstays of the meal, that if there is no foo-foo, the man has not been fed. She also talked about the importance of chi-chi (small crisscross pieces of pastry) to any celebration in Nigeria. It is not considered a truly festive occasion unless there is chi-chi.

As some 25 people share their food heritage, it highlights how various sides of the family pass down food patterns, how ethnic foods are treasured or lost, what central roles food played in people's lives, as well as gender differences. As one trainee remarked at the end of one sharing, "I didn't hear any stories about men being in the kitchen."

These three exercises are all various ways to bring an awareness of ritual possibilities with families into the curriculum. Not only do they create group cohesion through people learning about each other, but they make people more attentive to their own ritualizing capabilities.

Mid- and End-of-Training Exercises: Bringing in, Creating, and Scavenging Symbols

In talking about the importance of symbols to rituals, I have also asked trainees to bring in a *symbol of their relationship to their current family or their family of origin* to share with the group. As one group gathered to do this, one of the trainees, Portia, walked into the middle of the circle with a metal pole on a round stand covered with a woven feed sack. She said, "I need to go first," and took off the feed sack, showing a sign that said, "Funeral, No Parking." Portia said, "Today is the 12th anniversary of the funeral of my husband and daughter after they drowned. I thought long and hard about bringing this symbol in. It seems a little bizarre. I don't want anyone to think that we can't talk about the whole range of feelings that this event in my life brings up. This sign was given to me by my brother several months after the funeral. He stole it from out in front of the funeral parlor. He said to me, 'I don't know why I took it but I thought that you should have it.' So, at first it was out behind the barn, and then gradually I brought it out to the edge of the barn where I could see it and I began to use it. Whenever I felt really overwhelmed with grief I would bring it to the sign and say, 'Here, you take it for a while.' And I would hang it on the sign. It has come out into the barnyard more and people look at it, ask what it is for — and it has been a comfort for me as a place to hold that grief."

Another woman, Kelly, brought in a picture of her mother as she wanted to remember her (exuberant with arms thrown open on the beach) and her sister (more quietly contemplative). They had both died unexpectedly during the semester within a few weeks of each other. Kelly passed the pictures around the group to share with everyone and lit a candle she had brought. She talked about how the candle brings light but is also finite and burns down.

I have also asked training groups to *create symbols* and *symbolic actions* as a group to mark transitions. Four-person Bowen groups (where people coach each other on ways to rework some of their family-of-origin [FOO] relationships), after being presented with the information in Chapter 3 on how to design rituals, were asked to create a ritual to say good-bye. They had all been in a class together for one year, with the Bowen groups meeting separately for one semester. Ethnicity had been a theme during the year with ethnic caucuses, experiential exercises, and readings on cultural differences. People in the class were from South Africa, mainland China, Germany, Australia, Puerto Rico, and Venezuela, as well as from a range of immigrant backgrounds (Irish, French Canadian, African, Jewish, etc.). One Bowen group consisted of a Hispanic, Greek, Canadian and Chinese person. They came together before the class and each said good-bye in their language, noting that the form of good-bye that they chose connoted, "I will see you again" (such as *hasta luego*, until later). They then stated their appreciation of the learnings they had gained in class and in the Bowen group from people's willingness to share their ethnic background.

Another group created a sculpture out of three chairs, with two on the bottom and the third balanced delicately on top. They said that they chose chairs because the room was crowded with them, but yet there was always space for everybody. The chair on top also represented for them, in their study over the semester, the importance of balance in constantly monitoring the systemic view of a family (even when deliberately trying to unbalance a subsystem). Also, the three chairs made a triangle.

A third group, acknowledging that some people in the class would be going to take another two courses together, while others who were not specializing in family therapy would not continue, asked those who were leaving to form an inner circle with each individual facing out, and those who were staying in the group for more classes to form an outer circle around them, facing in. Then people were asked to make contact between the two circles with naming and any physical action that felt appropriate (shaking hands, hugging, etc.), as well as saying good-bye in their native language. Then the outer circle rotated around the inner circle until all had a chance to say good-bye.

In another class, which also worked in Bowen coaching groups over the semester, a group poem was written after they shared experiences and symbols. (Their symbols included a large blue bowling ball which was rolled back and forth across the classroom, because each time some group members told their families they were going to their "Bowen" group, their families thought they said "bowling" and would respond, "Since when did you take up bowling?" A few members together brought in fresh multicolored eggs from a variety of different chickens to symbolize all the colorful differences of the group, as well as the nurturing and hatching quality of the class. A third group came in wearing a number of different kinds of hats and talked about all the types of hats that family therapists have to wear. A lovingly worn Raggedy Ann doll was brought in by someone else to represent all the important childhood relationships and memories that were evoked by doing the Bowen work.) This Bowen group began the poem because they had provided their first critique of their work in poetry earlier in the semester.

> We would like to close this class with verse,
> since this is the ritual we started first.
> We invite you all to add a line of what
> Family Therapy II has brought to mind.

> Interconnectedness: individuals, systems and social change,
> A good way to get one's FOO rearranged.
> All individually part of a whole
> The joyfulness of communion, joined in soul

> Hugs to Raggedy Ann, hats off to us all,
> gathered round multicolored eggs with our "Bowen" Ball!

At the beginning of Family Therapy III in the following fall, this poem was read the first class as a link between the two semesters.

Food can also be used as a symbol at the end of Bowen groups. Evan Imber-Black has asked trainees to bring in food to share that represents their differentiation of self from their family of origin (for instance, food that they have created out of new traditions, or food prepared somewhat differently, or dishes that they would not have eaten in their families of origin).

Groups can also be asked to go on *scavenger* hunts and find items that represent what they have learned together over the year. I asked a group of school counselors and psychologists with whom I had been consulting to go out in groups of three and find something in the school in which we were meeting or immediately around it to create a collage of symbols for our last meeting in June. One group brought in tools from the workshop that represented various techniques that they had learned to help families rebuild. Another group brought wild buttercups they had picked and gave them to me, thanking me for the blossomings they felt I supported for everyone in the group. In turn, I gave each person in the group a few of the flowers, stating that the blossoming came from the group interactions. Other people brought in an empty picture frame, saying it was blank at the beginning of the year and now it was full of all the images and pictures that had been created as the group worked together, and they passed the frame around so that we could see ourselves framed by it. We kept adding symbols to a central table (a map, a mirror, sponge, plastic gloves, tennis balls, umbrella, pressure gauge, cactus, flashlight), placing them in such a way that each symbol informed the others. (For instance, the umbrella, which was a symbol of protection that people felt within the group, was opened up and placed leaning over the table.) Then, one person, who happened to have a camera in her car, took pictures of the three-dimensional collage that we had made to save it for the group.

Brief Example: Gift Giving and a Supervision Team

After working closely together for nine months with an O (observing) and T (treatment) team supervision model, the ten of us (two supervisors, six trainees, and two prepracticum students) decided to have a concluding ritual. Food had been an important marker for the group, with several people bringing snacks each week for the whole group to share behind the one-way mirror as we worked all day. There had been lots of jokes about the healthiness of the food, additives, kinds of food people would eat, not eat, etc. So we decided to end with a potluck, with everyone bringing something undesignated beforehand to share. We also drew names out of a hat and each person was to make or buy a gift for under $3.00 that was metaphoric of that person's work and relationship to the team. I received a pair of cotton work gloves to represent the caring hands that were always there to help people. The other supervisor received a kaleidescope to represent the usefulness of his way of seeing multiple realities in the world, as well as his playfulness. One of the prepracticum students who had just been observing received a budding plant.

Brief Example: Helping Individuals to Mark Transitions in Training Programs

Individuals can also be helped to design rituals that are unique to their particular changes. One student in our program at the University of Massachusetts, Amy Leos-Urbel, described her experience.

> During the time I was a full-time graduate student in family therapy one particularly important lesson for me personally was that the standards I considered necessary for any other person (for example, the things I would recommend for a client as basic elements of treating oneself decently), I needed to apply to myself as well. I did my clinical practicum in an alcohol treatment clinic where careful attention was paid to the nature of the team process, looking always to avoid replication of the "alcoholic system" we were trying to heal.
>
> In addition, I was aware of the value of marking significant life events with appropriate ritual. My experience with both traditional and newly created Jewish rituals has taught me that, and I have also witnessed the use of ritual as a powerful element in family therapy.
>
> With that as background, it made perfect sense to me when my faculty advisor suggested that since the C.A.G.S. program in which I was enrolled did not have a formal graduation, I might like to design a ritual to mark the completion of my period of study. I decided to ask my practicum supervisor, another member of the family therapy team, and my husband to participate in the ritual with my advisor and me. I asked each of them to be ready to talk about their sense of me and my work, my strengths, and their vision or hopes for my future. This format closely parallels the "self-estimation" format which I have used many times in Re-evaluation Counseling (RC), where self-estimation is done on a regular basis by all teachers and leaders, and as a part of the certification process for new teachers. I have had extensive involvement with RC for more than ten years, so including this element added a sense of integration for me.
>
> The day of my "graduation", we gathered at my advisor's (Janine Roberts) office. Before we began the sharing, Janine suggested that someone take notes on what was being said so I could take it with me, and she offered green paper to symbolize growth.
>
> Each person talked about aspects of my personal and professional development which particularly stood out. My advisor, for instance, talked about her experience of watching me find my own voice. Janine challenged me to discover the size of what I could do, which she suggested was much bigger than I had yet realized. After all of the others had given me their messages, I spoke to them.

To each of them, I gave a flower and talked about its symbolism in terms of what they had given me during my graduate school experience. I gave my advisor a red rose to represent the standard of excellence she sets for herself and her students. I pointed out that the rose also presented a paradox, saying, "I know you enjoy paradox, Janine. This rose has thorns which keep people from touching it, but I always found you to be warmly accessible."

Symbols are enriched by their use in other contexts and I was able to use a symbol for my husband which had layers of meaning. I gave him a giant white chrysanthemum, the flower we had used for our wedding decorations. We had chosen it then, and I chose it again on this occasion, for its uncountable number of petals, a symbol of infinity or immortality. I talked about his constant love and patience, and the timeless bond we share. My choice of flower symbols was given additional meaning by the fact that two of the participants in the graduation had brought me flowers as well, which they offered as symbols of growth and celebration.

The graduation ritual was moving and important for all of us who took part in it. Most obviously, it provided a chance for me to hear what each of these key people thought about my work up to that point, and about where I was heading. It also was an opportunity for us to say good-bye, not in a final sense, but to the particular form of relationship we had had up until that time. I saw that the experience of working together, or of witnessing the process (in the case of my husband) I had been going through, had been one of deep personal sharing, and the graduation ritual offered a time and place in which we could look at and express the bond we felt as a result of our shared experience.

These few examples presented here give some idea of the creativity that can be opened up in groups with just a few of the ideas presented earlier in the book on ritual design. It can be particularly important to use rituals to mark the creation of groups, transitions in groups, endings, as well as changes in group behavior. Out of these experiences, traditions can even evolve for programs. For instance, one year a student, when asked to bring in a symbol of what the class experience had been for him, wrote a song and had the group sing it (this was a class on strategic and systemic family therapy models[3]). I now bring in my violin at the end of this class each year, pass out copies of this song, and we sing it together:

The Meta-hymn of the Republic
(to the tune of "The Battle Hymn of the Republic")

Words by Tom Zink

Mine eyes have seen the glory of the coming paradigm,
It is trampling our perceptions of change and space and time,
It has loosened our thinking up to meta-levels so sublime,
And multiple truths go marching on.

CHORUS:
Family therapy forever, Family therapy forever,
Family therapy forever,
And families keep spiraling around and round and round and
round and round.

Does disengagement or enmeshment help you differentiate?
Rituals and paradoxes help to meta-communicate
That your morphogenesis you're going to have to punctuate,
As systemic truths go marching on.

(*Sing chorus*)
With the deviation-amplifying processes in class,
We are like an undifferentiated family ego mass,
And I have to ask the question at the risk of sounding crass,
"Is homeostasis enough?"

(*End with chorus*)

RITUALS IN THE THERAPIST'S FAMILY OF ORIGIN

In addition to consciously using ritual in ongoing groups, Evan Imber-Black, Dick Whiting, and I have been doing workshops where people come together for a few hours or one or two days to look at ritual use in their family of origin and current family. In the workshops, participants (most of them therapists) begin to identify some patterns that they would like to elaborate upon or modify in their experience with ritual. Our thought is that, as therapists become more aware of the roles of ritual in their day-to-day life, they will better understand how families in treatment may make use of it.

We begin with *day-to-day rituals* such as the family meal. We have shown clips from movies of family meals ("Breaking Away," "Saturday Night Fever," "Annie Hall") to highlight the possible range of interactional rules for allowable topics and affect, as well as the influence of ethnicity on these patterns. Then, people are asked to think about the ways mealtimes highlight family roles, including gender differences, family rules (including what can and cannot be talked about, who initiates conversation, who sits down for meals, how long they need to be at the table), and connections with extended family and others when they ate with them. In dyads, they ask each other the following questions:

1. Where did family members sit? Did they all sit?

2. What were the rules about topics and affect (e.g., "no arguing during dinner," "let your father eat before serious discussion")?
3. What were symbolic meanings of food (e.g., reward, punishment)?
4. What were symbolic meanings of food choices (e.g., giving and receiving, expression of preferences, expression of individual differences, control, power)?
5. Who was served first, last?
6. What expressions of ethnicity were involved in meals?
7. What gender rules were expressed via: shopping, cooking, serving, talking, cleaning up?
8. What were the differences in everyday meals and holiday meals?
9. What were the differences when company came for dinner?

Several common themes emerge as people share their discussions with the larger group. Women invariably sit closer to the kitchen. The position at the head of the table has special status. There is often only one head of the table, even though there are two ends. Men often get first choice of foods and frequently do the carving of any meats. Very young children usually sit closer to mothers. Available relationship options become clearer as well as various dyadic and triadic interactions.

One student, Ava, described in detail her family dinners:

Mealtimes: Hard to Swallow

My mother sat at the head of the table. My brother sat to her left, my father to her right, and I to the right of my father. When I was ten or so, perhaps already budding in my role as family therapist, I suggested that we had fallen into a rut and that we sit in different places at meals.[4] This new choreography upset the homeostasis and it became hard to talk. The experiment was short-lived—my parents treated it as an amusing nuisance—and we returned to our habitual places.

Dinners were the locus of the greatest family contact and conflict as my brother Brian and I tried to grow up into differentiated individuals. We were beginning to emerge with our own opinions, different from "the family opinion," and our own habits (I stopped eating meat). Both parents tried to dismiss our differentness ("I've been around a lot longer than you, so listen to me . . . " from my father; "If you eat something different from us, it's like you're not part of the family!" from my mother).

I carried much of the stress of the false front of family consensus, becoming secretly obsessed with food and somewhat ascetic. I greatly restricted what I ate, eliminating anything I viewed as impure (for three years I ate no ice cream!) and occasionally vomited after a family meal (symbolically relieving myself of the garbage I was being asked to swallow). Although my food problems were painful, I was happy to have a secret that separated me from my family. My parents had no inkling of my bulimia until I told them some three years later, while in psychotherapy. My mother's response was, "And here I thought we were all so happy! I never worried about you!" I believe my problems came to rest on food partly because dinnertime was the occasion when we were all together on a regular basis.

My mother's role as family switchboard was most evident at mealtimes. "Brian, do you want to say something?" "Fred, let him finish his sentence." "Have the last piece of broccoli, Ava." She managed the conversation and the meal like a corporate dinner for one hundred, not a family meal for four.

I formed an alliance with Ling (the live-in maid), helping her cook, putting the dishes on the table and clearing them. I found great comfort in the warmth and nourishment of Ling and the kitchen, which was in stark contrast to the dark, cold dining room (which doubled as my mother's home office). It didn't matter that Ling spoke little English—our communication was open and satisfying.

When Ava later had the chance to do a family sculpture, it was intriguing that she chose this dinnertime scene to recreate. As she worked on understanding it more, she asked people playing the roles of her family members to try out some different interactional patterns and looked at her own response to them.

Other daily rituals that could be examined usefully with similar exercises are bedtime rituals and daily entrances and exits from the home.

In another exercise, we look beyond daily interactions to special traditions that are created with the *family celebrations* of birthdays, anniversaries, vacations. These are events that are marked on particular days on the family's "inner calendar" (as opposed to the "outer calendar" of events such as Thanksgiving, Hanukkah, etc., which have the same dates for all families). This exercise is designed to go beyond just understanding the roles and rules and world view that are held within a ritual to understanding the evolving life of the ritual: how it has been passed down, modified, and what further changes the individual might want to initiate in a family ceremony. People are asked in the group whether they want to work on birthdays, vacations, or anniversaries, and then pair off in dyads to address questions from one of the following areas:

Birthdays

1. What birthday traditions have been passed down or would you like to pass down? How do they represent different sides of your families or origin or different ethnic traditions?
2. What do you know about how/why they have been passed down?
3. How has the celebration of birthdays for you or someone else in your family shifted over time in terms of *symbols, who gathers together, where you gather, foods, planning* (who creates the celebration)?

4. How do marking birthdays work for your family (by highlighting transitions, remembering the sacredness of birth, providing group cohesion and identity, or . . .)?
5. How would you like to be celebrating your or someone else's birthday in the future (perhaps pick a time frame that has special significance for you such as a decade birthday or a particular year)?

Vacations

1. What metaphors do the places you go on vacation convey for you and your family (e.g., camping as back to a simpler life)?
2. What roles do people take on in planning, anticipating the vacation?
3. How have vacations shifted over time for one of your families (current or family of origin) in terms of *place, time, activities, who goes*?
4. What kinds of activities on vacations do family members find restorative/relaxing? What meaning is given to these activities?
5. How do family rules and roles (including any gender roles) shift when you are on vacation?
6. What symbols have you brought home from vacations? Where are they kept? What use do they have in your non-vacation life?

Anniversaries (moving, deaths, cessation of drinking or smoking etc., weddings, divorces, living together)

1. What have you learned from your family of origin about the significance of anniversaries?
2. How has this influenced how you currently mark anniversaries?
3. Do others outside of the family members immediately affected by the anniversary (for instance, the married couple) mark it in any way?
4. What are some ways anniversaries are marked (*cards, special places, symbols, ceremonies*)?
5. Are there any anniversaries that are currently not acknowledged that you would like to mark in some way?

Common themes that emerge are a clearer awareness of what things have been passed on (rather than "things are just done this way"), developmental changes over time, more articulation of what sides of their families of origin they might be more joined to, and an understanding of their own roles. One school counselor, Bob, described a recent birthday ritual for his 20-year-old son, Robbie. Robbie was several hours away at college and so the family packed up the lasagna that was his favorite food and the same kind of cake (chocolate) that he had had throughout childhood, putting on top of it the baseball figure which had always been his birthday symbol. (Each of the eight children in the family has a birthday figurine in a special birthday drawer in the kitchen.) The first thing their son did when he saw the cake was to take the figure off, throw it away, and say, "I never want to see this again." His father later quietly took it out of the trash, took it home, and put it in the drawer with the ballerina and the other figures. As Bob talked about this event, he began to understand that the birthday ritual needed reworking to mark the developmental changes in the family. As a way to begin this process, he started to think about removing the baseball player from the drawer, putting it aside with other family mementos and perhaps passing it on to his son when he had children of his own.

We have also worked with examining *family celebrations* that exist more on the outside calendar, that is, religious and cultural events in the larger culture (Thanksgiving, Hanukkah, Easter, Passover, Fourth of July, etc.). Again, film clips have provided a way to look at families immersed in ritual. Excerpts from "Hannah and her Sisters" show how certain parts of that family's Thanksgiving ritual stayed the same over the years (music, kid's table, women in the kitchen closely connected, central place of alcohol, kibitzing), while developmental shifts were also marked as the children grew older, divorces occurred, and families regrouped.

It is useful to emphasize here the differences between the expectations surrounding holidays, which may be built up by media advertising and wishful thinking, and the actual reality. Notions about holidays that look like Norman Rockwell paintings only put more stress onto the actual celebration of events. As Dick Whiting reminds us, "Norman Rockwell paid those people to sit for those paintings."

To conclude our workshops, we often ask people to take all of the things we have been working with for the day (ritual typology, design elements, life cycle rituals, rituals of daily interaction, etc.) and use them to make beginning steps to redesign one ritual in their lives. One workshop participant, Kerry, decided to work on the occasion of his mother's 80th birthday coming up in several months. First, he identified that he felt the family had little ritual. The father abandoned the family when the three children were little, and the mother was very focused around daily survival. As adults, the three children were quite disengaged from each other. Kerry had never married himself and had felt very saddened when the family home was sold several months earlier because his mother was no longer able to live there alone. However, there had been no coming together of the family around this important transition in all of their lives. Kerry wanted to make the birthday celebration a time when he could reconnect with his siblings in relationship to his mother (rather than just a celebration of his relationship with his Mom). He also wanted it to be a time when they could mark, as a group, the loss of the family home. He carefully planned where he might stay and who he might ask to help with some parts of the birthday party as a way for him to begin to rebuild some sibling connections. Kerry also decided to ask each sibling to bring to the party one thing from his mother's home (many of her possessions had been divided up among them) that represented for him or her something important about the family homestead. In addition, he was going to bring pictures of the house.

SUMMARY

Working with rituals as part of the training process allows family therapists to learn about the use of ritual in families different from their own, to examine their own ritual making capacities, and to become more aware of times when ritual might not be as readily available to some families. In addition, the essential skills of creativity, playfulness, and humor are supported. By examining the ritual process, another template is introduced by which students can better understand both their own families and families in treatment. Further, the building of strong bonds within training groups can be facilitated. Various design elements of ritual are not just examined in the abstract, but worked with and applied. All of these experiences can help therapists to then work with rituals in therapy.

NOTES

[1] This idea came originally from Evan Imber-Black.

[2] This foo-foo was made from cream of wheat cooked with a small amount of water so that it was very thick. In Nigeria it is made from large yams.

[3] In classes taught by Evan Imber-Black, a food tradition evolved where students were asked to bring in a dish that represented strategic or systemic concepts. Some students brought in a pair of cooked ducks (paradox), chicken soup (more of the same wrong solution), and samosa's (an Indian appetizer made in the form of triangles). Others made fortune cookies with strategic messages inside of them.

[4] Try this at your own home, and see what happens. Or, without saying anything, sit in a different seat.

Afterword

THIS VOLUME HAS attempted to capture on paper the breadth of applications and the depth of meaning possible in therapeutic rituals. During the process of creating this book together as editors, we have become aware of changes in emphasis and direction in our own work with rituals. We have become increasingly interested in the normative or naturally occurring rituals in the lives of families, and how we may learn from these to enhance the course of therapy in general, and the design of therapeutic rituals in particular.

This focus on a family's own rituals, coupled with so many families' creative responses to our suggestions regarding therapeutic rituals, has influenced our choice to involve families as our collaborators in the creation of therapeutic rituals, moving away from an earlier position regarding rituals as *prescribed* to a position of rituals as *co-created*.

As we have explored the normative rituals in families and discovered the positive impact of such conversations, we have subsequently moved to an interest in exploring rituals in the families of trainees and practicing therapists. The powerful integration of the existential and the systemic has frequently emerged in this area of work with rituals.

All of these developments, along with the excellent research and clinical work in the area of rituals being done by both the contributors to this volume and many other colleagues we have met, lead us to conclude that there are multiple directions for further work with rituals.

The research of Wolin and his colleagues regarding rituals and the multigenerational transmission of alcoholism, along with our own repeated clinical impressions regarding the development of symptoms in families where normative rituals have gone awry, suggests a need for greater study of the interplay of rituals and symptoms. The questions occurring to us presently regard the impact of interrupted, lost, or abandoned rituals and of renewed, restored, or revitalized rituals on individual, family, and cultural functioning. Study of these issues may lead to useful prevention programs involving rituals with families experiencing chronic illness, divorce, migration, or other serious losses.

Since rituals are capable of providing stability while also facilitating change, we are especially interested in men's and women's differing experiences of normative and therapeutic rituals as a way of examining current gender issues of stability and change both in the small and intimate system of the family and in the larger society of work and the community.

Many other questions and areas for ongoing work with rituals will, no doubt, occur to readers of this volume. Janine Roberts, Richard Whiting, and I welcome dialogue.

Evan Imber-Black
New York, 1988

Index